In search of the catholic spirit

In search of the catholic spirit

Methodists and Roman Catholics in Dialogue

David M. Chapman

✠ EPWORTH

British Library Cataloguing in Publication data

A catalogue record for this book is available
from the British Library

0-7162-0588-2

First published in 2004
by Epworth Press
4 John Wesley Road
Werrington
Peterborough PE4 7ZP

Printed and bound in Great Britain by
William Clowes Ltd

To Susan,
Alexander, Sophie and Abigail

Contents

Foreword by Professor Geoffrey Wainwright

From the beginnings of Methodism our relations with Roman Catholicism have been mixed. On the one hand, John Wesley shared the political suspicions of most eighteenth-century Englishmen towards Papists and their allegiance to a foreign potentate; he engaged in theological and ecclesiological controversy with the Catholic bishop Richard Challoner; and the adverb in his 'Popery Calmly Considered' was something of a euphemism. On the other hand, Wesley's Letter to a Roman Catholic, written from Dublin in 1749, displayed an irenicism rare for its time, and summoned his addressee, on the basis of an extensive commonality in doctrine, to mutual help in 'whatever we are agreed leads to the Kingdom'. For their part, contemporary Catholics viewed Methodists as no better than the general run of Protestants.

With a few exceptions (notably the great German Catholic theologian of Tübingen, J. A. Möhler, in his *Symbolik*), negative attitudes predominated on both sides in the nineteenth century. The twentieth century, however, saw the start of a new evaluation by Catholics of Wesley and the Methodist movement, beginning with the treatise by the Belgian Franciscan Maximin Piette on 'John Wesley in the Evolution of Protestantism' (originally 1925). For their part, Methodists – typified by John R. Mott (1865–1955) – were prominent in the Ecumenical Movement from its early days and welcomed the Catholic entry into it, which became official with the Second Vatican Council and its Decree on Ecumenism, *Unitatis Redintegratio* (1964). The World Methodist Council was among the very first of the other Christian communions to respond to the Vatican's invitation to dialogue, and such a dialogue has been in progress since 1967. The two parties quickly found resonances between the universal call to holiness that marked Vatican II's

ix

Constitution on the Church, *Lumen Gentium*, and John Wesley's passion for personal and social sanctity. Under the heading 'An Olive Branch to the Romans', the American Methodist historian Albert Outler, an observer at the Second Vatican Council, included the Letter of 1749 in his much used anthology, *John Wesley*; the Irish Jesuit Michael Hurley brought unprecedented attention to the text by editing it, with his own commentary and a substantive preface by Cardinal Augustin Bea, as *John Wesley's Letter to a Roman Catholic*. The epistolary venture of Methodism's principal founder has since then provided a solid basis for continuing work. Catholics, moreover, have found inspiration in the hymns of Charles Wesley which for so long carried and shaped Methodist faith and spirituality.

In the present book David Chapman tells this entire story with skill and sympathy. He draws on multifarious sources at the individual, institutional and ecumenical levels. He expounds the theological issues with insight and narrates with enthusiasm the co-operative projects that have become possible between Catholics and Methodists. As a current member of the Joint Commission for Dialogue between the World Methodist Council and the Roman Catholic Church, he is well placed to write informatively about the work on the international plane. As co-secretary of the British Methodist–Catholic Committee, David Chapman is sensitive to the particularities of the national scene. He also shows himself well aware of the bilateral conversations with Roman Catholics in which the United Methodist Church, the Uniting Church in Australia and the Methodist Church of New Zealand are respectively engaged.

From my own participation in the English dialogues in the 1970s and then as co-chairman of the international dialogue since 1986, I would highlight two themes for present and future interest. First, the increasing urgency of a common witness between Methodists and Catholics in the contemporary religious and cultural situation. Despite some historical differences, and for all the apparent quaintness of some of John Wesley's formulations, there are some striking echoes between Pope John Paul II's call for 'a new evangelization' and Wesley's sermon 'On the General Spread of the Gospel'. There was perhaps a providential coincidence between the renewed confession of Jesus Christ as the sole Saviour of the world in the *Dominus Iesus* declaration of the Congregation for the Doctrine of the Faith in 2000 and the meeting of the World Methodist

Council and Conference at Brighton in 2001 under the banner 'Jesus: God's Way of Salvation'. That this substantial agreement on the core of the faith is not yet matched in the Vatican document by a full recognition of Methodism's ecclesiality is a stimulus to the continuing doctrinal dialogue.

My second, and related, theme derives from the invitation issued by John Paul II, in his ecumenical encyclical *Ut Unum Sint* of 1995, to 'a patient and fraternal dialogue' concerning the universal ministry of unity claimed and offered by the Roman see and the ways in which this Petrine function might be exercised in a new situation. Already in the Nairobi Report of 1986, *Towards a Statement on the Church*, the Joint Commission for Dialogue had held out the prospect that 'at some future date in a restored unity, Roman Catholic and Methodist bishops might be linked in one episcopal college, and that the whole body would recognize some kind of effective leadership and primacy to the bishop of Rome. In that case Methodists might justify such an acceptance on different grounds from those that now prevail in the Roman Catholic Church.' The exploration needs to be pursued.

And just a final thought: what a fillip it would be towards that 'full communion in faith, mission and sacramental life' between Methodists and Catholics which is envisioned as the goal of the international dialogue, if the Roman Church could solemnly and liturgically recognise the position that we know John and Charles Wesley enjoy in the communion of the saints.

Geoffrey Wainwright
Duke University, North Carolina

Ascensiontide 2004

Methodist Co-Chairman, Joint Commission for Dialogue between the World Methodist Council and the Roman Catholic Church

Foreword by Bishop Michael Putney

As a guest at the signing of the Covenant between the Church of England and the Methodist Church of Great Britain in London on Saturday, 1 November 2003, I was reminded more powerfully than ever before of how the relationship between Roman Catholics and Methodists always involves in some way the relationship of both parties with the Anglican Communion.

The signing of this historic Covenant was important not just for Anglicans and Methodists in Great Britain, but also for the larger communions to which they belong and for the Roman Catholic Church as well.

We are all inextricably bound to each other, not just at the deepest level of our existence by our common participation in the life of Christ through the Holy Spirit, but also historically and theologically. These two levels of relationship are intimately connected.

As we struggle to overcome the results of the historical divisions which have occurred between us and the theological interpretations of the Christian mystery which keep us apart, we are doing so in Christ through the power of the Holy Spirit. At the same time as the Holy Spirit moves us closer to each other in Christ, this will always lead us to engage with our history and our theological differences.

Despite the polemics, the prejudices and controversies of the past, Methodists and Catholics have never actually separated from each other. They have always dealt with each other in and around their respective relationships with the Church of England.

This means that their history of opposition is not as deeply grounded as that between the Catholic Church and the Churches of the Reformation, or between Methodists and Anglicans.

The new climate created by our ecumenical age makes it possible for Catholics and Methodists to explore each other's teaching, tradition, spirituality and structures with a freedom which is not found in other ecumenical relationships. This offers the possibility of a great fruitfulness, not just for the relationship itself, but for the ecumenical movement as a whole.

David Chapman's book enables us to understand the historical role the Church of England has played in the relationship between Roman Catholics and Methodists, and also the very distinctive characteristics of this relationship.

In the conclusion to his work he refers to Methodism as 'an ecclesial renewal movement in search of a Church'. One could perhaps equally refer to the Roman Catholic Church as a church searching for ecclesial renewal movements. No matter how focused dialogue between Methodists and Catholics may be on particular doctrinal questions, their approaches are often still those of a renewal movement and those of a church determined to hold fast to the apostolic tradition as it perceives it.

The struggle of Catholics and Methodists to understand each other and to learn from each other is potentially one of the most fruitful relationships in the contemporary ecumenical movement. The differing approaches of Methodists and Catholics are, in some ways, the fundamental ones which inspired the Reformation even before the doctrinal issues around which it coalesced.

David Chapman's work provides the resources that Methodists and Catholics have long needed to explore their relationship. He has shown how necessary it is to understand the complex approach of John Wesley to the Roman Catholic Church and to Roman Catholics, and then the sad century of polemics which followed his death.

The beginning of the ecumenical movement and then the Second Vatican Council created an entirely new context for their relationship. It is as if the partners to the relationship were each freed from a role which history had obliged them to play, but which fitted neither of them very well.

By God's grace, significant agreements have been reached. One cannot help but recognise the power of God's Holy Spirit, restoring the understanding and affection between Christians of which John Wesley himself so often spoke.

As Methodists and Catholics continue to work to overcome their differences, they are discovering that they need some of each other's gifts to be truly themselves, and in discovering this, they may well show other Christian communities a way forward.

+ Michael Putney
Bishop of Townsville, Queensland
Australia

Catholic Co-Chairman, Joint Commission for Dialogue between the World Methodist Council and the Roman Catholic Church

Acknowledgements

Every writer incurs a number of debts in producing a book and the present author is no exception. In particular, I should like to record my gratitude to the following:

Bishop Michael Putney and Professor Geoffrey Wainwright for kindly contributing a foreword and for their inspiring leadership in the international Methodist–Roman Catholic dialogue.

Professor Geoffrey Wainwright and Revd Dr David Butler for their insightful comments on an earlier draft of the manuscript. Any remaining faults in the script are entirely the responsibility of the author, as are the opinions expressed.

The members of the British Methodist–Roman Catholic Committee and the Joint Commission for Dialogue between the World Methodist Council and the Roman Catholic Church for their stimulating colleagueship and scholarship.

The following, who provided material relating to the national dialogues: Revd Dr Norman Young and Prof. James Haire (Australia); Revd Terry Wall (New Zealand); Revd Dr Bruce Robbins (United States).

Revd Professor George H. Tavard for permission to quote from his unpublished paper 'How Catholics have seen Methodists', written for the international Methodist–Roman Catholic dialogue (2002).

Revd John Bradley, Field Officer (South) for Churches Together in England, for information about Local Ecumenical Partnerships involving Methodists and Roman Catholics.

The library staff at Cambridge University Library; and Miss Janet Henderson, Librarian at Wesley College, Bristol, for their courteous and unfailing assistance.

The commissioning editor at Epworth Press, Dr Natalie Watson, and the staff at SCM-Canterbury Press.

Finally, I am deeply indebted to my wife, Susan, and our children, Alexander, Sophie and Abigail for their patience and understanding during the writing of this book, which is dedicated to them.

David M. Chapman
Horsham, England

Feast of John and Charles Wesley, Priests, Poets, Teachers of the Faith, 1791, 1788

24 May 2004

Abbreviations

BEM   *Baptism, Eucharist, Ministry* (Geneva: WCC, 1982)

CDF   Congregation for the Doctrine of the Faith

DMBI   *A Dictionary of Methodism in Britain and Ireland,*
         ed. John A. Vickers (Peterborough: Epworth, 2000)

LEP   Local Ecumenical Partnership

LJW   Letters of John Wesley, 8 vols,
         ed. John Telford (London, 1931)

PWHS   *Proceedings of the Wesley Historical Society*

WCC   World Council of Churches

WJW   *Works of John Wesley,* bicentennial edition
         Various editors (Nashville: Abingdon, 1984–2003)

Works   *The Works of Rev. John Wesley A.M.,* ed. Thomas Jackson
         (London, 1872) vols I–XIII

Introduction

The place of John Wesley in popular historical consciousness seems secure. In a nationwide poll televised by the BBC in 2002, Wesley was ranked in fiftieth place in the list of 'Top One Hundred Great Britons', scoring higher than any other religious leader in British history.[1] Since the purpose of the poll was primarily entertainment, its findings should not be taken too seriously. Even so, this unexpected result suggests that, three hundred years after he was born, the founder of Methodism continues to capture the public imagination in Britain.

Roy Hattersley adopts a more rigorous approach to history in his recent biography of John Wesley, timed to coincide with the Wesley tercentenary celebrations in 2003. Evidently, Hattersley does not warm to his subject as a person, nor has he any obvious sympathy for Methodism. However, he acknowledges the contribution of Wesley and Methodism towards the development of modern British society: 'Not in his own lifetime, but certainly by proxy during the hundred years which followed his death, Wesley was one of the architects of modern Britain.'[2]

Scholars, too, continue to be fascinated with John Wesley. A trawl through library catalogues reveals a vast amount of literature on almost every aspect of his life and the history of Methodism by admirers, opponents, historians and theologians. If the number of recent works is anything to go by, interest in Wesley and the rise of Methodism shows little sign of diminishing.[3] Besides published works, there is a wealth of unpublished academic theses in university libraries, especially in Britain and North America, where Wesley (and Methodist) studies are currently enjoying something of a renaissance.

In Britain, the Anglican–Methodist Covenant of 2003 has increased awareness of the historic relationship between Methodism and its parent, the Church of England.[4] Over the years, various authors have

1

studied the rupture between Anglicans and Methodists following Wesley's death, Methodism's subsequent lurch towards nonconformity in reaction to the Oxford Movement, and the failed unity schemes of the twentieth century. However, few studies have given more than cursory attention to Methodism's relations with other religious bodies, notably the Roman Catholic Church.[5] In particular, there is no comprehensive treatment of controversy and dialogue between Methodists and Roman Catholics from the death of Wesley to the present day.

This surprising lack of interest in relations between Methodists and Roman Catholics can be attributed to the higher priority that church historians and theologians have generally attached to studying the relationship between Methodism and the Church of England in an attempt to understand why the separation occurred and how the breach might be healed. Furthermore, it has often been assumed that Wesley had nothing particularly original to say about Roman Catholicism. As we shall argue, however, this assumption fails to take into account the diversity of Wesley's statements about the Church of Rome and his mixed legacy to successive generations of Methodists in Britain and America. At the very least, the history of dialogue between Methodists and Roman Catholics provides an illuminating case study in the budding relationship between Roman Catholics and Protestants as the fierce heat generated by Reformation disputes gradually cooled.

The present volume is not intended to be a definitive history of relations between Methodists and Roman Catholics, not least because the author is a Methodist theologian and not a professional historian. Its more modest aim instead is to sketch the historical and theological contours of controversy and dialogue between Methodists and Roman Catholics from Wesley's earliest letter on 'popery', written in about 1735, to the present day. The political dimension of relations between Methodists and Roman Catholics in the British Isles and North America would make a fascinating study but lies beyond our intended scope.[6] For the purpose in hand, it will be sufficient to mention political affairs only insofar as these illustrate the theological issues at stake.

As we shall discover, John Wesley's attitude towards the Church of Rome proved to be a formative influence on subsequent relations between Methodists and Roman Catholics. Thus in order to understand some of the underlying reasons for the continuing controversy between Methodists and Roman Catholics in later years, first we must account for Wesley's strong reaction to Roman Catholicism within the context of the Church of England during the eighteenth century. Our first chapter describes the seminal influences on Wesley's theological formation as a prelude to studying the controversy between Wesley and his chief Roman Catholic critic, Richard Challoner.

Wesley's immediate legacy meant that relations between Methodists and Roman Catholics in the nineteenth century followed the dismal pattern already established in his lifetime. In the second chapter we examine the period from the death of Wesley to the close of the nineteenth century, a convenient point at which to pause. Besides contemporary magazine articles, our principal sources are the American Methodist Charles Elliott, two British Wesleyans, Hugh Price Hughes and Benjamin Gregory, John Henry Newman and James Mason, 'a poor priest of Stourbridge'. Mason was a dedicated Methodist minister who subsequently converted to Roman Catholicism. His anti-Methodist tracts, written from a unique vantage point, provide a fascinating insight into the disputes between Methodists and Roman Catholics in the early decades of the nineteenth century.

After years of mutual hostility, revitalised historical scholarship led to more constructive exchanges between Methodists and Roman Catholics in the twentieth century. In company with Protestants generally, Methodists now recognised the inadequacy of viewing Christian history episodically. The long periods in the history of the Church between the decisive events of the New Testament, the Patristic era, the Reformation, and the Evangelical Revival thus began to attract serious attention from Protestant historians. As the powerful emotions released by the Reformation eventually subsided, Methodist scholars became aware of parallels between the rise of Methodism in the eighteenth century and earlier renewal movements within the universal Church. At the same time, Roman Catholic scholars began to reassess the inherited opinion in Catholic circles that Methodism was an eccentric Protestant sect. As a result, Roman Catholics were able to recognise the contribution of John Wesley and Methodism to the mission of the Holy Catholic Church in the West. In Chapter 3 we chart the changing perceptions of Methodists and Roman Catholics about each other during the twentieth century up to, and including, the Second Vatican Council.

The Second Vatican Council (1962–5) was a watershed for ecumenism. Since then, relations between Methodists and Roman Catholics have improved considerably, mainly as a result of the new climate created by the Council, which paved the way for an international Methodist–Roman Catholic dialogue sponsored jointly by the World Methodist Council and the Pontifical Council for Promoting Christian Unity. The Joint Commission for Dialogue between the World Methodist Council and the Roman Catholic Church has produced several reports containing convergence statements for study and reception in both churches. Yet the vast majority of Methodists and Roman Catholics remain unaware that an official dialogue exists between their two churches, and the reports themselves are not widely available. Furthermore, with the notable exception of Geoffrey Wainwright in his study of *Methodists in Dialogue* (1995), theologians have paid little attention to these significant ecumenical texts. Chapter 4 therefore investigates the reports produced by the Joint Commission.

Following the lead of the World Methodist Council and the Vatican, Methodists and Roman Catholics in Great Britain, the United States, Australia and New Zealand have established their own bilateral conversations to address issues of local and national interest. Again, few Methodists and Roman Catholics are aware of these conversations, and some of the reports are unobtainable. Chapter 5 chronicles the progress of the national conversations and assesses their contribution to Methodist–Roman Catholic dialogue.

In 1995 Pope John Paul II issued an encyclical 'On Commitment to Ecumenism', *Ut Unum Sint*. The Congregation for the Doctrine of the Faith then followed this in 2000 with a controversial declaration entitled *Dominus Iesus*. In the same period British Methodism published a major statement on the Church, *Called to Love and Praise* (1999), and then in 2003 approved a formal response to the reports produced by the Joint Commission, which is noteworthy for being the first Methodist statement on the theological content of the dialogue with Roman Catholics. The sixth and final chapter, 'Towards Catholicity', examines these recent developments and assesses their implications for future dialogue between Methodists and Roman Catholics.

The liturgical movement in the twentieth century has contributed to the catholicity of all the churches by uncovering the earliest Christian traditions of worship. Chapter 6 examines the influence of the liturgical movement on Methodists and Roman Catholics and considers its likely impact on continuing dialogue. Over the same period, the ecumenical

4

movement has led to improved relations between Methodists and Roman Catholics at a local level. We briefly analyse Local Ecumenical Partnerships in England in which Methodists and Roman Catholics both participate, before reflecting on some practical issues that arise in sharing sacred space for worship. Finally, the Conclusion investigates the place of Methodism in the Holy Catholic Church and argues the case for continuing theological dialogue between Methodists and Roman Catholics.

It has to be admitted that the reception of Methodist–Roman Catholic dialogue within the two churches has been disappointing. For reasons that remain unclear, Methodist and Roman Catholic authorities have signally failed to exploit areas of mutual agreement and convergence so painstakingly established by their nominated representatives. What is worse, many Methodists and Roman Catholics continue to hold outdated and erroneous views of each other. For instance, there are Roman Catholics who are convinced that Methodists deny the real presence of Christ at the Eucharist. Equally, some Methodists imagine that Roman Catholics believe the Mass to involve a repetition of the atoning sacrifice of Christ at Calvary. If the official dialogue between Methodists and Roman Catholics is to have an impact on the local situation, then these and similar misunderstandings must be addressed. This book is offered as a contribution to theological dialogue between Methodists and Roman Catholics and its wider reception within the two churches.

A word of explanation about terminology is appropriate. For the sake of consistency and clarity, throughout this study we shall refer to *Roman* Catholics and the *Roman* Catholic Church. No offence is intended to those Catholic Christians who generally describe themselves and their church simply as 'Catholic'. However, as will hopefully become clear in the course of our investigations, Methodists can justly claim to be catholic Christians, albeit in a tradition shaped by the Reformation. One of John Wesley's most famous sermons was entitled 'Catholic Spirit'.[7] In this same catholic spirit, the final goal of their bilateral dialogue is for *Roman* Catholics and *Methodist* Catholics to be visibly united within the Holy Catholic Church.

1

John Wesley and Roman Catholicism

In 2003 Methodists commemorated the tercentenary of the birth of John Wesley with a 'Service of Celebration and Thanksgiving' in Lincoln Cathedral attended by representatives from Methodist Churches around the world. In Britain and elsewhere hundreds of local events celebrated the life and ministry of the founder of world Methodism. The anniversary did not go unnoticed by ecumenical partners, among them Roman Catholics. Preaching at a service in the English-speaking Methodist Church in Rome to mark the tercentenary, Cardinal Walter Kasper, President of the Pontifical Council for Promoting Christian Unity, prefaced his homily with the tactful observation that 'John Wesley was a complex figure, and his relationship with and view of the Catholic Church was equally complex.'[1]

Wesley's 'complex' reaction to the Roman Catholic Church constitutes the most significant element in the historical baggage that continues to affect the relationship between Methodists and Roman Catholics today. Therefore it is important to be precise about what Wesley actually said about the Roman Catholic Church in his sermons, letters, theological treatises and journal. It is equally important to understand those formative influences that shaped Wesley's response to Roman Catholicism in the prevailing religious and political climate of the eighteenth century. At the outset, it is appropriate to sketch a few biographical details.

John Wesley was born on 17 June 1703 in Epworth, Lincolnshire, where his father, Samuel, the son of a Dissenting minister, was rector of the parish. His mother, Susanna, daughter of a famous Dissenter, Samuel Annesley, proved a formidable influence on his intellectual and spiritual development. Resourceful and independent-minded, Susanna provided her children with a rigorous school curriculum in the family kitchen. In later life John remembered with gratitude and affection his early education, especially the weekly sessions on moral and scriptural teaching.

The most famous episode of Wesley's childhood was the rectory fire of 1709 when five-year-old John was rescued from the burning house only after the rest of the family had escaped. Describing himself as 'a brand plucked from the burning' (Zechariah 3.2), Wesley subsequently interpreted his childhood deliverance as part of the providential rise of Methodism. The incident entered Methodist folklore as a sign that John had been preserved for an extraordinary mission. Whatever the reason for his good fortune, the boy suffered no ill effect from the fire and at the age of eleven became a pupil at Charterhouse.

In June 1720 John went up to Christ Church, Oxford, with an annual Charterhouse exhibition of £20 to support him. After taking holy orders in 1725 he was elected Fellow of Lincoln College, where he would probably have pursued a comfortable academic career had it not been for his growing involvement in the Holy Club, a group of earnest Christian students who met regularly for prayer and dedicated their time to acts of charity, earning themselves the derisory nickname 'Methodist'. Unusually, as part of their commitment to the welfare of the poor, members of the Holy Club took it upon themselves to visit prisoners in Oxford jail. Among the founder members of the Holy Club was John's younger brother, Charles Wesley (1707–88), who also took holy orders and later became Methodism's most prolific hymn writer.

After a short period as his father's curate in Lincolnshire, John volunteered to serve as pastor in the new colony of Georgia, where he hoped to make his mark by converting the Native Americans. However, his disastrous experience in America prompted him to return to England in a deep spiritual crisis, culminating in the famous 'conversion' experience of 24 May 1738, meticulously recorded in the *Journal*:

> In the evening I went very unwillingly to a society in Aldersgate Street, where one was reading Luther's Preface to the Romans. About a quarter before nine, while he was describing the change which God works in the heart through faith in Christ, I felt my heart strangely warmed. I felt I did trust in Christ, Christ alone for salvation; and an assurance was given me that He had taken away my sins, even mine, and saved me from the law of sin and death.[2]

Whether this was a conversion experience in the commonly understood sense of the term or an experience of *assurance* has been much debated. Whatever it was, Wesley was powerfully inspired to preach the Gospel with a strongly Arminian flavour, emphasising the availability of grace for all.

Less than a year later, George Whitefield (1714–70), who was currently enjoying some success in converting the miners of Kingswood near Bristol, urged Wesley to join him in his ministry of open air preaching. Wesley was reluctant at first, imagining that little good would come from such an irregular activity as 'field preaching', which contradicted his refined sense of ecclesiastical order. It was with strong misgivings that he eventually consented 'to become more vile' by preaching in the open air. In the event, the response soon convinced him that this was the right course of action. Abandoning all hopes of an academic career, Wesley embarked upon an itinerant preaching ministry, disregarding parish boundaries and the usual ministerial courtesies, to the annoyance of several diocesan bishops and parish priests who closed their pulpits to him.

From bases in London, Bristol and Newcastle, Wesley visited hundreds of communities in Britain and Ireland, preaching in the open air if necessary and founding Methodist societies wherever there was sufficient response to his message, with 'bands' (subsequently 'classes') for the most committed. In the course of a long and eventful ministry, Wesley travelled approximately two hundred and fifty thousand miles in Great Britain and Ireland, mostly on horseback, and preached more than forty thousand sermons, undeterred by scornful attack and occasional mob violence. Methodism, as Wesley was fond of saying, had been raised up by God to spread 'scriptural holiness' throughout the land.

Initially, the burgeoning 'connexion' of Methodist societies constituted an evangelical holiness movement within the Church of England. Horrified by the idea of schism in the Church, Wesley was intent on avoiding separation. Preaching services and class meetings were organised to allow Methodists to attend worship at their local parish church. At first, the new preaching house in Bristol (1739) had no communion table: the congregation processed to the nearby parish church in order to receive the sacrament. Writing just a few months before his death, Wesley resisted calls from some of his itinerant helpers for separation, insisting 'I live and die in the Church of England.'[3] Yet the impetus towards separation was irresistible, especially after he controversially ordained presbyters for North America (1784), Scotland (1785) and eventually England (1789), contrary to canon law, which required that presbyters be episcopally ordained. Even without such a serious step as this, separation became virtually inevitable as holders of the Methodist class ticket desired more and more the ministry of their own preachers, local and itinerant. The increasingly tenuous links between the Church of England and the Methodist societies could not long survive without Wesley to maintain the connexion by sheer force of personality.

John Wesley died on 2 March 1791 and was buried in a vault behind his chapel in City Road, London, in a burial ground 'as *holy* as any in England, and it contains a large quantity of "bonny dust" '.[4] Technically, this was unconsecrated ground, but Wesley disdained such 'idle Popish conceit'.[5] Over this issue, however, the brothers literally parted company. When Charles died in March 1788, he left instructions for his body to be buried in Marylebone Churchyard, prompting John to publish a short piece dismissing the notion of consecrated chapels and burial grounds as 'a mere relic of Romish superstition'.[6] In death, as in life, John would be 'guided, not by custom, but by Scripture and reason'. His indignant rhetorical question is typical in its forensic logic but somehow manages to miss the point:

'You say, this is consecrated ground, so many feet broad, and so many long. But pray how deep is the consecrated ground?' – '*Deep!* What does that signify?' O, a great deal: for if my grave be dug too deep, I may happen to get out of the consecrated ground: and who can tell what unhappy consequences may follow from this?[7]

This practical disregard for the conventions of a decent Church of England burial illustrates the strength of Wesley's Protestant convictions. Throughout his ministry, he consistently denounced the 'errors of the Church of Rome' and their residual influence on the Church of England despite the English Reformation. Using all available means, he vigorously opposed 'popery', attacking the 'idolatry' of Roman Catholicism as 'adulterated Christianity'. Even his brother's gift for poetry was pressed into the service of the Protestant cause: two of Charles's anti-Catholic hymns were appended to *A Word to a Protestant*. The following verses vividly convey their general flavour:

O how shall I presume,
Jesus, to call on thee,
Sunk in the lowest dregs of Rome,
The worst idolatry!

A murderer convict, I come
My vileness to bewail;
By nature born a son of Rome,
A child of wrath and hell.

Lord, I at last recant, reject,
Through thy great strength alone,
The madness of the Romish sect,
The madness of my own.[8]

Comparing the fallen human condition to being 'a son of Rome' may not have been the worst insult to be heaped upon the heads of Roman Catholics by a Protestant; nevertheless it was a virulent expression of abuse. It is no wonder, therefore, that Roman Catholic scholars have mostly taken it for granted that John Wesley was strongly anti-Catholic. Ronald Knox, in his influential study of religion in England during the eighteenth century, concluded that Wesley 'shared all the crude anti-Catholic prejudices of his day, and made no secret of it'.[9] Probably the most serious indictment comes from the Roman Catholic historian Eamon Duffy, who maintains that 'John Wesley detested Roman Catholicism.'[10] But, although there is ample evidence to support these claims, there are also signs in his sermons and other writings that Wesley could sometimes be conciliatory towards Roman Catholics. John Todd, a Roman Catholic layman and ecumenist, believed that 'Wesley was far more friendly to Catholics than most Englishmen at this time.'[11] Others have gone still further, describing the *Letter to a Roman Catholic* as a classic ecumenical text and proof that Wesley was the forerunner of the modern ecumenical movement.[12]

Whatever the ambiguities in Wesley's multifarious writings, Methodists have generally accepted that Wesley was to some extent anti-Catholic. Indeed, during the nineteenth century, Wesley's anti-Catholicism was a source of pride among Methodists and a selling-point in the fierce competition to attract new members. In these circumstances

10

Methodist scholars were in no position to reassess Wesley's attitude to the Roman Catholic Church, nor for the most part were they inclined to do so. Only in the course of the twentieth century did Methodist scholars begin to reconsider the received Protestant interpretation of church history and the controversies of the eighteenth century. Simultaneously, the ecumenical movement produced a thaw in relations between Roman Catholics and Methodists, which contributed on both sides to a collective loss of memory about past disputes. Nowadays Methodists are often uncomfortable at discovering their founder's hostile reaction to Roman Catholicism. David Butler candidly admits, 'It is embarrassing to realise just how wrong John Wesley was on the subject of Roman Catholicism and how prejudiced he was when he met it.'[13]

Whether or not to ease their embarrassment, some Methodists have distinguished between Wesley's opposition to Roman Catholicism as a theological system and his genuine esteem for those Christians who shared his 'religion of the heart', irrespective of their church allegiance. 'I know', said Wesley, 'some Roman Catholics who sincerely love both God and their neighbour, and who steadily endeavour to do unto everyone as they wish him to do unto them.'[14] This and similar statements have sometimes been seized upon in order to soften Wesley's anti-Catholicism. Henry Rack, for instance, concludes that John Wesley was 'equivocal' towards Roman Catholicism.[15] John Munsey Turner similarly refers to 'Wesley's strikingly ambivalent attitude to Catholicism'.[16]

While these are valid assessments, they tend to obscure the extreme tensions inherent within Wesley's reaction to Roman Catholicism, which stemmed from an unstable blend of opposites present in his personality and theology – prejudice and tolerance, hostility and sympathy, catholicity and exclusivity, subtlety of expression and an unfortunate tendency to broad generalisation when making a particular point. Far from being straightforward, Wesley's many and varied statements about Roman Catholicism require careful interpretation in the light of these personal traits and the particular circumstances in which he wrote. The fact that scholars from all ecclesial traditions have reached contrasting conclusions about Wesley's attitude to Roman Catholicism demonstrates how difficult it is to get to the heart of his ecclesiology and its theological presuppositions.

*

11

To understand the reasons for John Wesley's complex reaction to Roman Catholicism, it is essential to locate his theology in the intellectual, historical and political context of the eighteenth century. Three main influences can be identified as having contributed to shaping his attitude towards the Roman Catholic Church.

In the first place, there was Wesley's upbringing in the Church of England, which at the beginning of the eighteenth century was vehemently anti-Catholic. By a process of rigorous and at times brutal iconoclasm, the English Reformation had finally succeeded in dismantling the apparatus of Roman customs and practices, thereby effectively transforming the Catholic Church in England into what to many looked and felt like a Protestant church. More than a century before Wesley was born, parish clergy had removed the means of Catholic devotion from their churches for the last time with varying degrees of enthusiasm for Cranmer's Book of Common Prayer.[17] Protestant Primers had inculcated the new orthodoxy, cautioning the faithful against former superstitions. By the time Wesley was born, Protestantism had long since been fully absorbed into the bloodstream of the Church of England, and there was already a long tradition of anti-Roman polemic, as exemplified in such works as John Jewel, *An Apology or Answer in Defence of the Church of England* (1562), Richard Hooker, *Laws of Ecclesiastical Polity* (1594–7) and William Chillingworth, *The Religion of Protestants* (1637). To such as these, the Church of England was a *via media* between the extremes of the Roman Catholic Church on the one hand and the continental Reformed churches on the other. Though there was scope for debate about whether the English Reformation had gone too far, or not far enough, in leading the Church of England in a Protestant direction, the Caroline divines were united in their hostility to Rome.[18] Thus Wesley did not come to possess an anti-Catholic outlook as a result of unfavourable contact with Roman Catholics. On the contrary, anti-Catholicism was a significant element of the spiritual inheritance of the Church of England in the early eighteenth century.

The second factor to influence Wesley's attitude towards Roman Catholicism was the Enlightenment concept of 'toleration', which generally discouraged persecution and even permitted religious diversity, provided there were certain guarantees to civil order.[19] Some penal legislation against Roman Catholics had already been repealed under the Act for the Relief of Religious and Peaceable People (1650). In 1681

Oliver Plunket became the last Roman Catholic to be executed in England simply for his faith. The Act of Toleration (1689) put an end to state persecution by acknowledging the right of Protestant Dissenters (Baptists, Independents and Presbyterians) to worship freely and even accorded them some civil liberties.

In theory Roman Catholics were excluded from the provisions of the Act of Toleration, because the pope's territorial ambitions constituted a threat to civil society. Still, the high-water mark of anti-Catholic persecution had already passed, and during the eighteenth century practical toleration was extended to Roman Catholics under the benevolent spirit of Enlightenment thinking. Lacking any legal foundation, practical toleration was a fragile state of affairs, which could easily be shattered by changes in the political temperature, as happened at the time of the invasion scares in the 1740s. There were also a handful of notorious agitators like William Payne, 'the Protestant Carpenter', who in 1767 tried unsuccessfully to have Bishop Challoner (the Vicar Apostolic of the London District) and some of his priests indicted.[20] The Gordon Riots of 1780 were the last gasp of Protestant intolerance in response to the government's cautious and limited dismantling of the anti-Catholic laws.

As is often the case in such matters, political expediency rather than altruism provided the impetus for reform. To encourage the recruitment of Roman Catholics into the British Army in order to sustain the war against the colonialists in North America, the Catholic Relief Act (1778) removed certain penalties imposed by Parliament in 1700. Roman Catholics were now permitted to establish schools and buy and transfer land. In return, they were required to take an oath of loyalty to the Hanoverian succession, forswear the pope's temporal and civil jurisdiction in England, and deny the principle that 'no faith is to be kept with heretics'. A further Catholic Relief Act in 1791 even permitted Roman Catholics to build chapels. Although they remained second-class citizens until the middle of the following century, Roman Catholics were now free to consolidate their position in British society, to the alarm of more militant Protestants distrustful of their intentions.

The philosopher John Locke, in his first *Letter Concerning Toleration* (1689), provided the intellectual framework for religious toleration, which proved enormously influential on Wesley.[21] Briefly, Locke argued for individual liberty of conscience and freedom from state compulsion in religious matters. Since religion was about loving one's enemies, there could be no justification for torturing and killing others under the pretext of religion. Moreover, compulsion in religious matters was illogical since true religion consists in the inward persuasion of the mind. Instead, the law should tolerate every congregation, not just the state religion, because all were concerned with the salvation of souls. To avoid anarchy, the civil authorities had the right to control religious groups that threatened the peace and security of the realm.

Though he did not mention them by name, Locke excluded Roman Catholics from toleration for three reasons. First, it was impossible to secure the allegiance of Roman Catholics to Protestant civil authority. There could be no confidence in an oath of loyalty sworn by a Roman Catholic since it was a principle established at the Council of Constance (1415) that 'no faith is to be kept with heretics'. Thus despite a promise of safe conduct, John Hus was executed by order of the council, which felt under no obligation to honour its guarantee. Second, in the person of the pope Roman Catholics recognised an authority beyond that of the national government. Third, there was no reason to extend toleration towards Roman Catholics when 'they think themselves bound to deny it to others'. While Locke's concept of toleration was not the cause of long-standing anti-Catholicism in England, it provided intellectual respectability for more basic forms of prejudice against Roman Catholics.

Wesley frequently drew on Locke, though usually without naming his mentor. Paradoxically, Wesley's rejection of persecution, his liberal attitude towards religious dissent and his robust anti-Catholicism each had its intellectual basis in Locke's philosophy. In 'A Disavowal of Persecuting Papists' (1782) Wesley reflected on the subject of religious persecution. Unable to resist a credulous tale of Roman Catholic excess, he confided:

> Very lately, a person seeing many flocking to a place, which she did not know was a Romish chapel, innocently said, 'What do all these people want?' and was answered by one of them, with a great vehemence, 'We want your blood. And we will have it soon.'[22]

There again, Wesley genuinely hated the thought of Roman Catholics being persecuted in England, a view he held consistently for more than fifty years:

I set out early in life with an utter abhorrence of persecution in every form, and a full conviction that every man has a right to worship God according to his own conscience . . . And this I extend to members of the Church of Rome, as well as to all other men.[23]

The 'Disavowal' concludes with a declaration of support for the level of toleration enjoyed by Roman Catholics prior to the Relief Act: 'And the Romanists never have been persecuted in England since I remember. They have enjoyed a full toleration. I wish them to enjoy the same toleration still, neither more nor less.'[24]

What Wesley meant by 'the same toleration' is clear from a letter he wrote on 21 January 1780 to the printer of the *Public Advertiser* and from similar letters of 23 and 31 March 1780 to the editor of the *Freeman's Journal* in Dublin. Wesley insisted, 'upon principles of reason, no Government ought to tolerate men who cannot give security to that Government for their allegiance and peaceable behaviour'.[25] Protestants could have no security until Roman Catholics renounced the principle that 'no faith is to be kept with heretics'.[26] Oaths of allegiance to the British crown were 'light as air' because of the professed spiritual power of pope and priest to dispense the faithful from such promises and pardon even treason. Roman Catholics might take five hundred oaths of loyalty, but the same principle 'sweeps them all away as a spider's web'. Therefore, since Roman Catholics could guarantee neither loyalty nor peaceable behaviour, no government, 'Protestant, Mahometan, or Pagan' should tolerate them.[27] To Wesley's consternation, the Catholic Relief Act encouraged Roman Catholics to preach openly and 'make numerous converts day by day to their intolerant, persecuting principles', thereby threatening English liberty. In a vain attempt to turn back the clock, Wesley concluded: 'I wish them to enjoy the same liberty, civil and religious, which they enjoyed in England before the late Act.'[28]

Wesley's public opposition to the Catholic Relief Act of 1778 was a welcome development for Lord George Gordon's English Protestant Association, busily engaged in gathering signatures for a petition demanding that Parliament repeal the Act. Gordon was delighted to have the support of such an eminent preacher. But, although they shared the same objective, their methods were very different. In June 1780, at the instigation of Gordon, London was wracked by the most serious rioting of the eighteenth century. Directed principally at Roman Catholics, the Gordon Riots claimed the lives of nearly three hundred people, plus a number of rioters who were later hanged for their crimes. Horrified at the violence, Wesley became embroiled in a lengthy controversy with an Irish Capuchin, Father O'Leary, who accused him of being the inspiration behind the polemical works published by the Protestant Association.[29] Despite strong denials from Wesley, the false accusation proved difficult to bury, and the story subsequently became widely accepted among Roman Catholics. For the next fifty years, popular opinion among Roman Catholics in Britain and Ireland blamed John Wesley for stirring up anti-Catholic feeling in England.[30]

The third factor to influence Wesley's attitude towards Roman Catholicism was his experience of meeting Roman Catholics in the course of 21 visits to Ireland, one of the poorest and most isolated Roman Catholic countries in Europe. On his first visit in 1747 Wesley observed that the Protestant mission in Ireland had been a dismal failure: the Protestants in Ireland originated from England, and virtually all the native inhabitants remained in the religion of their forebears.[31] 'Nor is it any wonder that those who are born Papists generally live and die such, when the Protestants can find no better ways to convert them than Penal Laws and Acts of Parliament.'[32] Naively, Wesley proposed an alternative strategy for the Protestant mission in Ireland, which would yield better results. Since Roman Catholics recognised the apostles as having greater authority than the hierarchy, if the Church of Ireland clergy lived and preached like the apostles, then before long there would be no more Papists in Ireland.[33]

On his second visit to Ireland in 1748, Wesley was encouraged at the enthusiastic reception from the mainly Roman Catholic crowds.[34] The attentive and generally well-behaved congregations impressed him: 'So civil a people as the Irish in general I never saw, either in Europe or America.'[35] However, the burgeoning Methodist mission in Ireland was already generating tensions that soon spilled over into violence. Wesley's next visit in 1749 led to riots in Dublin and the most serious of all confrontations between Methodists and Roman Catholics in the British Isles. Whether or not as a result of this occurrence, ten years later Wesley had evidently changed his opinion of the inhabitants of Ireland. Preaching in a village outside Castlebar, Wesley was 'surprised to find how little the Irish Papists are changed in a hundred years. Most of them retain the same bitterness, yea, and thirst for blood as ever, and would as freely cut the throats of all Protestants as they did in the last century.'[36] The questionable loyalty of Irish Roman Catholics to the British crown was also a source of concern to Wesley, especially since the British military presence in Ireland had been reduced in order to cope with the demands of the American war. Wesley welcomed the establishment of the Protestant Volunteers in 1778 as a means to 'keep the Papists in order'.[37]

On the other hand, Wesley was genuinely sympathetic towards the uneducated peasants of Ireland, who could not be blamed either for their servility to the Roman Catholic hierarchy or for their economic plight. Responsibility lay with the priests who had oppressed the population. Fearful for their flocks in the face of marauding Methodist wolves, Roman Catholic priests in Ireland frequently intervened to prevent people attending Wesley's sermons, thereby breeding resentment on both sides. After preaching to the Protestant inhabitants of Ahascragh in May 1762 (the Roman Catholics having been forbidden by their priest to attend), Wesley observed in bitter tones: 'What could a magistrate do in this case? Doubtless he might tell the priest: "Sir, as you enjoy liberty of conscience, you shall allow it to others. You are not persecuted yourself; you shall not persecute them." '[38] Thus Wesley appealed indirectly to Locke's philosophy of toleration in defence of Methodist missions in a predominantly Roman Catholic country.

It appears Wesley even blamed the Roman Catholic Church for the economic plight of Ireland. On a visit in 1776 he noted the contrast in living conditions between the Roman Catholic south and Protestant Ulster. 'No sooner did we enter Ulster than we observed the difference. The ground was cultivated just as in England, and the cottages not only neat, but with doors, chimneys and windows.'[39] For Wesley, the lesson was obvious: only by accepting the Protestant faith could Ireland lift itself from economic distress.

Yet, despite his adverse experience of Roman Catholicism in Ireland, Wesley recorded several favourable impressions from meeting Roman Catholics. Travelling through Ireland in 1789, Wesley noted in the *Journal*, 'A Popish gentleman inviting me to lodge at his house, I spent a comfortable evening.'[40] Occasional encounters of this kind indicate that Wesley was by no means bigoted in his dealings with others, though they only served to strengthen his conviction that the Church of Rome was an unchanging and oppressive structure.

Wesley's choice of spiritual reading further demonstrates his sincerity towards individual Roman Catholics. Wesley read and appreciated various Roman Catholic spiritual writers, including: Thomas à Kempis; the Mexican hermit Gregory Lopez; Baron de Renty; and the Quietist Madame Guyon. These and similar writers Wesley particularly valued for their description of Christian holiness and perfection. For the edification of Methodists, he produced abridged versions of several Roman Catholic spiritual works, omitting anything 'popish'. Henry Rack describes Wesley's spirituality as being based on a synthesis of different strands of piety, conditioned as always by his own needs and experiences.[41]

The main theological influence on Wesley's attitude towards Roman Catholicism came from his reading of the Reformers, especially Luther and Calvin, though the picture is more complicated than is usually supposed. Luther and Calvin disagreed on important aspects of theology, and Wesley was neither wholly Lutheran nor totally Calvinist in his outlook. In certain respects, he was closer to Luther than to Calvin; in other ways the opposite was true. There again, by adhering to elements of the Catholic doctrine of salvation, Wesley parted company with both Reformers. The precise details are complex, and scholars have interpreted differently the character of Wesley's theology.[42] For our purpose, Wesley's understanding of grace and holiness illustrates the way in which his theology was related by comparison and contrast to Luther, Calvin and Catholic doctrine.[43]

Wesley was conscious of standing in the tradition of Anglican theology and was inclined to read the continental Reformers from the mediating perspective of the Church of England, which possessed a strong sense of continuity with the Church of the past. 'Primitive Christianity' of the first four centuries particularly fascinated Wesley. The New Testament and the early Church Fathers revealed to Wesley that primitive Christianity was not a system of doctrines but an inward change caused by the response of faith, resulting in outward righteousness and the fruits of the Spirit.[44] The early Church knew no universal head because no bishop was acknowledged as such at the Council of Nicaea (325).[45] In Wesley's eyes, the new-found status of Christianity under Constantine represented a kind of fall of the Church, which eventually led to widespread corruption through the abuse of privilege and power.[46] Echoing Luther's famous reference to the Babylonian captivity of the Church under the dominion of Rome, Wesley accused the Roman Catholic Church of being 'Babylon the great' (Revelation 17.6).[47] He yearned for the 'scriptural Christianity' of the early Church to become the religion of England.

A recurring theme in Wesley's writings, derived from Luther via the Church of England formularies, is the unique status and function of Scripture in the Church (*sola Scriptura*). Article Six of the Church of England refers to the sufficiency of Scripture for Christian faith and life. In 'The Character of a Methodist' (1742) Wesley placed belief in the sole authority of Scripture at the head of the distinguishing features of Methodism. 'We believe this written Word of God to be the *only and the sufficient* rule of Christian faith and practice; and therein we are fundamentally distinguished from those of the Romish Church.'[48] According to Wesley, though Christians were obliged to receive church doctrine that 'agreed' with Scripture, they were justified in doubting what was not clearly grounded in Scripture.

Not only did Luther emphasise the authority of Scripture, but he also insisted that Christians are saved exclusively through faith (*sola fide*) and not through performing works of piety and mercy. Differences in understanding the relationship between faith and good works in the doctrine of salvation provoked a substantial dispute between Luther and the Roman Catholic Church, which led to the most serious split in the Holy Catholic Church since the Great Schism separated East and West between the tenth and early thirteenth centuries. Wesley agreed with Luther that faith is the gateway to salvation, one of his favourite biblical texts being, 'By grace are ye saved through faith' (Ephesians 2.8), 'that great foundation of the whole Christian building'.[49]

In a classic sermon on 'Salvation by Faith', Wesley stressed that salvation stems from the free and unmerited grace of God. 'For there is nothing we are, or have, or do, which can deserve the least thing at God's hand.'[50] He regretted that, as a result of false teaching, Roman Catholics (and some Protestants) imagined that works of piety and mercy were more significant than faith itself.[51] Still, the doctrine of salvation by faith had successfully driven popery out of Britain, and only this doctrine could prevent the spread of the 'Romish delusion'.[52] Interestingly, Wesley did not regard the doctrine of 'salvation by works' as the fundamental doctrine of Roman Catholicism: that distinction he awarded jointly to the doctrine of the universality of the Roman Catholic Church and the supremacy of the bishop of Rome.[53]

Whereas Luther had insisted that God *alone* did everything to save human beings, Wesley retained a place for works of piety in his own theology of salvation. While agreeing with Luther that human beings are justified by grace through faith, he could not accept that Christians necessarily remain sinners (*simul iustus et peccator* in the Lutheran formula). As Wesley saw it, Luther 'in the fury of his solifidianism' had not sufficiently recognised what God's grace could achieve in sinners.[54] That God alone was responsible for the salvation of human beings did not exclude their active participation in that process. Crucially, Wesley's synergism gave the priority to God – every human action was in response to God's prevenient or preventing grace.

Wesley's sermon 'On working out your own salvation' contains a subtle account of the interaction between human agency and divine sovereignty, freedom and grace.[55] The text is Philippians 2.12–13: 'Work out your own salvation with fear and trembling; for it is God that worketh in you, both to will and to do of his good pleasure.' For Wesley, the meaning of these words 'removes all imagination of merit from man, and gives God the whole glory of his own work'.[56] At the same time, they lay an obligation on humans to 'work out' (that is, co-operate with) their own salvation through works of piety and mercy. Methodists were exhorted to ' "Search the Scriptures;" hear them in public, read them in private, and meditate therein. At every opportunity be a partaker of the Lord's Supper.'[57] Wesley cited with approval a maxim of St Augustine of Hippo: 'He that made us without ourselves, will not save us without ourselves.'[58]

Wesley explains thus the process of salvation, which 'begins with what is usually termed (and very properly) "preventing grace"':

Salvation is carried on by 'convincing grace', usually in Scripture termed 'repentance', which brings a larger measure of self-knowledge, and a farther deliverance from the heart of stone. Afterwards we experience the proper Christian salvation, whereby 'through grace' we 'are saved by faith', consisting of those two grand branches, justification and sanctification. By justification we are saved from the guilt of sin, and restored to the image of God. All experience, as well as Scripture, shows this salvation to be both instantaneous and gradual.

20

It begins the moment we are justified, in the holy, humble, gentle, patient love of God and man. It gradually increases from that moment as a 'grain of mustard seed, which at first is the least of all the seeds, but' gradually 'puts forth large branches', and becomes a great tree; till in another instant the heart is cleansed from sin, and filled with pure love to God and man. But even that love increases more and more, till we 'grow up in all things into him that is our head', 'till we attain the measure of the stature of the fullness of Christ'.[59]

Wesley insisted that grace is not merely *imputed* to the notional account of sinners (a metaphor borrowed by Calvin from accounting). Rather, through participation in the means of grace, including Holy Communion, grace is actually *imparted* to sinners so that they grow spiritually towards entire sanctification.

Wesley's doctrine of sanctification is summed up in *A Plain Account of Christian Perfection* (1777), which incorporates the following propositions dating from 1764:

(1) There is such a thing as perfection; for it is again and again mentioned in Scripture.

(2) It is not so early as justification; for justified persons are to 'go on unto perfection' (Hebrews 6.1).

(3) It is not so late as death; for St Paul speaks of living men that were perfect (Philippians 3.15).

(4) It is not absolute. Absolute perfection belongs not to man, nor to angels, but to God alone.

(5) It does not make a man infallible; none is infallible while he remains in the body.

(6) Is it sinless? It is not worth while to contend for a term. It is 'salvation from sin'.

(7) It is 'perfect love' (I John 4.18). This is the essence of it: its properties, or inseparable fruits, are, rejoicing evermore, praying without ceasing, and in everything giving thanks (I Thessalonians 5.16 etc.).

(8) It is improvable. It is so far from lying in an indivisible point, from being incapable of increase, that one perfected in love may grow in grace far swifter than he did before.

(9) It is amissable, capable of being lost; of which we have

21

numerous instances. But we were not thoroughly convinced of this till five or six years ago.

(10) It is constantly both preceded and followed by a gradual work.

(11) But is it in itself instantaneous or not? In examining this, let us go on step by step.

An instantaneous change has been wrought in some believers; none can deny this.

Since that change they enjoy perfect love; they feel this, and this alone; they 'rejoice evermore, pray without ceasing, and in everything give thanks'. Now, this is all that I mean by perfection; therefore, these are witnesses of the perfection which I preach.[60]

Wesley went on to address the objections that might be raised, but to discuss these would lead us away from our main objective. It is sufficient to note that, for Wesley, perfection meant 'purity of intention, dedicating all the life to God'. Put another way, 'it is all the mind which was in Christ, enabling us to walk as Christ walked'. Again, 'It is the circumcision of the heart in the whole image of God, the full likeness of him that created it.'[61]

In a letter to the Calvinist John Newton dated 14 May 1765, Wesley explained the inspiration behind his doctrine of Christian perfection:

In 1725 I met with Bishop Taylor's *Rule of Holy Living* and *Dying*. I was struck particularly with the chapter upon *intention*, and felt a fixed intention to give myself up to God. In this I was much confirmed soon after by the *Christian's Pattern*, and longed to 'give God all my heart'. This is just what I mean by *perfection* now. I sought after it from that hour.[62]

In a previous letter Wesley had enquired of Newton, 'Is not a Papist a child of God? Is Thomas à Kempis, Mr de Renty, Gregory Lopez gone to hell? Believe it who can. Yet still of such (though Papists) the same is my brother and sister and mother.'[63] Such obvious sympathy for certain Roman Catholic spiritual writers and their interpretation of the Christian life distinguished Wesley from the majority of his contemporaries in the Church of England, who were far more Protestant-minded, and inevitably invited the accusation of popery.

As if to reassure Newton, Wesley continued: 'I think on justification just as I have any time these seven and twenty years, and just as Mr Calvin does. In this respect, I do not differ from him an hair's breadth.'[64] Where Wesley did part company with Calvin, however, was over the doctrine of election. For Calvin, the effect of the Fall on the image of God in humankind was so profound and persistent that only God's prior election could overcome the effect of original sin. This belief provided the basis for Calvin's doctrine of double predestination. Thirty years earlier, Wesley and his brother had considered it 'our duty to oppose *predestination* with our whole strength, not as an *opinion*, but as a dangerous mistake which appears to be subversive of the very foundation of Christian experience, and which has in fact given occasion to the most grievous offences'.[65]

To Wesley's way of thinking, the doctrine of double predestination implies that God works in an arbitrary way. Moreover, it leads in the direction of antinomianism or moral anarchy, since there is nothing that an individual may do to alter his or her eternal destiny. As Calvin saw it, because God never goes back on his call, the elect must inevitably persevere in grace to the end. In contrast, Wesley held that 'perfection is amissable, capable of being lost', and in 'Serious Thoughts upon the Perseverance of the Saints' he established from Scripture that 'one who is holy or righteous in the judgment of God himself may nevertheless so fall from God as to perish everlastingly'.[66]

It has been suggested that Wesley's doctrine of salvation was 'a necessary synthesis of the Protestant ethic of grace with the Catholic ethic of holiness'.[67] In fact, Wesley's understanding of grace and holiness was not particularly original, but was very similar to the doctrine of salvation according to the *via media* of the Caroline divines in the Church of England. What distinguished Wesley however was that he drew immediate practical conclusions for the Christian life. In an age when the eucharistic life of the Church of England was generally at a low ebb, Wesley preached for more than 55 years on 'The Duty of Constant Communion' as a means of grace that led to Christian perfection.[68] Thus, in some ways, Wesley anticipated the sacramental revival of the Oxford Movement in the nineteenth century.

A powerful combination of all these formative influences produced in Wesley a complex reaction to Roman Catholicism, which varied according to the circumstances in which he found himself. As an itinerant preacher, Wesley was far too busy to engage in speculative theology. As a folk theologian, he was the tutor of Methodism, producing theology to help ordinary people face practical problems in the Christian life. Called to preach the Gospel to all people, and displaying a keen sense of the practicalities of Christian mission, Wesley wrote sermons and treatises on whatever topical subject seized his imagination. These were almost always occasional pieces, produced in response to a particular situation. Inevitably, there is a degree of inconsistency in this kind of material, not least because Wesley wrote over a considerable period of time. Therefore, a deal of caution is required when attempting to derive general conclusions from particular statements in Wesley's writings.

Wesley's earliest written challenge to the Church of Rome seems to have been his letter 'To a Roman Catholic Priest', which was probably written in May 1735.[69] Since the recipient is not named, it may have been an open letter. Wesley begins with the unlikely claim that he had 'neither time nor inclination for controversy with any; but least of all with the Romanists'. His professed reluctance to engage with Roman Catholics was because he did not trust the way in which they consulted historical documents and classical theologians – editing or omitting passages that might contradict the required outcome. All the same, he distanced himself from popular anti-Catholicism:

> I can by no means approve the scurrility and contempt with which the Romanists have often been treated. I dare not rail at or despise any man, much less those who profess to believe in the same Master. But I pity them much, having the same assurance that Jesus is the Christ and that no Romanist can expect to be saved according to the terms of his Covenant.[70]

Besides adding to the 'Book of Life', the Council of Trent broke the commandments by honouring religious images (Exodus 20.5). The charge is significant because Wesley believed it to be the root cause of other forms of idolatry in the Roman Catholic Church.[71] Whether Wesley fully understood the distinction that Roman Catholics draw between worship and veneration is difficult to say.

'To a Roman Catholic Priest' lists ten non-Scriptural doctrines which the Council of Trent had added to the 'Book of Life': '(1) seven sacraments; (2) transubstantiation; (3) communion in one kind only; (4) purgatory, and praying for the dead therein; (5) praying to saints; (6) veneration of relics; (7) worship of images; (8) indulgences; (9) the priority and universality of the Roman Church; (10) the supremacy of the Bishop of Rome'. Taken as a whole, these doctrines constituted the essence of 'popery'.[72] Wesley made no attempt in the letter to engage with popery, and it would be another twenty years before he produced a substantial theological challenge to Roman Catholicism. Nevertheless, an anti-Catholic marker had been put down early in his ministry, three years before his Aldersgate experience.

The principle that 'all articles of faith must be provable in Scripture' is central to the short pamphlet, *The Advantage of the Members of the Church of England over those of the Church of Rome* (1753).[73] Contrary to this principle, the Church of Rome had made Tradition equal in authority to Scripture, even denying lay people access to the Bible. Solely on the authority of Tradition, Rome had imposed various doctrines and practices without foundation in Scripture, including the withdrawal of the cup from the laity, seven sacraments, and ministerial celibacy. Furthermore, the papacy was nowhere proved in Scripture, where Christ alone is head of the Church. The so-called 'papal texts' (Matthew 16.19 and John 21.15–17) did not prove that Christ made Peter his vicar. Still less did they support the plenary power of the pope over the human conscience.[74] For Wesley, the chief 'advantage' of the Church of England was its adherence exclusively to those doctrines that were firmly grounded in the Scriptures.

Besides doctrine, the advantage of the Church of England extended to the conduct of worship. Public worship in the Roman Catholic Church, having degenerated from the 'simplicity' of early Christianity, now involved 'magnificent buildings, altars, images, ornaments and habits'. Essentially, the Roman liturgy consisted 'in splendid ceremonies; in processions and pilgrimages; and prayers in an unknown tongue; and in reciting the Creed, the Lord's Prayer, and the Ave-Maria, over and over, according to the number of their beads'. Even worse, the Church of Rome hindered the mediation of Christ by its doctrine of merit and the intercession of the Blessed Virgin Mary and the saints. Images and holy relics encouraged the ordinary faithful to rely on these means of devotion rather than trust in Christ and his mediation.

*

Wesley's most sustained attack on the Roman Catholic Church is found in a fiercely critical tract, *A Roman Catechism, faithfully drawn out of the allowed writings of the Church of Rome: With a Reply thereto* (1756).[75] This was in fact Wesley's abridgement of a much earlier polemical work by John Williams (later Bishop of Chichester), entitled *A Catechism Truly Representing the Doctrines and Practices of the Church of Rome with an Answer thereunto* (1686). Williams had not based his work on an actual catechism but on a compilation of Roman Catholic teachings about various subjects to which he had given Protestant answers arranged in catechetical form.

It would be tedious to examine the reply to each of the 89 questions posed in *A Roman Catechism*. Briefly, there is no evidence in Scripture to support the claim that the pope is the visible head of the Church (Q1). Nor has the pope any special power (Q2). Holy Scripture alone has authority in the Church (Q3–13). The replies challenge Roman Catholic teaching on: repentance (Q14); good works (Q15); indulgences (Q16–19); purgatory (Q20–28); as well as the worship of angels, Mary, the saints and religious images (Q32–49). One after another, the seven sacraments of the Roman Catholic Church are attacked for the 'fantastical' ceremonies that have debased them. Confirmation (Q58), penance (Q75), extreme unction (Q81), ordination (Q85) and marriage (Q87) are not sacraments at all. Transubstantiation (Q63–65) is unreasonable and false. Communion should be administered in both kinds (Q66). The self-offering of Christ at Calvary cannot be repeated in the Mass (Q68). The Eucharist is not a private but a corporate act (Q71), and the eucharistic elements should not be adored (Q72).

Wesley's second substantial treatise on Roman Catholicism, 'Popery Calmly Considered', was published in 1779 within a year of the Catholic Relief Act, presumably (since the timing can hardly have been coincidental) intended as an indirect response.[76] The arguments are identical to those deployed 23 years earlier in *A Roman Catechism*, though considerably condensed. Papists maintained that the pope was the visible head of the Church, though Scripture neither mentions such a figure nor that it is necessary for salvation to be subject to one. Roman Catholics insisted that the pope was Christ's vicar and Peter's successor, though Scripture reveals that Christ gave no such power to Peter. Nor was it certain that St Peter was ever Bishop of Rome. Jerusalem, rather than Rome, was the mother of all churches. For these reasons, the Church of

Rome had no right to require any person to believe what she taught on her sole authority. For good measure, Wesley attacked the use of Latin in the Mass as 'irrational and unscriptural'. Indulgences were a 'manifest prostitution of religion'. The sacrament of baptism had been made contemptible by the addition of 'idle ceremonies', and the doctrine of transubstantiation was 'nonsense, absurdity, and self-contradiction'.

Some of the theological issues Wesley raised in 'Popery Calmly Considered' today continue to divide Roman Catholics and Protestants. Others have been resolved as a result of reforms instituted by the Second Vatican Council. For instance, Wesley followed Luther in his criticism of the Roman Catholic Church for having deprived the laity of the cup at the Eucharist:

> It is acknowledged by all, that our Lord instituted and delivered this sacrament in both kinds; giving the wine as well as the bread to all that partook of it; and that it continued to be so delivered in the Church of Rome for above a thousand years. And yet, notwithstanding this, the Church of Rome now forbids the people to drink of the cup! A more insolent and barefaced corruption cannot easily be conceived.[77]

Among the liturgical reforms instituted by the Second Vatican Council, the revised order for the Mass restored the chalice to the laity.

Similarly, Wesley criticised the sacrament of extreme unction on the ground that it had little to do with the use of oil in the New Testament for healing the sick (cf. Mark 6.13 and James 5.14f.):

> It was used in the first Church for the body; it is used in the Church of Rome for the soul: It was used then for the recovery of the sick; now, for those only that are thought past recovery. It is easy, therefore, to see, that the Romish extreme unction has no foundation in Scripture.[78]

Again, the Second Vatican Council reformed the sacrament of extreme unction in line with a revised theology of healing. This sacrament, now known as 'The Anointing of the Sick', is no longer restricted to those close to death.

*

The role of Wesley as a folk theologian for Methodism is nowhere more evident than in his unsystematic approach to the doctrine of the Church.

Wesley's elusive ecclesiology has to be pieced together from various sources. Even then, gaps remain so that we are left with unanswered questions. What is certain, however, is that, despite his strong objections to Roman Catholicism, Wesley did not doubt that Roman Catholics belonged to the Holy Catholic Church.

The most substantial account of Wesley's ecclesiology is found in his sermon 'Of the Church' (1785).[79] In effect, this sermon is a study of Ephesians 4.1–6 in which Paul reflects on one body and one Spirit. Wesley agreed with Cyprian that, wherever two or three believers met together, there was a church in the narrowest sense of the word. For Wesley, the term 'church' signified 'a body of people united together in the service of God', whether in a city, a nation or universally. Accordingly, he proposed an inclusive definition of the Catholic Church:

> The catholic or universal church is all the persons in the universe whom God hath so called out of the world as to entitle them to the preceding character; as to be 'one body', united by 'one spirit'; having 'one faith, one hope, one baptism; one God and Father of all, who is above all, and through all, and in them all'.[80]

Any 'body of believers', large or small, could legitimately be described as a church. The Church of England, for instance, comprised those members of the universal Church who were inhabitants of England. To Wesley's way of thinking, this definition of the Church was 'exactly agreeable' to Article XIX of the Church of England, which states that 'The visible Church of Christ is a congregation of faithful men, in which the pure word of God is preached, and the sacraments be duly administered.'[81]

Characteristically, Wesley insisted that his definition of the 'church catholic' did not exclude those congregations in which the word of God was not *purely* preached or the sacraments *duly* administered:

> I dare not exclude from the church catholic all those congregations in which any unscriptural doctrines which cannot be affirmed to be the 'pure Word of God' are sometimes, yea frequently, preached. Neither all those congregations in which the sacraments are not 'duly administered'. Certainly if these things are so the Church of Rome is not so much as a part of the catholic church; seeing therein neither

is 'the pure Word of God' preached nor the sacraments 'duly administered'.[82]

Wesley included 'within the pale of the catholic church' all those possessed of 'one Spirit, one hope, one Lord, one faith, one God and Father of all', whatever their 'wrong opinions' and 'superstitious modes of worship'. For this reason, he professed to have no objection to receiving Roman Catholics as members of the Church of England.

In fact, Wesley's interpretation of Article XIX was more generous than its authors could ever have intended, embracing within the Church of England not only members of the established church, but also Dissenters and even Roman Catholics who shared 'one Spirit, one hope, one Lord, one faith, one God and Father of all'. At the same time, it was a much narrower interpretation, excluding from the Church those whose lives revealed that they were not true Christian believers. To Wesley's way of thinking, 'It follows that not only no common swearer, no Sabbath-breaker, no drunkard, no whoremonger, no thief, no liar, none that lives in outward sin; but none that is under the power of anger or pride, no lover of the world – in a word, none that is dead to God – can be a member of his church.'[83] Thus Wesley departed from the conventional Anglican approach, which was content to describe the Church as a *corpus permixtum*, a body that comprised both sinners and righteous. For Wesley, then, the true Church was neither a visible institution nor an invisible fellowship but 'the body of believers' who sought to live a holy life.

Whether Wesley's synthesis of 'institutional' Anglican and 'spiritual' Protestant ecclesiology is entirely successful is another matter. On the whole, it seems doubtful whether such an account of the Church is sufficiently stable to avoid lapsing into either an institutional or a spiritual model of ecclesial structures, though this would be contrary to Wesley's intention. While he attached greater significance to communion in faith than to structural unity, Wesley was far from indifferent to 'all the outward ties of Christian fellowship'. To his practical way of thinking, the concept of the Church as a 'body of believers' required visible expression. Furthermore, ecclesial structures were so bound up with the content of faith that 'a difference in opinions or modes of worship may prevent an entire external union'.[84] So far as the present study is concerned, it is sufficient to note that, whatever its deficiencies and ambiguities, Wesley's definition of the Church was sufficiently flexible for him to include Roman Catholics among the members of the universal Church, even if he remained highly critical of the Roman Church.

While the sermon 'Of the Church' represents Wesley's mature ecclesiology, it is consistent with his earlier statements on the nature of the Church. As early as 1743, a *Journal* entry described the Roman Catholic Church as 'part' of the 'whole' Church.[85] Even the otherwise polemical 'Popery Calmly Considered' concedes the ecclesial status of the Roman Catholic Church:

> The Church of Rome is no more the Church in general, than the Church of England is. It is only one particular branch of the catholic or universal Church of Christ, which is the whole body of believers in Christ, scattered over the whole earth.[86]

The metaphor of 'branch' in this context suggests Wesley believed that the essential features of the Holy Catholic Church were present in the Church of Rome. Typically, there was also an anti-Catholic point to be made. Wesley could see no reason to refer disputes to Rome since, 'neither the Bishop nor the Church of Rome is any more infallible than ourselves'.

The theological basis for these more generous statements about Roman Catholics lies in Wesley's subtle distinction between the 'essentials' of Christianity and those 'opinions' and 'circumstantials' of religion held by different churches.[87] Locke had defined 'speculative opinions' as disputed teachings that did not hurt members of different churches, and Wesley used the term 'opinion' in much the same way. For Wesley, the essentials concerned what were the 'undoubted, fundamental branches (if there be any such) of our common Christianity'.[88] Wesley himself was satisfied that there were indeed a small number of fundamental Christian doctrines, among them the doctrine of the Trinity. In the tradition of Anglican comprehensiveness (as distinct from Latitudinarianism) and Lutheran *adiaphora*, Wesley took the narrowest possible view of the irreducible essentials of Christian doctrine, while adopting a tolerant outlook on a broad range of theological traditions: 'As to all opinions which do not strike at the root of Christianity, we "think and let think".'[89] It was typical of Wesley's unsystematic approach that he should simply assume that Christians could agree about what constituted the essential core of the Christian faith.

Its systematic defects notwithstanding, Wesley's distinction between essentials and opinions allowed him to believe that some Roman Catholics were 'real, inward Christians', even though they held 'an heap of erroneous opinions . . . delivered by tradition from their fathers'.[90] In fact, true religion was not inconsistent with holding even ten thousand wrong opinions. What, asked Wesley, were all the 'absurd opinions' of Roman Catholics compared with Calvin's doctrine of double pre-destination?[91] To be sure, 'wrong opinions' often produced 'wrong tempers and wrong practices'. Nevertheless, even if people held erroneous or doubtful opinions, 'their hearts may cleave to God through the Son of his love, and be interested in his righteousness'.[92]

Tempting as it is, we should not take Wesley's inclusive definition of the Church as indicating that his criticism of the Roman Catholic Church applied only to its 'absurd opinions'. In a ferocious assault on the Church of Rome entitled *A Caution against Bigotry* (1750), Wesley came close to denying its ecclesial status. It should perhaps be pointed out that 'bigotry' in its eighteenth-century sense meant an irrational and excessive zeal arising from too strong an attachment to a particular religion, church, party, or opinion. Using Mark 9.38–39, where Jesus rebukes the twelve disciples for forbidding another to cast out demons because he 'followeth not us', Wesley launched a stinging attack on the Church of Rome:

> 'He followeth not us' who is not only of a different church, but of such a church as we account to be in many respects antiscriptural and antichristian: a church which we believe to be utterly false and erroneous in her doctrines, as well as very dangerously wrong in her practice, guilty of gross superstition as well as idolatry; a church that has added many articles to the faith which was once delivered to the saints; that has dropped one whole commandment of God, and made void several of the rest by her traditions; and that pretending the highest veneration for, and strict conformity to, the ancient church, has nevertheless brought in numberless innovations without any warrant either from antiquity or Scripture.[93]

31

At first sight, it is difficult to reconcile this statement with Wesley's conviction expressed elsewhere that the Church of Rome was a 'branch' of the universal Church.

Now the principal purpose of *A Caution against Bigotry* was not to attack popery so much as to warn Methodists against bigotry towards their fellow Christians, including presumably Roman Catholics. Wesley poses a question: 'What if I were to see a Papist, an Arian, a Socinian casting out devils? If I did, I could not forbid even him without convicting myself of bigotry.' Could this imply at least a degree of sympathy for Roman Catholicism? Certainly, though we must be cautious about drawing positive inferences that may have been far from Wesley's mind. On the whole, it is safest to conclude that this reference to Papists casting out demons was a memorable rhetorical device, intended to counsel Methodists against narrow partisanship. Fortunately, however, there are two pieces dating from about the same time in which Wesley was unambiguously positive towards the Roman Catholic Church.

Probably the first genuine Methodist attempt at dialogue with Roman Catholics was Wesley's 'Letter to a Roman Catholic' (Dublin, 18 July 1749), penned in the wake of severe rioting between Roman Catholics and Protestants in Ireland.[94] Aware that further riots could jeopardise his Irish mission, Wesley for once selected a conciliatory tone. The letter begins by acknowledging the bitterness of feeling between Roman Catholics and Protestants, which had utterly destroyed 'brotherly love' and led to such 'inhuman barbarities as are scarce named among the heathens'. What was needed on both sides was a 'softening of hearts' to restore a measure of love among neighbours and fellow citizens. Roman Catholics deserved the 'tenderest regard', because they had been created by God and redeemed by Christ. Furthermore, it could be shown that they shared, at least to a great degree, the faith of Protestants. To prove the point, Wesley sets out the true belief of a Protestant and invites Roman Catholics to recognise the essentials of their own faith in his account of 'true, primitive Christianity'. What follows is an orthodox summary of the classical doctrines of the Trinity and salvation, which draws extensively on the language of the historic creeds. Interestingly, Wesley included in the faith of a Protestant belief in the perpetual virginity of the Blessed Virgin Mary.

This conviction that Roman Catholics and Protestants shared in considerable measure a common faith singles Wesley out from the vast majority of his contemporaries, who were unwilling to concede anything of the kind. On this occasion Wesley passed over the opportunity to engage in controversy, pleading instead for Roman Catholics and Protestants to 'reason together' rather than engage in 'endless jangling about opinions'. The letter concludes with a plea to Protestants and Roman Catholics to join in resolving not to hurt one another; not to speak anything harsh or unkind of one another; to harbour no unkind thought or unfriendly temper towards each other; to help each other on towards the Kingdom. Given the circumstances of the letter and his own prejudices, Wesley's resolutions are quite extraordinary.

The 'Letter to a Roman Catholic' has been aptly described as an olive branch to the Roman Catholic Church.[95] All the same, it would be misleading to place too much weight on a single letter, written when there was considerable pressure on Wesley to avoid further trouble. Certainly, the letter reveals Wesley at his most irenical and conciliatory though it is unique in tone and content among his writings on Roman Catholicism. There is little evidence in subsequent works to show that Wesley made any attempt to fulfil its noble resolutions. However, even if he failed to live up to his own ideal, Wesley must be credited with a vision that transcended the eighteenth-century gulf between Roman Catholics and Protestants.

What Roman Catholics made of Wesley's open letter is impossible to say, for there is no record of any response from that quarter. In all likelihood, few would have bothered to read it, even if they could have obtained a copy. It was reprinted only three times in Wesley's lifetime: in 1750 (Dublin), in 1755 (London), and in the collected *Works* (1773). For various reasons, the call for Protestants and Roman Catholics 'not to speak anything harsh or unkind of one another' fell on deaf ears, and controversy continued unabated.

Although the 'Letter to a Roman Catholic' is without parallel in the Wesleyan corpus, its central theme was revived a few months later in the sermon 'Catholic Spirit' (1750).[96] The text is 2 Kings 10.15, which poses the question: 'Is your heart as true to mine as mine is to yours? . . . If it is, give me your hand.' Reflecting on this gesture of reconciliation between two Old Testament characters who held different theological opinions, Wesley concluded that differences in opinions and modes of worship need not prevent a 'unity in affection' even if they rule out visible unity:

'Though we can't think alike, may we not love alike? May we not be of one heart, though we are not of one opinion? Without all doubt we may.'

Alive to the danger of being misinterpreted, Wesley distanced the comprehensiveness of the catholic spirit from Latitudinarianism, as espoused by the Cambridge Platonists a century before and currently still in vogue among some Anglican divines. On the whole, Latitudinarian thought attached relatively little importance to matters of dogmatic truth, liturgical practice and ecclesiastical organisation. In contrast, Wesley insisted that the catholic spirit was not 'speculative latitudinarianism' (indifference to all theological opinions) for that was the 'spawn of hell'. A 'muddy understanding' in which theological opinions were jumbled together was closer to the spirit of antichrist, whereas a person of a truly catholic spirit was 'fixed as the sun in his judgement concerning the main branches of Christian doctrine'. The catholic spirit permitted liberty of thought and did not require others to embrace the same theological opinions, but instead encouraged a form of theological pluralism by occupying a middle position between extreme dogmatism and doctrinal indifferentism.

Nor was the catholic spirit practical Latitudinarianism or indifference to modes of worship, for this was a hindrance to the worship of God in spirit and in truth. The person of a truly catholic spirit held fast to a particular mode of worship and 'congregation', while accepting that everyone must follow 'the dictates of his own conscience' in such matters. 'I believe the episcopal form of church government to be scriptural and apostolical,' said Wesley: 'If you think the presbyterian or independent is better, then think so still, and act accordingly.'[97] Wesley did not agree that everyone born in England should become a member of the established Church of England, worshipping God in the form prescribed in that church. For a 'rule of fixity' in which church membership was determined by the place of one's birth would have allowed 'no Reformation from popery'.[98] Those possessed of a catholic spirit held fast to their theological opinions and modes of worship, while embracing 'with strong and cordial affection neighbours and strangers, friends and enemies. This is catholic or universal love. And he that has this is of a catholic spirit. For love alone gives the title to this character – catholic love is a catholic spirit.'[99] To reinforce the point, Charles Wesley's poem on 'Catholic Love' was appended to the sermon when it was first published.[100]

34

The catholic spirit, then, does not gloss over theological differences. Approaching these differences in a catholic spirit however involves regarding 'all of whatever opinion or worship or congregation who believe in the Lord Jesus Christ' with catholic love as brothers and sisters in Christ, fellow citizens of the new Jerusalem, fellow soldiers 'engaged in the same warfare under the same Captain of our salvation'. The catholic spirit involves praying for other congregations and working to strengthen their hand in God. By this means, theological differences can be significantly reduced and perhaps even doctrinal controversies settled. Though Wesley did not say so, the catholic spirit changes the nature of the encounter between separated Christians from confrontation to mutual respect. As such, the catholic spirit provides a framework in which Christians can work together to resolve their doctrinal differences. As an approach to ecumenical dialogue, the catholic spirit has much to contribute today and anticipates by more than two hundred years the method proposed by Pope John Paul II in his encyclical *Ut Unum Sint* (1995).[101]

Alas, the catholic spirit was in short supply on all sides during the eighteenth century. The Methodist movement soon began to attract hostile reactions, not only from Anglican bishops and clergy, but also from Dissenters whose Calvinist doctrine of double predestination was the antithesis of Wesley's Arminian theology of grace. Among those to challenge Wesley from a Calvinist perspective was the prominent Baptist writer Anne Dutton (1692–1765), who composed *A Letter to the Rev. Mr J. Wesley. In vindication of the Doctrines of Absolute Election, Particular Redemption, Special Vocation, and Final Perseverance. Occasioned chiefly by some things in his Dialogue between a Predestinarian and his friend; and in his Hymns on God's Everlasting Love* (1742). In the same year appeared *Methodism displayed: and enthusiasm detected; intended as an antidote against, and a preservative from the delusive principles and unscriptural doctrines of a modern set of seducing preachers* by William Mason (1719–91), a Church of England priest in Newcastle upon Tyne, Methodism's northern citadel.

Striving to follow a *via media* between Protestant and Roman Catholic approaches to the doctrine of salvation, Wesley was misunderstood on all sides to the extent that he was even accused of heresy. To ultra-Protestant ears, Wesley's distinction between justification and sanctification sounded dangerously Pelagian because of its corollary that humans co-operate with God in their salvation. Calvinist theologians in particular were incensed by this apparent slight to divine sovereignty. In *A Caveat against Unsound Doctrines* (1770), the Calvinist hymn writer Augustus Toplady launched a vicious attack on Wesley on account of his doctrine of salvation.

Curiously, Wesley was sometimes mistaken for a Roman Catholic. Ministering in Savannah in 1736/7, he gave 'the widespread impression that he was a Roman Catholic' on account of his zeal and strict discipline.[102] The most prominent Church of England bishop to attack Wesley in this way was George Lavington of Exeter, whose *Enthusiasm of Methodists and Papists Considered* (1749) accused Methodists of imitating the worst excesses of medieval Roman Catholicism in their supposed special providences, revelations, ecstasies, healings and exorcisms. Stung by this accusation, Wesley dashed off a vehement denial, assuring the bishop that, 'I have, by the blessing of God, converted several from popery, who are now alive and ready to testify it.'[103]

Even towards the end of his ministry, when Methodism was reasonably established and more widely known, Wesley remained the subject of salacious pamphlets describing him as a papist in all but name.[104] While the charge did not bear scrutiny, for those unable or unwilling to look closely, Wesley's emphasis on the means of grace, especially the Eucharist, invited the comparison with Roman Catholicism. At the same time, in the febrile atmosphere of the eighteenth century there were sound tactical reasons for Wesley's critics to accuse him of popery. The charge immediately put him on the defensive and was difficult to shake off in the prevailing climate of suspicion. The comparison between Methodism and Roman Catholicism, though superficial, proved persistent.

Between 1738 and 1800 anti-Methodist literature was published every year, and there was only one year (1797) when no new material appeared.[105] Altogether more than six hundred anti-Methodist publications emerged during the course of the eighteenth century.[106] Nor were attacks on Methodism confined to the written word. On more than one occasion Wesley was confronted by a violent mob, though providentially he usually managed to escape unscathed, his dignity more or less intact.[107] At one time or another, Methodists found themselves in the unenviable position of being attacked by the Roman Catholic mob in

Ireland for being ultra-Protestant, and by the Protestant rabble in England for being Papists. Surely, few other religious figures of the eighteenth century could have attracted the wrath of so diverse a collection of opponents as John Wesley.

Throughout the eighteenth century, Roman Catholics in England remained a small minority, socially isolated, politically powerless and constantly regarded with suspicion as potentially disloyal to the Protestant settlement. Periodic threats of a Jacobite rebellion aroused widespread fear of Roman Catholics among a large section of the population. Given that Methodists were regarded with equal suspicion, it might have been supposed that Roman Catholics and Methodists would at least find themselves on the same side as fellow sufferers at the hands of the established Church and Protestant Dissenters. Yet Roman Catholics, too, watched the growth of Methodism with alarm.

The most eminent eighteenth-century Roman Catholic to respond to the rise of Methodism was Richard Challoner (1691–1781), sometime Professor of Divinity at Douai and Vicar-Apostolic of the London District from 1758.[108] Challoner regarded the Methodist movement as a threat to the residual Roman Catholic community in England because it purported to derive from apostolic teaching. In *A Caveat against the Methodists* (1760), Challoner identified six areas of concern:

(1) The Methodists are not the People of God: they are not true Gospel Christians: nor is their new raised Society the true Church of Christ, or any Part of it.
(2) The Methodist Teachers are not true Ministers of Christ: nor are they called and sent by him.
(3) The Methodist Teachers have not the Marks by which the Scriptures would have us know the true Ministers of Christ; nor do their fruits any ways resemble those of the first Teachers of Christianity.
(4) The Methodist Rule of Faith is not the Rule of true Christian Faith.
(5) The Methodists' pretended Assurance of their own Justification, and their eternal Salvation, is no true Christian faith; but a mere Illusion and groundless Presumption.
(6) The true Scripture Doctrine concerning Justification.[109]

In a letter to the *London Chronicle* of 19 February 1761, Wesley rebutted each of Challoner's charges in turn, pointing out for good measure that the tract was really a caveat against Protestants in general.[110] Wesley denied Challoner's indictment that Methodists were neither the People of God nor true Gospel Christians and that the Methodist societies were not the true Church of Christ.

The *Caveat* cites more than fifty references from the Old Testament and a further twenty from the New to show that the Church founded by Christ is universal, one, holy and orthodox, with an unfailing succession of pastors and teachers under the direction of the Holy Spirit. In the face of such a formidable body of scriptural evidence, Wesley had little alternative but to agree with Challoner that these were the marks of the Church; but he then proceeded to define them very differently. For Wesley, the Catholic Church founded by Christ was 'the *whole body* of men endued with faith, working by love dispersed over the whole earth, in Europe, Asia, Africa and America'.[111] In all ages and nations the Church is the one body of Christ. This Church is holy 'for no unholy man can possibly be a member of it'. It is orthodox in all things necessary to salvation, secured against error in things essential by the perpetual presence of Christ and ever directed by the Spirit of truth.

Moving onto the offensive, Wesley claimed that these same ecclesial marks were lacking in the Roman Catholic Church, which in its present form was not founded by Christ.

> All the doctrines and practices wherein she differs from us were not instituted by Christ; they were unknown to the ancient Church of Christ; they are unscriptural, *novel* corruptions; neither is *that* Church 'propagated throughout the world'. Therefore, if either antiquity or universality be essential thereto, the Church of Rome cannot be 'the true Church of Christ'.[112]

Numerous instances of pope against pope and council against council convinced Wesley that the Church of Rome was not immune to error. Neither was the Church of Rome 'one' because it was torn with 'numberless divisions' and also because the 'Asiatic, African and Muscovite Churches' (presumably Wesley was referring to Coptic and Orthodox) had never been part of it. As for the supposed holiness of the

Church of Rome, 'the generality of its members are no holier than Turks or heathens'.[113]

Concerning ministry, Wesley agreed with Challoner that the true Church enjoyed a 'perpetual succession of pastors and teachers, divinely appointed and divinely assisted'. There was no lack of such pastors in the Protestant Churches, who 'convert sinners to God, a work none can do unless God himself doth appoint them therefore and assist them therein'. Similarly, Protestant teachers were 'the proper successors of those who have delivered down, through all generations, the faith once delivered to the saints; and their members have true, spiritual communion with the *one, holy* society of true *believers*'.[114] In comparison, Roman Catholic priests 'convert no sinners to God; they convert many to their own opinion but not to the knowledge or love of God. He that was a drunkard is a drunkard still; he that was filthy is filthy still . . .'[115]

Next Wesley turned his attention to Challoner's second charge that Methodist teachers were not true ministers because Protestants were not the people of God. According to Challoner, the Methodist teachers had no succession from the first apostles, nor had they received a commission from God, otherwise miraculous signs would have accompanied their ministry. On the contrary, argued Wesley, Protestant ministers, especially those of the Church of England, could claim to stand in the apostolic succession. He cites a Roman Catholic theologian who maintained that Anglicans had preserved the apostolic succession.[116] Even so, Wesley specifically rejected the idea of an uninterrupted apostolic succession: 'I deny that the Romish bishops came down by *uninterrupted* succession from the apostles. I never could see it proved, and I am persuaded I never shall. But unless this is proved, your own pastors, on *your* principles are no pastors at all.'[117]

Turning the tables on Challoner, Wesley fastened on the doctrine of intention in an attempt to subvert the Roman Catholic definition of apostolic succession. In the sacramental economy of the Roman Catholic Church, the required intention was the will to do what the Church did.[118] As Wesley put it, the 'intention of the administrator is essential to the validity of the sacraments which are administered by him'.[119] To Wesley's way of thinking, since there could be no guarantee as to the intention of the celebrant, there were necessarily doubts about the supposed effectiveness of the sacraments. Could Challoner be confident that he had received a valid Eucharist, or even that his baptism was valid? More to the point, could he be sure that he had been ordained a priest or bishop? If the required intention was lacking at his ordination, then the whole of Challoner's subsequent ministry had been defective. Even if a lack of intention had occurred only once in the past thousand years, what then had become of the uninterrupted succession?[120] A priest could hardly lead others to heaven if he himself was not on the right path: the blind could not lead the blind.

It would be unprofitable now to rake over the controversy between Wesley and Challoner. Some of Challoner's charges against Methodism remain the subject of dialogue between Methodists and Roman Catholics, though thankfully in a less confrontational manner. In other areas, such as the doctrine of intention, the debate has moved onto fresh ground. At least the doctrine of assurance is one area where agreement has been possible. Challoner objected to the Methodist doctrine of assurance on the basis that Scripture and the teaching of the early Church lent no support to the idea that anyone could be assured of justification or perseverance in the faith. More than two hundred years later, Methodists and Roman Catholics were able to agree that Christian assurance 'should not be seen as a form of certainty which removes the need for hope. Assurance, itself a gift of the Holy Spirit, was no guarantee of perseverance, nor even a necessary accompaniment of saving faith.'[121] In 1981 Methodists and Roman Catholics further agreed that 'Christian religious experience includes the assurance of God's unmerited mercy in Christ, the inner witness of the Spirit that we are indeed children of God, pardoned and reconciled to the Father (Romans 8.12–17).'[122]

If only Challoner and Wesley could have engaged in theological dialogue instead of controversy, some of their differences might have been resolved. As it was, in their literary sparring neither showed much generosity to the other. Plainly, Challoner could find nothing of value in the Methodist revival. For his part, Wesley appears to have forgotten his earlier resolutions in the 'Letter to a Roman Catholic'. Unfortunately, the controversy between John Wesley and Richard Challoner set the tone for relations between Methodists and Roman Catholics for the next two hundred years.

The relevance of John Wesley to the present study is beyond doubt. It is a matter of historical fact that he was the principal founder of

Methodism. As such, his views on Roman Catholicism must inevitably be a factor in dialogue between Methodists and Roman Catholics, whatever Methodists nowadays may feel about Wesley's theology. Furthermore, for reasons that will become clear in the next chapter, Wesley's anti-Catholicism, isolated from its historical context and shorn of its theological subtleties, struck a powerful chord with Methodists in the nineteenth century.

In the course of our investigation we have seen ample evidence from his two substantial treatises on the subject, together with the sermons and other writings, to show that Wesley strongly opposed the Roman Catholic Church. At the same time, he was more tolerant of individual Roman Catholics, though he did not always maintain the distinction as clearly as he might:

> We have not much more to do with the members of the Church of Rome [than with 'heathens, Mahometans and Jews']. But we cannot doubt that many of them, like the excellent Archbishop of Cambrai, still retain (notwithstanding many mistakes) that faith that worketh by love.[123]

Wesley claimed to know Roman Catholics who sincerely loved God and their neighbour. 'But I cannot say this is a general case; nay, I am fully convinced it is not. The generality of Roman Catholics, wherever I have been, are of the same principles, and the same spirit, with their forefathers.'[124] In the heat of controversy, Wesley could even assert that, 'the Roman Catholics, in general, are not "the people of God".'[125]

That John Wesley was stoutly anti-Catholic is undeniable, though this conclusion requires careful qualification. To begin with, he must be placed in historical context. Wesley was anti-Catholic in a way that was conventional but by no means extreme when measured by the standards of the eighteenth century. Opposition to the Roman Catholic Church was simply the duty of every loyal member of the Church of England. In mitigation, Wesley adopted the standard evangelical distinction between the rejection of Roman Catholic theology and opposition to its adherents. In Wesley's mind, the Roman Catholic hierarchy bore the greater responsibility for the errors of its followers whose plight Wesley viewed with some sympathy.[126]

Wesley's anti-Catholic attitude was tempered by his genuine abhorrence of persecution. This forbearance of Roman Catholicism, limited as it was, can be attributed to the eighteenth-century spirit of Enlightenment and in particular Locke's philosophy of toleration. Ironically, Wesley's intolerance of Roman Catholicism was also derived from Locke. Overall, Wesley's reaction to Roman Catholicism was neither bigoted nor irrational, but grounded in the classical theology of the Church of England, based on Tradition, Scripture, reason and experience as mediated through the lens of the English Reformation. Notwithstanding his high regard for 'primitive Christianity', Wesley was influenced by the spirit of the Enlightenment to a greater extent than he ever realised.

Regrettable as Wesley's anti-Catholicism now appears in the light of the ecumenical movement, it would be anachronistic to judge him by modern standards. Such prejudice was typical of his culture and era, which perhaps made him the more acceptable to ordinary people. At the same time, there was another dimension to Wesley's character, which sets him apart as a significant figure in the history of relations between Roman Catholics and Protestants. Remarkably, Wesley was able to transcend conventional Protestant attitudes towards Roman Catholicism and go much further than the vast majority of his contemporaries in recognising Roman Catholics as fellow Christians and members of the Holy Catholic Church. In particular, we should not lose sight of the fact that he incurred the wrath of many of his contemporaries by maintaining that Roman Catholics and Protestants, to a large degree, shared the same faith.

Concerning Wesley's theological formation, Henry Rack concludes that 'his ideas and language do bear a more positive affinity to the tradition of Catholic than Protestant spirituality'.[127] As his Protestant opponents frequently complained, this gave Wesley's theology a more Catholic 'feel' than was generally acceptable. His doctrine of sanctification in particular offended ultra-Protestant sensibilities. Albert Outler has described Wesley's theological perspective as *evangelical catholicism* inasmuch as it attempted to integrate the truth present in both the Roman Catholic and Protestant traditions.[128]

Following what he regarded as the example of unity present in biblical and patristic Christianity, Wesley tried to overcome the gulf between Protestants and Roman Catholics as typified in the Augsburg Confession and the Council of Trent.

In their stead, he proceeded to develop a theological fusion of faith and good works, Scripture and tradition, revelation and reason, God's sovereignty and human freedom, universal redemption and conditional election, Christian liberty and an ordered polity, the assurance of pardon and the risks of 'falling from grace', original sin and Christian perfection. In each of these conjunctions, as he insisted almost tediously, the initiative is with God, the response with man.[129]

It is this exciting theological method, rather than his personal limitations, which makes Wesley such a fascinating figure for continuing dialogue between Methodists and Roman Catholics.

2

From the Death of Wesley to 1900

After Wesley's death in 1791 Methodism finally became an independent ecclesial movement with an initial membership of around seventy thousand. Internal arguments concerning the relationship between the Methodist societies and the Church of England, crystallised in the celebration of the sacraments, immediately put the Connexion under great strain. The Conference of 1791 resolved 'to follow strictly the plan which Mr Wesley left us at his death'; but this was open to conflicting interpretation by competing factions.[1] The dispute was not exclusively between those who wanted to remain within the Church of England and those who urged separation. There was also the issue of whether the Methodist societies and their buildings would be controlled locally by the members or centrally by the Conference. In the event, the Conference asserted its authority over the societies.

The Conference of 1795 approved a Plan of Pacification, which marked a crucial stage in the separation of Methodism from the Church of England. Under its provisions, the itinerant preachers were authorised to celebrate the sacraments of Holy Communion and baptism in those Methodist societies where a majority of the trustees and leaders were in favour, subject to final approval from Conference.[2] Similar provisions were made for burial services and Sunday worship during parish church hours. Already tenuous, the remaining links between the Methodist societies and the Church of England swiftly dissolved as Methodism gathered momentum under the influence of a fervent evangelical zeal. Within fifty years of Wesley's death, the number of people holding a Methodist class ticket had risen to nearly 450,000; though by this time Methodism was seriously fragmented as the result of acrimonious arguments about church order and the respective roles of ministers and lay people.

As early as 1797 Alexander Kilham seceded to form the Methodist

New Connexion because the Wesleyan Conference would not allow lay representation. Based mainly in northern industrial towns, the Methodist New Connexion was always a small movement though it prided itself on having equal representation of lay people and ministers in the Conference. Eventually, the New Connexion joined with two other Methodist denominations in 1907 to form the United Methodist Church, the smallest of the three branches to come together at Methodist Union in 1932.

Methodist divisions multiplied during the first half of the nineteenth century, often provoked by tensions between a conservative leadership and some of the more colourful Methodist preachers. Hugh Bourne (1772–1852) formed the Primitive Methodist Connexion in 1811 following an earlier series of revivalist camp meetings at Mow Cop in Staffordshire, which had incurred the displeasure of the Wesleyan Conference:

> It is our judgement, that even supposing such meetings to be allowable in America, they are highly improper in England, and likely to be productive of considerable mischief. And we disclaim all connexion with them.[3]

Primitive Methodism expanded rapidly and at the time of Methodist Union was the second largest strand (behind the Wesleyans) to enter the merger. As the name suggests, Primitive Methodism was a conscious attempt by Bourne and his associates to recover the vitality of 'primitive' Christianity as a lay movement, the Wesleyans having supposedly forsaken their Methodist roots by adopting a quasi-sacerdotal ministry.

In 1815 a Wesleyan local preacher in North Cornwall, William O'Bryan (1778–1868), formed an independent denomination called the Bible Christians in an attempt to return to the original ethos of Methodism. Elsewhere, disputes often centred on the authority of the Conference. In Leeds the Protestant Methodists seceded from the Wesleyan Connexion because of the power of the (exclusively ministerial) Conference over local preachers and lay people. Similarly, the Wesleyan Methodist Association stemmed from a dispute in the mid-1830s in part about the autocratic power of Jabez Bunting in the Wesleyan Conference. Finally, the Wesleyan Reform Union was established in 1849–52 following the Fly-Sheet Controversy, which was a series of anonymous attacks on the motives and leadership of Bunting and the Wesleyan Conference.

Whatever internal disputes wracked Methodism in the course of the nineteenth century, Methodists were united in their opposition to Roman Catholicism. This stance was virtually guaranteed by an irresistible combination of factors, the most significant being the attitude of John Wesley. According to David Hempton, 'Wesley's anti-Catholicism was one of his profound and enduring legacies to the Wesleyan connexion, and the connexion's vigorous anti-Catholicism – in which it genuinely reflected its following – was a most important determinant of Wesleyan political attitudes during the nineteenth century.'[4] To make matters worse, without the moderating influence of Wesley's subtle distinction between essentials and opinions, it was almost inevitable that Methodism's strongly evangelical theology would slide into outright condemnation of Roman Catholicism. Sadly, subtlety of any kind was a scarce commodity in Methodism, not least because 'the Methodist system was based on a plentiful supply of half-educated itinerant preachers'.[5] In what became a vicious circle, Methodist preachers were drawn from, and appealed most to, the lower social groups, which generally harboured cultural prejudices against Roman Catholics.

The monthly magazines produced by the main branches of Methodism provide a revealing insight into Methodist attitudes towards Roman Catholics in the nineteenth century. Fear of papal aggression is a recurring theme. In 1810 *The Methodist Magazine* (Wesleyan) published a short commentary on an extract from an oath of allegiance sworn by Roman Catholic bishops.[6] Two clauses of the oath were reprinted in italics for added emphasis:

> *I will to my utmost, defend, increase, and advance, the rights, honours, privileges, and authority of the Holy Roman Church, or our Lord the Pope, and of his successors aforesaid.*

> *Heretics, Schismatics, and Rebels, to our said Lord the Pope, and to his successors aforesaid, I will, to the utmost of my power, persecute and destroy.*[7]

To the Methodist commentator, nothing could have been clearer: an 'honest popish bishop' would be obliged by the most solemn obligation (on pain of 'eternal misery') to aid any conspiracy to overturn the established Church of England. It was simply not within the power of a Roman Catholic bishop to be the faithful subject of a Protestant prince. 'If Protestantism is Christianity, Popery must be antichristian. Our Roman Catholics tell us, they can be at once faithful subjects of the Pope, and of a Protestant King. Our blessed Saviour tells us, "No man can serve two masters, for either he will hate the one, and love the other, or else he will hold to the one, and despise the other. Ye cannot serve God and Mammon." (Matthew 6.24) Whether it be right in the sight of God, to believe a Papist rather than God, judge ye.'[8]

In 1812 the launch of *The Catholic Magazine* attracted a review of its inaugural issue in the pages of *The Methodist Magazine*.[9] The leading article on the subject of the pope, by the unnamed Vicar Apostolic of the London District, contained this description of the Roman Catholic Church:

> In spite of all the falsifications and metamorphoses of the catholic works and the Bible [by the Protestants], the pope, cardinals and catholic ministers, still form that universal, indivisible, unsullied, catholic apostolic church, without spot or wrinkle, built upon a rock by Jesus Christ himself, and is to last so until the end of time; and the gates of hell (*the innumerable sects*) shall not prevail against it.[10]

For the reviewer, 'Such vile, ignorant calumnies, are not worthy of a confutation: their being merely recorded is sufficient for the purpose.' What rankled most was not the identification of Protestantism with the gates of hell, but the charge that Protestants had falsified the Bible. Moving over to the attack, the reviewer gives a potted description of 'a few of the characters who filled the papal chair; men who were so far from possessing the moral qualifications suited to the episcopal office, that they were utterly unworthy of a name in the Church of Christ'.[11] To believe that these men were holy or infallible was 'in direct opposition to Scripture, Reason and Common Sense'.[12] Papal indulgences were a 'blasphemous nonsense' which gave the lie to the doctrine of infallibility. The doctrine of transubstantiation was 'even more absurd and blasphemous, if possible, than that of indulgences'.

The Methodist reviewer also took exception to the following definition of the Roman Catholic Church:

> The body of Christ, which is his Church, is composed of members
> united together, not only by the profession of the same faith, and by
> the participation of the same sacraments, but also by their subordina-
> tion, and submissive attachment to lawful pastors, particularly to the
> visible head of this mystical body, the vicar of Christ on earth. How
> admirable is that subordination, divinely established in the Church of
> Christ! By which the faithful, in all nations on the earth, are subject to
> their respective and immediate pastors, and all, faithful and pastors,
> are subject to one head, to one supreme pastor of the whole, to whom,
> in the person of St Peter, the plenitude of power was given by Jesus
> Christ, to feed and govern all. He is the one shepherd, to whom the
> whole flock of Christ is entrusted; whoever is not subject to him, is not
> a sheep of Christ. He is the head of the whole body of Christ on earth;
> whoever is not united with him, is not a member of Christ.[13]

Drawing on the words of Archbishop John Tillotson of Canterbury
(1630–94), the reviewer made a counter accusation:

> The truth is, we would fain hope, because [Roman Catholics] still
> retain the essentials of Christianity, and profess to believe all the
> articles of the Christian faith, that, notwithstanding their corruptions,
> they may still retain the essence of a Church; as a man may truly and
> really be a man, though he has the plague upon him; and for that
> reason be fit to be avoided by all that wish well to themselves . . . It is
> they, I take it, that are concerned to prove themselves a true church,
> and not we to prove it for them . . . till they can clearly acquit them-
> selves from being idolaters, they shall never more, against their wills,
> be esteemed a true church.[14]

In a parting shot, the reviewer reminded Methodists that 'Popery is a
hideous *corruption* of the Christian religion, and that Protestantism is
the good *old* religion of the Bible.'

Also in the inaugural issue of *The Catholic Magazine,* the Vicar
Apostolic of the Midlands District, John Milner, attempted to reassure
Protestants about the intentions of Roman Catholics in England:

I ask what harm would the pope do you, if, instead of being friendly to you, as he positively is, he were hostile to you, while the Catholics devote their money and their services, while, in short, they perform every duty of allegiance to their king and country? Will he excite the Catholics to rebel? He has never attempted this in England, since the year 1588, in the reign of Queen Elizabeth; and then he attempted it on the ground that this queen was an *apostolic Catholic.*[15]

The Methodist reviewer was not reassured, however. The fact that the pope had not incited a rebellion in England since 1588 in no way abrogated the principle that 'the pope claims a power, which he may use at his discretion, of absolving subjects from their oaths of allegiance'.[16] What was more, the Church of Rome was a 'domineering, persecuting Church'.

The various Methodist magazines took every opportunity to remind their readers of the horrors of Roman Catholicism, whether through reproducing a firsthand account of Roman Catholic persecutions in France or by publishing a letter from a correspondent about the scarcity of Bibles in Rome.[17] Some of the jibes were unsubtle, to say the least. For example, *The Methodist Magazine* (1820) reproduced an extract from a polemical work entitled 'Popery the Religion of Heathenism', which ridiculed the doctrine of transubstantiation:

I cannot avoid noticing the simple answer which was given by a Chinese disciple to a Romish missionary, who, after having taken great pains to teach him Christianity, asked him, before a large assembly, 'How many gods there were?' To which the humble learner answered, 'None.' 'None!' exclaimed the astonished priest, 'why, have I not always told you there was one?' 'Yes Sir,' replied the new convert, 'but you know I ate him yesterday.'[18]

Marian devotion provided a frequent target for Methodists, especially after Pius IX defined the doctrine of the Immaculate Conception in 1854. To take just one example, a fire in 1864 at a Roman Catholic Church in Santiago, which claimed the lives of some two thousand people, was tacitly interpreted as a sign of divine disapproval of an event held to mark the climax of a Marian Festival. In sanctimonious tones *The United Methodist Free Churches' Magazine* declared: 'To what extent it was designed by heaven to be a protest against the senseless worship in which they were engaged when the angel of destruction passed over them, is not for us to say . . . but he must be mentally blind who does not recognise, in the event we deplore, a confutation of the impious pretensions put forth by [the organisers].'[19]

Economic fortune was also attributed to religious allegiance. In 1863 *The United Methodist Free Churches' Magazine* noted that in 'Protestant Great Britain' there was one mile of railway for every three thousand inhabitants, as compared with one mile in 'Romish Tuscany' for every twelve thousand. Conversely, there were four times as many priests and religious in Tuscany as in Great Britain. The lesson was obvious: 'The more priests the shorter the rail, the longer rail the fewer priests. This is a world of work, and surely the God of Nature . . . is better pleased that his servants should work with grateful hearts, rather than they should lead lives of lazy, useless, and unproductive devotion; shut up in convents and monasteries, or making genuflections before graven images, the work of men's hands.'[20]

Even towards the end of the nineteenth century, there were few signs that Methodists were softening in their attitude towards Roman Catholicism. An article in the *Methodist Monthly* for July 1895 noted the increase in the number of Roman Catholic educational institutions and suggested 'It might be a useful service if someone with the time would make it his business to conduct a careful enquiry into all the Roman Catholic schools, colleges, nunneries, and monasteries in the kingdom, and let us know precisely what is going on.'[21] In a brief account of Ushaw College in Durham, which had just celebrated its centenary, the writer expressed his disparaging opinion of the Roman Catholic Church: 'Her genius harmonises best with a despotic monarchy or a corrupt oligarchy, though in this country and in the United States she is doing her best to manipulate free institutions to her selfish ends. The present battle with her is in the schools.'[22]

Throughout the nineteenth century, the Irish situation continued to exert considerable influence on Methodist attitudes towards Roman Catholics. Successful missions in the early years of the century had created a sizeable Methodist constituency in Ireland, which the Wesleyan leadership could not afford to ignore. By the 1840s almost a quarter of Wesleyan Methodists in the British Isles lived in Ireland, most of them in

Protestant Ulster.[23] A Roman Catholic backlash heightened tensions and strengthened the hand of the more extreme Protestant elements within the Wesleyan leadership. Gideon Ouseley was an Irish Methodist preacher and a prolific writer of anti-Catholic tracts.[24] In 1828 he toured northern England under the auspices of the Wesleyan Methodist Missionary Society, where he proved particularly effective in reviving anti-Catholic feelings among Irish immigrants.[25]

In England, aspirations to social respectability made many Wesleyan Methodists politically conservative, which in practice meant upholding the Protestant Constitution. In the north of England areas of Methodist growth, such as industrial Lancashire, tended to coincide with areas of Irish settlement, leading to tension and confrontation between the two communities. According to David Hempton, 'Methodism in general was more stoutly anti-Catholic than the rest of Nonconformity because of its all pervading evangelical theology, its relatively uncultivated ministry, its appeal to the lower social groups, and its vested interests in Ireland.'[26]

Officially, Wesleyan Methodism maintained high ideals of friendship towards other Christian denominations, as this extract from the famous 'Liverpool Minutes' of 1820 shows:

> Let us ourselves remember, and endeavour to impress on our people, that we, as a body, do not exist for the purposes of party; and that we are specially bound by the example of our Founder, by the original principle on which our societies were founded, and by our constant professions before the world, to avoid a narrow, bigoted and sectarian spirit, to abstain from needless and unprofitable disputes on minor subjects of theological controversy, and, as far as we innocently can, 'to please all men for good unto their edification'. Let us, therefore, maintain towards all denominations of Christians who 'hold the Head', the kind and catholic spirit of primitive Methodism; and, according to the noble maxim of our fathers in the Gospel, be 'the friends of all and the enemies of none'.[27]

In practice, however, ecumenical goodwill was reserved exclusively for fellow Protestants. Being 'the friends of all and the enemies of none' did not apply in the case of Roman Catholicism. When it came to popery, Methodists of every shade found it all too easy to renounce the catholic spirit in favour of bigotry and sectarianism.

*

Anti-Catholicism was not exclusively a Methodist phenomenon in the nineteenth century. Popular historical consciousness, shaped by the experience of the English Reformation and its aftermath, had established a widespread suspicion and fear of Roman Catholicism which persisted throughout the nineteenth century, kept alive by folk memories of Mary Tudor and the Gunpowder plot. Despite successive Catholic Relief Acts, many laws discriminating against Roman Catholics remained on the statute books, prohibiting charitable bequests for 'superstitious' purposes such as saying masses for the dead. Extraordinary as it may now seem, Roman Catholic churches were not allowed steeples, their priests could not wear clerical attire in public, nuns were supposed to register with the authorities, public processions were banned, and Jesuits were prohibited from living in England. Although many of these laws were seldom enforced, they remained a constant threat, and their very existence reinforced the social inferiority of Roman Catholics in the minds of English people. Most inequitable of all, until Roman Catholic emancipation in 1829, Roman Catholics were prohibited from voting or standing for election to Parliament or local authorities.

It was in the arena of politics and education that Methodist opposition to Roman Catholicism in England was most obvious in the nineteenth century. For Methodists, the immediate problem with Roman Catholics was their allegiance to the pope, which made them potentially disloyal citizens. The steady growth in the number of Roman Catholics in England in the early years of the century, mostly as the result of Irish immigration, allied with a gradual easing of restrictions on their participation in society, caused alarm among Methodists and led to a flurry of speeches and controversial literature.[28]

However, despite considerable pressure from the grassroots, the Wesleyan Conference, under the iron leadership of Jabez Bunting, made no official protest against Roman Catholic emancipation, nor did it organise opposition to the bill. Believing that the legislation would inevitably be carried, Bunting was keen to avoid a humiliating defeat; and so he took refuge in the 'no politics rule', according to which the Wesleyan Conference remained impartial in political affairs.[29] Besides, there were strategic issues at stake: Bunting firmly believed that conceding Roman Catholic emancipation in England offered the best prospect for effective missionary work in Ireland. Opponents of this policy argued in vain that Roman Catholic emancipation was too important a matter of principle for compromise.

As Bunting well understood, the motive of the Peel government in granting civil liberties to Roman Catholics was primarily conservative – to undermine the movement for greater democracy and to maintain the peace and stability of the British Empire.[30] Ironically, far from easing religious conflict, Roman Catholic emancipation merely exacerbated longstanding Protestant fears of the pope's territorial ambitions in England. Let down by Peel, many Methodists reacted bitterly, thereby contributing to heightened sectarianism in Britain. Nevertheless, from the 1830s onwards Roman Catholic emancipation was an accomplished fact, and there could be no going back. Though progress was slow and erratic, political emancipation paved the way for the eventual full integration of Roman Catholics into British society.

Having lost substantial ground as a result of the emancipation bill, Methodists changed tack from opposing the political freedom of Roman Catholics to campaigning against legislation that would consolidate their position in society. From about the mid-1820s elementary education provided the main outlet for anti-Catholic feelings among Methodists. After a slow start, due to their preoccupation with erecting chapels, Wesleyan Methodists gradually recognised the evangelical opportunities afforded by elementary day schools. The first report of the Wesleyan Educational Committee, presented to the Conference in 1837, concluded: 'Should Popery and infidelity ever attempt, under any pretence, to take the direction of the youthful mind of this country, it is to be hoped that Methodism will resist the attempt, even to the death; and, in order that we may then be in a condition to resist with success, let us now hasten to the field, and, as far as possible, pre-occupy the ground.'[31]

Fearful as to the possible implications for the supremacy of Protestantism, the Wesleyan Conference opposed Lord John Russell's proposals of 1839, which would have relaxed restrictions on access to public funding for denominational schools. While Methodists would also have benefited from the proposals, the prospect of civic revenue being given to Roman Catholic schools was unacceptable to Wesleyan Methodism. As the *Watchman* explained:

It is far safer for our institutions and a policy far more magnanimous and worthy of a Protestant people, that the voluntary principle shall alone be confided in, and every denomination of Christians be left at liberty to educate their own youth in their own principles. Who amongst us would not cheerfully forgo Government grants in aid of education, if thereby Roman Catholic ambition, left to its own unassisted resources, shall be baulked of its contemplated prey?[32]

Despite the 'no politics' rule, the Wesleyan Educational Committee launched an effective campaign against the Government education scheme, sensing the possibility of a morale-boosting victory in an important matter of principle. Wesleyan Methodists were called upon to sign a petition against the scheme, and speeches and tracts were hastily prepared.[33]

Bunting attacked the proposed Government education scheme as a violation of the Protestant Constitution, because it would permit state aid for Roman Catholic schools in which 'the errors, the superstitions, and the idolatries of Popery will be inculcated'.[34] Horrified at the prospect of a Roman Catholic revival in England, the Wesleyan Conference denounced the scheme on the grounds that it would lead to the 'propagation of the corrupt and tyrannical system of Popery, highly detrimental to the best interests of this country, the security of the Protestant faith, and the spiritual welfare of the community at large, particularly of its children and youth'.[35] Such was the intensity of the opposition, led by Anglicans and Methodists, that the Government abandoned the scheme.

In the absence of Government funding, however, the Wesleyan Conference struggled to achieve its ambitious target of 700 Methodist day schools by 1850. In 1847 there were still only 395 Wesleyan day schools.[36] In order to reach the total, the Wesleyan Conference resolved to seek state aid for Methodist day schools, thereby reversing its earlier decision to oppose the use of public money for denominational schools. To assuage the opposition, the Conference passed a meaningless resolution promising to uphold Protestant Christianity. Inevitably, Roman Catholics soon followed suit by applying for government education grants, prompting frenzied concern among Methodists. An irate Wesleyan minister, lapsing into unintentional incoherence, declared that it was 'utterly impossible not to be without serious apprehensions as to where this may lead in future'.[37]

James Rigg (1821–1909) served as principal of Westminster College teacher training institute from 1868 to 1903. During this period he dominated Methodist education policy and was twice President of the Wesleyan Conference, in 1878 and 1892. Rigg was a firm advocate of denominational day schools as providing the only guarantee of religious education for British children. In the latter part of the nineteenth century, however, most other Wesleyan leaders had come to the conclusion that denominational schools were sectarian. Support grew within the Wesleyan Conference for a state system of education which would teach a non-denominational (and therefore a non-Roman Catholic) form of Christianity. Rigg was virtually alone in taking the view that an education system run by the state would lead to the impoverishment of religious education and eventually to the secularisation of schools.

Rigg's commitment to denominational schools made him more sympathetic towards Roman Catholics than most Wesleyans at that time. In an article in the *London Quarterly Review* of January 1870, he declared:

> it must not be forgotten . . . that if Roman Catholics receive a share of public money for educational purposes, they also pay their share of the national taxes . . . The priest may be trusted to keep his young people pretty well instructed in his and their religion and they may easily have an over-dose of it. But then we must not violate the principles of religious liberty, even to antagonise the Roman priesthood . . . it is a strong temptation to us to force Roman Catholic children into undenominational schools. But we must ask if we have any right to do this . . . As Englishmen we cannot refuse civil and educational rights to our Roman Catholic fellow-subjects.[38]

Rigg welcomed the 'candid, sound and friendly' contribution of the Roman Catholic representatives on the London School Board and complained that some Protestant members were provocative in their statements against Roman Catholicism.[39] Elsewhere, he wrote that he had 'all charity towards individual Roman Catholics . . . recognising that not a little that is good has always been found within the limits of the Roman Catholic Church and that the roll of hagiology includes many true saints as well as many false'.[40]

Nevertheless, despite his moderate approach to education issues, Rigg shared the opinion of the vast majority of nineteenth-century

Methodists that Roman Catholicism was a perversion of Christianity. In *A comparative View of Church Organisations, Primitive and Protestant* (1878), Rigg examined the patterns of church life in the New Testament and early Church, concluding that the Roman Catholic Church had lost, perverted and destroyed the primitive Christian fellowship.[41] Wesleyan Methodism, we should not be surprised to learn, represented a revival of primitive Christian fellowship and discipline: 'The peculiar excellence of the Wesleyan economy . . . is that it embodies more perfectly, and expresses more directly and fully, than any other, the genius, the spirit and tendencies of primitive Christianity.'[42] According to Rigg, Methodism, as the embodiment of biblical Christianity, had two forms of error to combat – Calvinism and the principles of Popish and Anglo-Catholic Medievalism.[43]

In September 1850 Pius IX restored twelve English dioceses, naming Cardinal Wiseman as the first Archbishop of Westminster. In some ways, the replacement of the previous system of Apostolic Vicars made little practical difference to parish life. However, the psychological impact on Roman Catholics and Protestants was immense. For Roman Catholics, the restoration came as a welcome acknowledgement of the steady growth in the number of churches, religious communities, schools and converts, which together betokened a revival in the fortunes of Roman Catholicism in England. In his famous sermon on 'the Second Spring' preached at Oscott near Birmingham in 1852, John Henry Newman inspired the Roman Catholics of England with a gloriously optimistic vision of the future. While Newman may have exaggerated the immediate prospects for Roman Catholicism in England, his confident tone heralded a new era of expansion.

The reaction from Protestants to news of the restoration of the Roman Catholic hierarchy in England was predictable. It was intolerable that the pope should arrogantly create Roman Catholic bishops to exercise spiritual and temporal power over the Protestant subjects of Queen Victoria. *The Times* newspaper exclaimed, 'If this appointment be not intended as a clumsy joke, we confess that we can only regard it as one of the grossest acts of folly and impertinence which the Court of Rome has ventured to commit since the Crown and people of England threw off its yoke.'[44] To uphold the rights of Church of England bishops and clergy against the territorial ambitions of the pope, the

Prime Minister, Lord John Russell, hastily passed the Ecclesiastical Titles Act.

Methodists, too, reacted angrily to the pope's latest act of 'insolent aggression'. In December 1850 *The Methodist New Connexion Magazine* printed an editorial article entitled 'The Papal Aggression, and the Duties of Protestants at this crisis'.[45] The editor pointed the finger of blame squarely at the liberal press for having softened public attitudes towards Roman Catholicism: 'Had it been in the pay of the Italian priest it could not more effectually have subserved his purpose.'[46] The government, too, was roundly condemned for handing out education grants in order 'to bribe and soothe the irritable temper of the Scarlet Lady'. The Church of England also came in for a share of the blame:

> The Church Establishment, too, has nurtured in her own bosom a brood of treacherous men. Not a few, while luxuriating in her glebes and fattening on her revenues, have turned recreant to her principles, and first covertly, and then openly, have assailed her doctrines and perverted her people. They have so far adopted the mummeries and defended the authority of Rome, that had they been Jesuits in disguise they could not have played their part more dexterously and successfully.[47]

For complacent Methodists, who took a more relaxed attitude to the crisis in the belief that the truth of Protestantism must inevitably prevail, the editor had this stark warning: when error is allied with human depravity and secular interests, truth 'maintains too often an unsuccessful contest'. It would be 'a melancholy day for England' if its ministers, the appointed guardians of religious truth, were 'indifferent to the aggressions of the apostate Church of Rome'.[48]

Is there just a hint of rebuke in the *Methodist New Connexion Magazine* that some ministers were perhaps inclined to adopt the attitude of 'live and let live'? If so, the Methodist people were left in no doubt about the 'monstrous delusions, the idolatries, the blasphemies, and the atrocities, unblushingly avowed by the Church of Rome'. The catalogue of Roman Catholic errors follows the tediously familiar litany: 'The idolatry of the mass, the glaring absurdity of transubstantiation, the worship of the virgin, the invocation of saints and angels, the doctrine of purgatory, the power to grant indulgences, the figment of infallibility . . .'[49]

The issue was not simply about the appointment of Roman Catholic bishops for England, but about their supposed jurisdiction:

> If the Roman Catholic people of this country desire bishops for themselves, by all means let them have such things; but let these bishops be stripped of every vestige of secular authority; let them have no titles involving jurisdiction, either temporal or spiritual, over protestants; and let them abjure the pretended power and authority of the Pope in relation to all secular and civil matters in this country. We have no desire whatever to infringe upon their religious liberty; but the assumption of jurisdiction over the protestant population, which the Pope's division of this country evidently implies, and which the language of the Pope's bull and the Cardinal's letter clearly expresses, we have both the right to deny and the power to resist.[50]

What did the Cardinal's oath of allegiance to the Queen matter 'when he has already taken an oath of allegiance to another sovereign, to whom he acknowledges higher obedience, and whose right and power he admits to absolve him from his allegiance to our sovereign?'[51] As a functionary of the pope, the Cardinal must inevitably exercise his jurisdiction in such a way as to overthrow the liberties enjoyed by Protestants. 'Loyalty to the British sovereign and constitution forbids us to acquiesce in such an appointment.'[52]

Behind the rhetoric lurked the fear that Methodists had gone soft on Roman Catholicism. In comparison, the puritan ancestors of Methodism combined 'pious magnanimity' with 'an intense hatred to Popery'. They had no tender words for the Man of Sin: 'Their masculine writings breathe instinctive abhorrence to the mystic Babylon; their allegiance to Christ admitted no complacent apologies for Rome.'[53] Continued opposition to Popery was the 'genuine offspring of enlightened and earnest piety'. But how should Methodists respond to the present crisis? First, they should humble themselves before God in prayer 'both for pardon for our supineness and unfaithfulness, and for the special interposition of Divine Providence and grace, to avert from our favoured land the threatened curse of popery and infidelity'.[54] Young people especially must 'be more thoroughly instructed in the doctrines of evangelical religion and in the principles of religious liberty', because the outcome of the 'fearful struggle between truth and error, betwixt Christianity and

Popery' would depend upon them.[55] Methodists must realise that 'The rising generation will be cast into the mould of the prevailing sentiments and principles of the times we live in.' Protestants were faced with the stark choice of preserving or betraying the truth which Providence had charged them to keep. In order to stiffen the resolve of its readers, *The Methodist New Connexion Magazine* maintained a barrage of anti-Catholic polemic in a series of articles during the first half of 1851.

The Wesleyan Conference reacted to the restoration of the Roman Catholic hierarchy in England by commissioning a string of pamphlets under the series title, *Anti-Popish Tracts for the Multitude* (1851). The first, entitled 'Popish Aggression', by an anonymous Wesleyan minister, claimed as its target the Roman Catholic 'system' rather than Roman Catholics themselves. Begrudgingly, the author conceded that some Roman Catholics had embraced and reflected the truths of common Christianity. 'These, however, I fear, have been exceptions to the general rule, and rather in spite of the peculiarities of Romanism, than by its legitimate influence.' Without a trace of irony, the author pompously declared that 'The papacy is a bigoted and exclusive corruption of Christianity under the dominion of the Pope of Rome . . . From this dominion we were delivered by the Protestant Reformation of the sixteenth century.'

In a separate initiative, the Wesleyan Book Committee published an inexpensive edition of a standard anti-Catholic work, *The Delineation of Roman Catholicism* by the American Methodist Charles Elliott (see below), adding a preface by John Hannah, tutor at the Wesleyan Theological Institution. This popular edition was serialised and a prospectus sent to all superintendent ministers inviting subscriptions from their circuits. What impact this mass circulation of anti-Catholic literature had on Methodist attitudes is impossible to say, though presumably the sales figures were considered sufficient to justify the Book Committee in taking a commercial risk.

Apart from any wider issues relating to politics and education in England, there were other reasons, closer to home, why Methodists found it expedient to oppose Roman Catholic aggression, real or imagined. Quite simply, anti-Catholicism earned Methodists recognition and respect within the Protestant constituency. With cynical appeal to base emotions among their supporters and the population at large, the various Methodist denominations vied to outdo one another in using crude anti-Catholic polemic to attract new members, attack enemies and rivals, and subdue internal quarrels by rallying support for a common cause.

Anti-Catholicism was also a trump card in the internal politics of Methodism. For instance, in the internal disputes within Wesleyan Methodism between the leadership and the reformers each side found it tactically advantageous to accuse the other of popery. The reformers charged the Conference with being a 'priestly conclave' for the promotion of 'popish protestantism'.[56] To sow disaffection among rank and file members, the reformers accused the Conference of being sympathetic towards the Roman Catholic Church, because of its reluctance to petition Parliament in 1850 for a more stringent Ecclesiastical Titles Bill. *The Wesleyan Times*, an anti-Conference weekly newspaper, complained that 'The Popery of Methodism is as rank as the Popery of Rome, and must come in for its share of condemnation . . . We think the reformers should meet and protest against Popery, not Roman only, but Anglo and Methodistic.'[57] By denouncing the Wesleyan Conference as papist, the reformers cleverly wrong-footed the leadership, at the same time establishing their credentials at the forefront of opposition to Roman Catholicism.

In response, the Wesleyan Conference attacked the reformers for behaving in a 'popish' way by denying the private judgement of the vast majority of Wesleyans, who wanted to maintain Methodism as it was. The reformers hid behind the anonymity of the Flysheets to persecute their leaders. Furthermore, they claimed 'an individual infallibility, which is worse than a Popish or aggregate one'.[58] Reaffirming its opposition to Roman Catholicism, the Wesleyan Conference urged the Methodist people to set aside their differences and support the leadership in their campaign against popery. The President of the Wesleyan Conference, John Beecham, even called for special days of fasting and prayer for an end to internal strife in the face of the serious threat posed by Roman Catholicism.[59]

Following his evangelical conversion in 1738, Wesley travelled extensively in Britain and Ireland but, wisely perhaps, never returned to North America, the scene of his disastrous early ministry. Methodism finally arrived in the American colonies with Irish immigrants in the

1760s, though at first it was slow to develop. In response to appeals, Wesley sent out itinerant preachers to consolidate the work. Principally through the ministry of Francis Asbury and Thomas Rankin, the scattered and isolated Methodist societies were gradually united into an American connexion, despite the disruption caused by the revolutionary war against Britain. Eventually, in September 1784 Wesley made provision for the oversight of Methodism in North America by ordaining Thomas Coke as superintendent; the plan being that when Coke arrived in America he would ordain Asbury as fellow superintendent. Precisely what Wesley intended when he laid hands upon Coke has been subject to intense debate because of the series of events it set in train. In November 1784 Coke arrived in New York and travelled to Philadelphia to meet Asbury, who insisted that his own appointment as superintendent be approved by a general conference of preachers.

With this on the agenda, the first Methodist Conference in the United States met in Baltimore at Christmas 1784. Sixty of the 81 preachers then active in America gathered under the leadership of Coke and Asbury to settle the constitution of American Methodism. The Conference resolved to 'form ourselves into an Episcopal Church and to have superintendents, elders and deacons', with Asbury and Coke being 'unanimously elected to the superintendency of the Church'.[60] Along with the *Form of Discipline*, the Conference adopted two other foundational documents: Wesley's *Sunday Service of the Methodists*, which was an adaptation of the Book of Common Prayer for use in America; and his *Twenty-Four Articles of Religion*, which were an abridgement of the Thirty-Nine Articles of the Church of England. Among the articles to survive intact were those with an anti-Catholic content.[61] Within a few years, Methodism had adopted the title 'Methodist Episcopal Church' and changed the title of superintendent to 'bishop', in spite of Wesley's intense disapproval.

If Wesley feared from this that Methodists in North America might neglect their Protestant identity, he need not have worried. For early Americans of Protestant extraction, anti-Catholicism was a natural part of their burgeoning national identity and democratic aspirations. Throughout the nineteenth century, Methodists in the United States, in company with Protestants generally, looked with suspicion on Roman Catholics as alien to the American dream by nationality, religion and class.[62] The view that Roman Catholics didn't belong was reinforced by differences in lifestyle. In contrast to the strongly puritanical ethos of Methodism, many immigrant Roman Catholics enjoyed Sabbath pleasures and liquor.

A policy of unrestricted immigration brought a flood of Roman Catholics to America from Europe, often from the poorest social classes. The exuberant growth in the number of Roman Catholics in America caused consternation among Methodists, who felt the social fabric of America was under threat, particularly in the sphere of public education. 'The Episcopal address [to the General Conference] of 1872 warned that the "Romish Church" was intent on destroying public education and asked Methodists to unite with "all intelligent Christians and all true patriots" to protect the "free institutions" granted by our "Protestant forefathers".'[63] Suspicion of Roman Catholicism as being un-American lingered well into the twentieth century. In 1922 one Methodist writer stated that 'Catholic' and 'Christian' could not be compared since the Roman Catholic Church was essentially pagan.[64] As recently as 1960, John F. Kennedy became the first Roman Catholic to be elected President of the United States, in the face of vociferous opposition from at least one prominent Methodist bishop.[65]

The most significant nineteenth-century American Methodist commentator on Roman Catholicism was Charles Elliott (1792–1869), whose *Delineation of Roman Catholicism* (1841) contains approximately one million words and took more than twenty years to complete. The size of a family Bible, the *Delineation* analyses Roman Catholicism as defined by the creeds, catechisms, councils, papal bulls and selected theologians. Throughout there are translations by Elliott of long extracts from the Council of Trent and papal bulls.

Elliott cited a number of reasons for undertaking such an enormous project. Above all, he believed firmly that 'the system of Popery . . . is at variance with the pure religion taught in the Bible, and is injurious to the public and private morals of this whole nation, and of the world; so that, if unchecked, it will retard or destroy true religion, and overturn the civil and religious liberties of the United States'. Part of his purpose, therefore, was to 'disabuse the public mind respecting the deceitful character of Popery' and 'to inform Protestants concerning the true nature, tendency, and design of Popery'. At the same time, Elliott hoped to reform those who were 'easily ensnared by the delusions of Popery'. It was believed that younger ministers in particular would find it beneficial 'to discover the Jesuitical shape into which Popery is now moulded'.[66]

Like many others before and since, Elliott claimed to distinguish between Roman Catholics and the Roman Catholic Church:

> Although [the author] is fully convinced, from the most careful examination which he can make, that Roman Catholicism is corrupt in its doctrines, morals, institutions, and practice, as a whole; yet he believes there is a remnant of truly pious persons among both the Clergy and the laity, who have not defiled their robes. The pious few, whether lay or clerical, are guided by the remains of truth buried in their system, and the portions of it which are forced on them through the influence of Protestantism. By these means, the effect of error and of bad example is counteracted. These persons are good Christians, not in consequence of Popery, but in spite of it.[67]

The *Delineation* is divided into four parts: Book I 'On the Rule of Faith' covers Scripture, Tradition, infallibility and the early Church Fathers; Book II analyses 'The Seven Sacraments of the Church'; Book III examines 'The Government of the Church of Rome'; and Book IV investigates 'Miscellaneous Doctrines'. There are just two brief references to John Wesley in the entire volume: the first occurs in a foot-note relating to the release of souls in purgatory; the second is Wesley's definition of true succession in the Church.[68] Luther receives 14 references; Calvin is not mentioned at all; and Richard Challoner is cited on 11 occasions. In comparison, there are copious references to the early Church Fathers – 34 references to Cyprian alone. Thus Elliott was not solely dependent upon Wesley and the Reformers for his critique of Roman Catholic doctrine. A considerable amount of material is intro-duced and discussed at length: the treatment of infallibility alone amounts to some thirty thousand words.

It would be impossible to do justice to such a massive work in the space of a few paragraphs. However, Elliott's treatment of the doctrine of the Church illustrates his general method. First, Elliott examined the use of the word *ekklesia* in Scripture, from which he discovered the scriptural marks of the true Church of Christ to be: (1) the apostolic faith or doctrine; (2) an apostolical ministry, which 'if not absolutely necessary to the existence of the church, was requisite to its well-being';

and (3) a congregation of holy persons to which unholy persons could be joined in 'external society'. In the light of these scriptural marks, the Roman Catholic definition of the Church, 'namely, profession of faith, use of the same sacraments, submission to the Pope' was 'peculiarly faulty'.[69] It meant, for instance, that pious Christians who denied the pope's authority were thereby excluded from the Church; whereas wicked or profane people were counted among the members of the Church, providing they acknowledged the authority of the pope. In contrast, it was clear from the New Testament that 'Wherever there is a true profession of Christianity, embracing at least a firm purpose to flee from sin and seek salvation, and where this purpose is fixed in the mind, it will be shown by its fruits.'[70] In practice, the fruits of a true profession of faith meant avoiding evil, undertaking works of piety and mercy, and attending to all the ordinances of God, including public worship, the Lord's Supper and the ministry of the word, private prayer, Bible reading and fasting. Those who habitually broke these regulations and showed no sign of repentance were to be separated from the communion of the Church. Providentially, these norms constituted 'the outlines of the General Rules of the Wesleyan-Methodist societies, which form the best system of church-regulations extant, because they are taken from the word of God. By enforcing these, the Wesleyan Methodists have preserved the purity of primitive Christianity in its doctrines and discipline for an entire century, without any material deviation.'[71]

Continuing, Elliott turned his attention to the four marks of the Church in patristic theology. No Protestant would deny that unity was a mark of the true Church. However, 'All unity is not of God; nor is all dissent derived from Satan. But the unity of sound doctrine and Christian love is especially enjoined.'[72] Emphatically, 'Adhesion to the Pope of Rome is no part of Christian unity.' Nowhere did the Scriptures support the Roman Catholic claim that the pope was the head of all Christians. The external unity that existed in the Roman Catholic Church was not the unity of faith, truth and love, of which the Holy Spirit is the source. There follows a long excursus on the tyrannical exercise of temporal power by popes. Second, the holiness of the Roman Catholic Church was defective, both in doctrine and also in the actions of the laity and clergy. Third, the Church of Rome could not properly be called catholic with regard to place, time or faith. In reality, the Holy

Catholic Church embraced all those who were or would be saved, in heaven and on earth: 'All of these were not in communion with the Roman Church; many of them lived and died in happy ignorance of the idolatry and superstition of the Popedom.'[73]

Turning to the last of these four marks of the Church, Elliott examined apostolicity and the question of succession. According to Elliott, there were three strands to succession in the Church – doctrine, morals and practice. For the early Church Fathers, the sign of episcopal succession was secondary in importance to continuity in doctrine, though the Bishop of Rome enjoyed a certain pre-eminence of honour in the Church. Therefore, 'Let modern Romanists demonstrate that they possess the same doctrines which the ancient Bishops of Rome held, and then their argument from succession will have weight.'[74] Surveying the history of the Roman Catholic Church, it was evident to Elliott that whatever kind of succession the Roman Catholic Church claimed for the papacy had been broken by illegitimate occupancy. Fortunately, however, 'There has been, independent of the Church of Rome, a succession or transmission of Christianity through a more holy channel, and in a purer state, than that of which she boasts.'[75] Through the ministry of the Protestant churches God has provided an extraordinary succession to reform and admonish the corrupt state of the Church.

Between 1841 and 1877 Elliott's *Delineation* went through four editions to take account of new developments, including the definition of the Immaculate Conception (1854) and the First Vatican Council (1869–70). Despite its density and the lack of concession to the general reader, the *Delineation of Roman Catholicism* became a popular source of reference for Methodism in America and Britain to refute the claims of Roman Catholicism, though it is difficult to know to what extent Elliott's theological arguments were understood by the average Methodist.

Methodism's Arminian theology, with its emphasis on the universality of grace, provided a powerful impetus for global mission. More mundane factors, including large-scale emigration and Protestant imperialism, also facilitated the spread of Methodism overseas. From the outset, anti-Catholicism was a common feature of Methodist missions.

By far the most important mission field for Methodism was Ireland. Between 1770 and Wesley's last visit in 1789, the number of Methodist members in Ireland grew fivefold to around 14,000.[76] The largest gains were made in those areas, mostly in the north of Ireland, where the influence of English Protestantism was already in evidence. As Wesley found to his frustration, Methodism made little headway among the bulk of the Roman Catholic peasantry in the south. While the rate of growth was spectacular, overall the Methodist community in Ireland remained tiny and without influence. Nevertheless, in the first half of the nineteenth century Methodism in Ireland assumed a strategic importance disproportionate to its size because of its key location in the global Protestant crusade against Roman Catholicism.

The Rebellion of the United Irishmen in 1798 caused considerable damage to Protestant churches, encouraging Methodists in their belief that peace in Ireland would come only when the bulk of the population became Protestant. In 1799 the Irish Conference appointed three full-time Gaelic-speaking missionaries to preach to Roman Catholics. It was an uphill task, even with the enthusiastic support of English Methodists. At the beginning of the nineteenth century, more than 3 million Irish people were still 'plunged in the deepest ignorance and superstition' by Roman Catholicism.[77] The appalling poverty of Roman Catholics in Ireland provided Methodism with a philanthropic veneer for its mission. Following Wesley's example, Methodists attributed the acute economic distress in southern Ireland to the influence of Roman Catholicism. By preaching the Gospel and spreading the Protestant faith throughout Ireland, Methodists hoped to remedy the dire economic situation and improve social conditions.

In 1866, when the worst years of the famine were over, William Crook, an Irish Wesleyan preacher, credited Protestantism with having improved conditions for the Irish people: 'It is popery that has im-poverished them and kept them down, shedding its baneful influence . . . over all . . . as seen in Spain, beneath the sunny skies of Italy, and in poor priest-ridden Ireland. On the contrary, it is Protestantism that has elevated . . . the sturdy inhabitants of Ulster.'[78] Twenty years later, the Wesleyan historian C. H. Crookshank described the purpose of the Methodist mission in Ireland as an attempt to subjugate 'Irish popery to the faith of Christ'.[79]

In the longer term, there were sound strategic reasons for the Methodist mission in Ireland. The high rate of emigration from Ireland throughout the century took Irish people to many different parts of the world. In particular, the years following the Potato Famine in 1845 saw a huge wave of emigration from Ireland to Britain, America and elsewhere. The export of Irish Methodists would greatly assist the development of Methodist missions in receiving countries. At the same time, energetic Irish preachers made a disproportionate contribution to the success of the Wesleyan Methodist Missionary Society. Writing in 1865, the American Methodist historian Abel Stevens credited Irish Methodists with a leading role in the establishment of Methodism in Canada, the United States, the West Indies, Australia, Africa and India.[80]

As Methodist missionaries and emigrants carried the Protestant faith from Britain and Ireland (and increasingly from America) to different parts of the world, part of their spiritual baggage was a crude anti-Catholicism that converts quickly assimilated. Frequently, intense rivalry between Protestant missionaries and Roman Catholic priests spilled over into confrontation, especially in predominantly Roman Catholic countries. A history of Methodist foreign missions written in 1909 contains numerous stories of attempts by Roman Catholics to scupper Methodist missions.[81] For instance, when American Methodists planted a mission in Italy in 1871 Roman Catholic priests 'tried to hinder the work in every way possible', even to the point of exercising a form of terrorism over the people.[82] All this only served to increase the determination of Methodists to establish and consolidate overseas missions.

In virgin mission fields in Africa and Australia, competition between Methodists and Roman Catholics was often intense. In December 1813 Thomas Coke ordained John McKenny for Wesleyan overseas missions. In 1836, following a period of service in Ceylon, McKenny was appointed Chairman of the New South Wales District. In a report to the Wesleyan Missionary Committee in 1838 McKenny suggested that the real question in Australia was whether the country would become 'a *protestant* or a *popish* colony'.[83] From the 'frightful' number of priests being sent to Australia, McKenny concluded that 'the Romanists are evidently organising a system to occupy, as far as they can, every part of the colony'.[84] As McKenny saw it, Australia had the potential to become the base for spreading the Gospel in the islands of the South Seas. However, more Protestant missionaries were needed to secure Australia against Roman Catholicism.

Given the high stakes involved, it is hardly surprising that Methodist and Roman Catholic missionaries were hostile to each other. Yet, there were Methodist missionaries whose reaction to Roman Catholicism was markedly more conciliatory than was generally the case. William Butler, an Irish Wesleyan minister, emigrated from Ireland to the United States in 1850 and later played a leading part in the development of Methodist Episcopal Church missions in India (1856–4) and Mexico (1873–8).[85] By the standards of the nineteenth century, Butler possessed an unusually enlightened attitude towards Roman Catholics. He criticised a great deal of Protestant evangelism in Mexico for being 'political and harshly controversial', especially sermons that amounted 'to little more than tirades against the Romish clergy and Church'. In Butler's estimation, 'Such conduct and such methods of missionary work are only calculated to irritate and disgust conscientious Romanists, and lead them to hate Protestantism, and even be willing to see it persecuted and driven away.'[86] To avoid unnecessary tension, Butler urged Methodist missionaries in Mexico to preach the Gospel in a non-sectarian manner 'without abusing the Romanists'. But, although he was more tolerant than many of his contemporaries, Butler was far from being an ecumenist. Indeed, his objective was to convert Roman Catholics to Protestantism. According to Butler, the best way to remove the 'darkness of superstition and sin' was to 'introduce the light of truth and holiness'.

Were Methodists in danger of embracing double standards by claiming their right to engage in mission, while resenting the freedom of Roman Catholics to do the same? The contrasting attitude of some Methodists in the United States to Roman Catholics and Negro slaves illustrates an apparent inconsistency. Methodism in the United States split over the slavery issue, and the Methodist Episcopal Church, South, was founded in 1844. In the North, Methodists adopted an anti-slavery position, while remaining implacably opposed to civil liberties for Roman Catholics. To the Methodist way of thinking, however, there was no contradiction. Slavery was physical bondage, whereas Roman Catholicism amounted to spiritual bondage. It was the duty of Methodists to deliver human beings from all forms of tyranny as the first step towards their evangelisation. In America, Methodist missions were faced with the bondage of human slavery, whereas in Ireland and other European countries the immediate enemy was Roman Catholicism. By this flawed process of reasoning, Methodists propagated anti-Catholic attitudes throughout the nineteenth century wherever the banner of Methodism was raised in overseas missions.

The most notable Methodist contribution to ecclesiology in the nineteenth century came from Benjamin Gregory (1820–1900) in his Fernley Lecture of 1873, entitled *The Holy Catholic Church, the Communion of Saints*.[87] From his reading of the New Testament and the history of the early Church, Gregory established as a first principle of ecclesiology that the Church was not a thing of rigid definition.[88] Therefore, it was a mistake to assert the divine institution of any particular form of church structure, whether episcopal or presbyterian.[89] On the contrary, 'The only Church-government which can justly claim a divine right is the government by sound, practical good sense, mutual compliance, and loving co-operation.'[90]

Gregory's second principle of ecclesiology held that the Church was a definite community with an object and reason for existence.[91] The doctrinal basis of the Christian Church was equally straightforward: 'Whatever amount of revealed truth is sufficient, when heartily believed, for the initiation of a rudimentary Christian experience, the enkindling and sustentation of the spiritual life and for tracing the outlines of a truly Christian character, is sufficient to entitle any individual to recognition as a member of the Christian Church.'[92] The scriptural baptism formula provided the basis for what Gregory called 'catholic inclusiveness'. Unitarians were excluded from the Church because the doctrine of the Trinity was an essential element of revealed truth.

Like Wesley, Gregory distinguished between the essentials and non-essentials of Christian faith. 'The rule of inclusiveness in the Christian Church, then, is to insist on faith in the fundamental facts of Christianity and to allow liberty of discussion on all other doctrines.'[93] The Holy Catholic Church was the communion or fellowship of the saints.[94] The unity of the Church was constituted by unity in the Spirit. Thus separate Christian denominations might obscure, but could not destroy, the visible unity of the Church. The historical continuity of the Church was located in the unbroken succession of true believers (the saints) and not the bishops. That Methodism occupied a special place within the Holy Catholic Church had been acknowledged by William Paley, whose *Evidences of Christianity* argued that Methodism represented the nearest possible approach to the primitive Christian 'mode of life'.[95]

Gregory made few references to Roman Catholicism, but 'sacerdotalism' was his chief target. According to Gregory, the primitive Church was based not on the temple with its hierarchical 'priestly' order but on the more egalitarian society found in the synagogue.[96] Its worship did not depend upon 'ordained officials', nor did it involve a 'merely ritual celebration of the Lord's Supper'. Any distinction between clergy and laity was foreign to the New Testament and therefore anti-scriptural.[97] The Gentile churches were granted their unrestricted freedom to self-determination by a decision arising out of 'an honest natural, *ex animo* concurrence of sentiment and judgement'.[98] The 'absolute unanimity' of this decision was clearly the work of the Holy Spirit: there was no 'make-believe' decision based on 'Popish unanimity' involving the suppression of personal conviction and the abandonment of Christian liberty and independence of thought. The notion of a succession of bishops was contrary to the New Testament. The pretensions of 'certain churches' to the exclusive title, privileges and powers of the Church – to the extent that they unchurched and excommunicated all others – was an insuperable barrier to visible unity.

Despite his tendentious attack on sacerdotalism, Gregory was not entirely without sympathy towards Roman Catholicism. Whatever their differences, Christians were invisibly united through a common baptism. The 'holy catholic Church' comprised countless churches throughout the world 'by whatever name they pass among men; not omitting one misled Roman Catholic who is loyal to his Saviour'.[99] Positively, if rather ungraciously, Gregory maintained that Roman Catholicism had been rescued from 'utter rottenness' by the presence of 'spiritual fellowships' that were similar to the Methodist societies.[100] He cited with approval the 'spiritual conferences' of the society of the Oratory of Divine Love sanctioned by Pope Gregory XIII in 1577. Likewise, the Bishop of Alet (died 1677) formed a system of fellowships within his diocese, known as the 'society of the Regents', which exhibited 'strong features of affinity with the Methodist Class-Meeting'.[101]

To Gregory's way of thinking, the ideal of 're-uniting' the churches could not be achieved by absorption, but instead would happen as a result of alliance, assimilation and coalescence arising out of mutual attraction. Conceiving the Church as a 'living organism' was more scriptural than the Roman notion of a Church 'whose vitality is so precarious, so skin-deep, and its unity so outward, superficial and mechanical, that a flaw in episcopal succession ruins all, and makes the body of Christ tumble to pieces'.[102] If the historic succession, rather than the atonement of Christ, were the only basis of unity, then the dogma of episcopal succession would become the 'foundation-truth' of the Church.[103]

Against what he described as Roman Catholicism's 'mechanistic' interpretation of Christian unity, Gregory contrasted his own very different vision for the future:

> A wide voluntary federation of churches, all holding the Head, yet various forms of government, and with a varying theological terminology and varying modes of worship, bound together by their common faith in fundamental doctrines, a common inner life and a common outer life; their common hope of sanctity in this world and rest with Christ in the world to come, is surely a grander ideal, and would be a grander spectacle than a colossal, rigid, hollow, external union, of which the bond is one particular mode of ordination to the Ministry, and an arbitrary limitation of grace and salvation to the officiations of men so ordained; a union, moreover, requiring, and often only too glad to secure the secular arm – in other words, brute force – to carry it into effect.[104]

But what would constitute the essential elements of a 'common outer life' in this voluntary federation of churches? We can only speculate, since Gregory did not elaborate. In his rejection of common structures and uniformity in ecclesial life, Gregory was an early advocate of Christian unity in the form of what has since come to be called 'reconciled diversity'.

Hugh Price Hughes (1847–1902) was probably the single most influential leader in Wesleyan Methodism in the final decade of the nineteenth century. A committed ecumenist, he has been credited with reversing Methodism's drift away from the Church of England caused by the influence of nonconformist thinking.[105] Against the mainstream of Wesleyan theology, which was conservative and inward-looking, he placed great emphasis on the need for Methodism to reflect the 'catholicity' of the Church. As Hughes saw it, Wesleyan Methodism at the end of the nineteenth century was faced with the stark alternatives of dwindling into a 'feeble stereo-typed sect' or growing into a national church. Fearful that Methodism would otherwise degenerate into a sect, Hughes was a strong proponent of Methodist reunion and thereafter a wider unity scheme involving English Protestants including, eventually, the Church of England.

A deep interest in the 'catholicity' of the Church led Hughes to appreciate the sacraments and the sacramental presence of Christ in his Church. One Christmas Day in Italy, Hughes came across a Roman Catholic church where the silent congregation lay prostrate in worship before the sacred host. Far from regarding such devotion as idolatrous, as many other Protestants would have done, Hughes was impressed that the worshippers were so powerfully aware of the presence of Christ in their midst.[106]

For a Wesleyan theologian, Hughes held a relatively moderate view of the Reformation, and his ecumenical vision encompassed the Roman Catholic Church. According to Hughes, 'at the root of the Roman error lay great truth, and what was required was to brush off and remove the accretions which hid the truth from view'.[107] He distinguished between the essential features of Roman Catholicism and subsequent additions, which had provided the Reformers with a legitimate target. In particular, Hughes had little time for the papacy, 'an excrescence – not a fundamental element of the Church of Rome'.[108] Likewise, papal infallibility was a modern phenomenon, the invention of Jesuits. In a display of sympathy for the Roman Catholic Church, unusual among Wesleyans, Hughes suggested that Christian 'Churchmen' must ultimately gravitate towards Roman Catholicism or Methodism, since these two ecclesiastical organisations were most suited to the needs of humanity and were also the most consistent.[109]

Hughes was among the first Methodists to observe certain similarities between the early Methodist preachers and the friars in the Roman Catholic Church. He was particularly impressed by the fact that, whereas Protestantism was bedevilled by fragmentation, the Roman Catholic Church had shown itself more adept at handling diversity:

In Anglicanism . . . or Methodism, or any of the other Protestant communities, if a man comes along full of the zeal of the Holy Ghost, willing . . . to use any method, conventional or unconventional, in the achievement of this purpose, he is scowled at . . . tied up here and tied up there, so that if in the end he wants to do his work in this world he has to clear out . . . But the Pope, on the contrary . . . welcomes him, ties a rope round his waist, and gives him more or less carte blanche to do as he pleases, i.e. he founds an order, and so keeps both himself and the whole concern alive.[110]

Could there possibly be a hint here that Hughes saw the future of Methodism as a religious order within the Holy Catholic Church? If so, in the prevailing climate of opposition to Roman Catholicism, it would have been difficult for him to express such a view more openly.

Although he was neither a systematic theologian nor an ecclesiologist, Hughes was probably more responsible than any other nineteenth-century Methodist for shaping the future of Methodism in the next hundred years.[111] His vision and groundwork made a major contribution to Methodist Union in 1932. Moreover, Methodism's ecumenical openness in the twentieth century owed a great deal to Hughes' vision of catholicity and his abiding influence on a rising generation of twentieth-century Methodist theologians. In particular, Hughes' moderate attitude made it easier for these younger Methodist theologians to engage positively with the Roman Catholic Church.

The Roman Catholic hierarchy in Britain marked the landmark event of Catholic emancipation by issuing a *Declaration of the Catholic bishops, the vicars apostolic and their coadjutors in Great Britain* (1829). Judging by its content, this was aimed primarily at Protestants rather than fellow Roman Catholics. In a dignified and measured response to widespread Protestant opposition to emancipation, the hierarchy professed amazement at all the fuss: 'When we consider the misrepresentations of the Catholic religion, which are so industriously and widely propagated in this country we are filled with astonishment.' The declaration refutes the indictment that Roman Catholic loyalties were divided between pope and sovereign: there was no conflict of loyalties because Roman Catholics owed spiritual obedience to the pope and civil obedience to the sovereign.

A further objection (and one held by Wesley) was that an oath of loyalty by a Roman Catholic was worthless because of the principle that 'no faith is to be kept with heretics'. The declaration challenges those who would interpret conciliar teaching in this way. It also rejects the

73

conventional Protestant charge that Roman Catholicism was idolatrous, superstitious and anti-scriptural. The bishops concluded: 'We confidently trust that this declaration and explanation will be received by all our fellow subjects in a spirit of candour and charity; and that those who have been hitherto ignorant of, or but imperfectly acquainted with our doctrines of faith, will do us the justice to acknowledge, that, as Catholics, we hold no religious principles which are not perfectly consistent with our duties as Christians, and as British subjects.'

To what extent the Roman Catholic hierarchy expected its *Declaration* to improve relations with Protestants is difficult to say. What is certain however is that it made little headway in changing Protestant attitudes towards Roman Catholicism. In all likelihood, few Protestants would even have been aware of the *Declaration*, let alone have read it with anything approaching an open mind. Of course, prejudice was not confined to Protestants. There was equal misrepresentation on both sides of the Catholic–Protestant divide, and Methodists similarly had cause for complaint that Roman Catholics had misunderstood them.

Roman Catholic attitudes towards Methodism in the nineteenth century were largely determined by a powerful combination of two forces – conventional disapproval of Protestantism in general as a schismatic movement and the particular legacy of the eighteenth-century controversy between Richard Challoner and John Wesley. Challoner's fierce attack on Wesley set the tone for Roman Catholic reactions to Methodism throughout the English-speaking world. For many years the *Caveat Against the Methodists* was a standard Roman Catholic reference work on Methodism. In total, six editions of the *Caveat* were published, the last appearing in 1817. An Irish edition was published in 1808 and an American edition appeared in 1817.

Even towards the end of the nineteenth century, when the Wesleyan Connexion was an established feature of the religious landscape in many parts of the world, Roman Catholic and Anglo-Catholic writers tended to dismiss Methodism as a sect of short duration, or else ignore it altogether. For example, the substantial *Catholic Dictionary* (1884) compiled by William Addis and Thomas Arnold contains articles on 'Calvin and Calvinism' and 'Luther and Lutheranism', but there is no entry on either Methodism or John Wesley.

Probably the most prolific Roman Catholic writer on Methodism in the nineteenth century was a former Wesleyan minister, James Mason (1785–1844), who converted to Roman Catholicism in 1819. His two substantial tracts *An Earnest Appeal to the People called Methodists and to the nation at large by the Rev. J. A. Mason formerly a Methodist preacher* (1827) and *The Triumph of Truth in the Conversion of the Rev. J. A. Mason from the Errors of Methodism to the Catholic Faith* (1827) provide us with an invaluable contemporary account of the controversy between Methodists and Roman Catholics in the opening decades of the nineteenth century.

Mason was born into a Methodist family where he was imbued with Methodist principles from infancy. As a 'Methodist among Methodists' he was zealously devoted to Methodism and subsequently described his conversion to Roman Catholicism in *The Triumph of Truth* in Pauline terms: 'No one, I appeal to those who knew me, was ever more prejudiced in favour of Methodism or hated with more decided aversion the religion I now profess.' Between 1808 and 1818 he served as a Methodist minister in a number of Midlands circuits, by his own account giving ten of the best years of his life in devoted service to the Wesleyan Connexion.

It was while serving in the Wednesbury circuit in the West Midlands that Mason first came into contact with Francis Martyn, a Roman Catholic priest of the Midlands District. Martyn was already engaged in a fierce controversy with a local Anglican rector, in the course of which he published a number of tracts defending Roman Catholic teaching on the Eucharist.[112] Presumably, Martyn enjoyed the confidence of the Roman Catholic hierarchy in England, since he preached the sermon at the funeral of the Vicar Apostolic of the Midlands District.[113]

One morning, probably in 1818, not long after Mason had arrived in Wednesbury, Martyn called at the Methodist manse to reprove the new minister for denying his servant girl permission to attend Mass. Intrigued by Martyn's direct approach, Mason 'felt it just to allow a Roman Catholic clergyman to explain his religion'. Thus began a yearlong dialogue, which culminated in Mason being confirmed into the Roman Catholic Church and then ordained priest.

The dialogue between James Mason and Francis Martyn, retold in *The Triumph of Truth*, centred upon the nature of truth. As a Roman Catholic priest, Martyn maintained the unity and unchanging nature of truth. In Roman Catholic teaching, the rule of faith was to listen to the living voice of the ministers appointed by Christ. The teaching authority of the Church was founded on the authority of Christ given to the apostles (Mark 16.15; Matthew 28.16–20). As a Methodist minister, Mason adopted Wesley's distinction between the essentials and non-essentials of faith, attacking those 'novelties of the faith' which had been introduced by Roman Catholics – purgatory, images, the invocation of saints, the sacrifice of the Mass. Mason agreed with Martyn that the apostles were infallible; but he could not accept that their successors, the bishops, were blessed with the same gift: Scripture alone was infallible.

Responding to Mason's point about the infallibility of Scripture, Martyn cited the doctrine of the Trinity to illustrate just how far the faith of the Church has guided its interpretation of Scripture. Whereas the Unitarians relied on certain texts from the Bible to deduce the Unitarian nature of God, the Roman Catholic Church read all the various biblical texts about the Godhead in the light of its traditional belief in the Trinitarian nature of God. Thus Martyn challenged the unreflective way in which Protestants often appealed to the authority of Scripture in matters of doctrine.

Though he did not mention Challoner by name, it is probable that Martyn had at least read the *Caveat against the Methodists*. At any rate, Martyn's four marks of the Church correspond very closely to those of Challoner. The true Church was: (1) one in faith; (2) holy in institution and in its requirement of members; (3) apostolic in order and mission, teaching all truths to all nations in all ages; and (4) possessed of infallible certainty in matters of faith and practice. As Martyn saw it, if the Christian religion is divine, then it is an unchanging and perpetual obligation, made known through a visible Church invested with authority to teach the Gospel infallibly as the guarantee of the unchanging nature of faith.

Martyn argued from Scripture (especially Matthew 18.18) that the bishops, as successors of the apostles, were infallible. Their infallibility came from the Holy Spirit dwelling in the Church in solemn council and was an essential mark of the Church. Otherwise, Christians could not be certain of the Gospel. When Mason enquired whether the doctrine of infallibility left any role for the Scriptures, Martyn assured him that Scripture served to confirm the Church's teaching and was a valuable source of instruction in the faith.

Rumours of Mason's conversations with a Roman Catholic priest soon reached the ears of his Superintendent. Horrified at this turn of events, the Superintendent urged Mason to read Wesley's *Popery Calmly Considered*. According to his own account, Mason read this treatise alongside a Roman Catholic Catechism whereupon he soon discovered serious errors in Wesley's understanding of Roman Catholic teaching.

Eventually, on 19 March 1819 Mason resigned from the Methodist ministry, handing over his circuit plan and society funds to the Superintendent, who exclaimed 'O! Mr Mason you astonish me: you will become a Roman Catholic and I had rather you had become anything else.' Mason was not persuaded by his Superintendent's advice that, if dissatisfied with Methodism, he should instead become a member of the Church of England. Two days later, Mason was confirmed into the Roman Catholic Church at St Thomas's church, Bloxwich.

Writing in later years as 'a poor priest of Stourbridge', Mason addressed *An Earnest Appeal to the People called Methodists*, 'because you are a people I was once proud to call mine. I was born among you; nurtured among you; educated in part among you; I mingled in all your assemblies, partook of all your spiritual benefits, ate of the same bread, drank of the same fountain.' Thus Mason wrote fondly and 'without the least unkind feeling' towards the Methodist people. Although he intended to expose the 'evils of Methodism', he wrote not from passion or prejudice, but because he 'wished the Methodist people well'. His appeal to the Methodist people was not based on emotion, but rather on Roman Catholic theological principles and the nature of truth. Whether Methodists received his *Earnest Appeal* in the same spirit must be seriously doubted.

As a convert from Protestantism, Mason regretted that Holy Scripture had been subject to the 'private opinion of every Protestant preacher'. Many years before the New Testament was written, the Gospel truth already existed in its full and unadulterated state within a living body of people led by pastors invested with authority to preach it to the world. The Church in every age is this same community founded by Christ, comprising all those who believe and teach the Gospel truth. Otherwise, the promise of Christ, that the gates of hell would not prevail against the Church, would have been proved false. Mason now realised that the key ecclesiological question was, 'What is truth and where is it to be found?' His conversion to Roman Catholicism could be attributed to the fact that 'truth is powerful and will prevail'. In his own words, 'I gave the

Catholic religion a candid examination, and the result was a painful but entire conviction of its truth.'

Although he was cut off from former friends, who failed to appreciate his reasons for leaving their society, Mason felt better able to assess Methodism from outside its ranks. For the first time he realised that there was a succinct proposition against which Methodism had to be tested: 'If the Christian religion be of God it must be uniformly the same; and if it be revealed for the use and benefit of man, then the same reasons which induced the Divine Being to reveal it at first must induce him to preserve it in such a manner that it may be infallibly identified and distinguished from error.' In other words, true Christianity was characterised by the unchanging nature of its doctrine and the perpetual visibility of its teaching authority.[114]

When measured against this standard, Methodism failed to satisfy Mason that it was the religion of God. In the first place, Methodism was manifestly not uniform because it had undoubtedly changed. According to Mason, Wesley was as changeable as the wind: having started out as a member of the Church of England, he embraced Moravianism before eventually forming a religion of his own. Wesley's claim that he was simply gathering souls into the Church was mere sophistry, since he was actually founding a religious sect. Likewise, Methodism was a 'hodgepodge' of teaching, which changed at the whim of its adherents. For instance, although the 1779 *Minutes of Conference* had declared that Methodist preachers were lay people, current Methodist practice was to permit its preachers to celebrate baptism and the Eucharist where a majority of the local trustees were in favour. (Mason was referring to the provisions of the Plan of Pacification.) The Methodist preachers further demonstrated the fickle nature of Methodism. Among the Methodist preachers there was such a variety of beliefs that scarcely two taught the same doctrine. Whereas some held to the necessity of baptism, others denied it. While a number taught perfect sanctification, others claimed this was impossible.

A further requirement for Methodism to be identified as the true religion of God was that it had been perpetually visible. But where was Methodism before Wesley? According to Mason, it was sophistry for Wesley or anyone else to claim that Methodism was primitive Christianity as found in the New Testament. Methodism, it was clear to Mason, did not possess a single mark of the Church, since it lacked unity in truth, universal extent, perpetual duration, and infallible doctrine and morals. As for the Methodist teachers, they had neither apostolic orders nor the apostolic mission, whether in an ordinary or extraordinary form.

In response to the supposed fruitfulness of Methodism in spreading scriptural holiness, Mason confessed to having little time for Methodist morality, which he regarded as defective and delusive, since a bad tree could not bear good fruit. On the surface, Methodism may have appeared worthwhile, but this was the outward appearance of a painted sepulchre. Love feasts and class meetings provided an occasion for self-deception and therefore corrupt morality among Methodists.

So much for the negative impact of Methodism on Mason, at least in his later perception, which was perhaps not entirely dispassionate. In what positive ways had Methodism contributed to his formation as a Roman Catholic priest? To what extent did he struggle to embrace those spiritual and devotional practices that formerly he rejected? Unfortunately, Mason did not address these and similar questions about his spiritual journey from Methodism to Roman Catholicism. Given the controversial nature of exchanges between Roman Catholics and Protestants in the nineteenth century, this was only to be expected. Still, it is a pity that Mason has not left us with any deeper spiritual insight into his unique experience as both a Methodist minister and a Roman Catholic priest.

While serving as a priest in Stourbridge, Mason produced several more anti-Methodist tracts; all of them intended to convince Methodists of their errors.[115] At about the time Mason was writing his *Earnest Appeal to the People called Methodists,* John Chettle, a Methodist preacher, attacked the doctrine of transubstantiation in a tract addressed to Francis Martyn, Mason's erstwhile dialogue partner and midwife to his Catholic conversion.[116] Mason responded to Chettle with a pamphlet defending the doctrine of transubstantiation.[117] When Edward Corser, a prominent local Methodist, converted to Roman Catholicism, Mason gleefully celebrated by publishing two tracts.[118]

Between 1828 and 1830 Mason produced a series of three substantial tracts, responding in detail to Wesley's *Roman Catechism* and challenging its 'numerous misrepresentations, false glosses, and gross falsehoods'.[119] Many of the arguments deployed in his earlier anti-Methodist tracts were amplified and extended. The effectiveness of Mason's anti-

Methodist literature seems to have been recognised by the Roman Catholic Church in Britain. At any rate, the Catholic Institute of Great Britain published two of Mason's anti-Methodist works as part of a series of anti-Protestant tracts by Roman Catholic writers, which were widely circulated in Britain and elsewhere in the middle years of the century.[120]

We have barely scratched the surface of the mountain of controversial literature produced by Protestants and Roman Catholics in the nineteenth century. This was the great age of polemical tracts, which could be produced quickly and cheaply for mass circulation. All denominations and parties invested considerable resources in pamphleteering as an effective means of attacking their enemies and encouraging members. With few exceptions, these tracts produced a dialogue of the deaf, since their authors usually made little or no attempt to engage in serious theological debate with opponents.

The following is one example of just such a 'dialogue' between a Methodist minister and a Roman Catholic priest. An anonymous Roman Catholic priest in Scarborough, known only by his initials 'J. L.', engaged in controversy with J. B. Holroyd, a Wesleyan minister. In 1827 Holroyd published some 'Remarks and Illustrations on a Letter from the Rev. J. L., Roman Catholic Priest, at Scarborough to a member of the Methodist Society, in that town'. Unfortunately, the original letter is not extant. Unimpressed at Holroyd's weak grasp of Roman Catholic doctrine, J. L. retorted with 'A Refutation of Remarks and Illustrations by J. B. Holroyd (Wesleyan Methodist Minister) on a Letter to A Member of the Methodist Society in which his Glaring Blunders, and Total Ignorance of Canons, Councils, Bulls etc. are exposed'. The following year, the industrious Yorkshire priest produced a further tract 'Methodism Unmasked', prompting Holroyd to respond with 'A reply to Methodism Unmasked by the Rev. J. L. Roman Catholic Priest at Scarborough, in which the abominations of the Church of Rome are further exposed'. Instead of shedding light on the theological issues at stake between Methodists and Roman Catholics, these and similar controversial exchanges tended to perpetuate mutual misconceptions and misunderstandings going back to the time of the Reformation.

As probably the most famous and erudite English convert to Roman

Catholicism in the nineteenth century, John Henry Newman was an influential theological commentator on a variety of subjects, including Methodism. Brought up in the Church of England under the influence of the Evangelical Revival, he later became the leading spirit of the Oxford Movement, producing 24 of the *Tracts for the Times* (1833–41). Directed 'against Popery and Dissent', these tracts argued that the patristic tradition of the Church of England represented a *via media* between Roman Catholicism and Protestantism. As regards the two traditions presently under discussion, Newman would concede only that 'Methodism and Popery are in different ways the refuge of those whom the Church stints of the means of grace; they are the foster-mothers of abandoned children.'[121]

In an essay originally written in October 1840, when he was still an Anglican priest and fellow of Oriel College in Oxford, Newman cast a critical, but not entirely unsympathetic, eye on the rise of Methodism in the eighteenth century:

> The history of Methodism is, we do not scruple to say, the history of a heresy; but never surely was a heresy so mixed up with what was good and true, with high feeling and honest exertion – never a heresy which admitted of more specious colouring or more plausible excuse – never a heresy in which partisan must be more carefully discriminated from partisan, persons from their tenets, their intentions from their conduct, their words from their meaning, what they held of truth from what they held of error, their beginnings from their endings. Being nothing short of a formal heresy, ultimately good could not come of it, nor will good come of it. We have not yet seen its termination, and therefore as yet can but partially argue *ab eventu*, which in theological matters is an evidence so solemn, so conclusive. 'Ye shall know them by their fruits,' is our Lord's canon concerning all schemes of doctrine, however attractive or fair of promise, which come not of the Catholic Church. Already has one of the two branches of Methodism, and that the principal one, borne, in the person of its most learned divine, the bitter fruit of error in the most sacred doctrine of theology.[122]

Newman was clearly referring to John Wesley as the founder of the largest branch of Methodism. Simultaneously fascinated and disconcerted by Methodism, he went on:

We hope nothing, then, we fear everything, from a religious movement, which nevertheless in its rise excites our sympathy, and of which we do not deny, as of any event in the world, the incidental benefits. Yet interest, pity and admiration we do feel for many of the principal agents in it; and if the choice lay between them and the reformers of the sixteenth century (as we thankfully acknowledge it does not), a serious inquirer would have greater reason for saying, 'Sit anima mea cum Westleio,' than 'cum Luthero,' or 'cum Calvino,' and 'cum multis aliis,' as the grammar has it, 'quos nunc perscribere longum est'.[123]

Newman did not distinguish between Wesleyan Methodism and the Calvinistic Methodism of George Whitefield: both were manifestations of a phenomenon that the Church of England in the eighteenth century was ill-equipped to comprehend. As a result of the thick fog created by the 'English Establishment', the guiding light of the Holy Catholic Church in England at that time was reduced to a 'wan and feeble ray' that exerted only 'languid influence' upon her children. In its enfeebled state, the established church was unable to engage seriously with the rise of Methodism:

Wesley and Whitfield [*sic*] doubtless had their places in her economy, as truly as St Francis, or St Philip Neri . . . Repentance and conversion have their place in the gospel and the Church; field preaching has its place; the poor have their place; and, if that place cannot be found in an existing system, which claims to be the Church, that system is, so far, but the figure of the narrow Jewish polity, not of that [Catholic Church] which overshadows the whole earth and penetrates into the recesses of the heart.

But such seems to have been, more or less, the English Church at that day. It saw that there was excellence in the Methodistic system, it saw there was evil; it saw there was strength, it saw there was weakness; it praised the good, it censured the faulty; it feared its strength, it ridiculed its weakness: and that was all. It had no clear consistent *view* of Methodism as a phenomenon: it did not take it as a whole – it did not meet it – it gave out no authoritative judgment on it – it formed no definition of it – it had no line of policy towards it – it could but speak of it negatively, as going *too far*, or vaguely, as wanting in

82

discretion and *temper*, whereas it on the contrary, defective as it was, was a living, acting thing, which spoke and did, and made progress, amid the scattered, unconnected, and inconsistent notions of religion which feebly resisted it.[124]

Newman disagreed with the opinion expressed by some of his contemporaries that the Church of England in the first decades of the nineteenth century was indebted to Wesley and Whitefield for its present vitality and seriousness of purpose. Although they were 'instruments in the hands of Providence', the founders of Methodism should be given no credit for their actions, since whatever spiritual gifts they possessed were mediated through the Church.

> She gave them the grace of baptism, *in order* that they might show forth their light, or rather her light in them; she ordained them, *in order* that they might preach repentance and gather souls into her bosom. As far as they did this, they only did what they had vowed to do; as far as they did something else, they did not benefit her, but were unnatural children and false priests.[125]

According to Newman, if the Church of England was a true branch of the Church, then its revival was inevitable, because of God's unfailing promises. Thus Newman was unwilling to attribute the rise of Methodism to an extraordinary mission from the Holy Spirit. However, he appears at least to have accepted that the ministry of Wesley and Whitefield in some unspecified way was derived from, and related to, the Holy Catholic Church.

By 1840 Newman was beginning to have doubts about his defence of the Church of England. Following a period in which he withdrew from public life altogether, in 1845 he was received into the Roman Catholic Church, where his chief theological contribution was to apply the idea of organic development to the growth of Christian doctrine. In 1871 he republished several essays dating from before his conversion to Roman Catholicism, among them his essay on Methodism. Although some of his views had shifted substantially, including his assessment of the Roman Catholic Church, there is little evidence to suggest that he ever modified his opinion of Methodism. Writing in 1851, following the restoration of the Roman Catholic hierarchy in England, Newman criticised English Protestantism in general as essentially a political rather than a theological or spiritual movement, which had vigorously opposed the rights of Roman Catholics. 'By Protestants,' declared Newman, 'I mean the heirs of the Traditions of Elizabeth; I mean the country gentlemen, the Whig political party, the Church Establishment, and the Wesleyan Conference.'[126]

Despite strained relations with Cardinal Manning and Rome, Newman's stature as a Roman Catholic apologist was eventually recognised by Pope Leo XIII, who in 1879 bestowed on him a cardinal's hat. Wide acceptance eluded Newman during his lifetime, but the quality of his mind was increasingly recognised after his death. With hindsight, Newman was the foremost proponent of Roman Catholic theology in England during the nineteenth century. Certainly, in the first half of the twentieth century, many Roman Catholics would have accepted unreservedly his judgement that the development of Methodism was essentially the history of a heresy.

If Methodist and Roman Catholic controversialists in Britain were ill-informed about their opponents, in Europe the situation was even worse. Here knowledge of Wesley and the Methodist movement was derived almost entirely from secondary sources, which were often misleading or based on ignorance and misconception. There was precious little knowledge of the origins of Methodism and virtually no acquaintance with John Wesley or his works.

The great German theologian Johann Adam Möhler (1796–1838) was the first Roman Catholic to evaluate Methodism in a reasonably positive way. His book *Symbolik* (1838) compared various Protestant traditions with Roman Catholic teaching.[127] Included in a survey of the 'smaller Protestant sects' was a short chapter on 'Herrnhutters, or community of Brothers, and Methodists' in which Möhler had the key facts about Wesley and Methodism mostly correct. Interestingly, he detected a similarity between the Wesleyan movement and 'that which led to the origin of the monastic institutes'.[128] Wesley was distinguished 'by great talents, classical acquirements and (what was still better) by a burning zeal for the kingdom of God'.[129] Möhler regretted, however, that Wesley had 'raised himself to the episcopal dignity and ordained priests ... The separation from the Anglican Church was now formally proclaimed'.[130] Of course, this last statement was an exaggeration, since the break did

not come until after the death of Wesley and it was never formally proclaimed. Noting the power of Methodist preaching to convert the
masses, Möhler observed that 'the Spirit delighteth at times even in
eccentric forms'.[131]

In France, J. P. Migne's influential *Encyclopédie théologique* (1847)
reproduced a brief article on (Calvinistic) Methodism, which had first
appeared in Nicholas Bergier's *Dictionnaire de théologie* (1788), adding
two short paragraphs on Methodism in North America.

> In the United States, Methodists are divided into Wesleyans, Whit-
> fieldians, Kilhamites, etc. The first attach themselves to the errors of
> Wesley, which the second set aside in order to embrace those of Calvin
> as taught by Whitefield. The Kilhamites, also known as reunion
> Methodists, separated from the old Methodists, who date from 1729,
> in order to establish a new form of government in which ordinary
> members of the sect share with the ministers.
>
> Of all the Methodist practices, the most remarkable is that which is
> repeated each year in the autumn and goes by the name of *camp meet-
> ing*. In the middle of the camp, which is established in an isolated
> place, is a kind of scaffold from where the ministers talk to the crowd,
> especially at night – the time judged favourable for the conversion of
> sinners. In response to the call of the minister, the young people of
> both sexes suddenly move forward to a reserved enclosure where they
> throw themselves on the straw prepared in advance; and in the middle
> of the hymns, exhortations and cries, finish by falling into con-
> vulsions, such as would only astonish those with a weak imagination.
> Such assemblies prompt the most excessive and revolting youthful
> licentiousness.[132]

This description of 'licentious' behaviour at an American Methodist
camp meeting can have done little to promote sympathy for Methodism
among French people.

In his influential *Histoire universelle de l'Eglise catholique* (1849), René
Rohrbacher drew extensively on bizarre anecdotes in order to portray
Methodism as an eccentric Protestant sect.[133] Apparently, a Cornishman
became mad due to Methodist sermons, while another committed
suicide after killing all his family. Several doctors had diagnosed that
'Methodism has multiplied the number of demented persons.'

Doubtless, this was due to the Methodist preachers, who were noted for their 'vociferations and gestures'. In North America Methodism had adopted even more hideous forms, including groups known as Jerkers and Barkers because of their peculiar behaviour. 'These ecstasies of delirium are held to be a revival of the religious spirit!' According to Rohrbacher, 'One sees here an image, an echo, not of the angelic hierarchies . . . but of that empire of confusion and disorder where the evil spirits reign.' Furthermore, John Wesley was a man 'who desired to be the leader of a sect, gave himself the authority to ordain priests and bishops, although he was neither.'[134] He embodied a principle that expresses the essence of Protestantism: 'The only authority in which I believe is myself, myself alone!'[135]

Rohrbacher's scheme of universal history placed Methodism at the end of the period 1606–1730 as yet one more example of the many Protestant sects that had brought chaos to the religious landscape of Britain. Commenting on the recent Roman Catholic emancipation in Britain, Rohrbacher expressed his conviction that, 'We should not be surprised to see, some twenty years from now, the English nation becoming the first and most fervent of Catholic nations, taking away this ancient glory from the French nation.'[136] On the whole, it is difficult to imagine what could have encouraged Rohrbacher to be so optimistic about the future of Roman Catholicism in England.

Rohrbacher wrote his universal history of the Catholic Church as a textbook for use in Roman Catholic seminaries in France, where its primary purpose was apologetic – to defend the Catholic, Apostolic and Roman Church. Altogether, ten editions were published between 1849 and 1903. It is sobering to think that generations of French-speaking Roman Catholic priests in Europe and Africa must have gained their only knowledge of Methodism from the work of René Rohrbacher.

In view of Rohrbacher's influence on French-speaking Roman Catholics, it is all the more remarkable that a Belgian-French Franciscan by the name of Maximim Piette was the first Roman Catholic theologian in the twentieth century to engage in a fresh attempt at evaluating John Wesley and the Methodist movement. After the stagnation of the hundred years following the death of Wesley, revitalised historical scholarship in the early years of the twentieth century resulted in significant developments in relations between Methodists and Roman Catholics, and to this key period we now turn our attention.

3

The Twentieth Century to the Second Vatican Council

In the opinion of one prominent Methodist theologian, suspicion of Roman Catholicism lingered in British Methodism until after the Second World War.[1] Even at the highest levels of Methodism, entrenched attitudes towards Roman Catholics were clearly in evidence throughout the first half of the twentieth century. Henry Bett (1876–1953) taught pastoral theology and church history at Handsworth Theological College in Birmingham and was President of the Methodist Conference in 1940. His Fernley-Hartley Lecture of 1937, published as *The Spirit of Methodism,* contains a stinging attack on Roman Catholicism.

Bett agreed with Hugh Price Hughes that Roman Catholicism and Methodism represented two basic alternatives. For Bett, this meant that the Christian was faced with a stark choice 'between the authority of tradition and the authority of experience, between a religion which stresses the continuity and validity of an ecclesiastical organisation through which alone the individual soul can be certified of salvation by a priestly absolution, and a religion which stresses the continuity and validity of a spiritual fellowship, in which each individual soul is certified of salvation by the direct action of the Holy Spirit'.[2] Methodism and Roman Catholicism were the very antithesis of each other. Roman Catholicism emphasised the institution of the Church, together with its ministry and liturgical rites. Conversely, Methodism stressed the role of personal experience within the Christian fellowship, and questions relating to ministry and rites were of 'secondary importance'. As Bett saw it, 'The absolute antithesis between Catholicism and Methodism is justified in the history of religious thought, for . . . Methodism may be said to be the last stage of the Reformation, in which the primitive attitude of Christianity is finally recovered.'[3] In short, Wesley was a 'thorough Protestant' with a 'thoroughly evangelical' view of the doctrine of the Church and its sacraments.[4]

As a regular contributor to the weekly *Methodist Recorder* and the author of a textbook for local preachers, Bett was an influential figure in British Methodism, though it is impossible to know to what extent his conservative view of Roman Catholicism carried weight with ordinary Methodists. Presumably, since he made no attempt to defend his position, Bett must have felt reasonably confident that the majority of Methodists shared his opinions.

Yet there were other Methodist voices in the early years of the twentieth century calling for a fresh approach to Roman Catholicism. In this chapter we shall briefly investigate four British Methodists – Agar Beet, Herbert Workman, John Scott Lidgett and Robert Newton Flew. Correspondingly, we shall then examine four Roman Catholic writers on Methodism from this period – Maximin Piette, Ronald Knox, Louis Bouyer and John Todd. Finally, we turn our attention to the Second Vatican Council and its dramatic impact on relations between Roman Catholics and Methodists.

J. Agar Beet (1840–1924) has been described as 'perhaps the greatest "forgotten" theologian of British Methodism'.[277] At a time when few Wesleyan theologians took much interest in sacramental theology, Beet drew attention to Wesley's Catholic understanding of the Church and its sacraments and the importance of the Eucharist in the Wesleyan revival.

In *The Church, the Churches and the Sacraments* (1907) Beet studied five biblical metaphors for the Church: the temple, the body, the fruit tree, the flock and the bride. These, he concluded, were complementary images, each one emphasising a different aspect of divine and human agency in the Church. All of them portrayed Christ as occupying a position of superiority towards the Church, and each was required for a full description of the Church.

To Beet's way of thinking, every ecclesial tradition (including the Roman Catholic) contributed to an overall understanding of the Church, since each enshrined one or more of these principal New Testament metaphors. This explains perhaps why Beet's writing was generally free of anti-Catholic rhetoric, though he criticised in fairly moderate tones certain features of the Roman Catholic Church. Thus, 'While recognising our deep obligation to that Church for preserving the light of Christianity, often obscured, but still burning, during the long night of the Dark Ages, I am compelled to believe that the claim of the Roman hierarchy to be the sole ordinary depository of the benefits symbolised and conveyed by the Supper has been not only a yoke hard to bear and needless, but directly and indirectly a source of terrible and widespread evil.'[6]

Beet also disagreed with the Roman Catholic assertion that the Church needs an infallible magisterium. On the contrary, the content of fundamental Christian doctrine and experience was sufficiently clear not to require validation by any authority in the Church.[7] He also attacked transubstantiation: 'A doctrine so unlikely, thus destitute of evidence, lies outside the range of intelligent religious thought.'[8] According to Beet, the basic difference between Roman Catholics and Methodists was not whether Christ was present at the Eucharist, but whether his presence was validated by the episcopal ordination of the celebrant, or authenticated by the faith of the recipient.

Sensitivity to the principal biblical images of the Church prompted Beet to adopt a pragmatic view of the various ecclesial traditions. In particular, he did not consider disunity in the Church and the development of separate ecclesial traditions to be entirely a disaster:

> Different churches embody different types of Christian life: and the types thus embodied are a lesson and an enrichment to the whole. This manifest gain reveals the hand of God even in the divisions of the one Church of Christ. These divisions, caused or made needful and inevitable by man's imperfection or sin, are God's way of purifying and perfecting his Church, and leading it to a higher and richer unity. And in many cases it is expedient or needful that the outward forms be retained till the types therein embodied have been appropriated by other communions.[9]

Beet's vision of separate ecclesial traditions combining to contribute their gifts to a reunited Church was partially fulfilled in the 1932 scheme of Methodist Union. Interestingly, the papal encyclical *Ut Unum Sint* (1995) echoed Beet's appreciation of the way in which different ecclesial traditions had embodied and preserved particular insights into the nature of the Church.

*

Herbert Workman (1862–1951) was a respected church historian and joint editor of *A New History of Methodism* (1909), which was intended to 'utilise the results of recent study upon the origins of the Methodist churches, manifest the sense of their oneness which all feel increasingly, and set forth worldwide Methodism as a branch of the Church Catholic with its own notes and an essential unity underlying its several forms in many lands'.[10] Workman contributed the opening chapter on 'The Place of Methodism in the Life and Thought of the Christian Church', which was subsequently published separately in a slightly revised and expanded form with the title, *The Place of Methodism in the Catholic Church* (1921).

Workman claimed a special place for Methodism in the progress and development of the one Holy Catholic Church, not as an ecclesial movement *sui generis,* but as the continuation or revival of several earlier movements. In particular, Methodism was a powerful manifestation of a second-century movement of itinerant preachers known as 'Prophetism'. By the end of the second century, Prophetism had been suppressed by growing sacerdotalism in the Church as the first wave of spiritual enthusiasm subsided. In their respective eras, Prophetism and Methodism testified to the 'liberty of prophesying' as a key element of living faith.

There was also a similarity between Methodism and Montanism, which was essentially a second- and third-century protest against the suppression of the itinerant prophets. Despite its excesses, Montanism bore witness to the freedom of the Holy Spirit to work outside sacerdotal channels. 'In some aspects Methodism was the Montanism of the eighteenth century; a protest against an age which had killed the doctrine of the Holy Spirit by frozen rationalism and deadly worldliness.'[11] In the West, Montanism had no dispute with Catholic doctrine or order, but sought to force both back to their 'apostolic simplicity and purity'. For Workman, 'The ideal of the Montanist and of the Methodist alike was spirituality; to ensure this both were prepared to turn the Church into 'societies', however few and insignificant, shut out from the world by rigorous discipline, and working upon the world not so much by intercourse as by challenge.'[12]

Besides these historical parallels with Prophetism and Montanism, in its emphasis on social religion Methodism resembled the medieval monastic movement, especially the Benedictine form. In Methodism, as in the monastic movement, people assisted one another in the Christian life under leadership and a rule of discipline, which applied to work and home as well as in spiritual affairs. Like Methodism, monasticism testified in a sacerdotal age that holiness was essentially a matter of Christian character rather than sacramental grace. Originally, the monastic orders were predominantly lay communities dedicated to a religious life – as expressed in the daily offices and the service of labour – in which the sacraments were of less immediate significance. Thus Methodism was a more recent example of the anti-sacerdotal protest of monasticism.

Even the structure of Methodism had its precedents in monasticism. The Cistercians and friars were the original founders of connexional-ism.[13] The abbots of Cistercian houses, being accountable to one another for the state of their own house, were required to attend their General Chapter held annually. Likewise, the Franciscan General Chapter was similar in purpose to the Methodist Conference, as it too was intended for mutual accountability and encouragement. Although very different in personality, John Wesley was the St Francis of the eighteenth century.[14] Both men preferred colloquial and simple sermons contain-ing a few central truths. Each looked upon the world as his parish and initiated a sacrificial ministry to the poor, uneducated and neglected. Like St Francis, Wesley renounced pomp and splendour in buildings and worship, and encouraged greater use of hymns and music. Wesley's *Twelve Rules of a Helper* resemble St Francis' rule for his Poor Brothers. Both Methodism and the Franciscans were principally lay fraternities, drawn from the lower social classes and espousing democratic principles in the face of stiff opposition even from within the Church.

As Workman saw it, the organisation of Methodism was essentially presbyterian. American bishops, British superintendents, the system of 'stewards', the annual Conference, the meetings of ministers and lay people in circuits were all consistent with a presbyterian order. In these structures Methodism had retained the vast majority of ministries present in the primitive Church. For example, Methodist church stewards corresponded to the apostolic deacons, and local preachers were equivalent to the prophets. What was more, Methodism had revived the primitive office of apostle. Far into the second century, the apostles had been the missionary evangelists of the Church, not assigned to individual communities but called to a life of poverty and itinerancy within the wider Church. In their role as itinerant evangelists, John and Charles Wesley, George Whitefield, Francis Asbury and Thomas Coke were authentic apostles.

We need not pause to evaluate Workman's thesis, though there is certainly some mileage in his observation of parallels between Method- ism and earlier renewal movements in the history of the Church. It is sufficient to note how seriously and imaginatively Workman investi- gated the Methodist movement as part of a recurring phenomenon within the Holy Catholic Church. His principal aim was to show that Methodism, far from being a sectarian movement, represented a dis- tinctive combination of spiritual emphases that had always been present in the life of the Church to a greater or lesser degree and in one form or another.

John Scott Lidgett (1854–1953) has sometimes been described as the greatest Methodist since Wesley.[15] A committed ecumenist, he was one of the architects of Methodist Union in 1932 and President of the Uniting Conference. His collection of essays entitled *God, Christ and the Church* (1927) contains a mature reflection on ecclesiology. In an essay on 'Reunion and the Advancement of Christ's Kingdom', Lidgett argued that catholic unity was the immanent ideal of ecclesial life, 'but the full realisation of this ideal is in the future, and must be the product of all the forces that make for fellowship, completed in perfect faith and full knowledge of the Son of God'.[16] Spiritual unity alone was insufficient, since this merely justified the existing state of disunity among Christians and was untrue to the source, goal and inner dynamic of the Church's life. But, while catholic unity was the inner dynamic of ecclesial life, it could not be achieved if artificial barriers were erected to impede its full embodiment. Crucially, catholicity was not the exclusive possession of any one Christian denomination, but the goal towards which all were called.

> [T]he one life of the Spirit, being heavenly, universal and catholic in nature, cannot be developed to perfection in national or sectional communities. All denominations, Roman, Eastern and Anglican as well as nonconformist, speak provincial dialects, which betray their lack of fulfilled catholicity. It is imperative that these provincialisms should be transcended, if the fullness of the 'truth as it is in Jesus' is to

be reached. And this communion can only be brought about in and through one communion, with its corporate organisation and life. Such catholicity as belongs to each denomination, be it more or less, can only be preserved in so far as it energises in pursuit of more.[17]

In another essay entitled 'Reunion: the progress made', Lidgett bemoaned the process by which the primitive organisation of the Church had become 'hardened and Romanised'. When the Roman emperor left for Constantinople, the pope substituted imperial government in the place of fellowship as a means of maintaining Christian unity in the world. This had led to the growth of ecclesiastical authority and the centralisation of church government in Rome.[18] As a result, faith and worship had come to be interpreted in terms of ecclesiastical law enforced by sanction. The primitive concept of Christian fellowship had been destroyed, except in the limited sense of participation in the rites and sacraments of the Church. In time the Roman Catholic Church bequeathed this 'fatal legacy' to the Reformed Churches by creating in them an undue emphasis on their own distinctive style of church organisation in protest against Roman claims. Each separate tradition claimed New Testament authority and primitive usage, which led to the exaggeration and hardening of differences. The problem was that all of these different forms of organisation (Episcopal, Presbyterian, Independent, Methodist) were based on a static concept of the Church, which ignored the evolutionary fact that a living organism preserves its identity by means of growth and such ordered change as promotes a fuller expression of its life and an increasing command over its environment.

Lidgett accepted that any surrender of the 'vital principles of the Reformation would create more divisions than it would heal'. There were important differences between the Evangelical Protestant interpretation of the Gospel and the Roman Catholic system of faith. The papal claims alone were a sufficient obstacle to reunion. Nevertheless, the followers of Jesus had to recognise the common Christianity of all who confessed the Lordship of Christ and press on to the goal of unity in faith and knowledge of the Son of God. According to Lidgett, 'The twentieth century cannot afford to let the Roman controversy remain where it stood in the sixteenth- and seventeenth-century statements of it. Both sides have moved since then and are still moving; both are under influences that make for change. Even our differences must be brought up to date.'[19]

In the final essay Lidgett compared Wesley and Newman, recognising their many theological similarities despite the ecclesiological gulf between them. Each regarded God as the supreme reality and the pursuit of God as the sole object of human life. They were men of uncompromising courage and sincerity, who were profoundly dissatisfied with the spiritual conditions of the Christian Church and the generally accepted outlook of their age. 'Each joined a movement that had already been initiated, and each came so to dominate it and personify it that John Wesley became the commanding genius and embodiment of the Evangelical, and John Henry Newman of the Catholic revival.'[20] In each case, their presuppositions were Christian, Catholic and Evangelical. As a result, their basic Christian beliefs and religious experience coincided to a great degree. However, by separate means of theological reflection stemming from contrasting personalities, they reached very different conclusions about aspects of their religious experience, which, by the application of systematic thoroughness and unswerving logic, led them far apart.

Newman regarded faith as being principally a matter of assent that Christianity as a system of thought and life was true and a corresponding willingness to act on it. For Wesley, faith was the trustful self-committal of the whole of one's being to the personal approach of God in Jesus Christ. Newman distrusted the place of reason in religion and represented the Catholic faith as being above it. Wesley, on the other hand, made bold appeal to reason in support of faith. For Newman, full assurance was the goal reached only at the end of a long life. For Wesley, assurance was the starting point of the process of justification. Given this divergence, asked Lidgett:

> Can a synthesis be found between the two contrasted points of view represented by Wesley and Newman? Some say that this is impossible, and that the Religion of the Spirit and the Religion of Authority must for ever confront one another in unreconciled antagonism. The chasm between the two is indeed too wide to be bridged by logic. Yet if, as we have seen, the oppositions take their rise in differences of emphasis and selection out of the vast realm of spiritual experience, may there not come a time when the birth of a new and more

comprehensive spirit, informed by fuller knowledge and with a wider outlook, may transcend them both in a larger apprehension and interpretation of Christ?[21]

As Lidgett clearly recognised, it is far from a straightforward task reconciling the positions of Wesley and Newman, because of their contrasting interpretation of religious experience. However, at a time when British Methodists were mostly absorbed in the pursuit of denominational reunion, Lidgett's broader theological vision kept Methodism in touch with the wider Church. In particular, his passion for the ideal of Catholic unity enabled Lidgett to envisage the possibility that the Holy Catholic Church would one day come to embrace all ecclesial traditions.

There was one further way in which Lidgett contributed to Methodism's understanding of its ecclesial identity. In 1932 the Wesleyan Methodist Church, the Primitive Methodist Church and the United Methodist Church came together to form the Methodist Church of Great Britain. Lidgett was the principal driving force behind the delicate negotiations that were required to make the founding Deed of Union acceptable to all parties, and the final text reflects his mediating influence. The Deed of Union explains how the British Methodist Church understands its ecclesial identity. As a foundational statement of Methodist ecclesiology, it is worth quoting at length:

> The Methodist Church claims and cherishes its place in the Holy Catholic Church which is the Body of Christ. It rejoices in the inheritance of the apostolic faith and loyally accepts the fundamental principles of the historic creeds and of the Protestant Reformation. It ever remembers that in the providence of God Methodism was raised up to spread Scriptural Holiness through the land by the proclamation of the Evangelical Faith, and declares its unfaltering resolve to be true to its divinely appointed mission.
>
> The doctrines of the Evangelical Faith, which Methodism has held from the beginning and still holds, are based upon the divine revelation recorded in the Holy Scriptures. The Methodist Church acknowledges this revelation as the supreme rule of faith and practice . . .
>
> Christ's ministers in the Church are stewards in the household of

God and shepherds of his flock. Some are called and ordained to this sole occupation and have a principal and directing part in these great duties but they hold no priesthood differing in kind from that which is common to all the Lord's people and they have no exclusive title to the preaching of the gospel or the care of souls. These ministries are shared with them by others to whom also the Spirit divides his gifts severally as he wills.

The Methodist Church holds the doctrine of the priesthood of all believers and consequently believes that no priesthood exists which belongs exclusively to a particular class or order of persons but in the exercise of its corporate life and worship special qualifications for the discharge of special duties are required and thus the principle of representative selection is recognised.

The Methodist Church recognises two sacraments, namely, Baptism and the Lord's Supper, as of divine appointment and of perpetual obligation, of which it is the privilege and duty of members of the Methodist Church to avail themselves.'[22]

Thus the Deed of Union sets out Methodism's Catholic and Protestant heritage. References to the apostolic faith and the historic creeds lay claim to Methodism's place in the Holy Catholic Church. References to the Protestant Reformation and the Evangelical faith specify the particular way in which Methodism has received the apostolic Tradition. To allay the fears of the more Protestant-minded Methodists, especially those in the non-Wesleyan traditions, the Deed of Union makes sabre-rattling noises against a 'priestly' (i.e. an ontological) understanding of ordination, with Roman Catholicism as the obvious, though unnamed, target.

Unfortunately, nowhere does the Deed of Union suggest how Methodism might set about integrating its Catholic and Protestant heritage into a coherent description of the nature and identity of the Christian Church. Nor does it attempt to explain how Methodism understands its place within the Holy Catholic Church in relation to other Christian churches. Such questions were referred to the Faith and Order committee for discussion and future report. Out of this process came a major Methodist statement on ecclesiology entitled *The*

Nature of the Christian Church (1937), which we shall examine in a moment.

In his presidential address to the Uniting Conference, *The Catholicity of Methodism*, Lidgett explained how he believed the Deed of Union should be interpreted. In the first place, the Deed of Union envisaged a wider fellowship for the Methodist people by claiming and cherishing Methodism's place in the Holy Catholic Church. Crucially, this meant that Methodism was not a 'self-contained communion'. Methodism had enriched and been enriched by other churches, and it continued to reach out to other Christians in the pursuit of closer fellowship. However, catholicity, as defined in terms of a common order and institutional unity, was merely 'the husk without the kernel'. Ecclesial structures by themselves could not give substance to Christian unity. For Lidgett, 'The spirit of true catholicity is the indispensable condition and the vital breath of all legitimate reunion.'

The Deed of Union also confessed a particular interpretation of the Christian faith by accepting the fundamental principles of the historic creeds and the Protestant Reformation. According to Lidgett, the fundamental principles of the historic creeds were the true deity and humanity of Christ (as expressed in the doctrine of the incarnation), his sacrificial and atoning death, the resurrection and the ascension. The fundamental principles of the Protestant Reformation were 'justification by faith, the completeness and self-sufficiency of our Lord's sacrifice and priesthood, the direct access of all believers to God through him, expressed as the priesthood of all believers'. Thus the Deed of Union located Methodism in the mainstream of Christian belief, with one foot firmly in both the Catholic and the Protestant traditions.

The Deed of Union further acknowledged and accepted the historic mission of Methodism to spread 'Scriptural holiness' by proclaiming the evangelical Christian Gospel as revealed by God in Christ and recorded in the Holy Scriptures. For Methodists, the Bible was the supreme rule of faith and practice to which everything else must be subordinated, including religious experience and venerable tradition. Finally, Lidgett appealed to the Methodist people to wait upon the Lord for 'greatness of catholicity, greatness of vision, for greatness of faith and courage, for magnanimity, for patience one with another and with all the followers of our Lord'. It was a visionary speech for an historic occasion in the development of British Methodism.

Today, the Deed of Union remains an essential reference point for British Methodism, though Methodists have tended to distort its subtle theological balance by neglecting the full implications of what it means for Methodism to belong to the Holy Catholic Church. All too often, the Deed of Union is interpreted as an enduring statement of Methodism's *Protestant* heritage in a way that fails to recognise and embrace its *Catholic* inheritance in the shape of the historic creeds and fifteen hundred years of shared Christian history and tradition prior to the Reformation. As a result, many of the treasures present in the Western tradition have been lost to Methodism and only now are beginning to be rediscovered as a result of recent historical and liturgical scholarship. What is more, Methodists generally approach the Deed of Union as if it were some kind of timeless statement, neglecting both the specific circumstances in which it was produced and its underlying theological presuppositions, which may no longer be entirely valid; thus ignoring Lidgett's advice that even the differences between Methodists and Roman Catholics must be brought up to date. As a product of its time, the Deed of Union must be interpreted in the light of its historical context and restated for a new era of greater understanding and closer relations between Methodists and Roman Catholics.

Robert Newton Flew (1886–1962) was a New Testament scholar and tutor at Wesley House theological college in Cambridge, where he was Principal from 1937 to 1955. He was a leading figure in the Ecumenical Movement in Britain in its early years and a major contributor to the inter-war Faith and Order Movement.

In an essay on 'Methodism and the Catholic Tradition' written in 1933, Flew agued that the defining characteristics of Methodism were authentic features of the Christian tradition, which had occurred in other movements in the history of the Church.[23] In particular, Methodism was driven by the same passion for holiness which characterised the Oxford Movement.[24] According to Flew, Wesley's devotion to the Eucharist was the sign and measure of his passionate striving after holiness. By stressing the constant duty of Christians to receive Holy Communion, Wesley anticipated the nineteenth-century Tractarians. Furthermore, the Methodist understanding of holiness, centred as it was on the cross, was entirely consistent with the Western Catholic tradition. Methodists believed that salvation was not the privilege of a few, but the inheritance of all the children of God. The Methodist quest for holiness or perfect love was a key feature of evangelism and personal devotion and, as such, a welcome return to apostolic Christianity.

Methodists were also unusual among Protestants for their rediscovery of the communion of saints. From being simply an article in the creed, the communion of saints had become a present reality for Methodism. Whereas some forms of Puritan piety were highly individualistic, the early Methodists valued their conversion as a means of immediate entry into the fellowship or communion of the saints. Methodist class meetings were the chief expression of this fellowship. As Wesley was fond of saying, the Bible knew nothing of solitary religion.

A further characteristic of Methodism was its Catholic doctrine as inherited from the Church of England. In all his sermons and writings, Wesley was not aware that he had ever substantially departed from Catholic doctrine as the Church of England had received it from the apostles. Indeed, Wesley's theology and the hymns of Charles Wesley were entirely orthodox from a classical Catholic perspective. At the same time, Methodism had introduced no new doctrines, though it had perhaps contributed a fresh emphasis on the work of the Holy Spirit.

Certain other historic features also suggested to Flew that Methodism could rightfully claim a place within the Holy Catholic Church in the West. For instance, biographers had long compared Wesley with the founders of religious orders within the Roman Catholic Church, because of his firm discipline over the Methodist societies. Also, Methodists agreed with John Henry Newman that the essential work of the Church was to receive and transmit the sacred flame of the Gospel, kindling in human hearts an enduring consciousness of a personal relationship with God. For Methodists, the Church was essentially the fellowship in which this flame was received and transmitted by various means, including the sacrament of the Lord's Supper. In the rich spiritual inheritance of the evangelical Protestant tradition, the apostolic succession of the Church was located in the succession of believers.

Flew made no attempt to justify Methodism's separation from the Church of England, which he regarded as an accident of history. Nevertheless, the break had occurred and Methodism now existed as a *de facto* church. As for its contribution to the Christian mission, Flew confidently appealed to the reality and experience of Methodism in

England, as demonstrated not so much on paper as in the fruitfulness of its work past and present. Methodists would have to be 'content in all humility to let the facts of our tradition, our history, our present experience, speak for us, while at the same time we recognise gratefully our growing debt to the other communions of the Catholic Church'.

Flew did not take it for granted that Methodism would continue as a separate entity. Methodist participation in unity schemes in Canada, South India and internally in Great Britain had already revealed the strong desire among Methodists for reunion with the wider Church. 'Perhaps these facts may count as evidence that Methodists are conscious of a deeper loyalty than even that which they owe to their beloved Methodism, that deep in their hearts is a desire to cherish its place in the Holy Catholic Church which is the Body of Christ, a faith in the catholic truths by which that Church lives, and a mission to spread Scriptural holiness throughout the land by the proclamation of the Evangelical faith.'[25] For Flew, the catholicity of Methodism compelled Methodists to develop closer relations with other Christians in the pursuit of visible unity.

Flew was a major contributor to the first statement on Faith and Order adopted by the Methodist Church of Great Britain. *The Nature of the Christian Church* (1937) was intended to help Methodists 'think more clearly and definitely about the nature and purpose of the Christian community' in the light of the Deed of Union.[26] From a Methodist perspective, conventional Roman Catholic and Protestant formularies did not adequately reflect the nature of the Christian Church. In fact, the 'conception of the Church' had been 'over-estimated in Catholicism and often under-estimated in Protestantism'. Methodists were anxious to avoid 'exaggerating the place of the Church, and clothing it, as Rome has done, with attributes that are properly predicable only of God himself'. Equally, Methodists disapproved of the Protestant tendency to transpose the Church into a 'remote and ideal realm'. The Christian community in the New Testament was imperfect, as its frequent lapses demonstrate. If this was true of the supposed golden age of the Church, history bore ample witness that the visible Church was still an imperfect instrument of God's will. Nevertheless, Methodists recognised the decisive element in the New Testament understanding of the Church to be the presence of the living Christ in its midst. Created by God, the Church was the instrument of God's divine purpose. It was not an association of individuals but the Body of Christ.

The Deed of Union had claimed a place for Methodism within the Holy Catholic Church by accepting the apostolic faith as contained in the historic creeds. *The Nature of the Christian Church* now affirmed the apostolicity of Methodism. Crucially, Methodism had preserved the sacraments of baptism and the Eucharist as being of 'divine appointment and perpetual obligation'. Methodism accepted the fundamental principles of the Gospel as established by the Protestant Reformation and had received a divine mission to spread scriptural holiness. True continuity with the Church of the past could also be discerned in the continuity of Christian experience, fellowship in the Holy Spirit, allegiance to one Lord, and the continued acceptance of his mission. Thus it was possible to trace the spiritual ancestry of Methodism through a multitude of saints to the Lord himself. This was the Methodist doctrine of apostolic succession.

> It is our conviction, therefore, that the continuity of the Church does not depend on, and is not necessarily secured by, an official succession of ministers, whether bishops or presbyters, from apostolic times, but rather by fidelity to apostolic faith. The office is contingent on the Word, and not the Word on the office. Indeed, the apparent discontinuity of office has sometimes been due to a reassertion of the true and essential continuity of experience, allegiance, message and mission.[27]

Methodism acknowledged its indebtedness to the Church of the past, which had endured throughout the years by the power of God, who would not suffer it to be destroyed by external assault or internal faithlessness. Even so, continuity in faith, experience, witness and sanctity within the Church had not prevented disastrous breaches of fellowship, which persisted to the present day. The Protestant Reformation was primarily an appeal to the revealed will of God against the corruptions that had infected the Church for centuries. The Reformers had stressed salvation by faith, Christ as the one mediator, and the priesthood of all believers. It was a tragedy that they had been cast out from the 'official Church' as heretics.

The Reformation led to the establishment of a number of separated Churches of which the Methodist Church was now one. Most of these had formulated their message in the shape of a confession of faith: Methodism had Wesley's sermons and *Notes on the New Testament* for its doctrinal standards. Raised by the Word of God, Methodism existed within the one Church of God and had done so since its inception. For historical reasons Methodists had been compelled to become a distinct religious community, although they had been guilty of no schism. Methodists accepted it was their duty 'to make common cause in the search for the perfect expression of that unity and holiness which in Christ are already theirs'. Significantly, the statement included the Roman Catholic Church among those Churches that could 'humbly claim to belong to the Body of Christ'; though none could claim to be 'the whole of the Catholic Church on earth'.[28]

From this brief summary of *The Nature of the Christian Church* it is evident that by the 1930s Methodism was increasingly willing to explore its place in the Holy Catholic Church in relation to other churches, including the Roman Catholic Church, even if it had not yet entirely overcome its inherited suspicion of Roman Catholicism. At about the same time, Roman Catholic writers were also beginning to show greater interest in Methodism as an ecclesial movement.

In 1925 Maximin Piette, a Franciscan student at the University of Louvain in Belgium, published his university thesis on Methodism and its relationship to other Protestant churches. *La réaction wesléyenne dans l'évolution protestante* was favourably received in theological circles, taking first prize in the 1926 Belgian Inter-University Awards. The following year the French Academy awarded Piette the prestigious Prize Marcelin Guérin. A second, slightly revised, edition appeared in 1927 under the title *La réaction de John Wesley dans l'évolution du Protestantisme*. Cardinal Mercier accepted the dedication of this second edition, effectively placing an official seal of approval on Piette's ground-breaking study.

Methodists, too, were swift to welcome Piette's work as a major reappraisal of John Wesley and the rise of Methodism. The *Wesley Historical Society* complimented Piette on a 'most creditable performance' in attempting to 'fix the Methodist movement in its true place in the life of the Church'.[29] In 1937 Piette's book was translated into English as *John Wesley in the Evolution of Protestantism*. In a foreword to the English translation, Herbert Workman praised Piette for his deep knowledge of Wesley and Methodism. Though Piette had restricted his study to the place of Methodism in the evolution of Protestantism, Workman detected a tacit recognition by Piette of the place of Methodism in the Holy Catholic Church.

In order to locate Methodism in its ecclesial context as a reform movement, Piette began by examining the evolution of Protestantism before and during the eighteenth century, commencing with the two principal reformers, Martin Luther (1483–1546) and Ulrich Zwingli (1484–1531). Piette identified three reform movements among the plethora of new sects and churches which characterised the evolution of Protestantism. The 'Anabaptist Reaction' comprised a number of different groups that reinstated the practice of believer's baptism. Vigorously denounced by Luther and Zwingli, and later by Calvin, the Anabaptists endured severe persecution at the hands of Protestants and Roman Catholics. The 'Nationalist Reaction' was evident in the powerful alliance of political and religious territorialism which resulted in the establishment of national churches in Germany and elsewhere. The third, and by far the most widespread and enduring, reform movement was the 'Theological Reaction' inspired by John Calvin (1509–64), whose *Institutes of the Christian Religion* remain the clearest and most systematic account of classical Protestant theology. However, these reform movements had run their course before the eighteenth century, so that Methodism was the fruit of a fourth reform movement inaugurated by John Wesley.[30]

Piette attributed the growth of Methodism to its 'marvellous disciplinary and religious organisation'. The key to the success of Methodism was not so much originality of ideas as their flexible and efficient implementation. Converts were organised into classes of up to a dozen members, which were 'the keystone of the entire Methodist edifice'.[31] Several classes formed a society, and these were grouped into circuits and districts watched over by Wesley and his itinerant preachers. The compact unity of the Methodist societies under Wesley's benevolent rule contrasted with the deplorable state of anarchy that broke out after his death. Leaving aside the ensuing fragmentation of Methodism, Wesley inaugurated a renewal of religious fervour in England to the lasting benefit of Protestantism in general.[32] Also, by giving a prominent place to hymn singing, Wesley established a liturgical pattern that was copied by Protestant churches throughout the world. Equally, Methodist missions breathed new life into Protestantism, not just as the result of reaching non-Christians, but also by appealing to the vast number of nominal Christians who had become detached from the practice of their religion.

Although Piette did not use the phrase 'reformer of the reform', it is a fair description of his interpretation of Wesley's reaction to Luther, Zwingli and Calvin. As seen by Piette, the Wesleyan Reaction distanced Methodism from Protestantism, bringing it closer to Roman Catholicism in key areas of doctrine. In particular, 'The justification by faith which Wesley preached was nearer the doctrine of the Council of Trent than what he contemptuously called Luther's crazy solafidianism. Similarly, his unswerving Arminianism puts him in direct opposition to Genevan predestination.'[33] Far from being a revolutionary, Piette's Wesley was a conformist in the sense that he remained loyal to the institution of the Church and was inclined wherever possible to revert to the usages of the primitive Christian community. Piette was impressed that 'In contrast with all the separatist movements of the sixteenth and seventeenth centuries, [Wesley] accepted unconditionally the doctrinal, disciplinary, and liturgical framework of his mother, the Anglican Church.'[34]

Piette noticed a number of similarities between the rise of the Methodist movement in the eighteenth century and the outpouring of the Holy Spirit upon the early Church. This was a bold step for a Roman Catholic scholar at that time, since it implied that Methodism was a *bona fide* ecclesial movement within the Holy Catholic Church. Unfortunately, Piette did not address the central question of whether Methodism was essentially a Catholic or a Protestant movement, though he demonstrated how in some respects Methodism was closer to Roman Catholicism than hitherto had been supposed. As such, Piette's sympathetic study of the Wesleyan Reaction to the Reformation and the place of Methodism in the evolution of Protestantism remains an important piece of revisionist Methodist history by a Roman Catholic scholar.

Despite Piette's endeavours, some Roman Catholic scholars continued to regard John Wesley as the founder of yet another Protestant sect. In a scholarly study of 'enthusiasm' in the seventeenth and eighteenth centuries, Ronald Knox (1888–1957) portrayed Wesley as a forceful eccentric whose legacy was an excessive individualism among his followers.[35] 'Enthusiasm' is a notoriously slippery term in theology; Knox used it as shorthand for a false emphasis on one particular aspect of Christian experience to the neglect of others.

In the eighteenth century, however, 'enthusiasm' meant a claim to extraordinary revelations or power from the Holy Spirit. Hence Bishop Butler's famous remark to John Wesley: 'Sir, the pretending to extraordinary revelations and gifts of the Holy Ghost is a horrid thing, a very horrid thing.'[36] In *The Enthusiasm of Methodists and Papists Considered* (1749), Bishop Lavington likened the 'wild and pernicious' enthusiasm of Methodists to the behaviour of some of the most eminent saints of the 'Popish communion'. In response, Wesley insisted that neither he nor his followers claimed any special revelation beyond what was contained in the Scriptures. Nor did they claim to possess any spiritual gifts and experiences besides those present in the primitive Church, which continued to be normative in the Christian community. Unfortunately for Wesley, the vast majority of his contemporaries argued that many of the charismatic phenomena present in the primitive Church (including instantaneous conversions) were confined to the apostolic age. In the post-apostolic age the Christian life was characterised by sound teaching, orthodox belief and a gradual process of nurture and development. In an age of reason, any kind of religious fervour was likely to be denigrated as enthusiasm, and the excitement generated among the early Methodists provided ample ammunition for Wesley's opponents.

Knox discerned two basic types of enthusiasm in the Church, which had occurred in various manifestations throughout its history.[37] 'Mystical enthusiasm' stemmed from an exaggerated emphasis on the incarnation, which evaded the atonement and a theology of grace in preference for an obsession with the 'interior' search for God. Conversely, by exaggerating the doctrines of the fall and the atonement, 'evangelical enthusiasm' attached undue weight to the experience of redemption, new birth and the assurance of forgiveness. Although both types of enthusiasm had enjoyed a long and colourful history in the Church, they assumed distinct shape only as a result of the Reformation. In his sharply observed study of the various manifestations of enthusiasm in the history of the Church, Knox devoted four chapters to the study of Methodism as a peculiar form of evangelical enthusiasm.

Knox accepted that the Evangelical Revival had had a powerful effect in 'waking up eighteenth-century England from its religious apathy'.[38] In an age when Deism was the fashionable heresy, Methodism in particular had recalled the Church of England to its roots in the Christian revelation. However, as far as its long-term effect was concerned, the Evangelical Revival had ultimately failed, because it had stirred up an unhealthy preoccupation with individual religious experience, sometimes of the most excessive kind, mistaking this for the true measure of a change of heart. The Evangelical Revival had sidelined Christian tradition in favour of religious experience; and, as a result, religion in England had come to be identified in popular thinking with a series of moods induced by revivalist preachers.

Particularly distasteful to Knox was the fact that evangelical preaching in the eighteenth century was often interrupted by paroxysms similar to the kind of phenomena that more recently have been associated with the charismatic movement. Falling to the ground, shouting, wailing and uncontrollable laughter were all familiar features of revivalism. Knox found numerous entries in the *Journal* to illustrate how Wesley's sermons provoked exactly this kind of response.

For instance, preaching in Bristol in April 1739, Wesley was moved to ask God for a sign that he had preached the true Word of God. 'Immediately one and another and another sunk to the earth: they dropped on every side as thunderstruck. One of them cried aloud. We besought God on her behalf, and he turned her heaviness into joy.'[39] Even more spectacular instances of the new birth were evidenced a few weeks later when Wesley preached to a society in Wapping.

> While I was earnestly inviting all sinners 'to enter into the holiest' by this 'new and living way' many of those that heard begun to call upon God, with strong cries and tears. Some sunk down and there remained no strength in them; others exceedingly trembled and quaked; some were torn with a kind of convulsive motion in every part of their bodies, and that so violently that often four or five persons could not hold one of them. I have seen many hysterical and many epileptic fits, but none of them were like these, in many respects.[40]

Knox identified a deliberate technique in Wesley's preaching to produce these symptoms in others. But, although Wesley sympathised with even the most violent forms of enthusiasm, he was never 'carried away by it'.[41]

As an experimentalist, fascinated by the phenomena of conversion, Wesley remained dispassionate in observing others' experience of the new birth. What Knox failed to point out, however, was that Wesley was severely critical of those whose conversion, vouchsafed by impressive signs and wonders, did not translate thereafter into holy living.

Knox challenged the view adopted by many Methodist writers that paroxysms were a temporary phenomenon from the early phase of Wesley's ministry and that in later years he neither sought nor encouraged such behaviour. On the contrary, throughout his ministry Wesley publicised instances of convulsions in the *Journal* as confirmation that his message was true. Two of Knox's examples will suffice to make his point. In September 1784 Wesley preached to the society at Coleford. 'They contained themselves pretty well during the exhortation, but when I began to pray, the flame broke out. Many cried aloud, many sunk to the ground, many trembled exceedingly, but all seemed to be quite athirst for God and penetrated by the presence of his power.' Again, preaching at the new chapel in London in February 1786, 'The power of God came mightily upon us, and there was a general cry. But the voice of two persons prevailed over the rest, one praying, and the other shrieking as in the agonies of death.'[42] For Knox, these and similar journal entries disproved the assertion that Wesley either regretted or discouraged such phenomena.[43]

Disparagingly, Knox attributed these Methodist 'swoonings' to a spirituality that was not content unless it saw results. In this type of spirituality the emotions must be stirred deeply at frequent intervals in order to be certain that God is at work. Wesley was one for whom 'grace must be something felt, or how could you be sure that it had any existence at all?'[44] Although the fires of spirituality sometimes burned low in the Roman Catholic Church, Knox preferred its institutional form of Christianity to the exaggerated phenomenon of Evangelical Protestantism. His assessment of the contribution of John Wesley and the Evangelical Revival towards religion in England is devastating for Protestants used to a more complimentary description:

If I have dealt at some length with this single side of Wesley's character – I mean his preoccupation with strange psychological disturbances now commonly minimised – it is because I think he, and the other prophets of the Evangelical movement, have succeeded in imposing

107

upon English Christianity a pattern of their own. They have succeeded in identifying religion with a real or supposed experience. I say 'real or supposed', because in the nature of things you cannot prove the validity of any trance, vision or ecstasy; it remains something within the mind. Still less can you prove the validity of a lifelong Christ-inspired attitude; in the last resort, all it proves is that certain psychological influences are strong enough to overcome, in a given case, all the temptations towards backsliding which a cynical world affords. But, for better or worse, the England which weathered the excitements and disappointments of the early nineteenth century was committed to a religion of experience; you did not base your hopes on this or that doctrinal calculation; you knew. For that reason, the average Englishman was, and is, singularly unaffected by reasonings which would attempt to rob him of his theological certainties, whatever they may be. For that reason, also, he expects much (perhaps too much) of his religion in the way of verified results; he is easily disappointed if it does not run according to schedule. It must chime in with his moods, rise superior to his temptations; a decent average of special providences must convince him that it works. Otherwise, though without rancour, he abandons the practice of it.[45]

According to Knox, Wesley and Newman headed two contrasting renewal movements: whereas the Evangelical Revival was 'charismatic', the Oxford Movement was 'institutional'. Even the personal styles of Wesley and Newman highlighted the disparity between their movements. Newman was painstaking in his judgements, whereas Wesley leapt to infallible conclusions. Newman was 'the apostle of religious authority': Wesley was 'a cheerful experimentalist who in all the hesitations of a lifetime never asked himself by what right he ruled, or on what basis or intellectual certainty he believed'.[46] Thus Wesley had no qualms about appealing to his own interpretation of Scripture.[47] As a result of the damage to the religious fabric of England caused by the Evangelical Revival, the Oxford Movement could only 'lock the door on a stolen horse'.[48]

Knox discerned a definite pattern to charismatic renewal movements. The history of the Evangelical Revival demonstrated a law of diminishing returns as the temporary effects of religious experience subsided. In every age, 'the enthusiast will always react against any form of institutional religion, whether it be Catholic or Protestant, and there is no Christianity with a hundred years of history that does not become, to a more or less degree, institutional'.[49] But does this indicate that 'evangelical enthusiasm' is essentially a cyclical process, as Knox seems to imply, or does it reveal that the Catholic Church always contains charismatic and institutional renewal movements in creative tension? Unfortunately, Knox did not pursue this question.

For Methodists, Knox's assessment of John Wesley and the Evangelical Revival makes sober reading. Knox could find few positive things to say about Wesley, apart from muted praise for his 'true and valuable' vision, which the heat of controversy then transformed into 'exaggerations and eccentricities'.[50] After an unfortunate ministry in Savannah, Wesley 'had thought of becoming a Catholic' as a result of reading the works of Cyprian.[51] According to Knox, although Wesley was far from experiencing the 'grace of conversion', unconsciously he was stirred by a faint desire that made him see the Catholic Church as a 'kind of mirage' on his mental horizon. Obviously the mirage disappeared, since Wesley later experienced another kind of conversion, which led him in the opposite direction. All the same, Wesley did not turn his back entirely on institutional Christianity, as Knox seems to suggest. As we saw in Chapter 1, Wesley's understanding of the Church involved a synthesis of institutional and charismatic forms of Christianity.

All things considered, it is difficult to avoid the conclusion that Knox simply failed to appreciate the full shape of Wesley's sophisticated reaction to religious experience. In comparison, the distinguished Methodist historian Henry Rack presents a more convincing portrait of Wesley's paradoxical spirituality. Rack agrees with Knox that Wesley gave far more credit to the supernatural claims of his followers than he was prepared to admit in his apologetic writings, though he tended to play down some of the more extraordinary experiences.[52] However, Wesley was a 'reasonable enthusiast', who combined a 'strong tincture of enthusiasm' with a 'benevolent pastoral despotism' and an autocratic preoccupation with orderliness and supervision, which became the hallmark of Methodism's structures. In the heady mix of personal religious experience that was typical of early Methodism, Wesley's overriding concern was 'to preserve the dynamic of religious revival without degenerating into its characteristic weaknesses of ephemeral emotion and individualism'.[53]

Tempting as it is to enter into a more detailed conversation with Ronald Knox about his assessment of John Wesley and enthusiasm in the eighteenth century, we must move on to consider alternative twentieth-century views of the Methodist founder from two other Roman Catholics who directly or indirectly contradict Knox's assessment of Wesley.

France in the 1950s was at the forefront of Roman Catholic theological renewal. Taking advantage of a more open climate, Louis Bouyer undertook a complete reassessment of Martin Luther and John Calvin and their relationship with the Roman Catholic Church.[54] In *The Spirit and Forms of Protestantism* (1956) he attempted to show that both men were inspired by entirely orthodox motives, and for this reason their reforms could only be completely fulfilled within the Roman Catholic Church. Although Bouyer devoted only a few pages to John Wesley, he made a serious attempt to locate and understand the Methodist founder in the wider reform movement.

Setting the scene, Bouyer described how the Wesleyan movement arrived in France and the French-speaking region of Switzerland in the early years of the nineteenth century. Its modest impact later extended far beyond the relatively small Methodist community and led directly to the rejuvenation of Protestantism in France and Switzerland, which would otherwise probably have died under the arid influence of rationalism.[55] Even in translation, the hymns of Charles Wesley provided a meaningful vehicle to express the heights and depths of Protestant spiritual experience.

Perceptively, Bouyer recognised how Wesley combined Luther's doctrine of justification with a Catholic doctrine of sanctification. On the one hand, Wesley 'was strongly possessed by the doctrine of salvation by grace alone and, through his dynamic temperament, this doctrine gained a marvellous increase of vitality'.[56] Wesley's emphasis on justification, more than any other contributing factor, gave Methodism its powerful impetus for mission. On the other hand, whereas Luther postulated a qualitative distinction between Christ's holiness and that of humans, Wesley believed that the realisable goal of the Christian life was entire sanctification. 'More penetrating than any of his predecessors, he criticized Luther's opposition of faith to works as a sophistry.'[57]

While Methodists have long valued the hymns of Charles Wesley, Bouyer was among the first Roman Catholics to appreciate them as a source of Catholic theology. The final two verses of the hymn 'Jesus, lover of my soul' were evidence in Bouyer's mind that Wesleyan theology embraced then transcended Luther's understanding of grace:

> Thou, O Christ, art all I want;
> More than all in thee I find;
> Raise the fallen, cheer the faint,
> Heal the sick, and lead the blind.
> Just and holy is thy name,
> I am all unrighteousness;
> False and full of sin I am,
> Thou art full of truth and grace.
>
> Plenteous grace with thee is found,
> Grace to cover all my sin;
> Let the healing streams abound,
> Make and keep me pure within.
> Thou of life the fountain art;
> Freely let me take of thee;
> Spring thou up within my heart,
> Rise to all eternity.[58]

These lines combine Luther's doctrine of justification with a Catholic emphasis on personal sanctification. Against Luther, Wesley maintained that grace was 'a power transforming our whole life and being, not a substitute for this change'.[59] Similarly, the hymn 'Soldiers of Christ arise' (based on the image of putting on the whole armour of God found in Ephesians 6.10–18) contains a synthesis of Luther's doctrine of justification with a Catholic description of the Christian life.

Given the similarities between Methodism and earlier reform movements, Bouyer concluded, rather cautiously, that Methodism was a true heir of Lutheranism.[60] The chief characteristic of Methodism was its theological grounding in the two doctrines of the divinity of Christ and the redemptive value of his death. The strength of Methodism was that Wesley had restored these two objective and fundamental elements of faith, not as abstract beliefs, but as real convictions essential to the

Christian life and sufficiently powerful to produce and sustain it.[61] The weakness of Methodism however was its failure to integrate these doctrines into a systematic theology.

Innovatively, Bouyer located Wesley at the beginning of a new and challenging era in the history of the Church. 'He was perhaps the first Christian to grasp the new problem set before the Church, that of the infidel community newly created within a devitalised Christendom by the birth of a proletariat.'[62] In developing his practical theology from a missiological perspective, Wesley anticipated the minority status of the Christian community within society in a way that deserves closer attention from modern theologians, at a time when the process of secularisation in Europe and North America presents an even greater challenge to the mission of the Church.

Since it was not part of his objective, Bouyer stopped short of investigating the place of Wesley and Methodism within the Holy Catholic Church. It was left to an English Roman Catholic layman, John Todd, to develop Bouyer's thesis and produce the first complete reassessment of John Wesley and his relationship with the Roman Catholic Church.

The reassessment of Calvin and Luther and their relationship with the Roman Catholic Church undertaken by Louis Bouyer directly inspired John Todd's corresponding study of *John Wesley and the Catholic Church* (1958). Todd aimed to discover the extent to which Wesley's motivation was 'identical with the inner force of the Catholic faith, and to see objectively whether the doctrines he preached were the same as traditional Catholic doctrine'.[63] Conscious that 'most Catholics probably think of John Wesley as a rabid revivalist preacher', Todd aspired to a more balanced assessment of his life and teaching.[64] The outcome was a 'new interpretation' of Wesley for English-speaking Roman Catholics, written from a 'frankly partisan' and 'ecumenical' approach in response to the 'special needs of the present'.[65] From this inventive perspective, Todd interpreted Wesley's life and ministry within the Church of England in a way that was significantly different from earlier attempts by Methodist apologists and Roman Catholic controversialists.

Educated in the theological tradition of the Church of England, Wesley never abandoned or opposed his Church, believing it to have received authority from Christ as the *de facto* Christian community in England. He was neither a heretic nor a schismatic, but intended

Methodism to be a revival or reforming movement within the Church. Furthermore, unlike some Protestants, Wesley did not believe in the divine inspiration of individuals independently of the Church, though he affirmed the presence of diverse spiritual gifts among the people of God. For Wesley, it was a basic principle of ecclesiology that the Church exercised jurisdiction over its members. While he would have agreed with the proposition that an individual might have to choose between obeying one's conscience and abiding by ecclesial rules, he successfully avoided having to make that hard choice and always acted within his authority as a priest of the Church of England. For Todd, this was a valid position to hold. Even Roman Catholics were sometimes called upon to decide whether the Church had acted *ultra vires*, thereby reducing its authority to that of a human agency.

According to Todd, in the context of the eighteenth-century Church of England, the original inspiration for Wesley's teaching was entirely orthodox, and for this reason it could properly be fulfilled only within the Roman Catholic Church.[66] Wesley believed in the 'old Catholic doctrines' as still maintained by the Church of England, and he affirmed the real presence of Christ at the Eucharist, even if his understanding of that presence was not philosophically identical with the Roman Catholic doctrine of transubstantiation. He also held the Catholic doctrine of grace in its essential details. Although Wesley lacked the doctrine of purgatory and a 'full understanding' of the role of Mary in the divine economy, these were 'omissions' rather than doctrinal errors.[67]

Leaving aside its omissions, Wesley's teaching was consistent with Roman Catholic doctrine, except where the nature and identity of the Church were concerned. As a Church of England priest, Wesley could hardly have subscribed to the Roman Catholic doctrine that the visible Church was a single juridical body. Even so, he remained in some doubt about the precise nature of the Church and never reached a final conclusion on the subject. Otherwise, Wesley demonstrated unswerving faith in the orthodox Christian revelation as contained in the historic creeds. Although he was not subject to the authority of the Roman Catholic Church, Wesley nevertheless exercised his ministry within a Church that he believed had received its authority from Christ.

If, as Todd believed, Wesley's motivation was entirely orthodox from a Roman Catholic perspective, then why had Methodism been so anti-Catholic? Unfortunately, Todd provides us with no answer to this question, though he ventured the opinion that anti-Catholic trends present within all Protestant bodies, combined with an invasive emotional and subjective attitude, tended to exert a stronger influence on Methodism than Wesley's dynamic interpretation of traditional doctrine – a case of 'bad money driving out the good'.[68] Despite the anti-Catholic tendency in Methodism, Todd was convinced that a proper understanding of Wesley would bring to light elements that were valuable for Christian traditions across the spectrum, from the 'highly formal legalised' tradition of Roman Catholicism to the 'largely irrational, emotional revivalism' found in some forms of Protestantism, including along the way complacent 'middle Anglicanism', which had largely lost the influence of supernatural religion.[69] As a distinctive combination of the 'institutional' and the 'individual', Wesley's theology was a 'happy mean' for the different Christian traditions.

> John Wesley, then, seems to occupy a providential middle position. Whilst never straying from the teaching passed on to him by Catholic tradition, the Trinity, the Incarnation, the Redemption, he yet emphasises the necessity of the inner experience, the call, which leads to an evangelical and apostolic life, a factor which had become dimmed in the English society of his time, though it had not disappeared altogether from the Anglican body itself.[70]

Todd disagreed with Knox that Wesley was a 'subjective Protestant visionary'.[71] Knox had objected to religious experience as a source of faith, because its validity could not be proved. In contrast, Todd questioned whether anything could be *proved* in religion. Besides, religious experience was an integral component of real assent. If faith were merely volitional assent to abstract doctrinal concepts, then it would lack moral force. Newman had been the first to distinguish between notional assent and the real assent of faith as an act of the whole person based on knowledge derived from a combination of sources, including religious experience. Roman Catholics believed the doctrines of the Church not because they could be proved, but because the authority of Christ guaranteed them; and the acceptance of Christ's authority involved a real assent of faith. Accordingly, Peter's confession of faith at Caesarea Philippi was neither an emotional impulse nor simply an intellectual response to a doctrinal proposition. Through his

114

experience of Jesus, Peter recognised the truth. Peter 'knew' in exactly the same way as Wesley taught that Christians in every generation continued to 'know' what was true. There was a danger, of course, that such knowledge could be perverted into hysterical subjectivism. However, in the Church there were checks and balances and the means of guiding individuals.

As Todd saw it, Wesley displayed a healthy scepticism about the validity of subjective experience. There were numerous occasions, even in his most subjective moments, when Wesley warned of the danger of being led astray by questionable religious experience. Preaching about the so-called French Prophets in 1739, Wesley cautioned that their supposed revelations were of a dubious nature and therefore should not be relied upon.[72] When a number of Methodists claimed to have felt the blood of Christ running down their arms and throat, he told them plainly that this was 'the mere, empty dreams of an heated imagination'.[73] In Todd's opinion, 'More or less hysterical visionaries in the Catholic Church both in the medieval times and at the present day have sometimes had an easier session with those who have had to judge them, than those judged by Wesley.'[74] Far from being the credulous evangelical enthusiast portrayed by Knox, Wesley displayed a healthy scepticism so far as religious experience was concerned.[75]

Todd was equally convinced that Knox had misjudged Wesley's doctrine of assurance, which was based on a specific form of religious experience. According to Knox, Wesley identified grace with a supposed knowledge that was based on mere *feelings*. Furthermore, Wesley was inconsistent in his beliefs about this 'cruel doctrine' of assurance. At the first Methodist Conference of 1744 the question 'Can a man be justified, and not know it?' was answered in the negative.[76] Subsequently, Wesley had to concede the possibility of exceptions to this general rule. As Todd saw it, however, this was a travesty of Wesley's doctrine of assurance. Wesley never identified grace with religious feelings, though he certainly believed the two were related as cause and effect. Moreover, it was doubtful whether Wesley ever held an unqualified doctrine of assurance for more than a few months in the early phase of his ministry. With an old man's disarming candour, Wesley acknowledged the shortcomings of his earliest description of assurance:

When fifty years ago my brother Charles and I in the simplicity of our hearts taught the people that unless they knew their sins forgiven they were under the wrath and the curse of God, I wonder they did not stone us. We preach assurance, a common privilege of the children of God, but we do not enjoin it under pain of damnation on all who enjoy it not.[77]

Whereas Knox considered assurance to be an immodest self-delusion on the part of some Protestants, Todd believed it was entirely normal at times for Christians to experience a certain inner peace and assurance. Indeed, Roman Catholic spiritual writers (including St John of the Cross) have prized this kind of experience as much as Wesley. Thus, in the dilute form held by Wesley, the doctrine of assurance was neither more nor less than traditional Catholic teaching.

After the caricature of Wesley presented by Knox, it is refreshing to come across Todd's more accurate account of the Methodist founder. Whereas Knox was unable to reach beyond the 'charismatic' Wesley, Todd discovered the 'institutional' side of Wesley, emphasising his respect for Christian tradition, especially in its patristic form. Unlike Knox, Todd was keenly aware that Wesley did not easily fit into the usual cycle of Protestant revival and schism. But what are we to make of Todd's thesis that Wesley's motivation was orthodox? If it were true, we should then have the makings of a theological framework in which outstanding doctrinal differences between Methodists and Roman Catholics might eventually be resolved.

Unfortunately, attractive as it might sound, Todd's hypothesis must be treated with considerable caution, because of his tendency to disregard evidence to the contrary. In referring disingenuously to Wesley's 'omission' of the doctrine of purgatory, Todd obscured the fact that Wesley rejected certain aspects of Roman Catholic teaching as neither scriptural nor part of the apostolic tradition.[78] On the whole, Wesley was more loyal to what the Methodist Deed of Union subsequently called 'the fundamental principles of the Protestant Reformation' than Todd was willing to acknowledge. If Wesley cannot be made to fit an ultra-Protestant mould as some have tried to do, still less can he be interpreted as a Roman Catholic manqué.

For reasons that can only be guessed, Todd consistently underestimated Wesley's opposition to Roman Catholicism. It is curious, to say the least, that Todd made no mention of Wesley's anti-Catholic writings, but chose instead to present the reader with a series of vague generalisations about Wesley's anti-Catholic attitude. Thus we are told that 'Wesley's sometimes depreciatory comments on Catholics and their doctrine were due, in the end, to ignorance of what they believed and practised, to lack of any substantial contact with Roman Catholic life.'[79] Likewise, 'Having inherited anti-Catholic convictions which had been confirmed during his studies at Oxford, like most men of the eighteenth century, [Wesley] retained them.'[80] Again, 'Wesley accepted the current assessment and criticism of Catholicism.'[81] By stressing the conventional nature of this reaction to Roman Catholicism, Todd virtually exonerates Wesley of any personal responsibility for his anti-Catholicism.

Ironically, Todd's Wesley comes across as a more enlightened figure than might have been supposed, in the light of these inherited prejudices. According to Todd, Wesley was 'more tolerant and more far-sighted than his contemporaries, looking as he did beyond the doctrinal battles of the moment to the problem of fidelity itself'.[82] Furthermore, his references to Roman Catholicism were 'frequently complimentary'.[83] Despite his mistrust of the motives of Roman Catholics in political matters, 'on the religious level Wesley saw Catholics in the first place as Christians – Christians whose beliefs in the end were not so very different from his own'.[84]

Now there is an element of truth in each of these claims. Wesley was indeed poorly informed about certain aspects of Roman Catholic doctrine and practice, and most assuredly he had inherited a good deal of anti-Catholic prejudice, though sometimes he could be genuinely sympathetic towards Roman Catholics. All the same, it is entirely wishful thinking to attribute Wesley's anti-Catholicism to the kind of prejudice and ignorance that was conventional among Church of England clergy in the eighteenth century. Wesley possessed sufficient independence of mind to make it most unlikely that he would ever unquestioningly have accepted the attitudes and theological views of others. Todd failed to recognise the extent to which Wesley first appropriated and then articulated a Protestant critique of Roman Catholicism, which in some respects remains operative today. Wesley may not have been particularly original in his thinking on Roman Catholicism, but he had a sound grasp of the substantive theological issues at stake and was able to communicate and defend his position with insight and consistency over a period of more than fifty years. While it is impossible to know with certainty the motivation of Wesley or anyone else, it could just as easily be argued that his inspiration arose out of a concern to safeguard the truths of Protestantism.

At the same time, there are a number of areas where Wesley's teaching converged with Roman Catholic doctrine, and Todd correctly drew attention to these. The doctrine of grace is probably the most obvious example; the communion of saints is another. Todd further believed that Wesley held a Catholic understanding of the sacraments.[85] What Todd chose to ignore, however, was the fact that Wesley criticised the Roman Catholic Church for having introduced unwarranted devotional practices, even though he shared the same basic doctrine.

The doctrine of the communion of saints illustrates how the appearance of doctrinal convergence actually disguised an underlying disagreement. Evidently, Todd considered John Wesley to be a profound spiritual teacher whose orientation towards the Roman Catholic Church transcended the limitations imposed by eighteenth-century controversy:

> A Catholic believes that every man who has followed his conscience will find himself eventually in heaven, with the saints, and able to do God's work, in and through his providence. As I have come to know Wesley I have believed him to be there and have prayed to God through him – not publicly as the Church prays through those declared to be saints – but privately as I pray for and to those who have been close to me.[86]

Wesley, however, strongly disapproved of the practice of praying to the departed saints, even though he held the communion of the saints in the highest esteem. His *Explanatory Notes on the New Testament* contain a blunt comment on the rich man's cry to Abraham for help (Luke 16.24), which is the only example in the Bible of praying to the departed saints: 'It cannot be denied but here is one precedent in Scripture of praying to departed saints: but who is it that prays, and with what success? Will any, who considers this, be fond of copying after him?' A further consideration for Wesley was that the invocation of saints was linked to the cult of relics and the treasury of merit, both of which had been discredited by the Reformers.[87] This practical divergence casts further doubt on whether Wesley's motivation was orthodox from a Roman Catholic perspective.

In stressing Wesley's loyalty to the Church of England, Todd chose to overlook inconvenient facts. Strangely, Todd deals with Wesley's ordination of presbyters in just a few sentences, on the grounds that 'Far too much emphasis has been laid on the almost incidental ordinations of priests undertaken by Wesley towards the end of his life.'[88] What was more significant for Todd was the fact that Wesley never broke from the Church of England, but always thought of Methodism as a revival or reforming movement within the Church. Yet, the matter was not as trivial as Todd made out. Far from being 'almost incidental', as Todd would have us believe, Wesley's ordinations were a serious breech of Anglican order. Methodists might wish to argue that these ordinations were justified in an extraordinary situation and vindicated by subsequent events. Still, Wesley's heartache and his brother's furious reaction testify to the potentially serious consequences. Only the lax discipline of the Church of England at that time saved Wesley from formal censure.

Despite the serious flaws in his thesis, Todd successfully challenged the notion that Wesley was just another rabid revivalist preacher. Building on the earlier studies of Piette and Bouyer on the continent, Todd was able to demonstrate to English-speaking Roman Catholics that John Wesley was a significant figure in church history and therefore of wider interest beyond Methodism. In this way Todd made a signification contribution to the improved reception of Wesley and Methodism among Roman Catholics in the latter part of the twentieth century.

When Todd published his book on John Wesley in 1958 it was still considered daring for a Roman Catholic to talk of an 'ecumenical' perspective, let alone engage in a sympathetic study of a Protestant church leader. Fortunately, events were about to unfold in Rome which would dramatically alter the situation. A decisive breakthrough in ecumenical relations was just around the corner in the shape of the Second Vatican Council.

On 11 October 1962 an immense crowd gathered in St Peter's Square, Rome, to witness an historic event, as nearly three thousand bishops from around the world filed into the basilica to open the first session of the Second Vatican Council. A theological and cultural sea change was about to take place in Roman Catholicism which would have been unimaginable only a few years earlier. When John XXIII was elected pope in 1958 the Roman Catholic Church was dominated by the mind-set of neo-scholasticism. Like a medieval fortress, the Church stood with its drawbridge raised against the world, besieged by the forces of modernity in the guise of historical methods and intellectual attitudes. The theology and philosophy of St Thomas Aquinas, free from the taint of modernity, constituted the approved basis for Roman Catholic scholarship. The Mass was still celebrated mostly in Latin, and the liturgy had remained virtually unchanged since the Council of Trent. Roman Catholics were forbidden to engage in ecumenical activities or dialogue. Extraordinary as it may now seem, they were even prohibited from joining Protestants in reciting the Lord's Prayer. Those theologians who deviated from the prevailing conservatism in an attempt to engage with the modern world soon found themselves in trouble with a hierarchy rigorously controlled by Rome.

The First Vatican Council (1869–70) had made it possible for popes to exercise effective control over the whole Church in a way that had never before been attempted. Pius IX had intended the Council to deal with a variety of subjects, including faith and dogma, ecclesiastical discipline and canon law, as well as the relationship between the Church and civil powers.[89] However, at a crucial juncture in proceedings, war broke out between France and Prussia, prompting the withdrawal of French troops from Rome. Italian soldiers swiftly occupied the city, forcing the Council to a hasty conclusion, its business unfinished.

The main achievement of the First Vatican Council in its short existence was the constitution *Pastor Aeternus*, which defined the jurisdiction of the pope as ordinary, immediate and truly episcopal. It further defined the pope's infallibility, though in a more restrained form than some had wanted. The pope was said to teach infallibly when he spoke in his office as Pastor and Doctor of all Christians (*ex cathedra*) to define a doctrine concerning faith or morals, which required the assent of the universal Church. The papal definitions represented a victory for the 'Ultramontane' party, which had campaigned energetically for the strengthening of papal authority.

In the years following the First Vatican Council, the Roman Catholic Church experienced a revival in confidence as Roman Catholics responded obediently to the authority of Rome. The concept of a papal monarchy, which had long dominated Roman ecclesiology, was given a new and more powerful lease of life. The intention at Vatican I had been to complement the papal definitions with further teaching on the role of the bishops. Conveniently for Rome, however, the council was suspended before this could be done. As a result, the ministry of the bishops became subject to intense scrutiny as the Roman bureaucracy gradually tightened its grip over the whole Church. For the first time in history, the *Code of Canon Law* (1917) provided a uniform legal constitution governing the whole of the Roman Catholic Church in every area of its life.

In many ways Pius XII (1939–58) exemplified the post-Vatican I era of the Church. A prolific speaker on almost any topic, he issued a stream of authoritative teaching in the form of encyclicals. His theologically conservative vision of the Church, contained in the encyclical *Mystici Corporis* (1943), was striking for its identification of the body of Christ with the Roman Catholic Church. For Roman Catholics, long used to thinking of their Church in triumphant terms, *Mystici Corporis* reinforced a sense of superiority over others who claimed to be Christians.

In *Humani Generis* (1950) Pius XII identified 'historicism' and 'evolutionism' as being among the non-Christian philosophies that had contributed to the spread of error in the Church. Several distinguished theologians were dismissed from their teaching posts soon afterwards, including a number of French Dominicans and Jesuits, among them Henri de Lubac, who was later created a cardinal in recognition of his contribution to Roman Catholic scholarship. Ignoring the disquiet felt in some quarters of the Church, on All Saints' Day 1950 Pius XII defined the Bodily Assumption of the Blessed Virgin Mary into heaven, which had no firm basis in Scripture or tradition, though it had been celebrated liturgically in the Church from the fourth century onwards.

At the forefront of theological renewal and ecumenism in France during the 1950s was a Dominican scholar by the name of Yves Congar. In 1937 Congar had argued that the Roman Catholic Church must engage in ecumenical dialogue precisely in order to become more *catholic*.[90] Catholicism stood in urgent need of reform and had much to learn from Protestantism. Inevitably, Congar was among those to feel the chill wind from *Humani Generis*. Suspected by the hierarchy of disloyalty to the anti-modernist oath sworn by Roman Catholic university teachers, he was expelled from his teaching post in 1954 and exiled to Jerusalem, forbidden to teach or publish his research. Distrustful of the new pope, Congar confided in the privacy of his diary, 'Rome is in need of a complete conversion. It needs to renounce its claim of running the whole show.'[91] Neither Congar nor anyone else could have imagined that, within a few months, Pope John XXIII would lay the foundation for the wholesale conversion of Rome by calling a council of bishops in response to a sudden inspiration from the Holy Spirit.

The aim of this Second Vatican Council was nothing less than the 'bringing up to date' (*aggiornamento*) or renewal of the Roman Catholic Church.[92] However, the omens for a successful outcome could hardly have been more inauspicious, given the power of a fiercely conservative Roman curia. When John XXIII announced to seventeen Roman cardinals his desire to call a council, instead of the enthusiasm he had hoped for, there was complete silence.[93] On hearing of the pope's decision to call a council, an astonished Congar remarked in his diary, 'It's either sheer madness – and therefore a complete catastrophe – or the work of the Holy Spirit, in which case anything is possible.'[94]

Two days after the opening ceremony, another historic event took place when the pope received 39 official observers from other churches, who had been invited to attend the general congregations and follow the work of the commissions.[95] Although they were not entitled to speak at the council, the observers could express their views in writing and more informally in conversations outside its sessions. Thus, for the first time, members of other churches were genuine participants in a Roman Catholic council with a real opportunity to influence proceedings. Among the official observers were three Methodists, the President of the World Methodist Council, Bishop Fred Pierce Corson, Albert Outler (United States) and Harold Roberts (Great Britain).[96]

The contribution of the conciliar texts to relations between Methodists and Roman Catholics is necessarily general, since Methodism is not specifically mentioned in any of the documents. In fact, the only church of the Reformation mentioned by name is the Anglican Communion. Nevertheless, two documents in particular are relevant for Methodist–Roman Catholic dialogue – the Dogmatic Constitution on the Church (*Lumen Gentium*) and the Decree on Ecumenism (*Unitatis Redintegratio*), promulgated by Pope Paul VI on 21 November 1964. Concerning the one holy catholic and apostolic Church of Christ professed in the creed, *Lumen Gentium* states: 'This Church, constituted and organised in the world as a society, *subsists in* [*subsistit in*] the

Catholic Church, which is governed by the successor of Peter and by the bishops in union with that successor, although many elements of sanctification and truth can be found outside of her visible structures.'[97]

Now the verb *subsistit in* (*subsists* in) was a deliberate change from *adest in* (is present in), which had appeared in the draft text prepared by the Roman curia.[98] Leaving aside the technical details, it is sufficient to note that *Lumen Gentium* adopts a fresh perspective on the Church. If the bishops had accepted the original wording, then they would have been adopting the position that the Church of Christ is found in the Roman Catholic Church and nowhere else; whereas the verb *subsists* affirms the presence of the Church of Christ in the Roman Catholic Church, but not necessarily in an exclusive way. Thus the bishops signalled their clear intention that the Church of Christ should not be identified *exhaustively* with the Roman Catholic Church. Bishop Christopher Butler, an English participant in the Council, is said to have remarked of the change: 'Before the Council, I knew where the Church was, and I knew where it wasn't; now I still know where it is, but I no longer know where it isn't.'[99] *Lumen Gentium* encourages a more inclusive understanding of the Church. Members of the Roman Catholic Church are said to be 'fully incorporated' into the Church of Christ.[100] Other baptised Christians are linked with them through the Holy Spirit 'in some real way'.[101] This revised interpretation of the relationship between the Roman Catholic Church and other Christians recognises the integrity of these ecclesial groups and, from a Roman Catholic perspective, creates the possibility of ecumenical dialogue.

The ecumenical implications of *Lumen Gentium* are spelled out more fully in *Unitatis Redintegratio*.[102] The third paragraph is particularly significant for relations between Methodists and Roman Catholics and is worth quoting at length. Concerning those 'quite large communities' which have become separated from the Roman Catholic Church as a result of widespread disagreements down the centuries:

> The Catholic Church accepts them with respect and affection as brothers. For men who believe in Christ and have been properly baptised are brought into a certain, though imperfect, communion with the Catholic Church. Undoubtedly, the differences that exist in varying degrees between them and the Catholic Church – whether in doctrine and sometimes in discipline, or concerning the structure of

the Church – do indeed create many and sometimes serious obstacles to full ecclesiastical communion. These the ecumenical movement is striving to overcome. Nevertheless all those justified by faith through baptism are incorporated into Christ. They therefore have a right to be honoured by the title of Christian, and are properly regarded as brothers in the Lord by the sons of the Catholic Church.

Moreover, some, even very many, of the most significant elements or endowments which together go to build up and give life to the Church herself can exist outside the visible boundaries of the Catholic Church: the written word of God; the life of grace; faith, hope and charity; along with other interior gifts of the Holy Spirit and visible elements. All of these, which come from Christ and lead back to him, belong by right to the one Church of Christ.

The brethren divided from us also carry out many of the sacred actions of the Christian religion. Undoubtedly, in many ways that vary according to the condition of each Church or Community, these actions can truly engender a life of grace, and can be rightly described as capable of providing access to the community of salvation.

It follows that these separated Churches and Communities, though we believe they suffer from defects already mentioned, have by no means been deprived of significance and importance in the mystery of salvation. For the Spirit of Christ has not refrained from using them as means of salvation which derive their efficacy from the very fullness of grace and truth entrusted to the Catholic Church.[103]

Every word in this dense statement carries weight. Forty years after the Council, many Methodists and Roman Catholics are surprised to discover that the Decree on Ecumenism has so many positive things to say about other churches and ecclesial communities.

The Second Vatican Council initiated a significant development in the way Roman Catholics regard other Christians. *Unitatis Redintegratio* positively encourages Roman Catholics to pray with 'separated brethren'.[104] Roman Catholics are called upon to participate in conversations with other Christians on an 'equal footing' and in a 'spirit of goodwill', with the aim of better understanding one another and smoothing the road towards Christian unity.[105] What is more, in the course of such dialogue, 'Catholics must joyfully acknowledge and esteem the truly Christian endowments from our common heritage which are to be found among our separated brethren.'[106] 'Nevertheless,' says the Decree on Ecumenism, 'our separated brethren, whether considered as individuals or as Communities and Churches, are not blessed with that unity which Jesus Christ wished to bestow on all those whom he has regenerated and vivified into one body and newness of life – that unity which holy Scriptures and the revered tradition of the Church proclaim.'[107] Again, use of the term *subsists* in a conciliar text suggests a particular understanding of Christian unity: 'This unity, we believe, *subsists* in the Catholic Church as something she can never lose, and we hope that it will continue to increase until the end of time.'[108] Thus elements of unity may exist outside the visible structures of the Roman Catholic Church.

There was much discussion at the Council about how to refer to the 'separated brethren' in the third and final chapter of the Decree on Ecumenism. The first part of this chapter deals with the relatively straightforward issue of the venerable Eastern Churches whose 'special position' is described with respect. 'Although these Churches are separated from us, they possess true sacraments, above all – by apostolic succession – the priesthood and the Eucharist, whereby they are still joined to us in a very close relationship.'[109] The second part of the chapter considers 'The separated Churches and Ecclesial Communities in the West'. This title reflects the more complex situation in the West, where certain Christian bodies lack at least some of those elements that would enable the Roman Catholic Church to recognise them as true churches. The Decree on Ecumenism does not specify what these elements are, though it makes it clear that the sacrament of order is essential to preserving the genuine and total reality of the Eucharist. Taken as a whole, the conciliar texts apply the term 'church' exclusively to those Christian bodies that have bishops in apostolic succession and hence true sacraments. Christian groups that lack these elements are referred to as 'ecclesial communities'.

In his scholarly commentary on the Second Vatican Council, Herbert Vorgrimler explained the background to the Council's distinction between churches and ecclesial communities: 'Whether the concept of "Church" in the theological sense, can also be applied if the episcopal ministry with apostolic succession is not (or not certainly) present, and where only some of the sacraments are recognised, as in the case of the Reformation Churches, was the subject of a difference of opinion among the Council Fathers.'[110] Naturally enough, *Unitatis Redintegratio* makes no mention of a difference of opinion, but simply notes: 'Since in origin, teaching and spiritual practice, these Churches and ecclesial Communities differ not only from us but also among themselves to a considerable degree, the task of describing them adequately is very difficult; we do not propose to do it here.'[111] Thus the question of what elements must be present for the Roman Catholic Church to recognise another ecclesial community as a 'true church' was left open for future study.

Shortly after the close of the Council, Albert Outler described *Lumen Gentium* as the 'masterpiece of Vatican II', partly because of its pastoral and ecumenical tone, but mainly because it was the first conciliar teaching document about the nature and identity of the Church.[112] Previous councils had defined Roman Catholic doctrine concerning various aspects of the faith, mostly in response to heresy, but never before had a council devoted as much attention and energy to describing the nature and identity of the Church. The result was a *magna carta* to inspire, reshape and direct the post-conciliar Church.

Enthusiastic as he was about the opportunity for ecumenical dialogue created by the Second Vatican Council, Outler was concerned that the Council's reception by the Roman Catholic Church as a whole would be crucial to the success of any future theological conversations. He foresaw the 'tragic possibility' that *Lumen Gentium* would suffer the fate of previous conciliar documents and be interred in the 'vast mausoleum of ecumenical literature' before it was fully implemented in the life of the Church. It would be equally disastrous if *Lumen Gentium* were subsequently interpreted and implemented piecemeal, in a way that gave priority to its more conservative content.

This is not the place to consider how the Second Vatican Council has been received in the Roman Catholic Church as a whole. Many commentators would agree that the *aggiornamento* inaugurated by the Council has yet to achieve its full potential.[113] Thus Outler's fears on this score have not proved groundless. Yet the Council was undoubtedly a watershed in the life of the Roman Catholic Church and a monumental landmark in the ecumenical movement as a whole. It is difficult now to appreciate the sense of excitement in the years immediately following the Second Vatican Council. In one sense, a new era had dawned in the Church, and Christians from all traditions began with great enthusiasm to exploit opportunities for ecumenical encounter and dialogue. Among its other achievements, the Council made it possible for Roman Catholics and Methodists to engage in a substantial theological dialogue, which is the subject of the next chapter.

4

International Methodist–Roman Catholic Dialogue

Following the close of the Second Vatican Council in December 1965, the Methodist observers lost no time in canvassing support in Methodism for an international bilateral dialogue with the Roman Catholic Church. The following summer, the World Methodist Council meeting in London accepted the Vatican's invitation to appoint representatives to a dialogue commission. The Joint Commission for Dialogue between the World Methodist Council and the Roman Catholic Church, to give its full title, met for the first time at Ariccia near Rome in October 1967.

Every five years the Joint Commission has presented a report of its work to its sponsors, the World Methodist Council and the Vatican Secretariat (now the Pontifical Council) for Promoting Christian Unity. For convenience, the reports are generally known by the name of the city in which the World Methodist Council was meeting at the time they were presented to it: Denver (1971), Dublin (1976), Honolulu (1981), Nairobi (1986), Singapore (1991), Rio de Janeiro (1996) and Brighton (2001). The next report is due to be presented to the World Methodist Council meeting in Seoul in the summer of 2006.[1]

Monsignor Richard Stewart was a member of the Vatican Secretariat for seven years and the Roman Catholic co-secretary of the Joint Commission from 1982 until his untimely death in 1985. Reflecting on the first ten years of the dialogue, Stewart noted certain features that he considered to be characteristic of conversations between Methodists and Roman Catholics.[2] His observations still provide a useful introduction to the general ethos of Methodist–Roman Catholic dialogue at the international level.

First, Stewart considered it significant that, although Methodism was very conscious of its 'Protestant heritage', there was no single moment of rupture from the Roman Catholic Church. Despite the 'real gap' between Methodists and Roman Catholics, their conversations were 'not complicated by those historical hard feelings and resentments, which so often linger on after the polemics of a schism'.[3] But, even without residual hard feelings, it was true to say that full visible unity between Methodists and Roman Catholics remained a long way over the horizon. Recognising the arduous path ahead, the Joint Commission in the early days had concentrated on correcting misunderstandings and mapping areas of agreement and disagreement.

As a senior Vatican official, Stewart was well placed to comment on the current state of relations between Methodists and Roman Catholics. However, it remains a mystery why the bitter controversies of the eighteenth and nineteenth centuries should have faded so completely from the collective memory of both communities. Perhaps there is something to be said for Geoffrey Wainwright's analogy with family relations: 'the relationship may sometimes be easier between a grandmother and her grandchildren than between a child and its parent (as would be the case between Anglicans and Rome, or between Methodists and Canterbury).'[4]

Even allowing for the progress that has been made in the twenty years since Stewart recorded his observations, it remains the case that conversations between Methodists and Roman Catholics are nowhere near becoming unity talks. No one should underestimate the work involved in overcoming the remaining obstacles to full communion. Encouragingly however despite their doctrinal differences, Methodists and Roman Catholics share what Stewart called the same 'spiritual wavelength'. In particular, Methodists and Roman Catholics have a great deal in common in their understanding and spirituality of holiness. This discovery prompted the Joint Commission early on to focus on the person and work of the Holy Spirit as a potentially fruitful area of theological convergence between Methodists and Roman Catholics.

The distribution of Methodists in the world makes it practicable for the Joint Commission to engage in an English-speaking dialogue, involving participants from Europe, North America, Africa and Australia. Inevitably, a common language makes discussion easier; and the primary sources of Methodist theology are all in English. However, Stewart felt that an English-language dialogue hindered its reception in parts of the world where the majority speak another first language. To overcome this problem, many of the Joint Commission's reports have now been translated into other languages, including Spanish and German.

Admittedly, an English-speaking dialogue may not be of immediate interest in Latin America, for instance, where recent tensions between Methodists and Roman Catholics in Mexico and elsewhere stem from the widespread attitude among the Roman Catholic majority that Methodism is a sect. It is possible that a further Latin American contribution to the Joint Commission could reduce this tension. (J. Miguez Bonino served on the Joint Commission from 1992 to 1996.) However, in parts of the world where relations between Methodists and Roman Catholics are strained, it is probable that local factors are mainly responsible. Perhaps a proper reception of the Second Vatican Council's teaching on ecumenism is needed in these places before Methodist–Roman Catholic dialogue can begin to bear fruit.

Tactfully, Stewart drew attention to an important difference between Methodists and Roman Catholics, which made it difficult to identify precisely areas of doctrinal agreement. While Methodists were far from being indifferent to doctrinal standards, they were 'less inclined to "definition" of doctrine' than were Roman Catholics. This complicated the search for a form of words to state exactly what Methodists and Roman Catholics could agree together. Fortunately, the ecclesiastical discipline present in Methodism helped Roman Catholics to identify areas of agreement from Methodist polity, even where there was no formal Methodist teaching. Inevitably, because of the nature of the Roman Catholic Church, Methodists had to be more exact in their conversations with Roman Catholics than they might otherwise be when speaking within their own community. This was bound to slow the process of dialogue as Methodists reflected on aspects of Christian doctrine which they had not previously considered in minute detail.

Behind the diplomatic language, it is easy to imagine Stewart's frustration at trying to pin down Methodist doctrine with the degree of precision required by Roman Catholics. It is just one consequence of the historical development of Methodism in Britain and America. As we saw in the first chapter, Wesley adopted the narrowest possible view of the essentials of Christian faith, while allowing considerable leeway in matters that did not strike at the root of Christianity. The Methodist ethos has been to tolerate diversity of belief, and even a certain ambiguity, in some of the minutiae of Christian doctrine. For example, while Methodists and Roman Catholics agree together that Christ is truly present at the Eucharist, Methodists have not thought it necessary to define the nature and mode of the real presence as precisely as Roman Catholics.

The autonomous nature of each national Methodist Conference complicated the reception of Methodist–Roman Catholic dialogue, according to Stewart. To an observer, the World Methodist Council could appear more like an ecumenical gathering than the assembly of a worldwide communion. As a consultative body, the council had no legislative or executive authority over its constituent members. It formally received the Joint Commission's reports; but these had no status in member churches without a separate act of reception by their Conference. The absence of a central authority in world Methodism therefore made it difficult to disseminate the results of Methodist–Roman Catholic dialogue, even though Methodists possessed a strong sense of corporate identity and shared a common ethos. As a result, few Methodists were even aware of the international dialogue with Roman Catholics, and the reports produced by the Joint Commission had been sadly under-utilised in world Methodism.

The problem of reception, however, has not been confined to Methodism. Stewart neglected to mention the indifferent reception that Roman Catholics had given the dialogue with Methodism despite sponsorship at the highest level. While the Vatican usually invites an eminent scholar to comment on the reports published by the Joint Commission, local churches have been free to decide how to use these and other ecumenical texts. The result has been disappointing. Reflecting on the extent and pace of Roman Catholic dialogue with other Christians since the Second Vatican Council, Tom Stransky remarked:

> The flood of results, with various degrees of consensus, convergence and agreements or disagreements, has done little more than trickle into the consciousness of local congregations. The printed results are often not easily available and, if so, they seem digestible only by the theological elite.[5]

Stransky was being no more than realistic about the fate of

131

ecumenical texts. Beyond the setting up of various national conversations between Roman Catholics and Methodists, there is little evidence to suggest that the Joint Commission has been able to make much of an impression on the consciousness of Methodist or Roman Catholic congregations and their mutual relations. For those engaged in Methodist–Roman Catholic dialogue at the international level, reception at the local level remains a real problem.

Still, ecumenical texts develop a life of their own and sometimes acquire new significance years after they were produced. In 1998 the Catholic Bishops' Conferences of England and Wales, Ireland, and Scotland issued a teaching document on the Eucharist entitled *One Bread, One Body*, which contains several quotations from ecumenical sources, including the reports of the Joint Commission.[6] By such means, the agreed statements arising out of Methodist–Roman Catholic dialogue may gradually become more widely disseminated among Roman Catholics. As we shall discover in Chapter 6 Methodists are also beginning to acquire an interest in the dialogue with Roman Catholics.

Unfortunately, there is as yet no detailed commentary available for those who might want to engage theologically with the reports produced by the Joint Commission.[7] Such a commentary would be a substantial undertaking, which limitations of space render impracticable in the present volume. Conscious of the danger of over-simplifying complex documents, in the following sections we shall examine each report in turn, drawing attention to areas of agreement and disagreement, convergence and divergence. Throughout the rest of this chapter the numbers given in parentheses correspond to the paragraph number in the report under discussion.

Growth in Agreement (Denver, 1971)

This first report produced by the Joint Commission was more a summary of the opening round of conversations than an agreed statement.[8] These early meetings were essentially exploratory and covered a wide variety of themes, identifying topics for further study. Reflecting on the question 'Why are we here?' the participants believed they were seizing the *kairos* moment for ecumenism (2), in the light of the 'spectacular change in atmosphere' between Methodists and Roman Catholics since the Second Vatican Council (3).

What is immediately striking about the Denver report is its silence about the past. No mention is made of the history of controversy between Methodists and Roman Catholics, beyond a muted reference to mutual 'aloofness and suspicion' in an earlier period (3). The fact that there had been no formal schism between the two churches was said to be an 'advantage' for the dialogue (6). Rather than revisit past disputes, the Joint Commission decided to concentrate on the present day by drawing on insights from the Second Vatican Council's Pastoral Constitution on the Church in the Modern World (*Gaudium et Spes*). Even in 1971 the challenge of secularism was considered to be an important factor in ecumenical dialogue, and the 'contemporary situation' provided the organising principle behind the Denver report.

The first three chapters address 'Christianity and the Contemporary World', 'Spirituality' and 'Christian Home and Family'. The report identifies several areas of broad agreement between Methodists and Roman Catholics, which facilitate a common mission to a 'nonbelieving world'. In particular, Jesus Christ is the supreme and final authority in the Church (35), and the Bible is God's living word (36). Methodists and Roman Catholics share a theistic world-view (37) and a common diagnosis of the human situation (42). Methodists find echoes of their own tradition in Vatican II teaching on human dignity and autonomy (46). Methodists and Roman Catholics place high priority on responsible living in community in the Church (47), though there are differences about divorce (75), contraception (76), abortion (77) and care of the aged (78). Lastly, Methodists and Roman Catholics share a sense of the importance of Christian spirituality (48), though there are differences concerning Mariology (62).

In the second half of the report, the Joint Commission turned its attention to 'Eucharist', 'Ministry' and 'Authority'. The chapter on the Eucharist notes the 'astonishing' measure of agreement between Methodists and Roman Catholics (82). 'Both Methodists and Roman Catholics affirm as the primary fact the presence of Christ in the Eucharist, the Mass or the Lord's Supper' (83). While the real presence 'does not depend upon the experience of the communicant', it is only by faith that he or she becomes aware of Christ's presence, 'mediated through the sacred elements of bread and wine over which the words of institution have been pronounced' (83). The bread and wine are said to be effective signs of the body and blood of Christ.

The Joint Commission proposed a particular definition of the Eucharist as a dynamic memorial (*anamnesis*). The Eucharist is 'a memorial which is more than a recollection of a past event. It is a re-enactment of Christ's triumphant sacrifice and makes available for us its benefits' (83). However, reference to the 're-enactment' of Christ's sacrifice was ill-advised in the light of the Protestant emphasis on its once-for-all nature. For this reason, the Joint Commission later added a rider to its definition of the Eucharist as *anamnesis*: 'Some would wish to link this dynamic view not with a "re-enactment of Christ's triumphant sacrifice," but with Christ's being present and bringing with him all the benefits of his once-for-all sacrifice for us' (Dublin report, 63).

One area of theological disagreement between Methodists and Roman Catholics concerns the mode of Christ's presence at the Eucharist in relation to his presence in other means of grace (84). Some Methodists are reluctant to distinguish between the real presence of Christ at the Eucharist and his presence in every other means of grace, especially the proclamation of the word. The Denver report calls for further study on the presence of Christ in his Church and the relationship between eucharistic sharing and ecclesial fellowship (85).

The chapter on 'Ministry' outlines areas of doctrine where Methodists and Roman Catholics agree. Christ is the one through whom the Church's ministry is identified and ultimately authorised (89), while the Holy Spirit calls individuals into ministry (90). The Church's ministry involves full-time dedication to Christ, and its basic functions include administering the sacraments, preaching the word, teaching Christian truth, defending the faith, nurturing souls, leadership in the Christian community, acts of reconciliation and Christian service (91). Through the power of the Holy Spirit, ministers are agents of Christ for bringing God into the lives of human beings (92). The various ministries in the Church are bound together through connexional systems to form a corporate ministry (94). The Joint Commission deferred several issues for future study, including the relationship between the ordained ministry and the laity, the 'authentic' nature of ministry in the Methodist Church, apostolic succession and special ministries in the Church (97).

The final chapter on 'Authority' acknowledges that problems in this area are implicit in some of the deepest divisions between Methodists and Roman Catholics. Longstanding disputes over the Marian doctrines, infallibility and indefectibility can be traced to a different understanding of authority in the Church. The report identifies a number of questions requiring further investigation: What constitutes the first rank among the 'hierarchy of truths' within Christian doctrine (101)? What form of authority is consistent with the incarnation (102)? How does conscience relate to authority (104)? What do Scripture and Tradition each contribute to the exercise of authority in the Church (105)? The Joint Commission would return to these questions in future conversations. Meanwhile, the commission agreed that 'Only an authority given in love and received in love expresses the deepest meaning of the word for Christians' (106).

At the end of the opening series of conversations, the Joint Commission was able to announce the discovery of 'exceptional affinities between Roman Catholics and Methodists in that religion of the heart which is the heart of religion' (129). It noted the 'central place held in both traditions by the ideal of personal sanctification, growth in holiness through daily life in Christ', and recognised the similarity between the Methodist idea of scriptural holiness and chapter 5 of *Lumen Gentium*, 'The Universal Call to Holiness' (7). For the participants, these exploratory conversations more than repaid earlier hopes that Methodists and Roman Catholics would be able to discover common ground.

Growth in Understanding (Dublin, 1976)

Adopting the theme of the WCC mission and evangelism conference held at Bangkok in 1972, the Joint Commission commenced its Dublin report with an agreed statement on 'Common Witness and Salvation Today'. Effective testimony to God's saving work in Christ is fundamental to the life of the Church, which is commissioned to preach the Gospel to all people (11). However, Christian witness is fully effective only when the different churches act together, not from expediency but for the sake of the truth being proclaimed and lived. Salvation has personal and corporate dimensions, which involve the transformation of individuals and society. Christian witness involves the reinterpretation of traditional descriptions of salvation to take into account the many ways in which people nowadays hope for, and seek, salvation (12–15). In response to the reality of sin, Methodists and Roman Catholics proclaim the grace of God (19) with a common emphasis on social concern (20), mission (21) and sanctification (22).

Reflecting on 'Christian Home and Family', the Joint Commission paid special attention to marriage. Roman Catholics and Methodists agree about the Christian understanding and practice of marriage, but disagree about the possibility of divorce and re-marriage and on ways of regulating conception (39). The 'problem' of inter-church marriage was postponed for a future report; though, following a change of direction initiated in the third round of dialogue, the Joint Commission has not yet returned to the subject of Christian marriage.

Christian ethics was another subject identified for further investigation, in response to a number of moral issues currently attracting public attention. The Joint Commission referred approvingly to a British Methodist statement which condemned euthanasia as an option in medical care (45).[9] The Roman Catholic members of the Joint Commission could 'wholeheartedly endorse this Methodist statement, especially the positive section on the Christian attitude to death and the pastoral care of the chronic sick and the dying' (46). Like the subject of marriage however Christian ethics was a victim of the change of direction adopted from the third round of dialogue and has not featured in any of the subsequent reports from the Joint Commission.

The two core chapters of the Dublin report on Eucharist and Ministry are the result of fruitful collaboration between the Joint Commission and the English Methodist–Roman Catholic dialogue. The chapter on the Eucharist takes account of the ARCIC statement *Eucharistic Doctrine* (Windsor, 1971), published a few weeks after the Denver report. Likewise, the chapter on ministry follows in the wake of the ARCIC statement, *Ministry and Ordination* (Canterbury, 1973).

One of the difficulties faced by the Joint Commission in producing an agreed statement on the Eucharist was the fact that Methodists have no official eucharistic doctrine, the nearest equivalent being the eucharistic hymns and sermons of Wesley (51). Drawing on these as the primary source of Methodist doctrine, the Dublin report notes areas of agreement and disagreement about the sacrificial nature of the Eucharist, the real presence of Christ, and eucharistic sharing.

References in the Eucharist to 'sacrifice' have long been a source of dispute between Roman Catholics and Protestants: in what sense can the Eucharist be described as a sacrifice? For Roman Catholics, the Eucharist makes present the once-for-all sacrifice of Christ in a sacramental way (66). For some Methodists, such language would imply that Christ is still being sacrificed. According to the Joint Commission however historical disagreements between Methodists and Roman Catholics concerning the sacrificial nature of the Eucharist were due in part to the different theological language adopted by the two traditions. Another historically divisive issue centres on the transformation of the bread and wine into the body and blood of Christ. Roman Catholics understand this transformation to involve a change in the inner reality of the elements (a process usually called transubstantiation), whereas Methodists tend to think in terms of the bread and wine acquiring additional significance (59). Doctrinal convergence depends on whether and how the 'additional significance' of the bread and wine can be equated with a change in their 'inner reality' (60). The Dublin report echoes the Denver report in calling for further study on this and the relationship between eucharistic sharing and ecclesial unity (68). The report also notes the different approaches adopted by Methodists and Roman Catholics to the question of eucharistic hospitality. Whereas Methodists welcome members of other churches to the Lord's Table, Roman Catholics allow this only in exceptional circumstances (69).

The chapter on 'Ministry' examines three contentious areas of doctrine – apostolic ministry, priesthood and ordination – building on the earlier affirmations about ministry contained in the Denver report. First, Methodists and Roman Catholics agree together that the Church's apostolicity involves continuous faithfulness to the New Testament in the areas of doctrine, ministry, sacraments and church life (84). For Roman Catholics, true apostolic succession in ministry is guaranteed exclusively through the historic succession within the apostolic college (85). For Methodists, a ministerial succession of this kind can be a valuable *symbol* of the Church's apostolicity but not the *criterion* or guarantee (87). This important difference in understanding the nature of ministry in the Church was left for future study and report.

The priestly nature of the Church provides the focus for one of the most contentious disputes between Protestants and Roman Catholics. Whereas Roman Catholics connect the priesthood of the Church principally with the ordained ministry, Protestants have emphasised 'The priesthood of all believers'; though this slogan can be and has been inter-preted in different ways. Whereas both Luther and Calvin identified the priesthood of the Church with the corporate ministry of the people of God, many Protestants have since come to interpret the priesthood of the Church in a highly individualistic way.

The Dublin report reflects little of this historical controversy and simply notes that Methodists and Roman Catholics usually refer to priesthood in different ways – Methodists in connection with the Church; Roman Catholics in connection with the ordained ministry (92). Behind this 'difference of emphasis', Methodists and Roman Catholics share a great deal in common in their respective understand-ing of priesthood (93). After surveying priesthood in the New Testament and the early Church (94-9), the report cites the teaching of *Lumen Gentium* that 'though they differ from one another in essence not only in degree, the common priesthood of the faithful and the ministerial or hierarchical priesthood are nonetheless interrelated' (97).[10] Together, ministers and lay people participate in the one priesthood of Christ, though in a way that is unique to their status as such.

Curiously, there is no hint in the Dublin report that some Methodists would find it difficult to accept any understanding of priesthood which involved a qualitative distinction between ministers and lay people. Yet, the theology of ordination is a prime example of diversity in Methodism, based on contrasting interpretations of the fundamental principles of the Protestant Reformation. Some British Methodists would argue that the Deed of Union excludes the possibility of a qualitative distinction between ministers and lay people in the priesthood of the Church. Others would maintain that the Deed of Union is based on a historically conditioned understanding of priesthood.

What the Dublin report says about the theology of ordination is mostly descriptive of the two traditions. Roman Catholic orders are 'indelible'; Methodist orders are 'irremovable' (99). In the Roman Catholic Church only those ordained to the priesthood are 'entitled' to preside at the Eucharist. In Methodism lay people are sometimes given authority to preside at the Eucharist in carefully defined circumstances, when church members would otherwise be deprived of receiving the sacrament (101). Roman Catholics ordain only men to the priesthood; Methodists ordain men and women to the ministry of word and sacra-ment (102).

Growth in Understanding marked the end of the first phase of the international dialogue, which had been in progress for ten yeas. During this time, the Joint Commission covered a huge amount of ground, making considerable progress towards identifying areas of agreement and disagreement. However, the agenda was impossibly long and the approach too broad for there to be much hope of reaching substantial agreement. A fresh approach was required, and the next round of dialogue provided the opportunity for a radical change in method.

Towards an Agreed Statement on the Holy Spirit (Honolulu, 1981)

For its third series of conversations the Joint Commission departed from the procedure adopted in previous rounds. Instead of addressing a wide range of topics, the conversations concentrated on a single theme. As a result of this more focused approach, the structure of the Honolulu report is sharper and clearer than in previous reports, and the content has greater theological substance.

The first series of conversations had discovered a 'notable rapport' whenever the participants talked of spirituality or life in the Spirit (7). The Joint Commission considered it significant that the doctrine of the Holy Spirit had never been a point of contention between Methodists and Roman Catholics. Equally, the Spirit was the driving force of ecumenism. In the light of these promising discoveries, the Joint Commission settled upon the person and work of the Holy Spirit as its theme for the third round of dialogue. As the title of the Honolulu report indicates, the modest aim was to outline areas of convergence. There was one further innovation for the third series of conversations. To encourage wider participation in its work, the Joint Commission published the two main sections of the Honolulu report in draft form and invited responses.[11]

The first section of the Honolulu report, headed 'Towards an Agreement on the Holy Spirit', outlines areas of convergence, beginning with a brief statement on 'The Holy Spirit in the Godhead'. The Holy Spirit is God and possesses all the divine attributes (8). 'He is not simply a mode of the Godhead; he is a Person, just as are the Father and Son, distinct from each other though one with both' (9). The relations among the divine persons in the Godhead are distinctive. 'The Father is the source

139

and fountainhead; the Son is eternally begotten of him and is related to him as Son to Father; the Holy Spirit is related to the Father and the Son, proceeding from the Father and the Son (or from the Father through the Son)' (10). All this is consistent with the historic creeds and would be universally accepted by Methodists as well as Roman Catholics.

The work of the Holy Spirit as Lord and Giver of Life is examined under four aspects – creation, justification and regeneration, the Christian community, and the human community. The mission of the Holy Spirit in creation is closely related to the mission of the Word. Throughout the Old Testament God's Word and Spirit act together (12). Likewise, in the New Testament, the Word made flesh in Christ by the power of the Holy Spirit does nothing without the Spirit. The Holy Spirit gives a variety of gifts to the Christian community (1 Corinthians 12.4), equipping its members for ministry (20). Since not every human work in the Church should be attributed to the Holy Spirit, discernment is also a gift of the Spirit (20). The Holy Spirit guides the Church, leading it into all truth and inspiring Christians to make disciples of the nations (21), so that the human community is transformed into the kingdom of God (22).

There is a great deal that Methodists and Roman Catholics can say together about the work of the Holy Spirit in justification, regeneration and sanctification. The particular work of the Holy Spirit is 'to maintain the divine initiative that precedes all human action and reaction' (14). Through this 'prevenient grace' (a favourite theme both of John Wesley and the Council of Trent), humans are moved to conversion and enabled freely to turn to God. 'Justification is not an isolated forensic episode, but is part of a process which finds its consummation in regeneration and sanctification, the participation of human life in the divine' (13). The Holy Spirit is present and active in the process of conversion from the initial awareness of God's goodness, through the experience of shame and guilt, sorrow and repentance, to the possession of new life (13). Sanctification leads to perfect love (18).

The second section of the Honolulu report explores 'The Holy Spirit, Christian Experience and Authority'. Christian experience includes the 'assurance of God's unmerited mercy in Christ, the inner witness that we are indeed children of God' (24). As we saw in Chapter 3 the doctrine of assurance is problematic for Roman Catholics inasmuch as it implies a doctrine of guaranteed perseverance. For Roman Catholics, the real possibility of falling from grace into a state of mortal sin means that no one can be *assured* of finally persevering to salvation. Wesley, too, rejected the Calvinist doctrine of the guaranteed perseverance of the saints (see Chapter 1). The Honolulu report accepts that Christian spirituality may sometimes include the experience of assurance, though this is neither a necessary accompaniment to saving faith nor a guarantee of perseverance in grace.

The Joint Commission had already discovered a convergence between Wesley's approach to Christian experience and 'mainstream' Catholic spirituality, which was now seen to have implications for the cause of Christian unity (25). In the years following the Second Vatican Council, Roman Catholics have adopted a more positive approach to Christian faith in the form of religious experience, where this is understood as intimacy with Christ through prayer. Methodists and Roman Catholics agree that the Holy Spirit is the 'prime artisan' of this 'heart religion' (27). Authentic Christian experience includes 'mystery and clarity, feeling and reason, individual conscience and acknowledged authority, charisms and sacraments, spiritual exercises and service, individual and communal discernment of spirits, local community and worldwide mission, fidelity to the past and openness to the present and future' (28). Christian experience and practical doctrine belong together, as correctives to a possible imbalance on either side (29).

Christ's authority in the Church is mediated through the Holy Spirit (33). One aspect of the Spirit's work in the Church is to maintain God's people in the truth (34). To this end, 'The Spirit moves the Church to constant reflection on the Scriptures which he himself inspired and on their traditional interpretation, so that she may speak with undiminished authority to men in different times and places, in different social and cultural settings, facing new and difficult problems' (34). Scripture and Tradition should not be thought of as being opposed to each other because 'Scripture in witness to the living tradition from which it arose has a normative role for the total tradition of the Church as it lives and is guided still by the Spirit of truth' (34).

The universal primacy of the pope poses 'special difficulties' for reaching agreement about the nature of authority in the Church. However, a shared understanding of the person and work of the Holy Spirit provides a theological framework in which it may eventually be possible to resolve disagreements about 'infallibility'. According to the

141

Honolulu report, 'The papal authority, no less than any other within the Church, is a manifestation of the continuing presence of the Spirit of Love in the Church or it is nothing. It was declared at Vatican I to be "for the building up and not the casting down of the church" – whether of the local Church or the communion of local Churches' (35). With further work, it may yet be possible for Methodists and Roman Catholics to agree that the pope exercises a universal primacy in the service of Christian unity (36).

Against a backdrop of lively debate within and beyond the Roman Catholic Church over the papal encyclical *Humanae Vitae* (1968), the third section of the Honolulu report on 'Christian Moral Decisions' focuses on conscience and Christian marriage. Conscience is a vital gift from God for the moral life (43). However, it is not an independent source of moral teaching, but must be open to guidance from authority so that it can be formed and informed. The normative authority for moral decisions is Scripture, as interpreted in the light of Tradition, reason and experience. 'People have both the responsibility to see that their conscience is open to authoritative guidance and the right freely and faithfully to follow that conscience' (44). There may come a point when exercising freedom of conscience puts an individual outside the Church. The Joint Commission noted an important difference between Methodists and Roman Catholics in this regard: 'some pronouncements of the Catholic Church are seen as requiring a higher degree of con-scientious assent from Catholics than the majority of pronouncements of the responsible bodies of Methodism require of Methodists' (47).

The Honolulu report confirms the agreement reached in earlier reports about the nature of marriage. Whereas Roman Catholics include marriage among the sacraments, Methodists (in company with other Protestants) do not generally refer to marriage as a sacrament. The Reformers were reluctant to describe marriage as a sacrament, prefer-ring to reserve sacramental language for the essential means of grace – baptism and the Eucharist. Nevertheless, Methodists accept that 'Marriage is sacramental in nature because it is the living and life-giving union in which the covenantal love of God is made real' (50). The sacra-mentality of marriage is grounded in the couple's daily love for each other in which their sexual union is itself sacramental (52). A married couple's love and continuing care for their children is a sacrament of God's love for all people. For this reason, the whole of marriage is sacramental and not just the wedding ceremony (49). Surprisingly, the Honolulu report makes no mention of inter-church marriages, despite the Dublin report having highlighted this as a subject requiring further investigation.

Towards an Agreed Statement on the Holy Spirit is an exemplary ecumenical text, the first from the Joint Commission to be of wider interest and application beyond Methodists and Roman Catholics. In the event, the theme of the Holy Spirit was an inspired choice for the Honolulu report. This powerful convergence statement about the person and work of the Holy Spirit provides a promising theological framework in which to discuss historically divisive aspects of doctrine, such as ministry and authority in the Church. Also, by emphasising the role of the Holy Spirit in salvation history, the Honolulu report encourages theologians from all traditions to locate the doctrine of the Church within the economy of the Holy Trinity. Subsequent reports from the Joint Commission have all adopted a distinctly Trinitarian structure.

Towards a Statement on the Church (Nairobi, 1986)

In January 1982 at a meeting in Lima, Peru, the WCC Faith and Order Commission produced the final version of a landmark ecumenical text entitled *Baptism, Eucharist and Ministry* (*BEM*). The outcome of a long history of study and dialogue reaching as far back as the first World Conference on Faith and Order held at Lausanne in 1927, *BEM* has since attracted an attention unprecedented in the history of the ecumenical movement.[12] The Faith and Order Commission believed that in the Lima text it had formulated a remarkable degree of ecumenical consensus in understanding baptism, Eucharist and ministry – three historically divisive areas of Christian doctrine.

The Joint Commission had already identified the nature of the Church as the theme for its fourth series of conversations, which began in 1982.[13] *BEM* provided a timely and invaluable set of convergence statements to assist the commission in its work. In particular, the section on 'Ministry' begins with the calling of the whole people of God as the proper context for theological reflection on the nature of the ordained ministry. Correlatively, according to *BEM*, the apostolic tradition is transmitted within the people of God in different ways, one of them being episcopal succession. Moreover, 'In churches which practise the succession through the episcopate, it is increasingly recognised that a continuity in apostolic faith, worship and mission has been preserved in churches which have not retained the form of historic episcopate.'[14] The addition of Geoffrey Wainwright to the Joint Commission in 1983 further strengthened the association between Methodist–Roman Catholic dialogue and the *BEM* process, since he was a principal editor of the Lima text.

The Nairobi report, *Towards a Statement on the Church*, deals with 'some of the most difficult questions Roman Catholics and Methodists have faced together' (preface). Mindful of past disputes, the Joint Commission remarked: 'As we reflect on a reunited Church we cannot expect to find an ecclesiology shaped in a time of division to be entirely satisfactory. Our explorations towards a more adequate ecclesiology have begun and are helping us to give proper recognition to each other's ecclesial or churchly character' (22). For the first time, the Joint Commission set out the goal of Methodist–Roman Catholic dialogue as being 'full communion in faith, mission and sacramental life' (20). The Nairobi report is in two distinct but related parts: the first contains an outline description of 'The Nature of the Church'; the second is devoted to 'The Petrine Office'.

Following the lead of *BEM* and the ARCIC I *Final Report* (1981), the Joint Commission introduced the concept of *koinonia* into Methodist–Roman Catholic dialogue, believing this to be the most valuable 'model' for understanding the nature of the Church (23):[15]

> For believers [koinonia] involves both communion and community. It includes participation in God through Christ in the Spirit by which believers become adopted children of the same Father and members of the one body of Christ sharing in the same Spirit. And it includes deep fellowship among participants, a fellowship which is both visible and invisible, finding expression in faith and order, in prayer and sacrament, in mission and service (23).

The Church is the visible *koinonia* of Christ's disciples (1). As such, it is not a self-appointed, self-initiated community but the assembly of God's people gathered in Christ by the Holy Spirit (3). The New Testament contains a varied set of images for the Church, including body of Christ, people of God, bride of Christ, temple, flock or sheepfold, and royal priesthood. While all of them reflect different aspects of the Christian community, no single image adequately expresses the complex reality that is the Church (4). In the New Testament the term *ekklesia* describes Christians meeting together in a house or living in the same city or, in a more universal way, the body of Christ, the communion of saints on earth and in heaven (18).

Living between the time of Christ's exaltation and his future coming in glory, the Church is empowered by the Spirit to be a 'sign, sacrament and harbinger of the Kingdom of God' (8). The Second Vatican Council taught that the Church is a kind of sacrament, but not all Methodists feel comfortable with this idea (9). Nevertheless, the mystery of the Word made flesh and the sacramental mystery of the Eucharist suggest that the Church also has a sacramental nature (10). Whether or not the Church itself is a sacrament, Methodists and Roman Catholics agree that baptism and the Eucharist are the two basic sacraments of the Church. While Methodists reserve the term 'sacrament' exclusively for baptism and the Eucharist, this does not necessarily preclude other rites from having a sacramental character (13).

Reflecting on 'Ways of Being One Church', the Joint Commission proposed four possible 'models' for organic unity between Methodists and Roman Catholics (24). First, within the Catholic Church there is room for various 'ecclesial traditions' (*typoi*) that demonstrate a 'basic agreement in faith, doctrine, and structure essential for mission', each tradition being characterised by its own 'particular style of theology, worship, spirituality and discipline'. Second, the history of Methodism suggests an analogy with certain religious orders in the Roman Catholic Church. Figures such as Francis of Assisi founded religious orders with their own distinctive forms of spiritual life and organisation. Although in communion with the pope, these orders relate to his authority in different ways and enjoy relative autonomy in their internal affairs. Third, the Methodist Church and the Roman Catholic Church could be regarded as 'sister churches'. However, in view of the recent CDF Declaration *Dominus Iesus,* this option would now appear to be a remote possibility (see Chapter 6). Fourth, Methodism could be regarded as a separate rite from the Latin (rather like the various oriental rites) but still in communion with the Bishop of Rome. This, too, would allow different styles of devotion and church life to be preserved within a single communion.

Of course, any form of organic unity which does not involve absorption into an existing ecclesial structure poses the question of what would constitute 'the acceptable range of variety and uniformity in the Church'. According to the Nairobi report, 'The Church should protect legitimate variety both by ensuring room for its free development and by directly promoting new forms of it' (26). However, 'There have to be limits to variety; some arise from the need to promote cohesion and cooperation, but the basic structures of the Church also set limits that exclude whatever would disrupt communion in faith, order and sacramental life' (28). The report raises, but does not address, the interesting question of whether legitimate diversity in the Church could be maintained within a single form of *episkope*, or whether overlapping jurisdictions would be required (27).

Continuing, the Joint Commission accepted that Methodists and Roman Catholics were still divided in their understanding of the ordained ministry. The threefold ministry of bishop, presbyter and deacon was firmly established during the second and third centuries (29). 'But we are not agreed on how far this development of the ministry is now unchangeable and how far loyalty to the Holy Spirit requires us to recognise other forms of oversight and leadership that have developed, often at times of crisis or new opportunity in Christian history' (29). For Roman Catholics, the threefold order of ministry is derived from the New Testament through the living Tradition of the Church, and valid succession in ministry is guaranteed by episcopal ordination in historic succession (31). Methodists regard ministerial succession as a valuable *symbol*, but not the *criterion*, of the Church's continuity. Thus Methodists and Roman Catholics give very different accounts of apostolic succession in the Church.

The second section of the Nairobi report on 'The Petrine Office' starts by recognising that the universal primacy of the Bishop of Rome has long been a source of dispute between Roman Catholics and Protestants. *Towards a Statement on the Church* explores the scriptural and historical background of the papacy in order to establish a measure of agreement about what functions the Bishop of Rome might legitimately exercise in a ministry of universal primacy, by what authority and under what conditions (40). The Joint Commission soon reached the conclusion that the universal primacy of the Bishop of Rome could not be established from Scripture in isolation from Tradition (55). Methodists however attach less significance than Roman Catholics to venerable tradition as a source of authority. For Roman Catholics, being in communion with the Bishop of Rome remains the 'touchstone of belonging to the Church in its fullest sense' so that reconciliation with the pope is a necessary element in restoring Christian unity (56).

The Joint Commission acknowledged that major differences between Methodists and Roman Catholics concerning the ministry of the Bishop of Rome were a serious obstacle to unity. 'For Methodists the concept of primacy is unfamiliar, even if historically John Wesley exercised a kind of primacy in the origins of the Methodist Church' (37). What is more important, in the absence of firm evidence in Scripture, Methodists find it difficult to accept that the universal primacy of the Bishop of Rome belongs to the *essence* of the Church. However, in a compromise formula devised by a British Methodist, A. Raymond George, the Joint Commission was able to affirm that 'Methodists accept that whatever is properly required for the unity of the whole of Christ's Church must by that very fact be God's will for his Church' (58).[16] Moreover, although Methodists cannot accept that the papacy is *essential* for the Church, 'A universal primacy might well serve as focus of and ministry for the unity of the whole Church' (58). Thus, 'It would not be inconceivable that at some future date in a restored unity, Roman Catholic and Methodist bishops might be linked in one Episcopal college and that the whole would recognise some kind of effective leadership and primacy in the bishop of Rome. In that case, Methodists might justify such an acceptance on different grounds from those that now prevail in the Roman Catholic Church' (62).

This remarkable vision for the future seems extraordinarily optimistic, unrealistic even, in view of the substantial doctrinal differences that would have to be resolved along the way, and not just concerning the ministry of the Bishop of Rome. Episcopacy itself remains a contentious issue in Methodism. The United Methodist Church (USA) has bishops, but they do not constitute a separate order of ministry.[17] British Methodism does not have bishops, though 'The Conference has declared that the acceptance of the historic episcopate would not violate the Methodist doctrinal standards.'[18] Indeed, the British Conference has gone so far as to express its readiness to embrace episcopacy, though with the freedom to interpret the historic episcopate in a way that is appropriate for Methodism. Nevertheless, this has not yet been tested in the form of practical proposals, and many British Methodists would be reluctant to institute an episcopal order of ministry in the absence of a scheme for wider unity in the Church.

Even if episcopacy were an established feature throughout world Methodism, it is difficult to imagine how Methodist bishops might be linked with their Roman Catholic counterparts in an episcopal college, not least because the universal primacy of the pope raises further complications. As the Joint Commission acknowledged, Methodists continue to have difficulties with the Roman Catholic understanding of infallibility (72). The Nairobi report suggests that the Methodist doctrine of assurance could provide a means to establishing convergence with Roman Catholics concerning infallibility (74). 'Methodists might ask whether the Church, like individuals, might by the working of the Holy Spirit receive as a gift from God in its living, teaching, preaching and mission, an assurance concerning its grasp of the fundamental doctrines of the faith such as to exclude all doubt' (75). But it is by no means obvious that the episcopal *charism* has much in common with the Methodist understanding of assurance. Since the Nairobi report raises many more questions than it answers, it was premature for the Joint Commission to tackle the Petrine Office at that stage.

The Vatican invited the distinguished French theologian and ecumenist Fr Jean Tillard to comment on *Towards a Statement on the Church*.[19] Tillard judged the Nairobi report to be 'a significant document of interest outside the context of Catholic–Methodist relations'. The first paragraph in particular 'deserves to take its place among the most beautiful definitions of the Church': 'Because God so loved the world, he sent his Son and the Holy Spirit to draw us into communion with himself. This sharing in God's life, which resulted from the mission of the Son and the Holy Spirit, found expression in a visible *koinonia* of Christ's disciples, the Church.'[20]

While Tillard praised the Nairobi report for its 'mature and nuanced expression' so 'honest and sober', he also made some astute observations about its limitations.[21] In particular, he noted the tentative way in which the report recognised the sacramentality of the Church yet failed to explore its full implications for the Church's role in salvation.[22] According to Tillard, such theological diffidence was characteristic of dialogue between Roman Catholics and Protestants. As such, the Nairobi report was far too discreet and failed to probe areas of convergence and divergence with sufficient rigour. As Tillard saw it, the Methodist doctrine of assurance had only 'very slight' similarity to papal infallibility.[23] Likewise, the comparison between Wesley's leadership of Methodism and papal primacy was simply 'not valid in this context'.[24] What was more, the report's description of the Church as a *koinonia* of disciples was misleading, because it failed to take into account the fact that the Church was a *koinonia* of local churches. As a result, the report said virtually nothing about the relationship between local churches and the universal Church.

To be fair however *Towards a Statement on the Church* was never intended to be more than a preliminary introduction to what is, after all, a huge topic in ecumenical dialogue. The Joint Commission was well aware that much more needed to be said about the nature of the Church. For the next round of dialogue, the commission chose to focus on the key subject of apostolicity.

The Apostolic Tradition (Singapore, 1991)

The Singapore report continues and develops the ecclesiological reflection started in the Nairobi report, addressing some of the issues outstanding from that and previous reports. Once again, the Joint Commission did not intend to address every aspect of its chosen theme, the apostolicity of the Church. Its aim instead was to outline a theological perspective, acceptable to both traditions, in which outstanding doctrinal and structural differences might eventually be resolved. In choosing to focus on the apostolicity of the Church, the Joint Commission was inspired by George Tavard's imaginative description of the apostolic tradition as *koinonia* in time.

The Nairobi report had revealed a significant difference between Methodists and Roman Catholics in the way they reflect theologically on the Church, especially in how each community uses the New Testament and early church history, as was evident from their contrasting approach to the Petrine ministry. In the absence of any confirmation in Scripture, Methodists attach little significance to the Petrine ministry in the apostolic tradition. Roman Catholics, on the other hand, regard the

149

apostolic tradition as authoritative, even where it cannot be verified from Scripture. Therefore, by focusing on the apostolicity of the Church, the Joint Commission hoped to provide a framework in which it might be possible to bridge the gap between these contrasting approaches to theological reflection on the nature of the Church. To move the conversation about apostolicity onto more fruitful soil, the Joint Commission introduced an innovation. Whereas it had been usual in ecumenical dialogue involving Roman Catholics to discuss apostolicity in the context of the Church's ministry and sacraments, the Joint Commission shifted the focus of apostolicity towards Christian teaching. Thus the Singapore report defines the apostolic tradition as the 'teaching, transmission and reception of the apostolic faith' (4).

Building on the Nairobi report, the Singapore report emphasises the important contribution of *koinonia* language and the doctrine of the Trinity to a correct understanding of the nature of the Christian Church. The Trinity brought the Church to birth. Election can be attributed to the work of the Father, while 'The Spirit is co-founder of the Church with the Son, by being the Church's principle of sanctification' (7). As such, the missions of the Son and Holy Spirit are extensions in time of their eternal procession in the Trinity (7). The Trinitarian relations are reflected within the ordered life of creation and 'in the pattern they establish and make possible for the community life of God's people' (49). The First Letter of John 1.1–3 suggests that the Church 'is a reflection of the life of the Godhead', so that Christian fellowship is nothing less than a sharing in the life of the Father and the Son in the Holy Spirit (50). Thus it is the Holy Spirit who makes it possible for Christians to live in communion (52), and the gifts of the Spirit are for the good of the *koinonia* (27). The setting apart of ministers in the New Testament was accompanied by the action of the Holy Spirit and, ever since then, the Spirit has been 'the invisible thread running through the work of the Church in the world' (52).

The first half of *The Apostolic Tradition* examines 'The Apostolic Faith: Its Teaching, Transmission and Reception'. In this context, the apostolic tradition signifies the living transmission of the Gospel of Christ by various means for the renewal of every generation, because 'The faith must be handed on' (18). Crucially, the living transmission of the Gospel does not involve the repetition of rigid formulae from the past. 'Rather, by recalling and holding fast to the treasured memory of the events of our salvation, we receive light and strength for our present faith as, under God, we seek to meet the needs of our own time' (5). Again, the Church is described in sacramental terms as the 'living sign' of Christ's victory over sin and death (1). At the same time, the Church is 'the place where the Word of God is spoken, heard, responded to and confessed' (15).

When the Church preaches today it is the same proclamation as when the apostles preached Christ crucified and risen (10). This can be said with confidence because the apostolic tradition continues an unbroken process of communication between God and human beings (16). The apostolic tradition cannot be divorced from Scripture, as if it were a separate source of authority, because there is a close dependency between them. 'Scripture was written within Tradition, yet Scripture is normative for Tradition. The one is only intelligible in terms of the other' (21). In other words, Scripture is the 'permanent norm' of the apostolic tradition (16). The criterion for hearing the Word with certainty is communion with those who have heard and obeyed the Word before us (18). Thus the Holy Spirit is the source of the Church's apostolicity. 'The Holy Spirit prepares the way for the preaching of the Word to those who do not believe, enabling them to respond in faith to know the saving grace of God' (28). Furthermore, the Holy Spirit establishes and maintains the unity of the Church, joining members of the body of Christ to their head.

It is the Holy Spirit who enables Christians today to confess with the people of God in every age the one true faith in Jesus Christ, the same yesterday, today and forever (21). *The Apostolic Tradition* identifies a convergence between Methodists and Roman Catholics in their understanding of 'Spirit and Church' (22–32), 'The Pattern of Christian Faith' (33–8), 'The Pattern of Christian Life' (39–48) and the 'Pattern of Christian Community' (49–52). By the power of the Holy Spirit at work within the people of God in every generation, the Church continues in the communion of the saints (33). This does not mean that the past has little or no significance for the present. On the contrary, in the Church 'an important place is given to those theologians who provided the earliest elucidations of the faith' (34). Methodists and Roman Catholics agree together that the Nicene Creed is 'a comprehensive and authoritative statement of Christian faith' and therefore one element of the communion they already share (38).

Recognising that Methodists and Roman Catholics describe differently those ministries that maintain the Church in the apostolic tradition, the second half of the Singapore report considers 'Ministry and Ministries: Serving within the Apostolic Tradition'. All ministries in the Church are at the 'Service of the Word' (54–57) and are made possible by the 'Gifts of the Spirit' (58–61). Ordained ministers 'represent the people before God' and 'act in Christ's name' (71). The ministry of oversight requires ministers to keep the churches faithful to apostolic teaching (74). The transmission of the Gospel is the work of the whole Church under the guidance of their pastors (76). Cautiously, the Joint Commission affirmed that 'Catholics and Methodists are at one in seeing in a divinely empowered ministry the guidance of the Holy Spirit and are moving in the direction of greater shared understanding of the nature of ordination and of the structure of the ministry in regard to the responsibility to teach and to formulate the faith' (77).

Already Methodists and Roman Catholics agree about various aspects of ordination. Both set apart ministers by the laying-on of hands with prayer for those gifts of the Holy Spirit appropriate to their order of ministry (80), and ministry is only effective by the power of the Holy Spirit (84). However, three unresolved issues require further investigation. First of all, Methodists and Roman Catholics disagree about whether ordination is a sacrament (88–91). Second, they disagree about the nature of *episkope* in the Church. For Roman Catholics, but not necessarily for Methodists, the succession of bishops 'serves the continued unity of the Church in the faith handed on from the apostles' (93). Third, Methodists and Roman Catholics disagree about who may be ordained (95–98). Unlike Methodists, Roman Catholics do not ordain women, believing that they have no authority to change the sacrament of order as it has been received in the apostolic tradition (97).

Despite these obstacles to full communion in sacramental life, *The Apostolic Tradition* concludes with an encouraging statement of the progress made by Methodists and Roman Catholics since the Second Vatican Council towards recognising the ecclesial status of each other:

While Wesley and the early Methodists could recognise the presence of the Christian faith in the lives of individual Roman Catholics, it is only more recently that Methodists have become more willing to recognise the Roman Catholic Church as an institution for the divine good of its members. For its part, the Roman Catholic Church certainly includes Methodists among those who, by baptism and faith in Christ, enjoy a 'certain though imperfect communion with the Catholic Church'; and it envisages Methodism among these ecclesial communities which are 'not devoid of meaning and importance in the mystery of salvation'. (*Unitatis Redintegratio*, 3) (100)

Full communion in faith, mission and sacramental life will depend not only upon doctrinal consensus but also on a 'fresh creative act of reconciliation' that acknowledges the activity of the Holy Spirit throughout the ages (94). As part of the Holy Spirit's continuing activity in the history of the Church, Methodists recognise Wesley's ordination of Francis Asbury and Thomas Coke to a ministry of oversight in American Methodism as a 'fresh and extraordinary outpouring of the gift of the Spirit' (93).

In welcoming the Singapore report, A. Raymond George (a former President of the British Methodist Conference and previously a member of the Joint Commission) expressed the hope that Methodists throughout the world would study it closely, since the report contained nothing contrary to Methodist doctrine.[25] In a short commentary he aired the opinion that, although there was nothing new in the report to astonish experts, 'the degree of convergence would come as a considerable surprise to the people "in the pew" in both Churches'.[26]

The official Vatican commentator on *The Apostolic Tradition*, Jared Wicks, responded with an appreciative and perceptive assessment in which he praised the Joint Commission for having advanced the ecumenical understanding of the nature of the Church.[27] The Singapore report was also 'remarkable for the extent and significance of the elements of consensus that surround its discussion of Methodist–Catholic differences over ministry'. Thus the report provided a valuable theological framework for further dialogue. However, before there could be substantial agreement in understanding the apostolic tradition, three issues arising out of the Singapore report required further investigation. First, the statement by the Joint Commission that Scripture was the 'normative' expression of Tradition suggested, misleadingly, that the Bible did not require any interpretation and that its authority was therefore independent of the Church. On the contrary, even as the normative expression of the apostolic tradition, Scripture was never free from interpretation.

Second, the Singapore report neglected to mention the fact that preserving the apostolic tradition had always been an immense struggle for the Church – as the content of the Pastoral Epistles demonstrates. The effort required to preserve the apostolic tradition without loss or contamination had naturally led Roman Catholics to recognise the spiritual empowerment of the bishops, as successors to the apostles, in order 'to resolve controversies in a binding way through teaching that in its solemn forms is maintained in the truth by God's Spirit'.[28]

Third, the Singapore report glossed over what Wicks called the fecundity of the apostolic tradition. For example, Roman Catholics looked upon the threefold structure of ministry as a providential development within the apostolic tradition. On the other hand, Roman Catholics did not accept the ordination of women as a legitimate development. For Wicks, the episcopal charism of truth was 'an empowerment for discerning innovative teachings and practices so as to test their homogeneity with the founding transmission to the apostolic Churches'.[29] However, Methodists would question whether the criterion of homogeneity with the past is strictly necessary in discerning the providential guidance of the Holy Spirit.

Wicks put his finger on some important omissions from the Singapore report. Once again, though, these were not due to an oversight on the part of the Joint Commission, which consciously decided to postpone the question of apostolic succession and the different ways in which Methodists and Roman Catholics transmit the apostolic tradition and teach authoritatively. The commission would eventually return to these subjects in its seventh series of conversations. However, before the Joint Commission could meaningfully study the transmission of the apostolic faith, it was felt necessary first to investigate the fundamental nature of Christian revelation and faith.

The Word of Life: A Statement on Revelation and Faith (Rio de Janeiro, 1996)

Previous reports from the Joint Commission had referred to the apostolic faith without paying much attention to the precise nature of revelation and faith. For its Rio report, the Joint Commission resolved to investigate the way in which God reveals himself to humankind and the response humans make. It was a wise decision to pause rather than press on to address some of the large issues looming on the horizon. By undertaking a painstaking analysis of the nature of revelation and faith, the Joint Commission was able to establish a firm foundation for future statements concerning the transmission of the apostolic tradition.

According to *The Word of Life*, the revelation of the Trinity and the human response constitute the substance of the Church's faith, mission and sacramental life, which are the core dimensions of full communion between Christians (4). A common account of revelation and faith is therefore an important step on the way towards full communion between Methodists and Roman Catholics. One immediately encouraging sign in this regard is that Methodists and Roman Catholics agree about the Trinitarian structure of revelation and faith (8).

The Word of Life is divided into five sections. The first section on 'Revelation' (11–26) sets out a shared understanding of God's self-communication to humankind in history. The New Testament asserts that God's self-revelation in history reaches its climax in the life, death and resurrection of Jesus Christ (17). Yet, it is only because of the earliest witnesses to Jesus that he is known today as the self-revelation of God (19). Christians nowadays are therefore dependent upon the first people to come to faith in Christ, especially those who wrote accounts of the meaning and significance of Jesus. Christians are also dependent upon those in the community of faith who have been faithful interpreters of the apostolic tradition.

The second (and longest) section on 'Faith' (27–72) explains the three ways in which faith can be understood. First, there is the faith by which Christians believe (*fides qua creditur*). It is not by human power that believers apprehend God's word addressed to them through Christ and thus come to salvation (30). Faith is entirely God's gift, freely given and received (31). The faith by which Christians believe is more than a dimension of human feeling. It is a response shaped by the nature and being of God so that what is believed is an integral part of faith (32).

In its second sense, therefore, faith refers to that which is believed (*fides quae creditur*). The Church has always expressed its faith in the form of creeds (34). Alongside sacraments and doctrinal teaching, creeds are one of the ways in which Christians appropriate for themselves the self-giving of God in Christ (35). Since creeds convey the Gospel in a way that is authoritative and life-giving, it would be a mistake to view them simply as collections of propositions requiring no more than intellectual assent (35).

In its third sense, faith involves a 'creative and dynamic fruitfulness' as humans respond to God's self-disclosure, not just through cognitive assent but also by a life of faith (37). As the community of faith, the Church is a 'seed', which grows with the support of the Holy Spirit in response to external stimuli in the form of different cultures and situations. However, there is no way of understanding the fruitfulness of revelation except within the community of faith (39). The fruitfulness of faith is more comprehensive than just the development of doctrine and includes confession (44–5), the spiritual life (46–8), worship (49–51) and service (52). It is the Holy Spirit who makes God's revelation in Jesus Christ fruitful for building up the Church and its individual members. Furthermore, the Spirit is the source of all authentic (i.e. authoritative) discernment (53).

The Word of Life identifies four criteria for authentic discernment. First, as the normative witness to revelation, the Scriptures have a central role in Christian discernment (54). Second, there is an inner harmony between personal conviction in faith and the teaching of the Church, as indicated by the Latin phrase *sentire cum ecclesia* (56). Long-term reception by the wider Church is a third criterion of discernment (59). Fourth, holiness is a criterion for the existence of truth in the process of the interpretation and development of doctrine, because holiness is the fruit of Christian moral and doctrinal truth (60). Thus it is appropriate to describe holiness as the source of subsequent developments in doctrine (61). Agents of authoritative discernment include the whole people of God (63), the prophets (64) and the Church's teaching office (67). Methodists and Roman Catholics identify differently the Church's teaching office, but the Joint Commission postponed discussion of this subject until its next round of dialogue.

The third section of *The Word of Life* on 'Mission' (73–93) is based on the premise that the Church, by its very nature, is missionary. The mission of the Church 'is none other than a sharing in the continuing mission of the Son and the Holy Spirit expressing the Father's love for all humankind' (73). Christians are 'Commissioned by Christ' (74) and 'Empowered by the Holy Spirit' (75). Since the Gospel is intended for all times and places, it should be proclaimed in ways that are appropriate to different cultures (90–3). But, whatever form it takes, Christian mission is both 'Word and Act' (77–80), for which the ministry of Jesus provides the pattern (78).

As the people of God have been sent into the world as witnesses to the Gospel, it is appropriate to speak of an 'Apostolic Mission' (84–8). Ever since the time of the apostles, there has been within the apostolic mission of the Church a ministry uniquely called and empowered to build up the body of Christ in the world (84). In the Roman Catholic Church this apostolic ministry is entrusted to bishops in the apostolic succession, assisted by presbyters and deacons. 'In the Methodist tradition, following Wesley, ordained ministry is held to be in succession to the apostles, though not dependent in the same way on the succession of bishops' (88). Aside from this structural difference, the fact that the apostolic mission is carried out by separate churches in isolation constitutes a 'serious obstacle to mission' in the world (89). Methodists and Roman Catholics recognise the integrity and faithfulness of each other's witness to the Gospel, and large areas of agreement permit a certain amount of shared mission. However, significant differences remain concerning key aspects of personal and social ethics (89).

The fourth section of the report on 'Sacramental Life' (94–107) develops the use of sacramental language in connection with the Church. In its Nairobi report the Joint Commission had spoken of the Church as 'a kind of sacrament'.[30] In the Singapore report the commission had referred to Christ as the 'primary sacrament'.[31] In *The Word of Life* the Joint Commission describes the particular sacraments as flowing from the sacramental nature of God's self-communication in Christ (98). Baptism is the 'basic sacrament of the Gospel' (102). The Eucharist builds up the Church into the body of Christ (100). Roman Catholics recognise five further sacraments (105), while Catholics and Methodists both recognise additional 'means of grace' (107).

The fifth section, 'Koinonia-Communion', explores some 'Basic Expressions of Communion in our Churches' (111–25). The essence of the Church is a sharing in the communion of love between the three persons of the Trinity, and the visible institution of the Church is a manifestation of this communion (109). Methodists and Roman Catholics live from the same Gospel and 'share the same faith' as summarised in the Apostles' and Nicene Creeds (112). This shared faith constitutes a basic form of communion. However, there is no agreement about what doctrines are necessary to constitute full communion in faith. Methodists distinguish between the 'essential doctrines' of the Gospel and 'different "opinions" about manners of worship, about ecclesiastical polity or even about the exposition of certain scriptural truths' (115). Methodists have not defined a fixed canon of 'essential doctrines', whereas Roman Catholics stress that the whole teaching of the Church constitutes an organic unity (116).

The sacrament of baptism constitutes a further manifestation of communion, and in many regions Methodists and Roman Catholics already recognise each other's baptism (119). However, it is not possible to share in eucharistic communion because Methodists and Roman Catholics identify differently the ministers appointed as witnesses to the truth of the Gospel and the kind of teaching authority committed to them (120). While this constitutes the 'most visible obstacle' to full communion, there is common ground in the shared belief that all sacramental life is rooted in Jesus Christ, the 'primary sacrament' (121).

Since 'The Church Universal' has dimensions in time and space, *koinonia* involves being in 'communion with the Church of those who preceded us in the faith throughout the ages', which communion extends beyond 'the fellowship of the members of the same congregation or the same local community' (126). Once again, however, Methodists and Roman Catholics differ in where they locate this *diachronic* and *synchronic* communion. For Roman Catholics, the ministerial hierarchy in episcopal succession guarantees the continuity and universality of the Church. For Methodists, continuity in the apostolic tradition is guaranteed exclusively by continued faithfulness to apostolic teaching, and authority in the Church properly belongs to conciliar structures. The Joint Commission considered that these differences constitute the 'greatest hindrances' on the way to full communion (130).

The official Vatican commentator, William Henn, observed a strong sense of continuity between *The Word of Life* and previous reports from the Joint Commission.[32] He noticed also that the structure and content of the Rio report bore a strong resemblance to the section reports from the Fifth World Conference on Faith and Order held at Santiago de Compostela in 1993.[33] For Henn, this resemblance was an example of the way in which multilateral and bilateral dialogues influence one another.

Henn commended some of the Rio report's general features. In particular, while not ignoring human weakness, *The Word of Life* was optimistic about the work of the Holy Spirit in the Church, an optimism reflected in the positive role attributed to the apostolic tradition as a criterion for discerning the faith. By consistently presenting revelation as the source of faith, mission and sacramental life, the report emphasised the historical expression of these core dimensions of *koinonia*. At the same time, the report established a theological framework for resolving outstanding doctrinal differences between Methodists and Roman Catholics concerning structures of unity, the ordained ministry and the number of sacraments.

However, there were a number of areas in the report where greater clarity was desirable. The similarity in practice between Methodists and Roman Catholics over the 'disputed sacraments' would benefit from further exploration. Also, it would be worthwhile to consider what it means for us to say that a sacrament was 'instituted by Christ', since Methodists and Roman Catholics identify differently the dominical sacraments. The relationship between eucharistic communion and communion in faith could usefully be studied in greater detail: what degree of communion in faith is required before divided churches can extend eucharistic hospitality to others?

Henn's warmest praise was reserved for the 'mature' way in which *The Word of Life* drew on a variety of sources, including liturgy, Church Fathers, historic creeds, early councils, Reformed confessions and the Council of Trent, as well as Orthodox, Roman Catholic and Methodist traditions and the Second Vatican Council. This implicit affirmation of the contemporary value of the apostolic tradition for the Church had been made possible by the Joint Commission's previous report. An important question still to be addressed was whether, or in what ways, post-biblical witness to revelation could be normative for the Church. Henn noted the lack of any direct reference in *The Word of Life* to the precise means by which revelation was transmitted from one generation to the next.[34]

In fact, the Joint Commission had already anticipated the need to consider the various ways in which the apostolic tradition is transmitted in the Church. In the seventh series of conversations, the commission took as its theme the subject of teaching authority in the Church.

Speaking the Truth in Love: Teaching Authority among Catholics and Methodists (Brighton, 2001)

The Brighton report addresses the specific question of 'how the faith which comes from the apostles is transmitted from generation to generation in such a way that all the faithful continue to adhere to the revelation that has come in Christ Jesus' (Preface). The focus of the report is the teaching ministry in the Church, which is responsible for transmitting the faith and ensuring fidelity to what Christians believe. In *Speaking the Truth in Love* the Joint Commission contributed one more piece to a 'mosaic' that had been slowly developed in earlier reports, illustrating the various interlocking elements that keep the Church as a faithful bearer of revelation to successive generations (Preface).

The Joint Commission turned to Ephesians 4.1–16 for guidance in its efforts to resolve doctrinal differences between Methodists and Roman Catholics over teaching authority in the Church (1). This passage suggests that unity in the Church has seven aspects: 'There is one body and one Spirit, just as you were called to the one hope of your calling, one Lord, one faith, one baptism, one God and Father of all, who is above all and through all and in all' (Ephesians 4.6). The purpose of the teaching office is to promote 'unity in faith and in the knowledge of God' (Ephesians 4.12–14). The apostle urges Christians to speak the truth in love (Ephesians 4.15). Truth and love are integral to each other because Christ incarnates both the love and the truth of God.

Speaking the Truth in Love is in two parts. The first part presents systematically what Methodists and Roman Catholics agree together about teaching authority, noting areas of divergence and posing questions each would wish to put to the other. Three substantial themes are introduced and developed: 'The Church as Communion in Love and Truth' (7–28), 'God's Prophetic Community Anointed with the Holy Spirit' (29–46), and 'Means of Grace, Servants of Christ and his Church' (48–84). The doctrine of the Holy Spirit is the common theme that links these sections, thus providing an overarching theological framework.

If the Church is a communion in love and truth, it is the Holy Spirit who preserves the truth of the Gospel in the form of Christian teaching (20). Methodists and Roman Catholics invoke the power of the Holy Spirit and trust in the Spirit's unfailing grace, albeit in different ways. For Roman Catholics, the locus of teaching authority is the episcopal charism of unfailing truth and faith, by virtue of which the Gospel is proclaimed indefectibly in spite of the sins and shortcomings of individuals. Occasionally, in carefully defined circumstances, a doctrine may be proclaimed infallibly by a council of bishops, or by the Bishop of Rome in his capacity as universal primate.

Methodists have sought assurance in the guidance of the Holy Spirit through godly individuals like John Wesley and by such providential means as the early councils, the Reformation and Methodist Conferences (21). However, assurance of the Holy Spirit's guidance falls short of a guarantee that Church teaching is free from error. Methodists affirm the Scriptures as containing all things necessary to salvation, whereas Roman Catholics maintain that further development of doctrine occurs through conciliar teaching and pronouncements made by the Bishop of Rome (22).

Methodists and Roman Catholics are united in the conviction that the Holy Spirit will lead Christians into all truth (29). The task of discerning the truth belongs to the whole people of God, lay and ordained, under the leadership of the Spirit. The Brighton report quotes from the ARCIC statement, *The Gift of Authority*: 'The Holy Spirit works through all members of the community, using the gifts he gives to each for the good of all' (33).[35] The Church is entirely dependent upon the Holy Spirit for its 'Abiding in the Truth' (36–8) and for its being 'Preserved in the Truth' (39–42). There should be no conflict between lay and ordained in the discernment of truth because they are 'Co-Workers in the Truth' (43–5). God works through individuals and communities, who are empowered by grace as signs and instruments of his presence and action (49). Among these instruments are authoritative agents of discerning and proclaiming the truth of the Gospel, who are the servants of communion in love and truth (51). For Roman Catholics, the bishops in union with the pope are empowered to teach authoritatively. In Methodism, the Conference has final authority for the formulation and interpretation of doctrine, though 'Methodists agree that God uses means of grace which are trustworthy channels' (53).

It is in identifying whether or how a particular means of grace is 'guaranteed' or 'trustworthy' that clear differences emerge. 'Catholics ask Methodists how and by what criteria they verify that a particular means is a trustworthy channel of God's grace. Methodists ask Catholics whether the idea of the guaranteed quality of a sacrament takes full account of the weakness, limitations and sinfulness of the human beings called to be agents of God's grace' (61). Despite various joint affirmations about 'Ordained Ministry' (63–8), important questions remain:

> Catholics ask Methodists whether they might not use sacramental language, such as has been used of the Church itself, of ordained ministry in the Church, and of its authoritative discernment of the truth of the Gospel. Methodists ask Catholics why, given human weakness and fallibility, they understand ordained ministry not only as a sign but also as a guarantee of the active presence of Christ by the power of the Holy Spirit, especially in particular acts of authoritative discernment and proclamation. These questions lie at the heart of ecumenical dialogue between our two communions (68).

In Methodism authoritative discernment of the Gospel rests finally with the Conference, even where Methodists have adopted an episcopal form of ministry in the office of bishop (74). For Roman Catholics, authoritative discernment is entrusted to the college of bishops united with the pope (75). This exposes a further difference concerning the role of lay people in the respective churches. In Methodist Conferences lay people sit in significant numbers with equal rights of participation and decision-making (78). Methodists ask Roman Catholics why lay people could not be involved formally in the process of authoritative discernment in the Roman Catholic Church (79). Roman Catholics ask Methodists why they cannot distinguish the role of the ordained ministry where authoritative discernment is concerned (80).

The second part of *Speaking the Truth in Love* describes the contrasting means by which Methodists and Roman Catholics authoritatively discern the Gospel. In Methodism the agents of discernment have been shaped by the historical origins of the movement in the eighteenth century (86). Methodists have mostly inherited the doctrines and order of the Catholic Church as mediated through the English Reformation and the Church of England. Originally, Methodism was a holiness movement aimed at proclaiming salvation to those with nominal religious adherence. Wesley's preaching and teaching focused on the doctrine of salvation as the best way to accomplish his mission of spreading 'Scriptural holiness'. The most authoritative agent of discernment in Methodism has always been the Conference (94–8).

In the early years of Methodism, the Conference of preachers exercised the functions of determining doctrine, exercising discipline and stationing the preachers, subject to final approval from John Wesley (91). Wesley counted 'Christian conference' among the prudential means of grace, a trustworthy channel used by God to mould the lives of God's people (94). After Wesley died, the Conference became the 'organising centre of ecclesial life' with final authority over doctrine (96). This is true even in North America where Wesley provided for a general superintendency, which quickly became an episcopate, albeit outside the historic succession. Eventually, lay people were admitted to membership of the Conference.

Roman Catholics recognise two related agents of discernment, 'Bishops' (101–10) and 'The Bishop of Rome' (111–16). The college of bishops continues the care of the apostles for all the churches. In the teaching of *Dei Verbum*, 'The task of authentic interpretation of God's Word in Scripture and Tradition has been entrusted only to the Church's living teaching office, whose authority is exercised in the name of Jesus Christ' (102).[36] Entrusted with this special service, bishops are not above God's Word, but instead serve it (103). As signs and instruments of Christ, who is head and shepherd of the Church, bishops share in the authority by which Christ builds up, teaches and sanctifies his Body (105). Bishops teach with authority in their churches through various means, including pastoral letters and homilies. However, 'The teaching of any individual bishop in itself is not guaranteed to be preserved from error by the Holy Spirit, and there have been and can be bishops whose teaching and way of life are contrary to the Gospel entrusted to them' (106). Bishops teach authoritatively only when united in communion with other bishops in the apostolic succession (108).

The college of bishops, in communion with the Bishop of Rome, is the final authority in the Roman Catholic Church. 'When bishops exercise their supreme teaching authority, the Holy Spirit guides and protects their discerning and proclaiming of the truth of the Gospel' (109). This charism from the Lord guarantees the Church's faithfulness to the Word of God, but it does not reveal new doctrines. When the bishops in communion with the Bishop of Rome solemnly define a doctrine relating to faith or morals, the Holy Spirit preserves them from error (110). This is what Roman Catholics mean by 'infallibility'. Although doctrine defined in this way is preserved from error, this does not mean that the form in which the doctrine is stated cannot be improved.

The second agent of discernment is the Bishop of Rome, who is head of the college of bishops and the focus of communion in the universal Church (111). The pope's ministry to his fellow bishops and their churches is a pastoral service to the Church's unity in love and truth (113). The universal primacy of the Bishop of Rome is exercised not to undermine the bishops but to support and sustain them in their ministry (113). The pope's teaching authority is an important aspect of his universal primacy (114). To serve the apostolicity and catholicity of the Church, the pope exercises, when necessary, his charism of infallibly proclaiming true doctrine. He does so as head of the college of bishops in whom the charism of infallibility is individually present. This is not to claim divine authority for everything the pope and bishops say (116). Roman Catholics consider their understanding of infallibility to be consistent with the belief that all forms of ministry in the Church derive from, and totally depend upon, divine grace.

In their different ways 'Both Methodists and Catholics trust the unfailing presence and grace of the Holy Spirit to preserve them in faithfulness and to protect the truth of the Gospel they preach and teach' (117). However, there can be no disguising the divergence over teaching authority. In particular, there remains a 'fundamental difference in the understanding of the degree to which one can attribute a guaranteed reliability to any human instrumentality exercising a ministry of teaching within the Church, even given the continuing presence of the Holy Spirit' (120). It is significant that Methodists and Roman Catholics interpret differently the role of the laity in relation to the ordained ministry in authoritative teaching. The relationship between ordination, authoritative teaching and the sure guidance of the Holy Spirit is therefore a topic for further discussion (120).

In his response to *Speaking the Truth in Love*, the official Vatican commentator, Ralph Del Colle, praised the Joint Commission for its 'delicate theological plodding (in the best sense)' over many years and for its achievement in having produced the Brighton report.[372] To assist the commission in its future work, Del Colle identified six areas for closer investigation.

First of all, greater awareness of the relationship between doctrine and

164

Church life would enhance the possibilities for further convergence. The Methodist and Roman Catholic traditions are different precisely because their histories involve a different reception of the apostolic tradition in diverse circumstances and cultural settings. For instance, the emergence of the Methodist Conference was Wesley's response to the urgent task of mission and ministerial formation. Del Colle observed a strong similarity between the Methodist Conference and a general chapter or congregation of a Roman Catholic religious order. In both cases, their purpose is to discern the apostolic work of the community and formulate the re-reception of its founding charism.

The second area for exploration is the way Methodists formulate their official teaching. When Methodists refer to their 'doctrinal standards' what exactly do they mean? What is the status of these doctrinal standards in Methodism and how are they used by Conference in the authoritative discernment of the Gospel? Third, the Brighton report's emphasis on the Holy Spirit provides future conversations with a theological framework for resolving the remaining doctrinal differences between Methodists and Roman Catholics concerning teaching authority in the Church. For Del Colle, the task of discerning and affirming the presence and activity of the Holy Spirit in both communities is a critical aspect of the Joint Commission's future work. The method of posing reciprocal questions in the Brighton report is a fourth area with the potential to assist the Joint Commission. This kind of mutual questioning will help clarify the key issues of faith and doctrine in a constructive and non-threatening way.

Ordination is a fifth area for further investigation. *Speaking the Truth in Love* identifies ordination as a major area of disagreement between Methodists and Roman Catholics. Del Colle urged the Joint Commission to continue its study of ordination and encouraged both sides to press their questions to the other. Of course, the Brighton report was not the first occasion that the Joint Commission had highlighted differences between Methodists and Roman Catholics in this area. However, the commission has consistently taken the view that intractable differences concerning the doctrine of ordination are more likely to be resolved by an oblique approach than by tackling the issues head-on. The Joint Commission remains committed to finding a suitable theological framework in which to address remaining differences over the doctrine of ordination.

Lastly, Del Colle raised the question of whether the corporate over-sight exercised by a Methodist Conference might in some sense be equivalent to the individual oversight exercised by Roman Catholic bishops. If the Church is a sacrament of the Trinity, then it is reasonable to suppose that the doctrine of the Trinity has something to tell us about the structure of the Church and its ministry. It has become fashionable in ecumenical circles to draw parallels between the Trinity and the Church, and there may be some merit in Del Colle's suggestion. However, envisaging just how the structure of ministry in the Church could correspond to the Trinity is far from straightforward. After all, the doctrine of the Trinity states certain rules governing the way in which Christians may appropriately refer to the divine persons, their mutual relations and missions. Applying those same rules to the life of the Church assumes an intimate correspondence between the Church and the Trinity which may not bear close theological inspection. On the whole, it is difficult to imagine how grammatical rules about the divine persons could meaningfully be applied to ecclesial relations. At the same time, the inner life of the Trinity remains a mystery to which the Church on earth has no access. For these reasons, appealing to the Trinity as a model for understanding the Church and the exercise of ministry remains highly problematic.

In its conclusion to *The Word of Life*, the Joint Commission noted that the international Methodist–Roman Catholic dialogue had already passed through two stages. The first stage was a process of mutual acquaintance and preliminary responses to doctrinal and ethical matters of shared interest. The Denver and Dublin reports represent the out-come from this preliminary phase. The second stage involved sketching broad theological perspectives in which it may eventually become possible to resolve the doctrinal and structural differences that continue to divide Methodists and Roman Catholics.[38] Thirty years after the dialogue first started, the Joint Commission believed the time had come to concentrate on some of the more detailed questions to emerge from earlier conversations. *Speaking the Truth in Love* was the first report to emerge from this third stage of dialogue.

Inevitably, the speed of progress has slowed markedly since the early conversations. As long ago as 1971, the Joint Commission noted: 'Further ecumenical progress becomes harder, not easier, because it cannot be a mere linear progress in the negotiating of differences.'[39] Thirty years later, the truth of this observation is readily apparent. It is unrealistic therefore to expect rapid progress or a sudden breakthrough in the near future. However, there is little sign of the dialogue running into the sand and no shortage of topics to occupy the Joint Commission profitably for many years to come. Nor is there any lack of enthusiasm among the membership of the commission, which is renewed at the end of each five-year period. 'Delicate theological plodding' remains an appropriate description of the painstaking work undertaken by the Joint Commission.

What has the Joint Commission achieved since 1967? Certainly, its reports demonstrate a degree of doctrinal convergence and agreement which would have astonished an earlier generation. Given the history of controversy between Methodists and Roman Catholics, this is a remarkable achievement. Of course, none of this would have been possible if the Second Vatican Council had not paved the way for Roman Catholics to engage in theological dialogue with other Christians. Beyond this general observation, however, a more thorough assessment of the dialogue's achievement is hampered by its indifferent reception among Methodists and Roman Catholics at every level of church life. This is a salutary reminder that there are limits to what a theological dialogue can achieve on its own. The challenge now for both churches is to find ways of encouraging local congregations to engage in their own dialogue, perhaps using some of the resources produced by the Joint Commission. Only then will the international dialogue become fully assimilated into the life of the churches.

Despite the continuing problems with reception, the international Methodist–Roman Catholic dialogue is a well-established and respected bilateral conversation, in its own way as productive as ARCIC. The seven reports produced so far by the Joint Commission constitute a rich source of material for the ecumenical study of the Church. The next report, due in 2006, will mark the fortieth anniversary of the start of the international dialogue between Methodists and Roman Catholics. For this current round of dialogue, the Methodist co-chair of the Joint Commission, Geoffrey Wainwright, suggested there were 'three fairly obvious topics' for discussion:

The most general would be an examination of the ecclesial claims each

167

partner makes for itself and, in relation to those, the way in which each views the other. The second possibility would be the question of the sacramentality of the ordained ministry and its role in the trans-mission of the Gospel and the maintenance of the faith as well as in the governance of the Church. The most particular possibility would be a consideration of the universal ministry of unity in the service of truth and love offered by the see of Rome. All three issues are mutually interlocking, and one might in fact consider the third as the way into the second and finally into the first.[40]

In the event, the Joint Commission chose the first of these options as the subject for discussion and report in 2006. At the present time, members of the commission 'continue their work towards a report on how Methodists and Catholics understand the Church and the extent to which they can recognise the one Church of Jesus Christ in each other'.[41]

In November 2003 Cardinal Walter Kasper, President of the Ponti-fical Council for Promoting Christian Unity, offered his personal assess-ment of what the international Methodist–Roman Catholic dialogue had achieved since 1967. It is a fitting tribute to the Joint Commission.

Thanks principally to the work of the International Commission, we have advanced significantly in our relations over the past four decades. While we both acknowledge that there are still important ecclesiological issues separating us, the gap between us is gradually being bridged. We have come to know and understand each other better; we have become friends, and recognise each other as brothers and sisters in Christ. Our goal, which will be achieved only by the grace of the Holy Spirit, is nothing less than full visible unity in faith, mission and sacramental life.[42]

5

National Methodist–Roman Catholic Dialogues

The impact of the Second Vatican Council on ecumenical relations was not confined to the setting up of international dialogues involving the Roman Catholic Church and various world communions. The *Directory for the Application of the Decisions of the Second Ecumenical Council of the Vatican concerning Ecumenical Matters* (1967/70) made a number of provisions to facilitate closer relations locally between Roman Catholics and other Christians. Bishops' Conferences and dioceses were encouraged to establish ecumenical commissions for their territory, and various national dialogues were initiated. Clergy were discouraged from conditionally baptising members of other churches who now wished to join the Roman Catholic Church. Approval was given to 'spiritual ecumenism' such as joint prayer for unity, and common worship with Protestants was allowed in appropriate circumstances. In cases of 'urgent need' priests were permitted to give the sacraments to members of Protestant churches, provided certain conditions were fulfilled, but Roman Catholics could not receive from Protestant churches sacraments that the Roman Catholic Church did not consider valid. Less tangibly, the Council created a new climate of openness in the Roman Catholic Church, which met a ready response from other Christians, who sensed the dawn of a new era of ecumenism. In the heady atmosphere immediately following the Council, anything seemed possible.

In this chapter we investigate the national bilateral conversations that have taken place between Methodists and Roman Catholics as a result of the Second Vatican Council. There are four such dialogues (in Great Britain, the United States, Australia and New Zealand), each with its own distinctive character and style, reflecting the diverse ecclesial and cultural contexts even among the English-speaking nations. Inevitably, some of the ground covered in the national conversations is familiar from the international dialogue. However, by responding to issues of local significance, the national conversations have extended Methodist–Roman Catholic dialogue into new areas.

Great Britain

On 2 December 1967 a group of Methodists and Roman Catholics met in Westminster Cathedral at the invitation of Cardinal Heenan to explore the possibility of developing closer relations between the two churches. Out of this initial consultation an unofficial steering committee was formed, which met for the first time in March 1968, its objective to develop mutual understanding through joint study by Methodists and Roman Catholics in England. In due course, the steering committee published a convergence statement, *Christian Belief: A Catholic/Methodist Statement* (1970).

To avoid the inevitable delay while it was vetted, *Christian Belief* was released without prior approval from the respective church authorities. With the benefit of hindsight, official endorsement by the Methodist Conference and the Catholic Episcopal Conference would almost certainly have encouraged wider discussion of the convergence statement among Methodists and Roman Catholics. As it was, *Christian Belief* failed to make much impact in either church. By today's standards the content is unexceptional, though at the time it must have appeared groundbreaking. The emphasis throughout was on those aspects of Christian faith and life which Methodists and Roman Catholics hold in common.

In November 1971 the steering committee, encouraged by the results of its early meetings, asked the Catholic Episcopal Conference and the Methodist Conference to appoint an official committee to progress the conversations on a more formal basis. Both Conferences agreed, and the English Methodist–Roman Catholic Committee met for the first time on 13 October 1972.[1] In 1990 the committee became the British Methodist–Roman Catholic Committee through the addition of representatives appointed by the Methodist Synod in Scotland and the Catholic Bishops' Conference of Scotland.

Almost the first task of the English Methodist–Roman Catholic

170

Committee was to assist the Joint Commission with its impossibly long agenda. The ARCIC agreed statements had just then begun to appear, and any report from the international Methodist–Roman Catholic dialogue would have to take these into account. At the request of the Joint Commission, the English committee set about examining the ARCIC statement on eucharistic doctrine (Windsor, 1971) and preparing an equivalent document *Roman Catholic/Methodist Statement on the Eucharist* (1974). Again, following publication of the ARCIC statement on ministry (Canterbury, 1973), the English committee prepared an equivalent document *Roman Catholic/Methodist Statement on Ministry* (1975). With few amendments, the Joint Commission later incorporated these documents into the Dublin report (1976).[2]

As part of its role, to increase mutual understanding between Methodists and Roman Catholics, the dialogue in Britain has endeavoured to make the work of the Joint Commission more widely known.[3] At the same time, the British dialogue has taken several initiatives of its own to complement the international conversations. In an early venture, two members of the English committee, Peter Stephens (Methodist) and John Todd (Roman Catholic) produced an introductory pamphlet, *Our Churches* (1978), to encourage local study groups. Over the years, several background papers prepared for the committee have been published to stimulate discussion among Methodists and Roman Catholics.[4]

In 1978 the committee submitted a brief report to its sponsors summarising what had been achieved in the first ten years of dialogue.[5] The report affirmed the future of Methodist–Roman Catholic conversations in England and defined their purpose as being 'to tackle major theological issues, always with awareness of the practical context and consequences of such study'. Without waiting for a formal report from the dialogue, the Methodist Conference had already resolved in 1975 'to explore the conditions on which communion might be established between the Methodist Church and the Roman Catholic Church'.[6] While this was premature, at least it shows how rapidly relations between Methodists and Roman Catholics in Britain had improved as a result of the Second Vatican Council.

A notable feature of the dialogue in Britain has been the strong emphasis given to discussing aspects of doctrine. Following on from its statements on the Eucharist and ministry, the English Methodist–Roman Catholic Committee turned its attention to the subject of authority. In a remarkably short period of time, these conversations yielded an *Authority Statement of the English Roman Catholic/Methodist Committee* (1978), which took into account *An Agreed Statement on Authority in the Church* (Venice, 1976) produced by ARCIC.[7] The English *Authority Statement* is in five sections: 'Agreed Principles'; 'Authority in the Roman Catholic Church'; 'Authority in Methodism'; 'Remaining Disagreement'; and 'A Future Pattern of Ministry'.

Among the agreed principles in the English *Authority Statement* was the belief that supreme authority belongs to Jesus Christ, who is the perfect revelation of the Father (1). The Scriptures are a 'permanent norm' for the Church, but they need to be interpreted to the people of God in every age and place (3). Thus a 'living voice' is required to proclaim the Gospel with authenticity. This living voice is in fact the voice of the whole Church, to which Jesus promised his presence and protection as well as the guidance of the Spirit of truth (4). Since God is the source of all authority, the Church is required to accept and exercise it (5).

The 'Remaining Disagreement' concerns the possibility of error in the Church. Roman Catholics believe that, under certain circumstances, the Church can make statements relating to fundamental aspects of faith and life which are free from error. Methodists, however, believe that even the most authoritative statements on such matters are not necessarily exempt from error. In view of the 'serious disagreement' between Methodists and Roman Catholics over the doctrine of infallibility, the English *Authority Statement* proposed the concept of indefectibility as a theological framework in which to establish convergence. The statement poses two rhetorical questions: 'To what extent did Christ's promise to his Church concern only ultimate freedom from failure or desertion of his message, and to what extent did it imply freedom from temporary error or failure to bring his message to the world (29)?'

In developing a future pattern of ministry in a united Church, 'Methodists might be guided by Catholics to a greater trust in God's unfailing promises for the Church of Christ' (34). On their part, 'Catholics might be led by Methodists to a greater awareness of the fallibility of the human response to the divine promise and guidance' (35). Altogether, the English *Authority Statement* sets out a bold vision for the exercise of authority in a future united Church, which goes further than any of the reports produced by the international dialogue. Thus 'A bishop ordained to the task in the historic succession would exercise the functions of teaching, leadership and pastoral care in the service of the unity of the various primary communities in a particular area' (36). The universal primacy of the Bishop of Rome would be exercised through his active presidency of a general council of the Church.

In the light of the substantial obstacles to be overcome, the vision for the exercise of authority contained in the English *Authority Statement* was precipitate in 1978, and even 25 years later it remains beyond the horizon of the international dialogue. In this instance, the more cautious approach adopted by the Joint Commission may yet prove to be the most realistic means of achieving a secure agreement on the nature and exercise of authority in the Church. Still, the English dialogue had set out a bold scheme that challenged Methodists and Roman Catholics to reassess their approach to authority in the Church.

Between 1983 and 1991 the English Methodist–Roman Catholic Committee devoted considerable time and energy to producing a convergence statement on justification, which subject has long been a source of dispute between Roman Catholics and Protestants. Responding to the Roman Catholic emphasis on the contribution of meritorious works towards salvation, the Reformers had insisted that justification was 'by faith alone' (*sola fide*). As we saw in Chapter 1, although Wesley agreed with Luther that sinners were saved by grace through faith, his teaching on salvation was closer to Roman Catholic doctrine than to the classical Reformers. In the light of this and the fact that the Joint Commission had mentioned justification in its Honolulu report without reference to any fundamental disagreement between Methodists and Roman Catholics, the English committee felt confident of being able to produce an agreed statement on the doctrine of justification.

Justification: A Consensus Statement was first published in 1988.[8] In response to criticism from some quarters of Methodism, the final paragraphs on purgatory, indulgences and holiness were later revised and expanded, and the whole document was reissued in 1991.[9] The consensus statement attributes historical clashes over the doctrine of justification to mutual misunderstanding and different usage by Roman Catholics and Protestants. Whereas justification was an important concept in the theology of the Reformers, it was much less significant for

Roman Catholics, who tended to use the term in a broad sense to refer to the whole process of salvation. What Protestants called justification, Roman Catholics more naturally thought of as forgiveness, thereby providing ample scope for confusion and disagreement.

To recap, the Reformers interpreted justification in terms of God's gratuitous pardon based on the *imputation* of Christ's righteousness and its benefits to believers. Imputation is a term borrowed from the realm of accountancy, where it refers to the transfer of credit or debit from one account to another. In this case grace was imputed to the individual account of sinners to cancel out their sin. The idea that grace was 'imputed' to believers had the twofold advantage of emphasising the divine sovereignty and initiative in redemption, while simultaneously making the point that works of piety did not acquire any credit value towards salvation. The Reformers abhorred the heresy known as Pelagianism, which maintained that human beings contributed towards their salvation through meritorious works. From a Protestant perspective, Roman Catholic teaching on the contribution of works of piety towards final salvation came perilously close to Pelagianism. On the contrary, insisted the Council of Trent, the Holy Spirit *imparted* sanctifying grace to believers, and individual works of piety were the essential bulwark against antinomianism or moral anarchy. Over time, the disagreement between Roman Catholics and Protestants concerning justification came to be focused on whether grace was *imparted* or *imputed* to sinners.

In fact, a close reading of the Council of Trent and the Reformers suggested that the two sides were not as far apart as they supposed, though the hostile climate of the Reformation disputes made constructive theological dialogue all but impossible. The *Consensus Statement* concludes that, 'difference in usage with regard to terms like justification and sanctification does not appear to indicate any real difference in overall belief'.[10] Roman Catholics and Protestants both accepted the priority of God's grace in human salvation. Although Protestants focused on justification and Roman Catholics emphasised sanctification, these ideas belonged together 'as two sides of one coin'.[11] Typically, Wesley combined both emphases. Accepting Luther's teaching on justification by faith alone, he nevertheless urged the importance of personal sanctification and works of piety.

Justification: A Consensus Statement identifies three Roman Catholic doctrines as requiring further study – merit, purgatory and indulgences. Taking these in turn, first the doctrine of merit draws on various biblical passages that imply a reward for virtuous human action.[12] The Council of Trent taught that, although works could not earn the grace of justification, those already in a state of grace who performed works of piety merited the award of additional grace. Moreover, a surplus of merit could be applied to others for the reduction of their penitential disciplines.

Protestants have generally attacked the doctrine of merit as an inappropriate idea in the Christian understanding of salvation, because it suggests a selfish incentive to moral behaviour, effectively creating a scheme of salvation by works. To the Protestant way of thinking, works of piety naturally follow justification, either as the result of spontaneous love or from the will to obey God. Roman Catholics, on the other hand, have defended the doctrine of merit as an incentive to good behaviour among weak human beings, the only alternative being to reject the moral law (antinomianism). They argue that the doctrine of merit does not deny the priority of God's grace. Recognising that all human merit rests ultimately on divine grace, St Augustine declared, 'When God crowns our merits, he crowns his own gifts.'[13] Even so, in their pursuit of a holy life, Christians can easily forget such a fine theological distinction. The question remains whether the concept of merit is an appropriate element of the doctrine of salvation, because it appears to offer an incentive to good behaviour.

The doctrine of purgatory is another contentious subject between Protestants and Roman Catholics. For Roman Catholics, the doctrine of purgatory represents the logical outcome of a considered theological reflection on the acute observation that most Christians appear not to have reached the point of entire sanctification before they die. The doctrine of purgatory allows Christians to believe that the process of sanctification is completed after death, if only for those who have died in the faith of Jesus Christ. Whereas Methodists envisage a more or less instantaneous transformation at death, the doctrine of purgatory postulates a searching post-mortem process in which the human soul is completely purged of all sin and any residual consequences before it can enter into the beatific vision of God. Many Roman Catholic spiritual writers have employed colourful images to depict this interim state, even though the Council of Trent excluded categories of time and place in the doctrine of purgatory. Whereas Methodists are generally reluctant to speculate about an idea that has very little, if any, grounding in Scripture, Roman Catholics argue that the doctrine of purgatory belongs within the hierarchy of truths as a sound deduction from the doctrine of justification.

A corollary of the doctrine of purgatory is the belief that the prayers of those who are still alive can assist the process of post-mortem sanctification. Over the centuries praying for the faithful departed has developed into a variety of practices centred on the Eucharist. However, the Reformers devoted considerable energy to challenging such practices, as a result of which prayer for the faithful departed ceased entirely in Protestant traditions. Interestingly, the early years of the twentieth century witnessed a revival of interest among Protestants in prayer for the departed. During the First World War, the mass slaughter on the Western Front, coupled with the frequently long delay in receiving news of soldiers killed in action, presented an urgent and widespread pastoral need on the home front for some form of prayer for the departed.

As the twentieth century progressed, official Methodist liturgies increasingly made provision for some form of prayer for the faithful departed, indicating a wider acceptance of this practice among Methodists.[14] Whereas the *Book of Offices* (1936) made no provision for prayers for the departed, the *Methodist Service Book* (1975) contained an optional general intercession for the faithful departed. More recently, the *Methodist Worship Book* (1999) provides various optional prayers for the faithful departed in the context of the Funeral Service.

Indulgences were another means available in the medieval Church for reducing the pains of purgatory. In the early Church strict penances in the form of temporal punishments were imposed on Christians who fell into serious sin. For a variety of reasons, including the prospect of imminent death, the baptised often sought to be excused or indulged all or part of their penance so as to be fully reconciled to the Church. By the fifteenth century the principle had been extended to include the sale of indulgences to aid those in purgatory. To avoid the appearance of moral laxity, church authorities appealed to the treasury of merit to assist the individual sinner. Despite this theoretical safeguard, the granting of indulgences was highly susceptible to misunderstanding and abuse. The ignorant easily imagined that they were purchasing forgiveness for themselves or their loved ones. As the medieval proverb put it, 'The moment the money tinkles in the collecting box, a soul flies out of purgatory.'[15] Geoffrey Chaucer's *Canterbury Tales* satirises the selling of indulgences by professional pardoners.

Luther attacked the abuse of selling indulgences in his *Ninety-Five Theses* (1517), though he conceded that if these had been granted according to the pope's intention, then there would have been no doubt about their validity (Thesis 91). Nevertheless, Luther raised such deep questions about the meaning and value of penance as to make it virtually impossible for the practice of indulgences to continue in any branch of Protestantism. It hardly need be added that, 'Indulgences do not play any part in Methodist teaching or practice.'[16] Nowadays the practice of indulgences in the Roman Catholic Church continues 'as a form of prayer to help the sinner in the Church make amends for the damage caused by personal sin'.[17] However, their vastly diminished use suggests a declining interest in indulgences as a means of assisting either the living or the dead. Overall, there has been little ecumenical progress in evaluating and understanding the practice of indulgences.

Justification: A Consensus Statement concludes that Methodists and Roman Catholics agree that perfect holiness is necessary before a person can see God face to face. In the light of the fierce controversy between Protestants and Roman Catholics over the doctrine of purgatory, A. Raymond George believed that the *Consensus Statement* had come up with a reconciling formula: 'When a person has reached in this life a measure of holiness which falls short of perfection, then it is believed that this perfection is conferred in the transition from this life to eternal life. Granted such basic agreement, some variety of attitudes and practices may be tolerated in a united Church.'[18] For many Methodists, however, the doctrines of purgatory and indulgences still raise strong feelings. Whether Methodists will learn to tolerate these Roman Catholic doctrines remains to be seen.

In 1992 the British Methodist—Roman Catholic Committee produced a short discussion paper: *Can the Roman Catholic and Methodist Churches be Reconciled?*[19] Taking account of the eventual goal of full communion in faith, mission and sacramental life, which was established in the Nairobi report, the paper identifies six essential components of unity between Methodists and Roman Catholics: (1) communion in the apostolic faith; (2) communion in sacramental life; (3) a mutually recognised ministry; (4) communion with a universal primate as the focus of unity; (5) structures of conciliar relations and common decision-making; and (6) common witness and service in the world. At present, there is 'real but imperfect communion' between Methodists and Roman Catholics, based on faith in the Holy Trinity, a common baptism, the Holy Scriptures, the historic creeds, a shared appropriation of the western spiritual tradition and the living tradition of worship, and a similar concern for holiness and social righteousness.

In 1992 the British Methodist Conference commended the discussion paper for study among the Methodist people, inviting responses from districts, circuits and individuals within two years. After a disappointing number of submissions, the deadline was extended by a further two years to encourage more responses. When these were finally analysed in 1996 reactions to the discussion paper were mixed.[20] For some Methodists the existence of a bilateral dialogue with the Roman Catholic Church came as a complete surprise. Others welcomed the goal of full communion in faith, mission and sacramental life, and spoke of a strong desire for closer relations between Methodists and Roman Catholics. Among the positive responses, most favoured 'unity in diversity' or 'reconciled diversity' as the best model for future relations between Methodists and Roman Catholics. A number of replies indicated a willingness to explore the papacy as the focus of Christian unity. Others revealed that some Methodists continue to harbour deep suspicions about Roman Catholicism.

The submissions in response to the discussion paper also revealed a great deal of confusion among Methodists about the Eucharist and Methodist doctrine relating to the sacrifice of Christ and the real presence. Informed responses identified the Eucharist, ministry and the papacy as subjects that continue to divide Methodists and Roman Catholics. A number of responses pointed out that the issues raised in the discussion paper were of no great interest to local churches. A few expressed concern for the experience of inter-church families. Probably the most positive response came from the West Yorkshire District, which suggested that it is not a question of whether Methodists and Roman Catholics *can* be reconciled – they *must* be.[21]

With hindsight, the failure of the discussion paper to attract widespread interest in British Methodism was due to a number of factors. Probably the most decisive was the Conference decision to *invite* submissions. Had the Conference *directed* districts and circuits to respond to a specific resolution, the discussion paper would have had far greater impact. At the same time, the failure of past ecumenical ventures involving the Methodist Church had undoubtedly caused Methodists to be wary of investing significant resources of time and energy in inter-church relations at a national level. Furthermore, for historical reasons, many Methodists do not consider Roman Catholics to be their most obvious choice of dialogue partner. Another factor may have been the lack of appropriate study material for local groups.

To be fair, it would have been unrealistic to expect the Conference in 1992 to take decisive action over Methodist—Roman Catholic relations when there were more immediate priorities on the horizon, including the human sexuality debate at the Conference in 1993. As an exercise in testing the water, *Can the Roman Catholic and Methodist Churches be Reconciled?* was modestly successful. That the Methodist Conference could receive such a report and commend it for study was a further indication of the substantial progress in relations between Methodists and Roman Catholics in Britain since the Second Vatican Council. The most significant achievement of *Can the Roman Catholic and Methodist Churches be Reconciled?* was to demonstrate that dialogue between Methodists and Roman Catholics no longer generated the heated controversy of past years.

Mary, the Mother of Jesus, has long occupied a unique place in the spiritual affections of Roman Catholics, who attribute to her various titles of honour, including Blessed Virgin Mary, Our Lady, and Queen of Heaven. In 1854 Pope Pius IX defined the doctrine of the Immaculate Conception, which states that 'from the first moment of her conception the Blessed Virgin Mary was, by the singular grace and privilege of Almighty God, and in view of the merits of Jesus Christ, Saviour of mankind, kept free from all stain of original sin'.[22] Biblical support has been found in Genesis 3.15 and Luke 1.28. Patristic testimony occurs in Justin Martyr and Irenaeus, who regarded Mary as the 'new Eve', just as Christ was the 'new Adam'. Belief in the Immaculate Conception of Mary has had a long and chequered history in the Church.

In another major development in Marian doctrine, Pius XII in 1950 infallibly defined the doctrine of the Assumption of the Blessed Virgin Mary, following a long process of consultation within the Roman

Catholic Church over a period of many years. According to the doctrine of the Assumption, having completed her earthly life, Mary was in body and soul assumed into heavenly glory. However, Protestants point out that there is no witness to this effect in Scripture, and the patristic testimony begins only in the sixth century.[23]

The Marian doctrines have come under particularly heavy fire from Protestants. As Gordon Wakefield put it, 'The whole problem for Protestants is the extent to which the cherished devotions of large numbers of Christians, unsupported by the unequivocal testimony of Scripture, should be given dogmatic status.'[24] Protestants have been deeply suspicious of Roman Catholic devotion to Mary, fearing it undermines the unique mediating role of Christ in salvation history. John Wesley scornfully remarked: 'To the Virgin Mary they pray in these words: "O Mother of God, O Queen of heaven, command thy Son to have mercy upon us!" . . . It is gross, open palpable idolatry, such as can neither be denied nor excused; and tends directly to destroy the love of God, which is indeed the first and great commandment.'[25] Characteristically, he was equally scathing of Protestant idolatry: 'They worship the picture of the Queen of Heaven; you the picture of the Queen or King of England.'[26] Interestingly, although he had little time for Marian devotion, Wesley held the Marian articles of the creed in high regard and included belief in the Virgin birth and the perpetual virginity of Mary among the articles of the Protestant faith.[27]

In company with other Protestants, Methodists have attached no special significance to Mary, beyond that of any other believer redeemed by Christ. Insofar as Methodists have honoured the mother of Jesus, it is as a witness to his humanity and not for her role in the drama of redemption. In recent years Methodists have generally maintained a puzzled silence about Roman Catholic devotion to Mary, though there has been criticism of the Marian doctrines in some quarters of Methodism. Neville Ward described the silence in Methodism about Mary as 'positively deafening', though he detected signs of 'a shy but nervous interest in her mysterious being'.[28] To his way of thinking, all Christians must love Mary because they love her son. However, Methodists 'fear being trapped by certain forms of Marian devotion which we suspect come dangerously near to superstition or suggest processes of psychological compensation which we want to question'.[29]

In a pioneering Methodist essay on Mary, Geoffrey Wainwright recognised that historically Methodists have shown little awareness of Mary.[30] In his view, 'Methodism remains firmly enough attached to some of the principles of Protestantism for the Roman Catholic attitude towards Mary to appear to Methodist eyes as in some directions excessive. It may be that these apparent excesses of Catholicism have frightened Methodists from developing a more positive appreciation of Mary.'[31] Nevertheless, he saw the potential for possible convergence. 'If Methodism truly marked a reaction in the direction of Catholicism, and if the Roman Catholic attitude towards Mary is a key to the specific nature of Catholicism, then it may be that there exists within Methodism the potential of an attitude towards Mary that could be regarded by Catholics as giving to Mary more of her due than is ordinarily the case within Protestantism.'[32]

The British Methodist–Roman Catholic Committee subsequently took up his implied challenge and in 1995 published a convergence statement, *Mary, Sign of Grace, Faith and Holiness: Towards a Shared Understanding*.[33] This significant ecumenical text skilfully handles its emotive subject with sensitivity and insight, boldly affirming that Mary, by God's election and grace the mother of Jesus Christ, is a powerful sign or icon of what the Church is, and can become, as the people of God (1). Whereas Roman Catholics affirm the Marian doctrines (Immaculate Conception, Perpetual Virginity and Assumption) as a legitimate development in church teaching, Methodists have not discussed these in depth but do not regard them as essential to Christian faith (2). There can be no avoiding difficult questions, however. Thus Methodists ask Roman Catholics whether their veneration of Mary comes close to the adoration due to God alone. Does not devotion to Mary risk obscuring her status as a human being redeemed by Christ, our sister in the Church? Does the conventional portrayal of Mary in Roman Catholic piety do justice to a Christian image of womanhood? For their part, Roman Catholics ask Methodists whether the response to the Marian doctrines among some Protestants is in fact linked to a rejection of any place for free co-operation under grace with God's saving work. Do Methodists respond positively enough to the scriptural call for all generations to call Mary 'blessed' (Luke 1.48)?

Methodists and Roman Catholics agree together that Mary has a unique role in the drama of redemption, which must not be seen in isolation but always in relation to her son and the community of disciples

181

(3). Thus the Marian doctrines are primarily doctrines about God's grace, Christ and his salvation, and the Church. 'Methodists who do not accept the Marian doctrines as such safeguard in other ways the faith which they seek to express and symbolise' (4). For Roman Catholics, the Marian doctrines proclaim the central truths of the doctrines of justification and sanctification so that Mary is a sign or icon of God's prevenient grace, the human response and the Spirit's work of sanctification (5). They 'see Mary in the Church and the Church in Mary' (6).

Like other believers, Mary was redeemed by the death and resurrection of Christ and received into glory by him at the end of her life (6). She was prepared by God's grace for the responsibility of being the redeemed mother of the Redeemer. By her faithful and obedient response to the grace of God, Mary became a model for the individual believer and for the Church as a whole; because she is nothing apart from the grace of God, Mary is a sign of 'grace alone' (*sola gratia*) (8). From all eternity, Mary was chosen or predestined in Christ for the unique task of becoming the mother of God's Son (10). Since the central figure in the story of Mary is the Holy Spirit, her acts were those of the Spirit (9). Mary is a powerful symbol of all that the Church is called to be and become (13). She is the perfect example of one who heard the word of God and put it into practice (14). By obeying, even though she did not understand, Mary has shown us the path of faith (15). Mary did not become the mother of the Lord against her will: she freely consented to become the human instrument of the incarnation of the Son (16). The title 'Mother of God' is a fitting way to affirm the reality of the incarnation and the full humanity of Christ (21).

Mary's pilgrimage of faith provides the pattern for the Christian life. By prevenient grace, humans are free to accept or reject God's offer of grace. 'The sovereignty of God's grace does not deny human freedom: it is grace that makes our free response to God possible and fruitful, and it is grace that changes our hearts and makes truly holy our lives' (16). With Mary, Christians are called to respond freely under grace to God's will for the salvation of the world, opening their lives in faith to the transforming work of God. 'Catholics and Methodists recognise the need for human beings to co-operate with God in the mystery of salvation' (16).

Roman Catholics formulated the doctrines of the Immaculate Conception, Perpetual Virginity and Assumption of Mary in response to the following theological questions: 'How did God fittingly prepare Mary to be the mother of his Son?' 'Was not Mary perfectly fulfilled in life by this awesome vocation?' 'What was fitting at the end of Mary's life, as the mother of the Risen One?' (21). Roman Catholics believe that God 'graced' Mary from the first moment of her existence to prepare her for becoming the mother of Christ (23). Ever 'full of grace', she was preserved from the original sin by which humankind lacks the right relationship with God. Properly understood, the doctrine of the Immaculate Conception teaches that Christ redeemed Mary from the first moment of her existence (25). Mary, 'all holy', is sanctified and perfected by the Holy Spirit. As a symbol of what Christians will become, Mary is a sign of the universal call to holiness (26).

Methodists do not accept the Immaculate Conception as a scriptural doctrine, but affirm much of what it says about the doctrines of salvation and the Church (24). Methodists and Roman Catholics agree that Mary was a virgin when she conceived Jesus (27). This is a way of affirming that the work of new creation begun in Christ is entirely the work of God (28). Roman Catholics further believe, as did John Wesley, that Mary continued a virgin, though 'many Methodists today do not accept the perpetual virginity of Mary' (30).

Roman Catholics believe that at the end of her life Mary was assumed, body and soul, into heaven (31). In recognition of her unique role in the incarnation, it was fitting (though not strictly necessary) that God should welcome her into his presence to share the risen life of her son. Nevertheless, Mary's assumption was entirely dependent upon his resurrection and ascension. If Christ was raised as the first fruits from the dead (1 Corinthians 15.20), then Mary was 'the second fruits from the dead', but only through God's grace. While Methodists do not accept the bodily assumption of Mary as a scriptural doctrine, they affirm much of what it says about Christ's saving work and his Church (32). The assumption of Mary anticipates what Christians hope one day to share (33). It also testifies to the belief that everything of real value in human existence will be transfigured and taken into glory by God, including our bodies (34).

Methodists and Roman Catholics believe in the communion of saints as a practical fellowship of mutual prayer (35). Within this communion of the saints, Mary is our sister in the Church and fellow disciple who prays for us; but, at the same time, she is still the mother of Jesus and her prayers therefore have a special value (36). Roman Catholics distinguish between the adoration (*latreia*) due to God alone and the veneration (*dulia*) given to Mary and the saints. However, 'Catholics have not always been careful enough to ensure that their devotions to Mary exclude any idea of her being between Christ and ourselves, or even taking his place, rather than being a special member of the Church who joins us in prayer' (37). Similarly, the honorary titles given to Mary are open to misunderstanding if used in isolation from Christ and his Church (40).

As its full title indicates, *Mary, Sign of Grace, Faith and Holiness* does not claim the final word on Mariology. Nevertheless, it is an astute contribution towards an ecumenical understanding of Mary and her unique role in salvation history. Grounding the study of Mary in the doctrines of Christ and the Church established a sound theological framework in which outstanding doctrinal differences between Methodists and Roman Catholics about Mary may eventually be resolved.

An exception to the British Methodist–Roman Catholic Committee's usual focus on matters relating to doctrine has been its longstanding interest in the experience of couples in inter-church marriages. For many years the committee has included members of the Association of Inter-Church Families, so that its conversations have often dealt with practical questions relating to marriage between Methodists and Roman Catholics and their subsequent participation in the life of both churches. While it is probably only in a small minority of cases that both partners are equally committed to membership of their respective churches, for such couples being unable to share fully in the life of both communities leads to considerable pain and distress. On a more positive note however we should not lose sight of the fact that the increasing number of marriages between Roman Catholics and Methodists in recent years is a further sign that Roman Catholics have become fully integrated into British society.

The Methodist Church of Great Britain has no special regulations governing marriage between Methodists and Roman Catholics, but the Roman Catholic Church lays down strict rules that must be followed in the case of 'mixed marriages'. As recently as 1970, Pope Paul VI referred to the Church's duty of discouraging 'mixed marriages'.[34] Under the Code of Canon Law (1983), it is prohibited for a Roman Catholic to marry a person from another church or ecclesial community without permission from the competent authority (Canon 1124). However, provided certain conditions are fulfilled, permission can be granted for a just and reasonable cause (Canon 1115). Where the marriage takes place in a Roman Catholic church, a minister from another Christian tradition may be invited to take part in the ceremony. In certain circumstances, permission can be given for the non-Roman Catholic party to receive Holy Communion during the nuptial Mass. Roman Catholics require permission ('dispensation from the canonical form') for the marriage service to take place in another Christian church or ecclesial community. In such cases, Roman Catholic priests are permitted to take part in the marriage service.

Since the full provisions for inter-church marriages are complex, Methodist ministers and Roman Catholic priests are not always aware of what is permitted under canon law. To guide ministers and priests in conducting inter-church marriages, the committee published a leaflet written by A. Raymond George entitled *Marriages of Methodists with Roman Catholics* (1980), which explained what was permitted under Roman Catholic rules.[35] Following publication of the new Code of Canon Law in 1983 and revised norms for 'mixed marriages' in England and Wales, the leaflet was updated and reissued under the title, *Marriages with Roman Catholics* (1990).[36]

Of course, the problems faced by inter-church couples and their families do not end with the marriage service. The partners in an inter-church marriage experience in an acute way the pain of division between their churches, through being unable to share fully in the life of both communities. The Methodist Church practises an 'open table policy', while the Roman Catholic Church does not.[37] Rites of passages in the Roman Catholic Church, such as baptism, first communion and confirmation, can therefore be occasions when the non-Roman Catholic marriage partner feels excluded. While it is sometimes possible to obtain permission for a non-Roman Catholic to receive Holy Communion on these and other special occasions, there is no standard practice across the dioceses, and permission is usually only given to allow an exception to the rules for a single occasion. The Association of Inter-Church Families, which is now an international organisation, conducts a dignified campaign for a sensitive interpretation of the norms for eucharistic sharing in the case of inter-church marriages.

Realistically, there is little that the British Methodist–Roman Catholic dialogue can do by itself to influence the Roman Catholic hierarchy in the British Isles in this sensitive area of ecclesial discipline. However, the dialogue provides an official forum in which members of the Association of Inter-Church Families are able to express their thoughts to representatives of both churches. The committee listens with interest and sympathy and from time to time discusses particular issues of practical interest to the association. As we shall discover, the issue of inter-church families is not confined to Britain. In Australia there has been a great deal of ecumenical work in the field of inter-church marriages, which may yet be of wider benefit within the Church.

The United States

In the aftermath of the Second Vatican Council ecumenically minded Methodists in the United States regarded Wesley's *Twenty-Four Articles of Religion* as a problem for relations with Roman Catholics. Yet, the articles could not simply be discarded from the official corpus of American Methodism as if they had never existed; nor could they easily be rewritten. In the event, the *Twenty-Four Articles of Religion* were retained intact in recognition of their historical status as a landmark document in American Methodism. However, to facilitate closer relations with Roman Catholics, the United Methodist Church adopted a *Resolution of Intent*, which valued the history of Methodism in the United States while acknowledging that circumstances had changed.

The *Resolution of Intent* was based on a principle used at the Second Vatican Council to interpret historical texts. This involved distinguishing between a valid legal document and a historically conditioned statement of convictions no longer held or no longer held in a particular form. Sensing the theological possibilities in this distinction, a specially convened theological commission reported to the General Conference:

It would be more constructive for us to propose a *Resolution of Intent* with respect to an appropriate contemporary interpretation of the Articles concerned. This is not merely or even chiefly on account of the constitutional difficulties involved in piecemeal deletion of Articles, but much more because it belongs to the spirit of modern ecumenism that separated Christian brethren receive and trans-valuate their historical traditions rather than by repudiating some and not others suggest that the remainder stand in no need of contemporary reinterpretation.[38]

The General Conference of 1970 agreed, and the *Resolution of Intent* was duly approved and delivered to Cardinal Willebrands, President of the Vatican Secretariat for Promoting Christian Unity. Responding on behalf of Pope Paul VI, the Vatican Secretary of State, Cardinal Villot, welcomed the United Methodist action as a spur to Christian unity. Roman Catholic members of the Joint Commission similarly made 'grateful reference' to the 'noble' *Resolution*.[39]

Bilateral Methodist–Roman Catholic conversations in the United States began in 1966 under the auspices of the Bishops' Committee for Ecumenical and Interreligious Affairs of the National Conference of Catholic Bishops and the Ecumenical Concerns Division of the Board of Global Ministries of the United Methodist Church. Since it began, the dialogue has considered a range of subjects, mostly from a practical perspective.[40] There have been five rounds of dialogue, varying in length between four and seven years, which have all resulted in a substantial report.

Early conversations between Methodists and Roman Catholics in the United States covered a variety of topics, including salvation, justification, sanctification, works of piety, and glorification. The commission did not consider it necessary to issue a comprehensive report of this first round of dialogue, but instead released a joint statement about education in America in response to a crisis in the public sector provoked by the federal government's threat to ban state aid to private schools.[41] As sponsors of church schools and universities, United Methodists and Roman Catholics had a substantial stake in private education in the United States.

Shared Convictions about Education (1970) affirms the public sector as the 'chief instrument' for providing adequate education in the United States, but defends private schools as 'important contributors to the common good'.[42] It is the responsibility of society to make it possible for every child to obtain an adequate education through public schools, which must be 'open to all on an equal basis, without discrimination because of race, religion, national origin, sex, or economic class'. At the same time, parents have the right and responsibility to choose the kind of education their children shall receive in public or private schools, 'particularly what understanding of the nature and duty of man they shall be taught'.

Funding allocated to education out of tax revenue should remain under public control and should not be used to finance the teaching or practice of religion. However, private schools that meet certain minimal standards deserve recognition and encouragement as a legitimate part of the education system in America. Children in private schools should also be entitled to receive the welfare benefits provided by the government, including school lunches, bus transportation and secular textbooks. The statement concludes, 'It is conceivable that some way can be found to enable private institutions to serve a public purpose with public resources without losing their autonomy or distinctiveness, without sacrificing public control of public funds, and without risking discrimination among children.'

Interestingly, nowhere does *Shared Convictions about Education* refer to either the United Methodist Church or the Roman Catholic Church. There is no mention of Christian doctrine, and the secular nature of education in the public sector is assumed without question. This suggests that the intended readership was not United Methodists and Roman Catholics so much as local, state and federal authorities. This being the case, *Shared Convictions about Education* is a rare example of Methodists and Roman Catholics uniting to lobby national and local government about an issue of shared concern.

The second series of conversations (1971–6) took as its theme 'spirituality in the ministry'. Among the questions the commission sought to address was whether the holiness to which ministers were called was different in kind from that to which all Christians were called, and whether new disciplines were needed to express and support the spirituality of ministers. The report *Holiness and Spirituality of the Ordained Ministry* (1976) describes God's holiness in terms of separateness, love and righteousness.[43] The vocation of the Church, individually and corporately, is to accept God's gift of holiness and manifest it in Christian spirituality. Among the people of God, ministers have a special duty to lead a holy life of service.

United Methodists and Roman Catholics agree together that there is no difference in kind between the holiness of ministers and that of lay people. In the Roman Catholic tradition, the chief means to holiness for bishops and presbyters is the celebration of the Eucharist. The United Methodist tradition does not specify the means to personal holiness for its ministers, though they are required to make a commitment to the pursuit of Christian perfection, and some form of daily prayer and devotion is assumed. But, whatever means are employed, the commitment to holiness makes a 'simple way of life' most appropriate for Christian ministers, whose lives should be characterised by approachability rather than privilege. Ministers of word and sacrament should be people of prayer, whose life is one of simplicity and humility in harmony with their high calling to be a symbol of the Church's holiness. At the same time, ministers should be alive to the danger of falling into hypocrisy or arrogance:

> Much of the modern world reacts negatively to the assertion of the holiness of the Church because of its apparent hypocrisy. Hence, the need to emphasise that real compassion and true humility are an integral part of holiness. If they are honest, the Church's ministers will acknowledge that they share the anguish of men and women who, like them, are unable to live up to the Gospel and to achieve in themselves the holiness to which they aspire.[44]

This recognition of ministerial frailty takes on a more poignant significance in the light of recent sexual abuse scandals involving Roman Catholic priests in the United States and elsewhere. The holiness of the ordained ministry remains a pressing pastoral issue for Christians of all traditions.

According to the report, the form that Christian holiness takes will vary according to the particular culture in which the Gospel has taken root. Adaptation to indigenous cultures is essential if faith in Christ is to become a real possibility for all people. Throughout the world, rapid changes in technological societies have created problems for people seeking authentic holiness of life. Ministers need the gift of discernment in order to recognise signs of the Holy Spirit directing the human quest for a holy life in the modern world. Contemporary paths to Christian holiness include the search for personal authenticity, a return to simple ways of living, the investigation in depth of human motives, and the adoption of devotional practices such as meditation and fasting. These and other manifestations of the 'human spirit' should be viewed positively, as long as the danger of bondage to the 'elements of this world' is also discerned. But, whatever form it takes, Christian holiness for today is appropriately expressed in compassion for those who suffer, in practical assistance to the needy, in the struggle for political, social and economic justice, and in the promotion of peace and reconciliation within and among families, races, classes and nations.

The backdrop to *Holiness and Spirituality of the Ordained Ministry* was the range of alternative non-Christian spiritualities on offer in America in the late 1960s. The New Age movement had not yet come to birth, though it had its antecedents in various popular movements of the 1960s. Presumably, the need for sympathetic awareness of contemporary society and alternative forms of spirituality had practical implications for ministerial formation. However, the report made no recommendations about ministerial training or the discernment of new forms of spirituality within the ordained ministry. Instead, *Holiness and Spirituality of the Ordained Ministry* maps out areas of agreement between United Methodists and Roman Catholics concerning the role of the Church's ordained ministry in the service of holiness. Interestingly, both churches are urged 'to work toward full utilisation of and respect for women in all forms of ministry'; though what this actually meant is open to interpretation.[45] Though short on practical advice, the report was offered to all who sensed 'a need to formulate and to live a spirituality that is both faithful to the gospel and appropriate to our time'. Thirty years later, the holiness and spirituality of the ordained ministry is once again a topical issue, as Christians in all traditions wrestle with issues relating to morale and stress in the ministry, as well as the problems caused by abusive clergy.

The third round of dialogue in the United States studied the meaning and practice of the Eucharist in the light of the Denver and Dublin reports. The final report *Eucharistic Celebration: Converging Theology – Divergent Practice* (1981) notes that twentieth-century reforms in Roman Catholic and United Methodist eucharistic liturgies are mostly the outcome of a common approach to biblical, liturgical, historical and theological studies.[46] Greater knowledge of patristic sources in particular

190

has enabled United Methodists and Roman Catholics to escape from Reformation and Counter-Reformation propaganda by rediscovering their roots in a common liturgy. As a result, eucharistic liturgies in the main Christian traditions have converged in recent years, in the process overcoming an imbalance between word and sacrament, which was a notable feature in the past. By comparing the General Instruction of the Roman Missal and the Great Thanksgiving in the United Methodist liturgy for Holy Communion, the commission discovered a remarkable degree of convergence in the structure of the Eucharist and the content of the central eucharistic prayer, though popular piety and liturgical practice did not always reflect this convergence.

Eucharistic Celebration examines three historically divisive subjects: the real presence, the sacrifice of Christ, and the role of faith at the Eucharist. Methodist belief in the real presence of Christ at the Eucharist found powerful expression in the eucharistic hymns of Charles Wesley, and many but not all United Methodists understand the elements to be the locus of this presence. 'For their part, Roman Catholics have begun to see that the doctrine of transubstantiation is itself an historically conditioned theological formulation that seeks to avoid misunderstanding about Christ's Eucharistic presence.'[47] But, despite the convergence in doctrine, eucharistic practice and popular piety still tend to reflect earlier disagreements. Whereas Roman Catholics emphasise the significance of the eucharistic elements, some United Methodists stress the proclaimed word of God as the locus of the real presence. Any future agreed statement between United Methodists and Roman Catholics concerning the real presence at the Eucharist will have to take into account these and other differences in eucharistic practice and popular piety.

References in the Eucharist to the sacrifice of Christ are more complex than we can do justice to here. United Methodists emphasise the once-for-all sacrifice of Christ at Calvary, whereas Roman Catholics stress the sacrifice offered by the Church down the centuries. United Methodists are generally uncomfortable with Vatican II teaching that the Eucharist 'perpetuates the sacrifice of the cross throughout the centuries' (*Constitution on the Liturgy*, 47) and would ask 'Who is offering what at the Eucharist?' Thus Roman Catholics and United Methodists do not yet agree about the precise sense in which the Eucharist is a sacrifice and how this relates to the historical sacrifice of Christ. The report asks

191

whether the fact that United Methodists generally celebrate the Eucharist less frequently than Roman Catholics suggests a different theological understanding of the nature of 'sacrifice'.

Roman Catholics and United Methodists affirm the role of personal faith in the celebration of the Eucharist, but place a different emphasis on the corporate and individual dimensions of faith. Roman Catholics stress that the presence of Christ at the Eucharist is not realised solely through the faith of the individual, whereas United Methodists maintain that, to be effective tokens of the real presence, the elements must be received in faith. Though not irreconcilable, these different emphases have led United Methodists and Roman Catholics to adopt contrasting positions on the possibility and desirability of eucharistic devotion. Nevertheless, there is a fundamental agreement that God's grace present in preaching and the Eucharist both activates and elicits a faith response.

Eucharistic Celebration highlights the eschatological and ethical dimensions of the Eucharist as being worthy of further investigation. Describing the Eucharist as a foretaste of the messianic banquet has implications for the way in which United Methodists and Roman Catholics understand each other, because it suggests solidarity among all those people on earth who eagerly await God's reign. The ethical dimension of the Eucharist is reflected in the post-communion prayers present in Roman Catholic and United Methodist liturgies. These prayers, before the dismissal, establish a link between the sacrament and Christian service in the world. United Methodists and Roman Catholics agree that the individual's response to the Eucharist appropriately includes good works, which proceed from faith in Christ.

The report invites United Methodists and Roman Catholics to take a fresh look at their own ecclesiology and doctrines of the ministry and authority. The challenge for Roman Catholics is to appropriate into their ecclesiology those images of the Church contained in the documents of the Second Vatican Council and subsequently incorporated into liturgical reforms. The challenge for United Methodists is to develop a more ecumenical understanding of the Church in the light of their Anglican and Wesleyan roots, setting aside those historical and theological factors that presently inhibit a sacramental understanding of the Church and its ministry.

In an unusual departure from the more familiar topics of ecumenical dialogue, the fourth round of United Methodist–Roman Catholic conversations (1982–8) turned to the subject of biomedical ethics. The final report *Holy Living, Holy Dying* (1988) focuses on 'ethical issues in the Christian care of the dying'.[48] As providers of the most extensive healthcare networks in the United States, United Methodists and Roman Catholics have a shared interest in this sensitive area of pastoral care and therefore had much to gain from a joint approach.

The first section of the report sets out 'Theological and Ethical Principles' and the second section deals with 'Pastoral Care' of the dying. *Holy Living, Holy Dying* affirms all human life as a gift from God. Human beings are called to exercise stewardship over life, while fulfilling the purposes for which God made humankind. In its actual condition, humankind is subject to disease and death, exacerbated by sin and moral failure. In the face of the mystery of why human beings suffer and die, Roman Catholics and United Methodists affirm that God has entered into human suffering through the incarnation. What is more, through the healing ministry and sacrificial death of Christ, God seeks to turn human suffering and death into wholeness and life. The mystery of human suffering and death finds its complete answer only in the wholeness and holiness of the resurrection community. Meanwhile, the Church is called to share compassionately in healing the sick and comforting the dying, guided by the principle of loving stewardship of human life.

Pastoral care of the dying means entering into a relationship with them so that they can experience the signs of God's presence and thus face death realistically and 'wholely'. For Roman Catholics, pastoral care of the dying includes the sacraments of Reconciliation (Penance), Anointing of the Sick, and Holy Communion as signs and sources of spiritual growth. For United Methodists, pastoral care of the dying includes Holy Communion, the laying on of hands and informal prayers of repentance, reconciliation and intercession. In addition to the Church's sacramental and spiritual resources, other appropriate forms of pastoral care include offering the insights of Christian faith in any discussion about organ donation, advance directives for treatment (now commonly called 'living wills'), and the kind of life-prolonging treatment that raises quality of life issues.

Holy Living, Holy Dying is a rare example of an ecumenical statement on a specific moral issue. In encouraging local churches to reflect on ministry to the dying, and by offering practical recommendations, it is a valuable pastoral resource for United Methodists and Roman Catholics. However, its usefulness is diminished to some extent by its failure to resolve two important theological questions relating to pastoral care of the dying. The Roman Catholic participants and a number of the United Methodists unequivocally rejected suicide and euthanasia as contrary to Christian stewardship of life because of their absolute dominion over human existence. However, some of the United Methodist participants argued that there could be exceptions to this norm in certain circumstances. Furthermore, the participants failed to agree on a Christian understanding of death. From a theological perspective, is death part of finite human existence as ordained by God, or is it a consequence of the Fall and therefore intrinsically evil? The way in which these questions are answered has pastoral implications for the Christian care of the dying.

The most recent document published by the United Methodist–Roman Catholic dialogue is a study guide designed to promote local dialogue in communities across the United States. *Yearning to be One: Spiritual Dialogue Between Catholics and United Methodists* (2000) is a glossy publication, containing material for group discussion and reflection in six sessions:

1 Getting to know one another and discovering our need for one another.
2 Exploring the spirituality of dialogue and the attitudes and behaviour that help or hinder dialogue.
3 The meaning and practice of baptism in the United Methodist and Roman Catholic traditions, and common understandings of baptism.
4 Worship in each faith tradition.
5 The ways in which we grow in faith.
6 The mission of the Church and our role in it.

Each session takes the form of a guided exploration of a particular aspect of the United Methodist and Roman Catholic traditions. For instance, in the session on worship in each faith tradition, the group is invited to compare the order of Mass in the Roman missal with the 'Service of Word and Table' in the *United Methodist Book of Worship*

(1992). Participants are encouraged to ask one another questions about their faith community and to identity aspects of either tradition which they would like to explore in greater detail. The study guide suggests resources, including useful websites, for further research. A short glossary explains a number of terms commonly used by United Methodists or Roman Catholics.

The modest aim of *Yearning to be One* is the attainment of three preliminary steps on the way to full communion. The first step is to gather United Methodists and Roman Catholics together locally for dialogue. The second is to encourage group members to learn the listening and speaking skills for dialogue. The third step is for participants to experience the 'fruits of dialogue', which include a growing understanding and positive reception of the beliefs and experience of the dialogue partner (even when full agreement is not reached), a change in personal attitudes concerning those aspects of ecclesial life which currently prevent unity, and greater appreciation of the degree of unity that already exists, based on the Scriptures and the creeds. Sharing together in prayer and service are also among the fruits of dialogue. The final session on the mission of the Church includes an outline for a 'Service of Commissioning as Ecumenical Christians'.

Yearning to be One rightly sees the healing of divisions in the Church as ultimately the work of the Holy Spirit. The duty of United Methodists and Roman Catholics is to be open to the Spirit in order to participate in the process of healing. In almost every county of the United States there is both a Roman Catholic and a United Methodist congregation. In many places they already co-operate in ministry and mission in local community projects. Dialogue at the local level therefore has the potential to become a significant means of strengthening and deepening the communion that already exists between United Methodists and Roman Catholics.

Yearning to be One is a groundbreaking ecumenical text, which offers an accessible programme of joint study and reflection for small groups of United Methodists and Roman Catholics. What is more, there is very little, if anything, in this study guide which could not readily be applied outside the context of North America. In the absence of other equivalent resource material, local conversations involving Methodists and Roman Catholics in Britain and elsewhere would benefit from using this useful publication.

Australia

In Australia, among the first ecumenical ventures following the Second Vatican Council was the establishment of a Working Group appointed by the Australian Council of Churches and the Roman Catholic Church, which led to the establishment of several bilateral dialogues in the early 1970s, including the Methodist–Roman Catholic conversations. As it happens, this last dialogue was short-lived, because of a significant ecumenical development in the form of a unity scheme. Five years after the bilateral conversations started, the Methodist Church of Australasia became part of the Uniting Church in Australia. Nevertheless, in its short existence the Methodist–Roman Catholic conversations in Australia produced two agreed statements, which subsequently provided a starting point for dialogue between the Uniting Church and the Roman Catholic Church.

The first fruit of Methodist–Roman Catholic dialogue in Australia was a *Joint Statement on Baptism* (1973).[49] There were two main reasons for such a statement. First, the participants in the dialogue recognised that baptismal union in Christ was the basis for all ecumenical endeavour. Second, among Methodists and Roman Catholics in Australia in the early 1970s there was a shared concern about indiscriminate infant baptism and its long-term effect upon the well-being of the Church.

The *Joint Statement on Baptism* comprises six short paragraphs setting out common beliefs about the nature of Christian baptism. For Methodists and Roman Catholics, baptism was a sacrament in which the action of Christ drew believers into his suffering and glorification. Those baptised in Christ were united in a shared experience of the mystery of salvation as a priestly people offering spiritual sacrifices to God, declaring the wonderful deeds of him who called them out of darkness into his marvellous light (1 Peter 2.9). Methodists and Roman Catholics prescribed the use of the Trinitarian formula in the baptismal rite (Matthew 28.19–20) and the ritual washing with water of each candidate. The baptised person was thereby drawn into the community of believers, within which his or her faith was nurtured and deepened through the Holy Spirit. Since baptism began the process of Christian initiation, it was unrepeatable.

Methodists and Roman Catholics in Australia differed in their baptismal practice in one important respect. In the Methodist Church, baptism was usually celebrated in the context of the main Sunday service. Among Roman Catholics, baptism often took place in a private ceremony outside the Sunday Mass. For pastoral reasons, the joint statement declared: 'Because it is the Church which receives the baptised person in the name of Christ, we regard it as important that a congregation of Christians be present at the celebration of the sacrament whenever this is practicable.' This was ambiguous, however. Did a 'congregation of Christians' refer to the local church or merely to the guests gathered for a private ceremony? Also, the caveat 'whenever this is practicable' provided an obvious loophole. From a Roman Catholic perspective, such guidelines for good practice in baptism services were all very well in theory. In practice, Methodists were seldom faced with the situation in some Roman Catholic parishes, where the large number of baptisms made it impracticable for these to take place during the Sunday Mass. Still, the *Joint Statement on Baptism* encouraged Methodists and Roman Catholics to find ways of establishing a more visible link between baptism and the community of believers.

On the basis of a shared belief about the sacrament of baptism, the joint statement made several practical recommendations, which were subsequently accepted by the Methodist Church of Australasia and the Roman Catholic Church in Australia. The most far-reaching of these was that Methodists and Roman Catholics in Australia officially recognise each other's baptism. In the case of infant baptism, the report recommended 'adequate pastoral counselling of the parents concerning their responsibilities'. To assist in the mutual recognition of baptism, the statement proposed that Methodists and Roman Catholics adopt a common baptismal certificate and make their baptismal records readily available to each other.

Shared concern about the disintegration of family life in Australia and the increasing number of divorces prompted the Methodist–Roman Catholic dialogue to publish a convergence statement on *Christian Marriage: Its Meaning and Pastoral Implications* (1973).[50] *Christian Marriage* affirmed the estate of marriage as a sacred gift from God to provide a stable environment for family life, allowing both partners and their children to grow and mature. Christian marriage signified the mystery of the unity between Christ and his Church. It was also a means of grace. For Roman Catholics, marriage was one of the seven sacraments of the Church. For Methodists, marriage had a 'sacramental nature' (3).

Within the new covenant in Christ, the relationship between husband and wife was itself a covenant, sealed and sustained in union with Christ. 'Christian marriage exists so that a man and a woman, united in Christ, may give to each other life-long companionship, help and comfort, both in prosperity and adversity; that God may hallow and direct the sexual love created by himself; and that children may be brought up in families in the knowledge of our Lord Jesus Christ to the glory of God' (5). Methodists and Roman Catholics agreed that lifelong marriage was the will and purpose of God for the welfare of human society, but they disagreed about the possibility of divorce. The Roman Catholic Church did not permit the remarriage of divorced persons, whereas the Methodist Church did so in appropriate circumstances.

The second half of *Christian Marriage* considered the subject of 'mixed marriages', more as a problem for the Church than as a sacred gift from God: 'We affirm that marriage most readily reaches its fulfilment where the partners are of the same tradition and allegiance' (7). Since mixed marriages sometimes led to a lack of mutual assistance in spiritual growth and the nurture of children, ministers of both churches had a clear responsibility to help couples make realistic and responsible decisions about marriage. 'The decision to enter a mixed marriage must be made in the context of the right to marry, the inviolability of conscience, the joint obligation of the parents for the care and education of their children, other mutual rights and obligations in marriage and the teaching of the Churches involved' (8). When, out of 'natural affection', a couple were considering a mixed marriage, it was 'a pastoral responsibility to impress upon them the need to consider whether such marriage is one in which they are able to satisfy their obligations in conscience before God' (8).

It is difficult to imagine how any but the most theologically competent couples could have navigated their way through these criteria to make an informed decision about whether to marry. Worse still, the tone of the statement suggested that love – a word used only rarely in the text – was primarily a matter of the will rather than the heart. On the whole, *Christian Marriage* gives the impression that a loving relationship between a man and woman was much less important than preserving the doctrinal purity of the Church, though it conceded that 'A marriage between sincere and dedicated Christians who share a common baptism can show forth the love of Christ (cf. Ephesians 5.25) and be a sign of the unity that Christ wills for his Church' (9).

Christian Marriage made a number of recommendations regarding good pastoral practice. Both churches were asked to develop a programme of education and guidance to help people discover the 'validity and richness of Christian marriage'. Wherever possible, Methodists and Roman Catholics were encouraged to organise joint courses in marriage preparation. Ideally, ministers would be trained ecumenically in understanding human relationships, mixed marriages and 'marriage problems'. Family life groups should be established on denominational lines as mutual support groups. In the case of mixed marriages, the statement recommended that both partners be encouraged to practise their faith to the full, with their ministers working together to offer appropriate pastoral care. *Christian Marriage* asked the Roman Catholic Church in Australia to administer its regulations governing mixed marriages in such a way as to 'maintain a uniform and generous discipline throughout Australia', especially with regard to providing dispensations from the canonical form.

Although *Christian Marriage* contained some worthy observations on the nature of marriage, it was curiously devoid of warmth and feeling in its treatment of human love, especially in its approach to mixed marriages. In considering mixed marriages to be a problem for the Church, the statement was following the lead of Pope Paul VI, who discouraged such marriages. With the passage of time, however, has come a softening of attitudes, and the description of mixed marriages contained in *Christian Marriage* now comes across as pastorally insensitive and therefore inappropriate. Fortunately, the Uniting Church–Roman Catholic dialogue has been much more creative in its approach to marriage between Christians who belong to different churches.

The Uniting Church in Australia was inaugurated in June 1977, incorporating the Congregational Union of Australia, the Methodist Church of Australasia and the Presbyterian Church of Australia. Almost immediately, the Uniting Church established a Joint Working Group with the Australian Episcopal Conference of the Roman Catholic Church to continue the dialogue started by the Methodist–Roman Catholic and Presbyterian–Roman Catholic conversations. Between 1978 and 1992 the dialogue was based in Melbourne, where it produced three reports. In 1993 the dialogue moved to Brisbane, where so far it has produced one report.

There are sound reasons for including the Uniting Church–Roman Catholic dialogue within the scope of the present volume. First of all, the dialogue continues and develops the Methodist–Roman Catholic conversations in Australia. Furthermore, the Uniting Church in Australia is a full member of the World Methodist Council and as such remains in close contact with Methodism. At the same time, the conversations between the Uniting Church and the Roman Catholic Church bring a different perspective to dialogue between Methodists and Roman Catholics.

The Joint Working Group, in its initial series of conversations, chose to examine the separate agreed statements on baptism made between the Roman Catholic Church in Australia and the Methodist and Presbyterian Churches. The first document produced by the Uniting Church–Roman Catholic dialogue was *An Agreed Statement on Baptism* (1979) which updated these earlier reports to take account of the new situation brought about by the formation of the Uniting Church.[478]

An Agreed Statement on Baptism tightened the rules governing the administration of baptism in response to the more informal baptismal practices that had been commonplace in at least one of the constituent traditions of the Uniting Church. Ministers were now required to use an approved order of service for baptism, comprising twelve essential elements, none of which caused problems for Methodists. In response to continuing pastoral concern over indiscriminate infant baptism in Australia, the Joint Working Group concluded that the baptism of children was appropriate only when 'there is a founded hope for their Christian upbringing'. The pastoral recommendations made previously by the Methodist–Roman Catholic dialogue in Australia were repeated in the *Agreed Statement on Baptism*. The 1979 Assembly of the Uniting Church and the Episcopal Conference of the Catholic Church in Australia both approved the statement. As a result, the Uniting Church and the Roman Catholic Church in Australia today recognise each other's baptism and are able to issue a common baptism certificate.

In its next statement, *Make Straight His Way: Stages on the Road to Unity,* the Joint Working Group addressed popular stereotypes that had often been the cause of misunderstanding and prejudice among Christians in Australia. While overcoming stereotypes would not automatically lead to agreement, nevertheless the Joint Working Group hoped to advance the cause of Christian unity in Australia.

Make Straight his Way identifies doctrine, the sacraments and liturgy as areas in which mutual misunderstanding among Christians in Australia has been especially divisive. In the case of doctrine, Christians often misconstrue the intentions of other ecclesial traditions. Thus Roman Catholics tend to regard themselves as defending Christian doctrine against Protestants who reject some of its essential aspects. Conversely, Protestants regard themselves as recovering the original proclamation of the biblical faith against Roman Catholics who have distorted it. In reality, both Protestants and Roman Catholics have been concerned, in their different ways, to preserve the central doctrine of God's saving work in the person of Jesus Christ. The Reformation produced a gulf between the Protestant emphasis on faith and the Roman Catholic emphasis on good works. While both traditions uphold the divine initiative in human salvation, neither has been able to propose a commonly acceptable way of reconciling the sovereignty of God with the moral responsibility of human beings.

Different approaches to the sacraments, especially the Eucharist, have also been a prime cause of disagreement between Roman Catholics and Protestants. Whereas Roman Catholics commonly refer to the Eucharist as a sacrifice, Protestants stress the once-for-all nature of Christ's sacrifice, preferring to avoid sacrificial language in connection with the Eucharist. According to *Make Straight his Way,* however, these two emphases need not be mutually exclusive. Different devotional and cultural practices associated with the Eucharist have also led to sectarian antipathy between Roman Catholics and Protestants. The different traditions relating to architecture, the conduct of worship and devotional aids such as rosaries, statues and incense were identified as expressions of substantial difference.

Fortunately, past controversies now seem more remote from the situation today. Shared study, worship and prayer have led to a growing spirit of mutual trust between Roman Catholics and Protestants in Australia. *Make Straight His Way* calls for further growth in mutual understanding and respect for the heritage of different Christian traditions. Roman

Catholics and Protestants need one another in order to place past events and doctrinal formulations in their proper historical perspective and to recover their shared heritage of faith. Since ecumenical encounters can sometimes appear to threaten ecclesial identity, growth towards unity will inevitably develop in parishes at different rates, according to local circumstances.

To affirm and consolidate ecumenism in Australia, *Make Straight His Way* identifies ten preliminary 'stages' on the long road to full unity: the mutual recognition of baptism; common acceptance of the biblical witness to Christian revelation; shared acceptance of the historic creeds and ecumenical councils as authoritative statements of the Christian faith; ecumenical translations of the Bible; similar regard for the contribution of the apostolic tradition to Christian life and thought; a standard church calendar and lectionary; convergence in eucharistic liturgies, based on the earliest Christian traditions; fellowship in prayer; united witness to Christ on issues of importance in Australian society; and collective action for justice in the world. Each stage represents a modest, but nonetheless significant, achievement towards the goal of Christian unity.

Make Straight his Way is rooted in the ecumenical situation in Australia, where strongly held prejudice against unfamiliar Christian traditions has been a major obstacle to closer relations between the churches. In other places, such as Ireland, where there is still deep suspicion between Roman Catholics and Protestants, the approach adopted in *Make Straight his Way* may help Methodists and Roman Catholics to engage in constructive theological dialogue. The allusion in the title to the biblical image of God's highway cutting through the desert is a powerful reminder that the path of ecumenism is God's will for the Church.

The role and expectations of women in Australian society have changed considerably in recent years, and the rate of divorce has increased dramatically. In 1986 the Joint Working Group noted that, although 60 per cent of Australian marriages were celebrated in church, almost a third ended in divorce, and one in five children lived in 'non-traditional family units'. The number of marriages between Roman Catholics and members of the Uniting Church had also steadily increased. In response to the challenges presented by these changes in Australian society, the

Joint Working Group published a discussion paper *Towards Agreement on Marriage* (1989).

Towards Agreement on Marriage reflected the significant shift in outlook towards mixed marriages in the fifteen years since the Methodist–Roman Catholic dialogue in Australia had reported on the subject. In fact, the discussion paper made no mention of 'mixed marriages' as such, but referred instead to 'inter-church marriages'. Far from being a problem for the churches, such marriages were now said to hold certain 'ecumenical advantages'. The paper posed two questions: 'What can an inter-church family as a "domestic church" contribute to the wider Church?' And, 'How can our Churches give sensitive and constructive pastoral care to inter-church marriages and re-marriages?' With regard to this last question, the paper acknowledged with regret that the pastoral recommendations made fifteen years earlier in the Methodist–Roman Catholic report had been implemented only to a very limited extent.

When the Joint Working Group moved its base from Melbourne to Brisbane in 1993, the dialogue continued to focus on the subject of Christian marriage. Besides studying the teaching of both churches, the working group commissioned a series of interviews with married couples and a survey of Roman Catholic and Uniting Church ministers. The outcome of this process was a substantial report on inter-church marriages, which the Australian Catholic Bishops' Conference and the Uniting Church Assembly approved and subsequently published under the title *Interchurch Marriages: Their Ecumenical Challenge and Significance for our Churches* (1999).

The opening chapter of *Interchurch Marriages* investigates 'The Phenomenon of Interchurch Marriage', noting the scarcity of marriages in Australia which fulfil all the requirements to be truly inter-church. Only in a small number of cases are both partners equally committed to following their separate religious convictions. The pain of separation experienced by these couples in worship is not their fault. It is a case 'not of the Church having to forgive them, but of asking them to forgive the Church'. How different this approach is to the discouraging tone adopted in the Methodist–Roman Catholic statement on mixed marriages in 1973.

In a novel departure from the norm, the chapter on 'Marriage' consciously uses the language of covenant relationship in preference to that of sacrament, for reasons of convergence. As the statement explains, 'While our two communions use the language of *sacrament* in different ways, members of both Churches could find that in a covenant theology of Christian marriage many apparent differences implied in the language of *sacrament* are overcome.'[52] In the covenant relationship of marriage the ultimate source of love between a man and woman is the circulation of love within the Holy Trinity. 'In this smallest of Christian communities the love of God for all human beings and of Jesus Christ for the Church is expressed through the mutual love of husband for wife and wife for husband.'[53] Again, this is a much richer description of Christian marriage than anything found in the Methodist–Roman Catholic statement of 1973.

Interchurch Marriages goes on to explore the difficulties faced by inter-church families in belonging to the Church. Although the Uniting Church and the Roman Catholic Church agree that all the baptised are members of the Holy Catholic Church, they have a different understanding of what it means to belong to the local church. Thus the Roman Catholic Church in Australia is unable to permit the non-Roman Catholic partner in an inter-church marriage to receive Holy Communion, except on rare occasions. *Interchurch Marriages* outlines the possibilities for inter-church families seeking baptism and tentatively proposes an ecumenical service at which an authorised minister from either church could baptise all the candidates, committing them to membership in a specific community. The chapter on 'Eucharistic Hospitality' considers the general norms established by the Roman Catholic Church in 1993 in the case of inter-church marriages. Finally, the report provides practical guidance for ministers on the pastoral care of inter-church families, including marriage preparation, planning the ceremony and living as a 'domestic church'.

Overall, this latest report from the Joint Working Group between the Uniting Church and the Roman Catholic Church in Australia contains a great deal that is of interest and value for partners in inter-church marriages, as well as for those charged with their pastoral care. Clearly and sensitively, the report explains the respective positions of the two churches concerning various aspects of inter-church marriage and what is permissible under current rules.

It is interesting to observe how specific pastoral concerns have set the agenda for the dialogue between Methodists and Roman Catholics in Australia, and thereafter between the Uniting Church and the Roman Catholic Church. Furthermore, the Joint Working Group has deliberately opted to tackle the principal doctrinal disagreements between Roman Catholics and Protestants as these present themselves in Christian baptism and inter-church marriage. It has done so from a firm conviction that baptism and inter-church marriage present a microcosm of ecumenical relations between separated churches. The partners in inter-church marriages in particular are 'living ecumenism on behalf of the Churches in the most significant manner possible'.[54]

New Zealand

Dialogue between Methodists and Roman Catholics in New Zealand began as recently as the 1980s, following a long history of mutual suspicion and misunderstanding reaching back to the days of the earliest Christian missionaries. The first participants in the dialogue shared a sense of excitement that this was an historic moment for all Christians in New Zealand, and their initial conversations sought to establish a new relationship between the two churches in a spirit of genuine commitment to openness.

The first series of bilateral conversations between Methodists and Roman Catholics in New Zealand was essentially exploratory in nature and quickly led to the discovery of shared basic convictions concerning faith and discipleship. The dialogue was able to establish considerable common ground, noting a shared emphasis on the centrality of grace and spiritual growth. The outcome of these conversations was expressed in the form of pastoral letters sent to Roman Catholic and Methodist parishes to promote local dialogue. Unfortunately, there is little firm evidence of what this achieved, beyond the establishment in a few places of local study groups.

Building on the 'strong relationship of trust' that was established in the first series of conversations, the second round of dialogue took place between 1994 and 1999.[55] This time the discussion focused on issues 'more resistant to resolution', and the ecumenical spirit of the conversations was tempered by a greater realism about what could be achieved. The final report from this second phase of dialogue reflected that 'We have become aware that our differences time and again focussed on ecclesiology'.[56] The theological details are familiar by now and need not be repeated here.

Responding informally to *Speaking the Truth in Love* (Brighton, 2001), the Methodist co-secretary of the dialogue, Terry Wall, highlighted certain elements in the report which Methodists in New Zealand would welcome.[57] Briefly, these were: the primacy of the Word in the Church; the Church as a communion; the emphasis on the Holy Spirit animating the Church; and 'the greatly enhanced recognition given to the place of the laity within the Church'. At the same time, he identified a number of issues that continue to be problematic for Methodists in New Zealand. For instance, the report's assertion that 'Methodists affirm with Catholics that ordination establishes the minister in a new and permanent relationship with the Risen Christ' (Brighton report, 77) raises difficulties for Methodists in New Zealand which are 'not easily resolved'. Likewise, 'the notion that there are doctrines which the Church requires its members to accept sounds strange' to New Zealand Methodists. Most serious of all, 'There is a sense that the language in which *Speaking the Truth in Love* is written adopts a Catholic accent. Many of the terms and phrases would not be familiar within our parishes, and the language appears to come from another tradition.' The response further questioned whether Methodists in New Zealand would be able to recognise their own experience of Methodism from *Speaking the Truth in Love*:

> There are aspects of the report that push into territory that is unfamiliar. For example, we could question the claim that 'Methodists' reading of the Scriptures is guided by the early Creeds and Councils and certain standard texts, such as the Sermons of John Wesley, his Notes on the New Testament, and the Articles of Religion' (paragraph 22). This may be so in other parts of Methodism, but it is not strongly apparent in the New Zealand context.

These remarks demonstrate that the various Methodist Conferences around the world are by no means certain to receive the reports of the international Methodist–Roman Catholic dialogue in precisely the same way. As Wall points out, 'each Methodist Church is autonomous and prizes its independence'.

The tone of the response to *Speaking the Truth in Love* from New

Zealand vividly illustrates Richard Stewart's experience, derived from his participation in the international dialogue, that Methodists are much less inclined than Roman Catholics to formal definition of doctrine. According to Wall:

> Most Methodist people are cautious of grand schemes, tidy treatments and conclusive statements. They are not comfortable with the view that truth can easily be tied down in doctrine and official formulations. They tend to want to keep things open, aware of the ambiguity that seems an inevitable part of life. So many Methodists will be suspicious of final words, imposed formulas and an insistence that there is only one way to see an issue. While holding to the great central convictions of our faith concerning creation and incarnation, cross and resurrection, Trinity and Eucharist, they will be less eager to tie things down in what seem to be a final formula. This applies to theology and liturgy, ethics and spirituality. A dogmatic approach is not favoured.

Clearly, Methodists in New Zealand approach the dialogue with Roman Catholics in a robust spirit that combines relaxed candour and independent thought.

Thus a notable feature of the dialogue in New Zealand is its reflective insight into the nature and purpose of conversations between Methodists and Roman Catholics and the perceptions both sides have of the other. From a New Zealand perspective, dialogue between Methodists and Roman Catholics is necessarily a lengthy process involving two very different partners that have adopted contrasting approaches to the way they identify, discuss and resolve doctrinal issues. Their characteristic methodologies in dogmatic and systematic theology are derived from the normative ways in which the two churches express their ecclesial identity and existence. Thus bilateral dialogue between Methodists and Roman Catholics requires a 'reflexive' approach in which the beliefs of both communities are related back to the respective ecclesial structures in which they were embedded.[58] If theological language and concepts are divorced from their original framework and translated into another setting, there is a high risk of distortion and misunderstanding.

A further difference between the dialogue partners is that the Roman Catholic Church and the Methodist Church in New Zealand are 'not in the same place in relation to the nature, goal, and possibilities of dialogue'. The participants in the dialogue relate to their sponsoring churches in different ways: the Methodists belong to the Methodist Church in New Zealand, which is governed by an autonomous Conference; the Roman Catholics report to the Catholic Bishops' Conference of New Zealand, which relates to the wider Roman Catholic Church through the Vatican. Whereas Roman Catholics in New Zealand consider it vital not to compromise unity by becoming 'out of step' with Roman Catholics elsewhere, 'It is less important to the Methodist side how they stand to Methodists elsewhere in the world.'[59] The Roman Catholic members of the dialogue are primarily concerned to investigate how a particular position relates to Roman Catholic teaching, while the Methodists have to judge whether the Conference could accept a particular development.

Methodists and Roman Catholics also diverge in the way they approach the past. 'Catholics want to profess the same beliefs as the Church of the past in a reasonably detailed manner. Methodists have a more relaxed approach to the detail of past belief, at times frankly admitting that circumstances may demand change on quite fundamental notions e.g. the power to ordain.'[60] This does not mean that Roman Catholics are bound to approach their tradition as static or closed; still less that Methodists necessarily fail to preserve the integrity of their tradition over the course of time. Even so, Methodists and Roman Catholics have certain perceptions of each other. Thus 'Catholics tend to feel that Methodist openness will inevitably finish by bending to current pressures in society. Methodists tend to feel that Catholic positions are simply too inflexible to relate to the contemporary world, or that they cover up *de facto* changes under unchanging formulas. While such views could easily become simplistic stereotypes, there is some truth in them.'[61]

A third phase of the dialogue in New Zealand began in 2001; but as yet no report has been published. Reflecting on the conversations so far, the Roman Catholic co-secretary, John Owens, made an observation that is both an apposite comment on the particular method adopted in New Zealand and a suitably positive note on which to end this survey of the four national dialogues:

Dialogue forces us back to our roots. That is, in talking to one another, we discover better who we ourselves are, and this becomes part of the changing life of the respective believing communities, whose lives develop through their conversations. Dialogue can lead to a process of mutual modification, which is always enriching. No one would pretend that there is any immediate prospect of full unity. The dialogue exposed too many points of impasse which do not offer any immediate hope of resolution. But if we remain open to Christ's word as we develop, who knows what God will deliver?[62]

6

Towards Catholicity

Addressing the British Methodist Conference in June 1998, the then President of the Pontifical Council for Promoting Christian Unity, Cardinal Edward Cassidy, declared: 'We have such a lot to thank God for: the change in our relationships over the last forty years is a great grace of God.' He went on,

> We are now so much more aware of the ties that bind us together because of our common baptism. Catholics and Methodists have come to appreciate what an important bond is the concern both have for sanctification and the life of grace. We openly admit to the many gifts we see in each other and are able to share. Now we see that we are indeed sisters and brothers in Christ and that we can and should give greater common witness to him. Our communion, though not yet all it should be, is nevertheless real.[1]

Forty years earlier it would have been unthinkable for Methodists to invite a Roman Catholic leader to address the Conference. It is a sign of how things have changed in recent years that, even among conservative evangelicals in Methodism, the presence of a Roman Catholic cardinal at the Conference hardly raised an eyebrow.

Cardinal Cassidy reminded the Conference of some of the encouraging developments in ecumenical relations in recent years, including the way in which the churches have become accustomed to entering into each other's lives by participating in special events. As a result of this increased contact, the different churches now understand one another better than ever before and realise more fully what they have in common, including shared problems, such as the influence of secularisation. The significance of sharing a common faith is too easily overlooked.

The cardinal also praised the international Methodist–Roman Catholic dialogue for its 'deepening conversation, in which we have attempted to listen to each other, to find common ground and recognise that there are areas that are not contentious in order then to look at similarities and differences'.[2] It was the cardinal's belief that the overly optimistic early reports had been followed by a more realistic process of engagement, which involved carefully refining areas of agreement in order to narrow the points of disagreement.

Although sanguine about past gains from ecumenical dialogue and the future possibilities, Cardinal Cassidy drew attention to certain difficulties that still face Christians on the way to full communion. Leaving aside doctrinal matters, which are well documented, the cardinal noted the existence of 'other sources of tension and disagreement that cannot be overcome by arguments based on logic or calm reasoning'. At the root of these lie 'psychological difficulties'. In Europe, for instance, unhealed memories of the past, often stemming from appalling experiences in religious wars, pose an immense psychological difficulty for ecumenical dialogue. There are many such memories on all sides, which have left deep wounds. Thankfully, a process of healing is under way; but it would be foolish to underestimate the challenge involved in overcoming raw memories from the near or even distant past. Though the cardinal gave no illustrations, one example that comes to mind is the former Yugoslavia, where the bitter history of conflict between Christian and Muslim is further complicated by longstanding rivalry between Roman Catholic and Orthodox. Closer to home, past feuds between Roman Catholics and Protestants in Northern Ireland have created a legacy of political and religious sectarianism.

Suspicion and mistrust, arising from unhealed memories, create an immense psychological difficulty for ecumenical dialogue, especially among people who have remained isolated or distant from moves towards greater communion and unity by their churches. People are easily led astray by misinformation, and suspicion is quickly generated by news media. Again, Cardinal Cassidy did not elaborate; but we do not have to look far to find evidence of lingering suspicion and mistrust between Christian traditions, even in the comparatively healthy ecumenical climate of England. As a participant in Methodist–Roman Catholic dialogue, just occasionally I receive letters from people who are evidently out of touch with ecumenical developments during the past

211

forty years. Methodists who write usually insist that Protestants have no business talking to Roman Catholics, unless to challenge their misguided and false doctrines. Such letters from Roman Catholics generally advise Methodists to return to the Roman Catholic Church without delay, if they want to be certain of salvation. Plainly, while there is plenty of goodwill in local ecumenical relations, some Methodists and Roman Catholics continue to hold views about each other which are no longer officially held by their respective churches.

Fear of unity is a recurring psychological difficulty in ecumenical dialogue. Everyone fears the unfamiliar, preferring the *status quo* to a daunting challenge. Numerous people in all the churches resist moving beyond their traditional way of being Christian because they are afraid of unknown territory. Elsewhere, the cardinal spoke of the need to move out into the deep.[3] Anyone with experience of ecumenical relations will know what the cardinal meant when he referred to fear of unity. In 2002 the British Methodist Conference consulted circuits about the proposed Anglican–Methodist Covenant so that Conference knew the mind of the Church before reaching a final decision. The Covenant envisaged closer collaboration between Anglicans and Methodists and a renewed commitment to overcoming the obstacles to full unity; however, it was not a unity scheme. Even so, some of the submissions expressed anxiety that the Covenant would inevitably lead to a loss of denominational identity. In the event, both the Methodist Conference and the General Synod of the Church of England approved the Anglican–Methodist Covenant, which is still in its infancy.

According to Cardinal Cassidy, none of these psychological difficulties can be overcome by theological dialogue alone, though patient ecumenical encounter will certainly help. In the end, only true Christian love will overcome them. Such love does not look for an immediate response or reciprocal action but is determined to overcome all suspicion and opposition with unfailing respect and consideration. When it comes to dealing with past memories, Christian love knows how to pardon and be pardoned. Interestingly, the cardinal's reference to Christian love contains a strong echo of what John Wesley called the 'catholic love' that is at the heart of the catholic spirit.[4]

From a Roman Catholic perspective, Cardinal Cassidy reaffirmed the goal of dialogue between Roman Catholics and Methodists as being full communion in faith, mission and sacramental life. Further progress towards full visible unity will be the gift of the Holy Spirit, who leads Christians into all truth, heals past memories, takes away the fear of unity, and smoothes over ethical, cultural and historical differences.

Among recent developments that give hope and encouragement for better relations between the churches, Cardinal Cassidy singled out for special mention the encyclical letter of Pope John Paul II on commitment to ecumenism, *Ut Unum Sint*. Since this document provides a theological framework in which Roman Catholics are able to converse with other Christians, it is a significant text for Methodist–Roman Catholic dialogue.

Ut Unum Sint (1995) is the most important of the various Roman Catholic teaching documents that have attempted to apply or explain the Second Vatican Council's teaching on the Church. What is striking about this encyclical is its positive evaluation of the various multilateral and bilateral dialogues in which the Roman Catholic Church has been involved since the Council. That a papal encyclical should describe these ecumenical texts as 'a sure foundation for further study' and 'useful tools' for the ecumenical movement (17) is a heartening sign of deepening communion in faith. Overall, *Ut Unum Sint* adopts a conciliatory tone, showing warmth and appreciation for the life and witness of other churches and ecclesial communities.

The encyclical is structured in three chapters. The first explains 'The Catholic Church's Commitment to Ecumenism' with extensive reference to the teaching of Vatican II, especially the Decree on Ecumenism (*Unitatis Redintegratio*) and the Decree on the Church (*Lumen Gentium*). These two documents acknowledge that many elements of sanctification and truth exist outside the visible community of the Roman Catholic Church. John Paul II is equally positive in *Ut Unum Sint*: 'It is not that beyond the boundaries of the Catholic community there is an ecclesial vacuum. Many elements of great value (*eximia*), which in the Catholic Church are part of the fullness of the means of salvation and of the gifts of the grace which make up the Church, are also found in the other Christian communities' (13). 'Indeed the elements of sanctification and truth present in the other Christian communities, in a degree which varies from one to the other, constitute the objective basis of the communion, albeit imperfect, which exists between them and the Catholic Church. To the extent that these elements are found in other

213

Christian communities, the one Church of Christ is effectively present in them' (11).

The ecumenical journey towards the goal of unity requires 'interior conversion', individually and corporately, within all Christian communities. Such conversion is intimately related to renewal and reform (16). Following interior conversion, 'Love builds communion between individuals and between communities' (21). While love is the undercurrent that gives life to the ecumenical movement, the capacity for dialogue is rooted in the nature of the person (28). Since human beings find themselves through self-giving, dialogue is an indispensable step towards the self-realisation of individuals and communities. 'Although the concept of "dialogue" might appear to give priority to the cognitive dimension (*dia-logos*), all dialogue implies a global, existential dimension. It involves the human subject in his or her entirety; dialogue between communities involves in a particular way the subjectivity of each' (28). In other words, dialogue is never simply an exchange of ideas: it is the sharing of gifts.

Pope John Paul II envisages a close relationship between dialogue and prayer. A change of heart, which is an essential condition of the authentic search for unity, flows from prayer (26). 'Deeper and more conscious prayer makes dialogue more fruitful' (33). With profound emotion, the pope remembers praying together with the leaders of other churches and ecclesial communities in the course of his ecumenical visits. The proper spirit for ecumenical dialogue is a prayerful awareness of the sinful human condition that is the cause of disunity. Such awareness creates an 'interior space' where Christ, the source of the Church's unity, can act with all the power of the Holy Spirit. When approached in the proper spirit, ecumenical dialogue is first an examination of one's own conscience and thereafter a 'dialogue of consciences' (34).

Inevitably, ecumenical dialogue puts before the participants real disagreements in matters of faith. These have to be faced in a spirit of love towards the dialogue partner and humility with regard to the truth, which requires assertions and attitudes to be reassessed. Full communion will only come about through accepting the whole truth into which the Holy Spirit guides Christ's disciples. Tempting though they are, all forms of reductionism or facile 'agreement' must be avoided (36). A further problem for ecumenical dialogue stems from the different formulations of doctrine which can be found in the various Christian

214

communities. Sometimes, 'Intolerant polemics and controversies have made incompatible assertions out of what was really the result of two different ways of looking at the same reality' (38). In such cases, the task of dialogue is to uncover the underlying agreement. In other cases, a formula is required that will enable Christians to move beyond partial readings and eliminate false interpretations. In all disputed matters of doctrine there are two essential reference points for an eventual con-sensus – Sacred Scripture and the apostolic tradition of the Church, in the interpretation of which Roman Catholics are able to call upon the assistance of the Church's magisterium (39).

The second chapter of *Ut Unum Sint* considers 'The Fruits of Dialogue' during the past thirty years (41–76). Thankfully, Christians no longer regard those of another tradition as enemies or strangers, but as brothers and sisters. Even the Vatican II expression *separated brethren* tends nowadays to be replaced by phrases such as 'other Christians' or 'Christians of other communities', which more readily bring to mind the deep communion that continues to exist through Christian baptism and shared faith, in spite of historical and canonical divisions (40). Likewise, the 1993 *Directory for the Application of Principles and Norms on Ecumenism* refers diplomatically to 'Churches and Ecclesial Com-munities that are not in full communion with the Catholic Church'. Increasing awareness that Christians are united in baptismal commu-nion is a significant fruit of ecumenical dialogue. Others include greater ecumenical co-operation in social affairs (43), joint translations of the Bible and liturgical renewal (44), and greater awareness of the truly Christian endowments present among separated brothers and sisters (47).

A long section considers 'Dialogue with the Churches of the East' (50–63), before the pope turns his attention to 'Dialogue with other Churches and Ecclesial Communities in the West' (64–76). Here we find extensive quotations from *Unitatis Redintegratio* affirming the elements of truth and sanctification present in these communities. There is said to be a special affinity between the Roman Catholic Church and other churches and ecclesial communities in the West because of the long span of centuries when there was ecclesial communion (64). On the other hand, weighty differences in the interpretation of revealed truth emerged at the time of the Reformation, especially with regard to the Church, the sacraments and the ordained ministry. Still, the hopes expressed by the Second Vatican Council are being met in the various bilateral dialogues involving the Roman Catholic Church (69).

In the final chapter, Pope John Paul considers the way forward for continuing and deepening dialogue, with the ultimate goal of full visible unity among all the baptised. The path towards unity requires Christians to avoid false irenicism, theological indifference, half-hearted commitment, and defeatism (79). Five areas require further study before a true consensus of faith can be achieved:

1) The Relationship between Sacred Scripture, as the highest authority in matters of faith, and Sacred Tradition as indispensable to the interpretation of the Word of God; 2) the Eucharist as the Sacrament of the Body and Blood of Christ, an offering of praise to the Father, the sacrificial memorial and Real Presence of Christ and the sanctifying outpouring of the Holy Spirit; 3) Ordination, as a Sacrament, to the threefold ministry of the episcopate, presbyterate, and diaconate; 4) the Magisterium of the Church, entrusted to the Pope and the Bishops in communion with him, understood as a responsibility and an authority exercised in the name of Christ for teaching and safeguarding the faith; 5) the Virgin Mary, as Mother of God and Icon of the Church, the spiritual Mother who intercedes for Christ's disciples and all humanity (79).

Continuing dialogue in each of these areas must further exploit the theological agreements already achieved. 'These cannot remain the statements of bilateral commissions but must become a common heritage' (80). Above all, what is required is a 'dialogue of conversion' in which individuals recognise their own faults, confess their sins and place themselves in the hands of Christ (82).

As a sharing of gifts and not just the exchange of ideas, ecumenical dialogue is a reciprocal process in which communities offer to supply and receive what each needs in order to grow towards fullness and unity (87). The pope is aware of how much the Roman Catholic Church has benefited from other ecclesial communities – from their witness to certain common Christian values, their study of those values, and even from the way in which they have emphasised and experienced them. Quoting from an address he gave to the cardinals and the Roman curia in 1985, the pope urges his fellow Roman Catholics: 'We must take every care to meet the legitimate desires and expectations of our Christian brethren, coming to know their way of thinking and their sensibilities ... The talents of each must be developed for the utility and the advantage of all' (87).

Naturally, Roman Catholics also possess gifts to share with other Christians. In particular, it is the conviction of the Roman Catholic Church that in the ministry of the Bishop of Rome she has preserved, in fidelity to the apostolic tradition and the faith of the Church Fathers, the visible sign and guarantee of unity in the Church. Pope John Paul II acknowledges that his ministry is a stumbling-block for most other Christians. However, it is a hopeful sign that the universal primacy of the Bishop of Rome has become the subject of study within the ecumenical movement as a whole. After centuries of bitter conflict, Christians in all traditions are taking a fresh look at this ministry of unity (89). Accordingly, the pope invites church leaders and their theologians to engage with him in 'a patient and fraternal dialogue' on the universal primacy of the Bishop of Rome (96).

It is too early to assess the impact of *Ut Unum Sint* on ecumenical relations. Roman Catholics will need time to absorb its teaching before responding in appropriate ways. Protestants often fail to appreciate that the teaching contained in a papal encyclical is expected to remain current for a considerable number of years. For those engaged in dialogue, *Ut Unum Sint* will long continue to provide a rich source of Roman Catholic teaching on ecumenism. Perhaps its most enduring contribution to dialogue between Christians will be the statement that ecumenism is an organic part of the Roman Catholic Church's life and work, and not merely an 'appendix' to its activity (20). Equally, in its description of the necessary conditions for fruitful ecumenical encounter, *Ut Unum Sint* is an unambiguous expression of the Roman Catholic Church's commitment to what John Wesley called 'the catholic spirit'.

Many Christian groups and individuals responded warmly to *Ut Unum Sint*, accepting the pope's invitation to join him in dialogue about his ministry of universal primacy. Geoffrey Wainwright, writing from a Methodist perspective, welcomed the fact that the encyclical eschews the language of the First Vatican Council about the pope's 'universal power of jurisdiction' and 'infallibility in defining doctrine'.[5] Methodists will more readily appreciate the language of John Paul II when he speaks of 'a ministry which presides in truth and love' so that the ship of the Church 'will not be buffeted by the storms and will one day reach its haven'.[6] These same scriptural categories of truth and love are also present in the hymns of Charles Wesley from where they have found their way into Methodist ecclesiology. Furthermore, Methodist ecclesiology has structures and organs that serve the maintenance of truth and the furtherance of love. So it is conceivable that, despite historical sensitivities, Methodists will eventually come to accept the Petrine function as belonging historically and theologically to the Bishop of Rome. Meanwhile, Wainwright makes the following practical suggestion:

> [T]he pope should invite those Christian communities which he regards as being in real, if imperfect, communion with the Roman Catholic Church to appoint representatives to cooperate with him and his appointees in formulating a statement expressive of the Gospel to be preached to the world today. Thus the theme of the 'fraternal dialogue' which John Paul II envisaged would shift from the *theory* of the pastoral and doctrinal office to the *substance* of what is believed and preached. And the very *exercise* of elaborating a statement of faith might – by the process of its launching, its execution, its resultant form, its publication, and its reception – illuminate the question of 'a ministry that presides in truth and love'.

In 1997 the Faith and Order Committee, responding on behalf of the British Methodist Conference, welcomed *Ut Unum Sint* as the first positive encyclical on ecumenism. Faith and Order rejoiced at the Roman Catholic Church's commitment to ecumenism, looked forward to ongoing dialogue on the issues raised in the encyclical, and made a number of comments and suggestions on specific theological issues.[7] Concerning the pope's statement that disagreements should be resolved in the light of Scripture and Tradition, Faith and Order pointed out that Methodists also recognised reason and Christian experience as additional sources of authority though the relationship between Scripture and the Church was crucial. The Committee endorsed the pope's advocacy of fellowship in prayer. Noting the Pope's experience of the presence of Christ in the course of his ecumenical visits, Faith and

Order suggested that the Eucharist could be a means, as well as an end, of Christian unity.

In 1998 the British Conference reached a number of conclusions concerning the implications of *Ut Unum Sint* for the Methodist Church. First, Methodist–Roman Catholic dialogue in Britain should continue, nationally through the British Methodist–Roman Catholic Committee and locally through *Churches Together* groups.[8] In response to the invitation from Pope John Paul II, these conversations could usefully involve a dialogue about his office and ministry of universal primacy. Second, Local Ecumenical Partnerships and the Association of Inter-church Families must be supported and encouraged as a means of deepening Christian unity. Greater priority needed to be given to increasing awareness of the agreed statements produced by the international and national dialogues. Above all, Methodists and Roman Catholics should continue in dialogue and prayer in order to grow closer together. Since the Nairobi report had established the goal of Methodist–Roman Catholic dialogue as being 'full communion in faith, mission and sacramental life', Methodists must not lower their sights, even though there will be many difficulties along the way.

The warm response from the British Methodist Conference reflects a conviction widely held among the churches that *Ut Unum Sint* marked a significant change in attitude on the part of the Vatican. The previous encyclical on ecumenism, On Fostering True Religious Unity (*Mortalium Animos*), had been issued by Pius XI as long ago as 1928. This forbade Roman Catholics to take part in ecumenical conversations, such as the conferences then being organised under the auspices of the Faith and Order movement. *Mortalium Animos* envisaged an alternative form of ecumenism, whereby other Christians would meekly return to the fold of the Roman Catholic Church. Nearly seventy years later, *Ut Unum Sint* irrevocably committed the Roman Catholic Church to ecumenical dialogue among equal partners, each with gifts to offer the other.

To many observers, *Ut Unum Sint* appeared to herald the beginning of a new and promising phase of ecumenical dialogue in which the Roman Catholic Church would participate with a renewed sense of openness to other Christian traditions. Alas, the mood of optimism was short-lived. In 2000 the Congregation for the Doctrine of the Faith stunned even seasoned Vatican watchers by publishing a controversial

Declaration on the Unicity and Salvific Universality of Jesus Christ and the Church (*Dominus Iesus*).

If *Ut Unum Sint* is the most promising document on ecumenism to emerge from Rome since the Second Vatican Council, *Dominus Iesus* is probably the most discouraging. Not since the encyclical *Humanae Vitae* appeared in 1968 has a teaching document emanating from the Vatican provoked so much adverse reaction. *Dominus Iesus* immediately caused controversy as Christians from other traditions responded angrily to what they interpreted as a decision by the Roman Catholic Church to renege on its previous commitment to ecumenism. Articles in the secular press mostly interpreted the document as reinforcing the divisions between Roman Catholics and Protestants. However, many of the responses to *Dominus Iesus* were misinformed and unbalanced. In fact, the text is much more subtle than its detractors have generally been willing to acknowledge. In view of the strong feelings aroused by *Dominus Iesus*, it is important for the sake of Methodist–Roman Catholic dialogue to try and make sense of the Declaration in order to understand its real significance and why it has been so roundly criticised in ecumenical circles.

Contrary to popular perception, *Dominus Iesus* is primarily a response to inter-faith dialogue and certain trends observed by the CDF in its role as doctrinal watchdog for the Roman Catholic Church. The Declaration attempts to clarify the Roman Catholic principles of inter-faith dialogue as set out in the teaching of Vatican II, especially in the Declaration on the Relationship of the Church to non-Christian Religions (*Nostra Aetate*). Its principal target is the phenomenon of relativism, which rejects the uniqueness of the divine revelation in the incarnation. According to relativists, the salvific significance of Jesus Christ is limited to his followers. Other world religions are based on different revelations of the divine, which may equally lead to full salvation for their adherents.

Against relativism and widespread indifferentism towards Christian doctrine, *Dominus Iesus* sets out a robust defence of the salvific universality of Jesus Christ and his Church as taught by the Second Vatican Council. Whatever constructive things Roman Catholics want to say about world religions (and *Nostra Aetate* says a great deal about other faiths that is positive) must not be at the expense of undermining the uniqueness of the incarnation. 'The Church, guided by charity and respect for freedom, must be primarily committed to proclaiming to all people the truth definitively revealed by the Lord, and to announcing the necessity of conversion to Jesus Christ, and of adherence to the Church through baptism and the other sacraments, in order to participate fully in communion with God the Father, Son and Holy Spirit' (22). Twenty-one out of a total of 23 articles in *Dominus Iesus* are devoted to describing the salvific universality of Jesus Christ and his Church as the doctrinal basis for Christian mission and dialogue with other religions. These articles affirm the unique truth of the Judaeo-Christian revelation in the Holy Scriptures in relation to other world faiths and their writings.

Now there are many Christians from all traditions who would similarly regard relativism as a threat to the integrity of Christian faith. They would agree with the CDF that 'As a remedy for this relativistic mentality, which is becoming ever more common, it is necessary above all to reassert the definitive and complete character of the revelation of Jesus Christ' (5). Others would argue in favour of an alternative theological basis for inter-faith dialogue. For reasons of sensationalism, however, any debate concerning the approach to inter-faith dialogue advocated in *Dominus Iesus* has been eclipsed by reactions to the two remaining articles on the unity of the Church.

Articles 16 and 17 of *Dominus Iesus* are devoted to the 'Unicity and Unity of the Church'. Unicity is a technical term for the indivisible uniqueness of the Church. In these two articles the Declaration attempts to clarify the teaching of *Lumen Gentium* that the Church of Christ *subsists* in the Roman Catholic Church. First of all,

> With the expression *subsistit in*, the Second Vatican Council sought to harmonise two doctrinal statements: on the one hand, that the Church of Christ, despite the divisions which exist between Christians, continues to exist fully only in the Catholic Church, and on the other, that 'outside of her structure, many elements can be found of sanctification and truth', that is, in those Churches and ecclesial communities which are not yet in full communion with the Catholic Church. (16).

Certain ecclesiological implications of the Council's use of the term *subsists* are spelled out in a footnote: 'The interpretation of those who would derive from the formula *subsistit in* the thesis that the one Church

221

of Christ could subsist also in non-Catholic Churches and ecclesial communities is therefore contrary to the authentic teaching of *Lumen Gentium*' (footnote 56).

According to the CDF, those churches that have maintained the apostolic succession and a valid Eucharist are 'true particular churches' (17). The Church of Christ is said to be 'present and operative' in these churches, even if they lack full communion with the Roman Catholic Church. Then comes the most problematic statement: 'On the other hand, the ecclesial communities which have not preserved the valid episcopate and the genuine and integral substance of the Eucharistic mystery, are not Churches in the proper sense [*sensu proprio Ecclesiae*]; however, those who are baptised in these communities, are by Baptism incorporated in Christ and thus are in a certain communion, albeit imperfect, with the Church' (17).

On the whole, Christians do not take kindly to the implied suggestion that they belong to an *improper* Church. Despite the reference to 'a certain communion' between Roman Catholics and other Christians, it is hardly surprising that *Dominus Iesus* was greeted by strong protests from Protestants. To be fair, the Declaration is written in the technical language of Latin ecclesiology, where words signify neither more nor less than their precise meaning. The English translation 'Churches in the proper sense' in no way does justice to the Latin *sensu proprio Ecclesiae*. In particular, use of the word 'proper' to translate *proprio* is fraught with difficulty because it replaces a technical term with an everyday word, which is easily misunderstood. It would be incorrect therefore to interpret *Dominus Iesus* as saying that Anglicans, Methodists and others belong to 'improper' churches in any sense that would render them devoid of salvific meaning. Indeed, the Declaration repeats the teaching of *Unitatis Redintegratio* that 'elements' of the Church exist outside the visible structures of the Roman Catholic Church and that other ecclesial communities also contain the means of salvation.

The Declaration's interpretation of the technical term *subsists* prompted more scholarly debate in academic circles. The fine details are complex, which is almost certainly why the secular press failed to register the debate. Briefly, according to *Dominus Iesus*, the Church of Christ exists *fully only* in the Roman Catholic Church. The Church of Christ is said to be 'present and operative' in certain local churches (principally Orthodox) that are not in communion with the Bishop of

Rome. However, because such churches lack this essential sign of communion, it is not possible to say that the Church of Christ *subsists* in them. While it is appropriate to refer to local churches as 'sister' churches, the Catholic Church has no sisters precisely because there can only be one *subsistence* of the Church of Christ in the world.[9] Thus in addition to its primary purpose of providing a framework for inter-faith dialogue, *Dominus Iesus* is also a protest against the increasingly common practice in some ecumenical circles of describing the Roman Catholic Church and other churches and ecclesial communities as *sister* churches.

There is a cool logic in *Dominus Iesus* which is consistent with certain aspects of the teaching of the Second Vatican Council though the question is by no means settled beyond all doubt. Seemingly, the CDF was surprised by the fierce response to what it regarded as a relatively straightforward clarification of what the Council had taught. If this is true, then the CDF should still have been aware that Declarations of this kind are not just read and absorbed by theologians and scholars. Whatever subtleties of doctrine may be involved, the failure of *Dominus Iesus* to acknowledge other Christian communities as sister churches has a detrimental emotional impact, not least because of longstanding sensitivities in this regard. Understandably, Christians from other traditions, including Orthodox, will interpret the Declaration as a return to an exclusive definition of the Catholic Church, which is incompatible with the spirit of Vatican II. Despite assurances from Pope John Paul II in *Ut Unum Sint*, some will suspect that behind *Dominus Iesus* lurks an old-style view of ecumenism, which requires other Christians to return home to Rome. If the Roman Catholic Church no longer wishes to be described as having sister churches, then it must be because she intends to reassert her historical claim to be their mother. For many Christians, this approach to ecumenical relations would be unhelpful at the present time.

Leaving aside the media frenzy, how should *Dominus Iesus* be interpreted by Christians from other traditions? On behalf of the Methodist participants in the international Methodist–Roman Catholic dialogue, Geoffrey Wainwright issued a measured statement in response to the declaration, which made a number of helpful observations.[10] First of all, Wainwright agreed that the Declaration said little that was not already familiar from the teaching of the Second Vatican Council:

When one considers the larger context of ecumenical statements from the Roman Catholic Church, the pronouncements of this recent Declaration can be viewed in their proper perspective as a restatement of the Catholic position on many disputed matters. Such a statement, made with the integrity, love and humility that we consistently find in our dialogue partners, can only help further our mutual understanding.[11]

Methodists, Wainwright suggested, must recognise their own need of further reformation and be willing to engage in a self-critical and honest dialogue with the Roman Catholic Church. Still, it was regrettable that the Declaration made no mention of ecumenical developments since the Council. If there had been some acknowledgement of what has already been achieved through ecumenical dialogue, then Methodists and others might have felt less aggrieved by the restatement of the Roman Catholic Church's position on the unity of the Church.

Diplomatically, the Methodist response pointed out that, since the Declaration was intended for internal use, others might not understand its context in the life of the Roman Catholic Church. Greater awareness among Protestants and others of Roman Catholic teaching and the present state of ecumenical dialogue could have prevented some of the controversy surrounding *Dominus Iesus*. On the other hand, the CDF has a responsibility to anticipate how a wider audience than the one principally intended may interpret a document. It should also take account of the rapid transmission of documents and the intense (though often brief and shallow) interest from news media and other Christian communities. Protestants must hope that future documents produced by the CDF will be more balanced and contain an explanation of their wider context in Roman Catholic teaching.

Nor was it solely Protestants who were likely to misinterpret the content of *Dominus Iesus*. Around the world, Roman Catholics will have heard the text differently, according to their own cultural and theological context. 'In some places where the relationships between Catholics and Protestants have been marked by suspicion, even by hatred and violence, the Declaration has actually done harm to the very cause of responsible ecumenism that it seeks to promote.'[12] Thus *Dominus Iesus* risked reversing the progress of ecumenism at the local level.

Although he agreed with the main thrust of *Dominus Iesus* about the dangers of relativism, Wainwright observed that an excellent opportunity had been lost for united Christian witness to the salvific universality of Jesus Christ in a pluralist world. In the face of cultural fragmentation, joint witness by Christians would have profound implications for the unity of Christ's Church. As it was, the general public, encouraged by the news media, had wrongly interpreted the Declaration as reinforcing the divisions between Christians.

While *Dominus Iesus* may contain little, if anything, that is substantially new, its bleak tone hardly reflects the generosity present in *Ut Unum Sint*. Nor does it give due recognition to the progress made in ecumenical dialogue during the past thirty years. That said, Christians from other traditions have no real grounds for complaint when the CDF draws their attention to the more awkward aspects of *Lumen Gentium*. Enthusiasts for ecumenical dialogue often underestimate the remaining obstacles to full visible unity. In that regard, *Dominus Iesus* is a timely reminder that the path towards full communion between Christians is neither straight nor smooth.

Even when every allowance has been made, there can be little doubt that *Dominus Iesus* was written from a conservative standpoint. But, whatever the intention of those responsible for this Declaration, it is beyond the ability of the CDF or any other organ of the Roman Catholic hierarchy to turn back the clock to an earlier age when ecumenism meant persuading other Christians to return home to their mother, the Roman Catholic Church. The controversy surrounding *Dominus Iesus* should not obscure the fact that the Roman Catholic Church is now irrevocably committed to the process of ecumenical dialogue.

In 1999 the British Methodist Conference adopted a new statement of Methodist ecclesiology entitled *Called to Love and Praise*. This latest document supersedes the 1937 statement on *The Nature of the Christian Church* which had served Methodism well in the intervening years. *Called to Love and Praise* serves four main purposes. First, it will 'help the Methodist people, and perhaps others, to think more clearly about the nature and purpose of the Christian community' (1.3). Second, it promotes greater understanding between Methodists and Christians of other traditions. Third, it contributes toward the *apologetic* task of explaining to non-Christians the nature and purpose of the Church.

Fourth, it encourages deeper discipleship, since reflection on the Church necessarily involves a review of personal commitment to Christ. Thus *Called to Love and Praise* has a direct bearing on dialogue between Methodists and Roman Catholics.

Typically, the statement begins with the situation facing Methodism today. The first section surveys the recent social changes that have created a secular society in which religion, seen as the private affair of a minority, is increasingly marginalized. During this period there have also been many changes in the Church: the ecumenical situation is different today, and biblical scholarship has continued to develop, contributing new insights and challenges. Also, there are fresh perspectives on the Church from Black theology, liberation theology and feminist theology. All this makes a revised Methodist statement on the Church both necessary and timely.

Called to Love and Praise assumes that whatever is said about the Church must be tested against Scripture in conjunction with tradition, since 'tradition is the context which shapes our use of Scripture, and Scripture is the resource by which the tradition is deepened and purified' (1.2.9). Since Scripture and tradition engage with and inform each other, the issue of authority in the Church is complex. Three things need to be said about authority, however. First, Christ is the supreme authority, though there are dependable witnesses, of which Scripture is the most important. Second, because Christians travel by faith, which is not the same as certainty, an eschatological perspective is vital. Third, 'our experience and discernment, nurtured, stimulated and corrected by the witness of Scripture and tradition help to confirm the truth that is in Christ' (1.2.10). Thus equipped, Christians have *sufficient authority* by which to travel.[13]

For Methodists, God's mission and kingdom are the primary given factors in ecclesiology. Scripture and tradition provide the key to understanding the Church as 'one, holy, catholic and apostolic'. The description of God's kingdom provided by the Gospels, together with a Trinitarian understanding of God, demonstrates that the Church is a community for worship and mission. The various images of the Church found in the New Testament illustrate part of the truth. In recent years biblical scholarship has uncovered the rich diversity of ecclesial life in the New Testament, which provides the norm for directing, purifying and enriching the Church today. The unity of the New Testament precludes an 'anything goes' attitude in the Church, while its diversity excludes a narrow rigidity that would impose unnecessary uniformity on the Church.

Questions about the nature and identity of the Church can only be answered in the light of God's relationship with the world and presence in it. 'Whatever way we think of the Trinity, we cannot have an adequate ecclesiology without a proper Trinitarian doctrine, since the Church is called to mirror, at a finite level, the reality which God is in eternity' (2.1.9). Thus the Church is one because God is one, and it is holy because it belongs to God. The Church is catholic because there is one universal God who embraces all nations and peoples without regard to human distinctions. Also, the Church is catholic in the sense that it embodies *authentic* Christian faith. The Church is apostolic insofar as it maintains its continuity with Jesus through his apostles and their successors. Crucially, 'such continuity is not dependent upon, nor guaranteed by, an unbroken succession of ministers, whether presbyters or bishops, from the apostolic period' (2.4.6). Instead, continuity consists in the Church's loyalty to Christ, its mission and experience of fellowship in the Spirit.

While baptism and the Eucharist are essential characteristics of the Christian community (2.4.8), the task of defining the Church and its boundaries is not straightforward. Methodists are reluctant to define the Church with reference to a particular ministerial order (the Roman Catholic approach), or as the community where the word of God is purely preached and the sacraments duly administered according to Christ's institution (the Lutheran and Anglican approach). *Called to Love and Praise* proposes instead an alternative, less tightly drawn criterion for identifying the Church: 'wherever people join together to respond to Christ as Lord – there is the Church' (2.4.9). Visible margins are not unimportant in this definition of the Church, though it would be a mistake to describe in too precise detail the boundaries of the Church as a whole.

Called to Love and Praise draws on recent ecumenical dialogues to describe the unity and catholicity of the Church, attaching particular importance to the WCC Faith and Order Commission's use of *koinonia* language to describe the essential nature of the Church.[14] *Koinonia* implies unity, mutuality and reciprocity based on mutual recognition and a common acceptance of each other's identity (3.1.8). As such, *koinonia* is fundamentally an *experience* and not an abstract concept. Quoting from the Methodist–Roman Catholic Nairobi report, *Called to Love and Praise* asserts that *koinonia* is 'more important than any particular model of Church union that we are yet able to propose . . . For believers it involves both communion and community' (3.1.9).[15] What is more, the unity of the Church is unmistakably related to mission, since God seeks to reconcile the world through unity in Christ. The Church is therefore called to be 'a sign, foretaste and instrument of God's kingdom' (3.2). This ecumenical vision challenges Christians to realise that separation makes them incomplete.

Offering the Gospel in different cultures provides the opportunity for dialogue with people of other faiths. 'To refuse opportunities for such dialogue would be a denial of both tolerance and Christian love . . . People of other faiths can hardly be said to belong to the Church. But the Church has to be understood in a way which does not deny the signs of God in their midst' (3.2.16). It is not our intention to compare the methodology for inter-faith dialogue proposed in *Called to Love and Praise* and that adopted by *Dominus Iesus*. However, on the face of it, the two approaches would appear to be compatible.

The most interesting section in *Called to Love and Praise* addresses 'The Methodist Experience and Understanding of the Church', starting from the premise that 'The Methodist Church has always considered itself to be part of the whole Church of Christ' (4.1). The statement traces the *ad hoc* development of Methodism from a 'connexion' of religious societies within the Church of England into a 'denomination or Church'. Two factors in particular were mainly responsible for this development. First, the Methodist ministry changed from an extra-ordinary mission of travelling preachers into a more settled pastorate. Second, the idea of membership in Methodism evolved from the early days of belonging to a religious society into membership of a fully-fledged denomination or church.

The societal origins of Methodism have left their mark. Some of the distinctive characteristics of Methodism in the present day derive from its roots in a connexion of religious societies. For instance, the issue of membership tickets goes back to the days when the class ticket was required for admission to society meetings. Another legacy from the past is the prominent role of the laity in worship and church government. The past, however, can turn a church into a prisoner of its own cultural identity, creating a cosy sectarianism. 'Great discernment is needed in order to distinguish between those features of Methodist history and tradition which should be cherished and handed on to the wider Church, and those which need to be abandoned, or adapted, because they no longer contribute creatively to contemporary Christian life' (4.2).

The enduring legacy of Methodist ecclesiology lies in its distinctive emphases (4.7). Above all, it is a received truth in Methodism that the nature of the Church incorporates interdependence and reciprocity. The idea of 'relatedness', as expressed in the connexional principle, is therefore integral to Methodist ecclesiology (4.6). An emphasis on fellowship and mutual discipline in small groups reflects the societal origins of Methodism. The development of Methodist ecclesiology has also been influenced by the conviction that the Church should be structured for mission and thus able to respond pragmatically whenever the need or opportunity arises. From the outset, Methodists have adopted a practical approach to questions of ecclesial order. For this reason, the structures of Methodism, including circuits and districts, are not necessarily regarded as essential.

Referring to the national and international Methodist–Roman Catholic conversations, *Called to Love and Praise* acknowledges that Methodists and Roman Catholics are not agreed on what is 'essential for the whole Church'. Concerning the ministry of the Bishop of Rome, however, the statement demonstrates the willingness of Methodism to receive insights from other traditions:

> Methodists could not accept all aspects of papal ministry as it is currently exercised, but would be more open to a universal primacy understood as a ministry of service and unity rather than primarily as a seat of authority. In effect, Methodists rule out no development compatible with our ethos which strengthens the unity and effectiveness in mission of the Church. (4.6.11)

Even the continuing existence of the Methodist Church of Great Britain is not taken for granted in the quest for further progress towards visible unity (5.4).

The statement concludes with a vision of what kind of community the Church should be (5.5). Ideally, the local church will be a community incorporating all ages, races, social backgrounds and occupations – richly diverse but united around the Lord's Table. It will be nourished each week by great songs of faith, prayers and preaching that engages with contemporary experience. There will be warm fellowship, matched by a hospitable welcome and a commitment to Christian service. Its members will sustain one another through love, prayer and forgiveness so that the local church is characterised by joy in the Lord.

A detailed examination of *Called to Love and Praise* lies outside the scope of the present study.[16] However, what little the statement has to say about the essential characteristics of the Church raises questions for Methodist dialogue with Roman Catholics. Noting that certain Christian groups, such as the Society of Friends and the Salvation Army, do not celebrate the sacraments, the statement declares: 'Methodists have been reluctant to unchurch other denominations, and for this reason, whilst affirming these sacraments [baptism and the Eucharist] as "of divine appointment and of perpetual obligation" (*Deed of Union*), would probably wish to say that they are normative, even essential for the whole Church, but not necessarily for every part of it' (3.1.12).

This reluctance to 'unchurch' other Christian groups is a longstanding Methodist trait that goes back to John Wesley. Such sensitivity is commendable in some ways, but inevitably it draws questions from Roman Catholics and others, which *Called to Love and Praise* does not even begin to address. Is it theologically coherent to talk about *essential* features of the 'whole Church' which are not necessary in every 'part' of the Church? What understanding of unity is implied when *essential* features need not be present in every part of the Church? How would the various parts of the Church recognise each other as such? What does 'essential' mean in this context? How do Methodists understand the relationship between the universal Church and local churches? Furthermore, how can the Church *mirror*, at a finite level, the eternal reality of God, when the Church has no knowledge of the interior life of the Trinity? Roman Catholics would press Methodists for unambiguous answers to these questions, in the firm belief that the essential marks of the Church must unquestionably be present in every local church. Although *Called to Love and Praise* provides no answers to these questions, at least it accepts the need for further work on the characteristics necessary for the unity of the Church (3.1.11).

*

In its 1998 response to *Ut Unum Sint*, the British Methodist Conference accepted that eventually it would have to give some kind of official recognition to the statements produced by the international Methodist–Roman Catholic dialogue, if these were not to become totally neglected in British Methodism. Accordingly, in 2003 the Conference accepted a report prepared by its Faith and Order Committee on the content of the international Methodist–Roman Catholic dialogue.[17] As Faith and Order admitted, 'Thirty years of dialogue is a long period to review in a short space.' After a brief analysis of the six statements produced by the Joint Commission between 1971 and 1996, Faith and Order presented a short digest of the main issues to emerge during this period. The most recent statement, *Speaking the Truth in Love*, was treated separately.

Briefly, Faith and Order noted with approval that the Joint Commission had identified many areas of common witness between Methodists and Roman Catholics. Key areas of agreement included Christ's authority in the Church, the Bible as God's Living Word, the importance of Christian spirituality, holiness, and the Holy Spirit. The Methodist doctrine of entire sanctification was consistent with Roman Catholic teaching on continuous growth in perfection. There was also agreement with respect to certain aspects of the Eucharist, though one unresolved difference concerns the precise nature of Christ's presence in relation to the bread and wine. Some Methodists would maintain that there is no qualitative distinction between Christ's presence at the Eucharist and his presence in other means of grace such as preaching.[18] Methodists and Roman Catholics converged to some extent in their understanding of apostolicity and ministry, though the Methodist practice of ordaining women was noted as a major area of disagreement.

To assist the Joint Commission in its future conversations, Faith and Order offered its own observations on some of the key issues to emerge in the course of Methodist–Roman dialogue. Concerning the ordained ministry, divergence between Methodists and Roman Catholics in this area reflects a fundamental disagreement about the nature of the Church and its structures. As seen from Britain, the Joint Commission's theological reflection on ministry in the Church has been dominated by the doctrine of ordination to such an extent that the ministry of the whole people of God has received insufficient attention. The Joint Commission could usefully reassess the way in which it perceives and values lay ministry in the Church alongside ordained ministry.

Episcopacy is another potentially fertile field for dialogue between Methodists and Roman Catholics. Faith and Order pointed out that British Methodism has recently introduced a diaconal order of ministry and continues to consider an episcopal order, though the Conference historically has exercised an episcopal ministry in Methodism. In view of this, it could be argued that Methodism has no need of a separate episcopal order of ministry. Alternatively, the historic role of the Conference could provide an appropriate model for an episcopal ministry exercised by Methodist bishops collegially and alongside lay people. If so, the collegial exercise of episcopal ministry is an area where Methodism might learn from other traditions. While the nature of apostolic succession remains a sticking-point, the Joint Commission was commended for keeping alive the challenge to Methodists and Roman Catholics of revisiting their understanding of apostolic continuity and faithfulness to the New Testament.

Noting that recent statements by the Joint Commission had ignored Christian ethics, Faith and Order accepted that it made sense for Methodist–Roman Catholic dialogue to avoid becoming bogged down in disagreements about Church teaching on moral issues. Even the question of what constitutes a major moral issue can be posed and answered in different ways. However, one subject that deserved more attention from the Joint Commission was language. Awareness of how language can obscure theological issues has grown considerably in recent years. By the standard of today's inclusive language, the gendered language contained in the Denver and Dublin reports seems dated. The Joint Commission might usefully consider further how the use of language both influences and reflects belief, and how the words in which Christian doctrine is expressed might better reflect the fact that the Church incorporates women and children, as well as men.

Thirty years after the Denver report had first identified the problem of reception, Faith and Order expressed the same concern that Methodist–Roman Catholic dialogue should not remain the preserve of theologians, but that its results should be widely available in both churches. The formal response from British Methodism, though late in the day, was intended to help the international Methodist–Roman Catholic dialogue become more widely known in Britain. However, it is difficult to imagine just how a Conference report of this kind could stimulate interest in Methodist–Roman Catholic dialogue in local churches.

The Faith and Order Committee addressed the Brighton report separately, so as to establish a precedent for the Conference to receive and comment on future reports produced by the Joint Commission. Again, for the benefit of the Joint Commission, Faith and Order made a number of observations and comments on the content of the Brighton report. Conference adopted the report from Faith and Order as its official response to *Speaking the Truth in Love.*[19]

In the judgement of the British Methodist Conference, *Speaking the Truth in Love* follows in the tradition of earlier reports from the Joint Commission in being 'an open and honest attempt to locate both agreements and disagreements between the two traditions'.[20] The conversational approach to dialogue, especially the use of mutual questions, has more scope for establishing convergence than a confrontational approach. The emphasis on the Holy Spirit challenges Methodists and Roman Catholics to examine more closely the way in which God guides the Church as it seeks to remain faithful to the Gospel it has received. Methodists and Roman Catholics fundamentally agree that 'God accompanies our appointed leaders, our recognised teachers and our communal gatherings as they undertake their work of teaching and discernment.'[21]

The British Methodist Conference further agreed with the Brighton report that there is a certain similarity between a Methodist Conference and the college of bishops in communion with the Bishop of Rome. From a Methodist perspective, however, the participation of lay people in the Conference is a significant feature. Both traditions affirm that the Holy Spirit works through the whole Church, even though some are called and set apart by God for special service. To the Methodist way of thinking, the process of discernment will be most effective when it involves the whole people of God. Methodists therefore remain strongly committed to 'conferencing' as a vital means by which the Holy Spirit guides the Church.

British Methodism is willing to accept the challenge posed in *Speaking the Truth in Love* for fresh thinking on the role of the bishop. The Conference was pleased to learn that, in the Roman Catholic Church, 'The first task of bishops, especially when together as the college of bishops, is to proclaim the Gospel in its integrity to all' (Brighton report, 65). The gifts and insights that each tradition brings to ecumenical discussions on episcopacy will influence the eventual form in which British

233

Methodism could appropriately receive the historic episcopate into its ecclesial system.

Concerning the disagreement between Methodists and Roman Catholics about what doctrines constitute the 'essentials' of Christian faith, Conference welcomed the Joint Commission's unambiguous affirmation of Scripture as the 'primary and permanent norm' for all doctrine, 'to be interpreted authoritatively by the living voice of Tradition' (Brighton report, 39). However, certain issues arise when trying to determine the precise nature of the relationship between Scripture and Tradition. In particular, the ways in which Scripture can be used as the normative standard for Christian doctrine are many and diverse. In theory, the 'living voice of Tradition' is none other than the living Word, the eternal Logos, to which Scripture bears witness. To complicate matters, the different means of receiving and appropriating the apostolic Tradition within the two communities has a direct bearing on the way it is subsequently handled.

The Conference was of the opinion that, in the current ecumenical climate, it was not easy to envisage a future united Church that embraces and values different ecclesial traditions. It further recognised the fact that in every tradition there are Christians who do not regard institutional unity as the primary goal of ecumenism. Nevertheless, the Conference welcomed the Brighton report as the latest contribution from the 'patient, long-standing conversation' between Methodists and Roman Catholics. Whatever obstacles still remain before full visible unity can be achieved, *Speaking the Truth in Love* signalled a continuing willingness to listen and talk, agree and disagree, which is a crucial feature of the Church's future and its mission.

In the history of the ecumenical movement as a whole, the official response from British Methodism to the reports produced by the Joint Commission is a small gesture, though nonetheless significant for what it represents, if not its substance. For it demonstrates to Methodists and others that the dialogue with Roman Catholics is sufficiently important to warrant consideration in the highest decision-making forum in British Methodism. The Conference's constructive approach to the content of the international dialogue with Roman Catholics is a reminder of how far things have moved on since the nineteenth century, when the Wesleyan Conference and its counterparts in the other branches of Methodism actively tried to impede the growth of Roman Catholicism in Britain.

We have almost come to the end of our survey of recent developments in Roman Catholicism and Methodism and their impact on continuing bilateral dialogue. However, there are two other areas of church life outside the formal channels of dialogue which have contributed indirectly to improved relations between Methodists and Roman Catholics. The first is the Liturgical Movement, where the ecumenical study of the origins and development of Christian worship has had a considerable impact on Methodists and Roman Catholics in the latter part of the twentieth century, leading to a significant convergence in liturgy. The second is the ecumenical movement as a local phenomenon and the practical experience of Methodists and Roman Catholics engaged in joint ecumenical ventures.

In *Ut Unum Sint* Pope John Paul II described liturgical renewal as being among the fruits of ecumenical dialogue (44). The twentieth-century Liturgical Movement had its antecedents in different strands of liturgical renewal in the latter part of the nineteenth century. In Britain, the Anglo-Catholic Revival in the Church of England produced a surge of interest in liturgical sources and the revitalisation of worship in many parishes. Prosper Guéranger (1805–75), a Benedictine monk, was the leading advocate of liturgical renewal within the Roman Catholic Church. In 1832 Guéranger re-founded the abbey of Solesmes in France as a centre dedicated to the study of liturgy, especially Gregorian chant. The groundbreaking research of Guéranger and his monks prompted a revival of interest in the study of liturgy among Benedictines and spurred the investigation into the origins and history of the liturgy. By today's standards, Guéranger's focus was narrowly medieval, based on the somewhat dubious assumption that the Middle Ages represented the golden age of the Church's worship and liturgy. His lasting achievement, however, was to inspire in the Church of his time an interest in the liturgy as something to be prayed and lived.

The beginning of the Liturgical Movement in the twentieth century is usually traced to the address of Lambert Beauduin (1873–1960) at the Roman Catholic pastoral congress in Malines, Belgium, in 1909.[22] Whereas Guéranger had been intent on recovering and restoring historic liturgical texts, Beauduin gave the Liturgical Movement a pastoral orientation. For Beauduin, the active participation of lay people in the liturgy constituted the best means of nourishing their spiritual life, besides exposing them to a basic form of instruction in the faith. He believed that a better grasp of the Church as the body of Christ would encourage a deeper sense of community in worship and the Christian life. For all this to happen however the Roman missal had first to be translated into the vernacular. Although Beauduin was aiming for a moderate renewal of worship rather than its radical overhaul, the Liturgical Movement aroused considerable opposition from more conservative Roman Catholics. Yet, the movement flourished and began to spread throughout Europe and North America.

By the end of the Second World War, the Liturgical Movement was a powerful force for renewal within the Roman Catholic Church. In his encyclical *Mediator Dei et Hominum* (1947), Pius XII gave official recognition to the Liturgical Movement, while simultaneously seeking to curb its more radical demands. The pope expressed a desire that lay people should participate more actively in the liturgy, even conceding that vernacular languages would facilitate this. In the following decade the Easter Vigil was restored to the liturgical calendar and further modest reforms were introduced in other Holy Week services.[23] The major rites were restored to evening hours so that the majority of people could attend. To meet the needs of people living in industrial urban areas, the rules on fasting before the Eucharist were relaxed and evening Masses were permitted. The rubrics governing the conduct of services were simplified, making it easier for lay people to participate. Even so, the framework of the liturgy was proving too restrictive to meet the needs of Roman Catholics in post-war Europe. The demand for further reforms in the liturgy was one of the factors that led John XXIII to summon the Second Vatican Council.

It was at the Second Vatican Council that the Liturgical Movement achieved its greatest success. On 4 December 1963 Pope Paul VI promulgated the Constitution on the Sacred Liturgy (*Sacrosanctum Concilium*), the first constitution to come out of the Council. One of its main purposes was to present a theology of the liturgy as a framework for introducing wholesale liturgical reforms in response to contemporary needs.[24] In many ways, *Sacrosanctum Concilium* articulated the manifesto of the Liturgical Movement, setting out the theological principles and pastoral objectives of liturgical reform in the Roman Catholic Church. The emphasis throughout the Constitution on the Sacred Liturgy is on the celebration of the Eucharist by the whole people of God as participants in Christ's priesthood. One of the most far-reaching provisions was for the use of vernacular languages in the liturgy, so as to facilitate the active participation of the laity. At the same time, the Constitution's implicit understanding of the Church as the people of faith gathered in unity round the bishop provided a fundamental ecclesiological perspective for other conciliar documents, including the Dogmatic Constitution on the Church and the Decree on Ecumenism.

Immediately following the Council, steps were taken to implement *Sacrosanctum Concilium* by establishing various commissions to reform the liturgy (including the Eucharistic Prayer, which few bishops had envisaged) and translate it into various languages. Among a host of reforms, the rites of Christian initiation (baptism and confirmation) were revised, and communion under both kinds (i.e. the bread and wine) was restored to the Eucharist (*Sacrosanctum Concilium*, 55). The structure and content of the Eucharist was also modified in the light of recent liturgical scholarship. The ancient Roman canon was retained as the first Eucharistic Prayer, but the Tridentine Mass was effectively banned.

Inevitably, not all Roman Catholics have been happy with the extent of the liturgical reforms initiated by the Council, and there is evidence of a conservative reaction. Some claim that the Liturgical Movement has had an adverse effect on the Roman rite, allowing twentieth-century cultural norms to invade the liturgy. The English translation of the liturgy has proved particularly contentious. Conservatives maintain that any translation into English should faithfully reproduce the exact meaning of the Latin in the Roman rite. Others argue that this results in a translation that is stilted and inelegant. What is required, they say, is a translation based on the principle of 'dynamic equivalence', which would render the essential meaning of the Roman rite into appropriate and contemporary English. The debate cannot be pursued here.

Even reforms in the rubrics have been hotly debated. To take just one example, the Second Vatican Council reversed the direction faced by the celebrant at the Eucharist. In the Tridentine Mass, during the Eucharistic Prayer the celebrant faced the altar, his back to the congregation, thereby emphasising the eschatological dimension of the Eucharist, as priest and people together looked eastwards in anticipation of Christ's return in glory. The present rubric requires the celebrant to face the congregation across the altar, thereby emphasising that he acts *in persona Christi* as the whole community celebrates the Eucharist. This very visible change, based on a different (though complementary) theological perspective, provides considerable scope for debate among Roman Catholics about the merits of the liturgical reforms.

In 1938 Ernest Rattenbury, a leading Methodist preacher and scholar, declared in words that remain apposite today, 'Methodism seems to be standing at the crossways. Much of her distinctive denominational life has gone, and she is feeling, perhaps subconsciously, after Catholicity.'[25] In Chapter 3 we saw how Methodist theologians in the early years of the twentieth century were beginning to explore the catholicity of Methodism. Participation in the Liturgical Movement had broadly the same effect: it brought Methodism into greater contact with the long history of the Church prior to the Reformation. Liturgical developments in Methodism in Britain and the United States during the twentieth century, especially with regard to the Eucharist, provide a practical illustration of how Methodism has continued to feel its way towards greater catholicity, with obvious implications for relations with the Roman Catholic Church.[26]

It is sometimes forgotten that early Methodism in England was as much a eucharistic revival as it was a renewal and holiness movement. At a time when parish churches typically celebrated the Eucharist three or four times a year, John Wesley observed the sacrament much more frequently, stressing in a classic sermon 'The Duty of Constant Communion'.[27] However, for a variety of reasons, eucharistic practice among Methodists diminished after the death of Wesley. Many of Methodism's itinerant preachers were temperamentally and theologically inclined more towards evangelical preaching than the celebration of the sacraments. Later, the powerful eucharistic emphasis at the heart of the Anglo-Catholic Oxford Movement in the Church of England reinforced in the minds of Methodists the negative association between a sacramental economy and Roman Catholicism. For most of their history, Methodists have tended to separate word and sacrament, often neglecting the Eucharist in favour of preaching services as the most cherished means of grace.

During the nineteenth century, the various Methodist denominations in Britain developed their own service books, based to a greater or lesser extent on Wesley's revision of the 1662 Book of Common Prayer for use in North America. Following Methodist Union in 1932, the first major publication authorised by the Conference was *The Methodist Hymn Book* (1933). The second was the *Book of Offices* (1936) which attempted to integrate the liturgical preferences of the main branches of Methodism. The text of the service of Holy Communion followed very closely Wesley's service and so was directly related to the earliest rites in English. A second 'alternative' form was much shorter, reflecting the liturgical style of the non-Wesleyan traditions, though in practice the celebration of the Eucharist in Primitive Methodism and the smaller Methodist bodies had seldom made use of a printed liturgy. Since Sunday worship for the vast majority of Methodists meant a preaching service, use of the *Book of Offices* was confined for the most part to the monthly observance of 'the sacrament' or Holy Communion.[28]

The *Methodist Service Book* (1975) was a landmark development in British Methodism, the result of Methodist involvement in the Liturgical Movement during the 1960s. Its chief architect was A. Raymond George (1912–98), a participant in the international and national Methodist–Roman Catholic dialogues, a member of the WCC Faith and Order Commission, and a WCC observer on the commission that revised the Roman Catholic liturgy following the Second Vatican Council. The various 'experimental liturgies' that eventually found their way into the *Methodist Service Book* had been circulating in British Methodism since 1967. Circuits, churches and individuals were given the opportunity to comment on the draft liturgies, and many chose to do so, thereby contributing to the service book's subsequent reception by the Methodist people.

The *Methodist Service Book* contained a completely revised order of service for Holy Communion in contemporary language, entitled 'The Sunday Service'. The choice of title reflected Wesley's ideal that the Eucharist should be celebrated weekly; though the general directions made no comment on how frequently the sacrament should be observed.[29] The Service Book also contained a lectionary and collects prepared by the Joint Liturgical Group. For the benefit of traditionalists, the complete order of Holy Communion from the 1936 service book was reproduced in full. Among the few provisions in the rubrics for liturgical symbols was the optional presentation of a lighted candle at baptism, which provoked much comment at the time, especially among more conservative Methodists, fearful at what they regarded as the encroachment of Romish practices into Methodism. However, by providing the vast majority of British Methodists with access to an authorised eucharistic liturgy, based on the best insights of the Liturgical Movement, the *Methodist Service Book* proved to be a powerful influence on the continuing development of Methodist spirituality and devotion to the Eucharist. In so doing, the service book was a victim of its own success. Less than twenty years after it was published, the Conference resolved to prepare a successor containing a greater variety of liturgical material for use in Methodist worship.

Just as the *Methodist Service Book* was beginning to make its mark on British Methodism, the WCC Faith and Order Commission published *Baptism, Eucharist and Ministry*. Among its seminal achievements, the Lima text endorsed the Liturgical Movement as a means of bringing the churches closer together in their celebration of the Eucharist: 'The best way towards unity in eucharistic celebration and communion is the renewal of the Eucharist itself in the different churches in regard to teaching and liturgy.'[30] According to *BEM*, 'As the Eucharist celebrates the resurrection of Christ, it is appropriate that it should take place at least every Sunday.'[31]

In its official submission to the WCC, the British Methodist Conference admitted that, due to the influence of the 1975 service book, Methodists in Britain would read the section in *BEM* on the Eucharist 'with far more interest and understanding than would have been possible a decade ago'.[32] The Conference accepted that liturgical reform was 'the most striking example of convergence between the churches'.[33] In the case of the Eucharist, Methodists had moved closer to their founder, who had urged frequent celebration. However, 'the history and the structure of Methodism make weekly celebrations in all our churches all but impossible'.[34] As a matter of statistical fact, there had never been sufficient ministers for every Methodist service to be led by an ordained minister. Accordingly, 'Methodists have learnt to nourish themselves on [preaching services] and many would not now wish to see the balance altered in favour of more frequent communion.'[35] The Conference then raised a question that has yet to be fully investigated in

Methodist–Roman Catholic dialogue: 'Christ's presence in the Eucharist is unique in the sense that every means of grace is unique, but is it unique in the sense that it is superior to all others?'[36] With these reservations, the Conference welcomed the timely guidance offered by *BEM* on the subject of the Eucharist, which continued to inform Methodist thinking on the subject throughout the 1980s.

Following extensive trials of draft services based on contemporary liturgical scholarship and the ecumenical insights of *BEM*, the British Conference authorised the *Methodist Worship Book* (1999) for use in Methodist churches.[526] This latest worship resource contains several liturgies and elements hitherto unknown in British Methodism, thereby supplying striking evidence of the influence of the Liturgical Movement. There are offices for Morning and Evening Prayer, following the pattern of the Book of Common Prayer. Altogether, there are eight full orders for Holy Communion in different seasons, plus a further seven orders for particular occasions such as Holy Week, the Covenant service, the marriage service, healing services, and ordination services. There is greater provision for the use of liturgical symbols, including seasonal colours, candles and the pouring of water at baptism. The service for Ash Wednesday includes the imposition of ashes, and the service of healing provides for the laying on of hands and anointing with oil. For the sick and housebound, there is a form of reserved sacrament or 'extended communion'. There is an 'Easter Vigil' complete with instructions on how to insert nails into the Paschal Candle. An extensive set of funeral liturgies includes a Vigil (familiar to some Methodists outside Britain) and optional prayers for the departed. At the last moment, the Conference withdrew from the Funeral Service an option for a white pall to be placed over the coffin. 'An Order for the Blessing of a Home' prompted discussion about the theology of blessing, and whether it was appropriate to bless inanimate objects.

Until recently, some of the liturgical rites, symbols and gestures contained in the *Methodist Worship Book* would have caused considerable consternation in many Methodist congregations. In fact, some Methodists continue to regard the liturgical innovations in the worship book as contrary to Protestant principles and an undesirable intrusion of Roman Catholic elements. Yet, sales of the *Methodist Worship Book* had already exceeded 250,000 by 2003, and it is now in regular use in Methodist churches throughout Britain, providing an impressive liturgical resource for ministers and lay people in their public worship and private devotions.

The development in the twentieth century of more sophisticated liturgical rites to accompany entry into the Methodist community illustrates Methodism's transition from society to church. Historically, Methodists have been unsure about the merits of confirmation and have usually preferred some form of dedication as the effective liturgical sign and seal of entry into full membership of the community. The 1936 *Book of Offices* contained a short service for the 'Public Reception (Confirmation) of New Members', which invited new members to 'confirm your response to his gracious call' in a short act of dedication.[38] The 1975 service book included a service of 'Public Reception into Full Membership, or Confirmation', which contained a prayer of invocation, accompanied by the laying on of hands, asking the Lord to confirm his servants by the Holy Spirit.[39] The *Methodist Worship Book* contains various services of 'Confirmation and Reception into Membership', all of which invoke the Holy Spirit to confirm those to be received into membership. Coyly, the Worship Book describes confirmation as 'a significant point along the journey of faith' but declines to say what kind of rite it is.[40]

Methodists tend to view their liturgical history as maintaining a proper emphasis on the word through preaching services and show little obvious regret that Wesley's emphasis on the Eucharist soon faded in Methodism after his death.[41] Interestingly, however, there is firm evidence to indicate a revival of interest in the Eucharist in British Methodism. In 2003 the Faith and Order Committee presented a major report to the Conference *His Presence Makes the Feast: Holy Communion in the Methodist Church.*[42] Intended as an 'overall expression of our practice and beliefs' about Holy Communion, *His Presence Makes the Feast* is not a formal teaching document as such, but is based on a survey of current practice and beliefs within the Methodist Church.[43] Among other things, the survey revealed that Holy Communion was celebrated at least once a month in 90 per cent of Methodist churches. While some respondents expressed a desire for more frequent celebration of the Eucharist, others expressed concern that the sacrament would lose its special character if it were celebrated too often. A large majority of the responses expressed belief in the real presence of Christ at the Eucharist, though some were cautious about the idea of Christ being either uniquely or specially present. There were also a few Methodists who claimed not to believe in the real presence of Christ at the Eucharist, though it is impossible to know for certain what it was they imagined they were rejecting. Most respondents attached great value to the Eucharist, though a few claimed not to value it at all. Altogether the survey confirmed, not entirely helpfully, that 'there are many and various views about Communion' within British Methodism.[44] The report concluded that 'Methodists would benefit from a programme of thorough and high quality teaching concerning the meaning and value of Holy Communion and its place in our spiritual lives.'[45]

Interestingly, the findings from the internal Methodist questionnaire were confirmed by the National Church Life Survey, which questioned a sample of around 10 per cent of people worshipping in Methodist churches in England on the day of the survey in 2001. Among the Methodists questioned, Holy Communion was valued significantly more highly than preaching.[46] If this is typical of Methodism as a whole (and there is no reason to doubt the reliability of the statistics), then it is reasonable to suppose that more frequent celebration of the Eucharist during the past thirty years has influenced the spirituality of many Methodists. The long-term implications of this trend remain to be seen; but it is potentially significant for ecumenical conversations with other Christians, including Roman Catholics, in whose lives the Eucharist has a central role.

In North America practical and cultural difficulties associated with life in the colony meant that the Wesleyan eucharistic revival never really got under way.[47] *The Sunday Service of the Methodists in North America with Other Occasional Services* (1784) was Wesley's adaptation of the *Book of Common Prayer* (1662).[48] Wesley encouraged the ideal whereby the Service of the Lord's Supper, including a sermon, would always follow Morning Prayer on Sundays. However, since there were never sufficient presbyters, the reality was that Methodists in America were mostly unaccustomed to a weekly Eucharist. What is more, the vast majority of the Methodist people had little education and even less appreciation for liturgy. In 1792, barely a year after Wesley died, the American Conference drastically shortened his *Sunday Service.* As in Britain, American Methodists adopted a Sunday preaching service with hymns, prayers, Bible readings and sermon. Contrary to Wesley's intention, for most practical purposes the Eucharist became one of the 'other occasional services'.

During the course of the nineteenth century, the main branches of American Methodism continued to use variations of the 1792 service, despite their divisions over race, slavery and church governance. There were a few minor changes here and there, though none of great theological significance.[49] For instance, the influence of the temperance movement became apparent in 1876 when the Methodist Episcopal Church rubric for communion first recommended the use of unfermented grape juice.[50] Following the growth of the Liturgical Movement in the United States, the 1932 Methodist Episcopal *Book of Discipline* contained three orders for communion, one of which was a deliberate attempt to reconstruct Wesley's *Sunday Service*. These orders provided the basis for the liturgies that were subsequently adopted by the (reunited) Methodist Church in 1939 and included in the *Book of Worship for Church and Home* (1945).

A major revision of American Methodist worship occurred in the 1965 *Book of Worship*, partly in response to a recognised need to make Wesley's service more than a museum piece. However, the timing of the service book was unfortunate, inasmuch as it appeared just three years before the Methodist Church united with the Evangelical United Brethren to form the United Methodist Church. Furthermore, the thinking behind the *Book of Worship* had not benefited from the research that resulted in the Vatican II Constitution on the Sacred Liturgy (*Sacrosanctum Concilium*). In order to catch up with the latest research in liturgical studies, the United Methodist Church initiated a further process of revision that eventually led to the publication of a 'Service of Word and Table' (1972). For the first time in American Methodism, there was now a distinct eucharistic shape to Sunday worship, whether or not the service included the sacrament of Holy Communion. Following a series of minor amendments, the revised service was published separately in 1984 as the 'United Methodist Lord's Day Service'. The final text appeared in the *United Methodist Hymnal* (1989) and thereafter in the *United Methodist Book of Worship* (1992).

The structure of the Lord's Day Service does not rely on Wesley's *Sunday Service*. Based on the results of recent liturgical research, it follows the classic shape of the Sunday liturgy in what many scholars believe to be its primitive form, as found in Justin Martyr and

244

Hippolytus' *Apostolic Tradition*.[51] In their introduction, the compilers of the United Methodist Worship Book declared:

> Since New Testament times, this Basic Pattern has had a long history of development. At times this pattern has been obscured and corrupted, and at times it has been recovered and renewed. The Wesleyan revival continued this emphasis on Word and Table, taking the gospel into the world by preaching and singing and by celebrating the holy meal. Today the United Methodist Church is reclaiming our biblical and historical heritage, as we seek in this Basic Pattern to worship God 'in spirit and in truth'.[52]

Although Wesley would not have recognised the structure of the Lord's Day service, he would presumably have approved of the method by which it was produced. In 1784 he assured the Methodists in North America that they were 'at full liberty, simply to follow the Scriptures and the Primitive Church'.[53]

In its official response to the WCC Lima text *Baptism, Eucharist and Ministry* in 1986, the United Methodist Church admitted that 'Like other Protestants, we have allowed the pulpit to obscure the altar. Now, without minimising at all the preaching of God's word, we more clearly recognise the equivalent place of the sacrament.'[54] With commendable honesty, the United Methodist Church also confessed to having omitted core elements of the Eucharist, as described in *BEM* (Section III, para. 27), 'for reasons of carelessness, neglect or lack of informed understanding'.[55] In contrast to the more cautious British reply, the United Methodist response accepted the arguments set out in *BEM* for a weekly celebration of the Eucharist: 'Although we fall short of a weekly celebration, we acknowledge that the Church's long experience shows it to be normative. We intend to urge our congregations to a more frequent, regular observance of the sacrament.'[56]

In this section we have observed how the Liturgical Movement, through its study of the origins and historical development of Christian worship, has led to a remarkable degree of convergence between Roman Catholics and Methodists in the way they understand and celebrate the Eucharist. To some Roman Catholics, the liturgy now has a more Protestant feel to it. Equally, there are Methodists who are convinced that their worship has become much more Roman Catholic. This is due to the fact that when Methodists and Roman Catholics celebrate the Eucharist it is no longer immediately obvious just what the differences are. This striking convergence in eucharistic liturgy may well have far-reaching implications for the way in which ordinary Methodists and Roman Catholics view each other as they increasingly experience each other's worship. Indeed, as a result of the ecumenical movement and changing patterns of church allegiance, it is now more common for Christians to participate in worship in traditions previously unfamiliar to them.

Besides the Liturgical Movement, the phenomenon of local ecumenism is the second of our indirect factors, other than formal dialogue, to have influenced relations between Methodists and Roman Catholics in recent years. Unfortunately, there has been very little research in this field, and a full treatment of the subject must await a future study. However, no account of dialogue between Methodists and Roman Catholics would be complete without at least some reference to the ecumenical experience of Methodists and Roman Catholics at a local level.

In many places in Britain Methodists and Roman Catholics find themselves sharing in local Churches Together groups where they participate along with other Christians in various ecumenical activities and projects. Typically, these would include united services during the Week of Prayer for Christian Unity and on other occasions, joint ventures in mission and service, such as ecumenical drop-in centres or church coffee shops, and ecumenical house groups. The value of these informal contacts between Methodists and Roman Catholics, even on an infrequent basis, should not be underestimated, since they help erode the sense of 'us' and 'them', which for so long has been a feature of the Christian landscape in Britain.

As far as more formal arrangements are concerned, in 2003 Churches Together in England recorded 207 Local Ecumenical Partnerships (LEPs) in which Methodists and Roman Catholics were both partici-pants.[57] Table 6.1 shows the breakdown of these, according to the six types of LEP identified by Churches Together in England:

Table 6.1   LEPs involving Methodists and Roman Catholics (2003)

Type	Description	Total	Comments
1	Single Congregation	21	Indicates Methodist Church is in partnership with a third denomination
2	Shared Building	109	
3	Covenanted Partnership	40	
4	Chaplaincy	42	Hospital (9); Education (27); Prison (6)
5	Mission Partnership	23	Industrial (9); Community (13); Rural (1)
6	Education	4	

Note: Some LEPs are officially registered in two or more categories, so the above figures add up to more than 207.

Two of the above types of LEP require a brief word of explanation. Canon law prevents Roman Catholics from becoming full partners in a Single Congregation LEP. In the above table, a Single Congregation LEP denotes one in which the full partnership is between the Methodist Church and a third denomination. To record the participation of Roman Catholics, these LEPs are also registered as Covenanted Partnerships, and they are also listed in Table 6.1 under the appropriate category. From the information supplied by Churches Together in England, it is not easy to establish the difference between Education LEPs and Chaplaincy LEPs in educational institutions. However, since the number of these LEPs is very small, any ambiguity has little effect on the overall picture. With these provisos, the table illuminates the range of ways in which Methodists and Roman Catholics are involved in formal ecumenical relationships in England.

Since each LEP is unique it is difficult to generalise about the way they operate. Nor is it possible here to provide examples of every type of LEP. Even within the same category, LEPs take many different forms. However, the type of LEP most likely to generate regular contact between Methodists and Roman Catholics is the category of shared buildings. It is interesting to note that in 2003 there were 109 Local

Ecumenical Partnerships in which Methodists and Roman Catholics shared a building. In most cases, these were places of worship, though in a few places shared buildings were used for some other purpose. There are also a small number of church buildings shared by several denominations, including Methodists and Roman Catholics.

As yet, there has been no detailed research into the experience of Methodists and Roman Catholics in Local Ecumenical Partnerships where both are constituent members, not even in the case of shared buildings. Anecdotal evidence gathered for the British Methodist–Roman Catholic Committee reveals mixed experiences within each type of LEP. For the most part, those involved in such partnerships consider them to be effective and worthwhile, though there are often tensions because of different expectations. Even where a building is shared between two worshipping communities, the existence of an LEP sometimes makes little practical difference to local Christians, apart from those who are ecumenically minded. Moreover, the pace of ecumenism varies greatly: something that is considered daring in one situation may be commonplace in another. It is hardly surprising that the most successful experience of collaboration seems to occur where the principal personalities, usually the clergy, are able to work together in a spirit of mutual respect.

The shared use of buildings for worship by Methodists and Roman Catholics presents both opportunities and challenges. To take just one example, in a small town in Cumbria, Methodists and Roman Catholics successfully share a building that is owned by the Methodist Church.[58] Roman Catholic Mass is held on Saturday evening, and the Methodists worship on Sunday mornings. The notice board outside the church proclaims its dual function. Apart from informal contacts, the congregations share in special events as appropriate.

The challenge involved in sharing this and any other building for worship stems from the fact that places of worship constitute sacred space. Insofar as Methodists and Roman Catholics hold a different theology of sacred space, tensions can arise in how the building is used. Great sensitivity is required on all sides if problems are to be avoided. For instance, it is second nature for Roman Catholics to bow towards the altar on entering and leaving a church. Methodists would not dream of doing so, not out of disrespect, but because they hold a different theology of sacred space. It would be very easy for Methodists and Roman

Catholics to misunderstand each other's actions and take offence where none was intended. Similarly, tabernacles, altar lights, holy water stoups, bells, statues and other church furnishings can be a source of friction. Even displaying the symbol of the cross in shared churches raises questions. Crucifixes are virtually unheard of in Methodist churches, though an empty cross is usually displayed prominently as a witness to the resurrection of Christ. For Roman Catholics, the crucifix offers powerful testimony to Christ's sacrifice at Calvary. It is not unknown for Methodists and Roman Catholics to interpret each other's liturgical rites, symbols and gestures as indicating irreconcilable theological differences, which in fact may not be the case.

In most of the above instances, awareness of the issues involved and a corresponding sensitivity on the part of both communities will probably be sufficient to avoid controversy. However, when one community uses sacred space for a purpose that is contrary to the doctrine of the other, the issues are more complex and the scope for anguish correspondingly higher. A case in point concerns the remarriage of divorced persons in a shared church building. Whereas a Methodist minister is permitted to conduct such a marriage in appropriate circumstances, Roman Catholic priests are only allowed to do so where the Church has already granted an annulment. How can the doctrinal integrity of both communities be safeguarded when their sacred space is used for liturgical rites in these circumstances? This and related questions could usefully be explored further.

To date, a theology of sacred space has not featured in the international Methodist–Roman Catholic dialogue or in any of the national conversations. Even if it had, the response of theologians is likely to be somewhat different to that of ordinary Methodists and Roman Catholics, who react to sacred space from an experiential, rather than an academic, perspective. The cause of ecumenism would benefit from further research into the experience of Methodists and Roman Catholics in sharing sacred space for worship. Of course, there are risks involved in sharing any resource, buildings perhaps especially. However, through sharing these and other resources, and by reflecting on the experience, Methodists and Roman Catholics will come to experience a deeper form of spiritual communion.

In this regard, a recent pioneering development is the construction of church premises in Nelson, Lancashire, for shared use by Methodists

249

and Roman Catholics. The new church was first used for worship on Trinity Sunday in 2004, a fitting occasion in the church calendar to celebrate and affirm the real but imperfect communion in faith, mission and sacramental life which already exists between Methodists and Roman Catholics. Furthermore, it is tangible evidence of how far relations have improved between Methodists and Roman Catholics since the earliest controversy between John Wesley and Richard Challoner. During the nineteenth century, Lancashire saw some of the worst sectarian rivalry between Methodists and Roman Catholics in the whole of England. Those nineteenth-century Methodists and Roman Catholics who traded insults and violence could hardly have imagined that one day their descendants would join together to build a church. The opening of the first church in Britain specifically for shared use by Methodists and Roman Catholics is a hopeful note for the future of local ecumenism.

Conclusion

During the course of our study of dialogue between Methodists and Roman Catholics, one obvious question has kept appearing on the horizon only to be postponed: in theological terms, what is the place of Methodism in the Holy Catholic Church? In a letter to the editor of the London Chronicle dated 19 February 1761, John Wesley set out a general claim on behalf of the Protestant churches, among which he naturally included the Church of England: 'Their teachers are the proper successors of those who have delivered down, through all generations, the faith once delivered to the saints; and their members have true, spiritual communion with the *one, holy* society of true *believers.* Consequently, although they are not the *whole* "people of God", yet are they an undeniable *part* of his people.'[1] The particular question before us now concerns what *part* the Methodist people have within the *whole* people of God.

In Chapter 4 we learned how the 1986 Nairobi report from the international Methodist–Roman Catholic dialogue identified various elements that contribute to a 'model of organic unity' between Christians. From these basic elements Geoffrey Wainwright identifies four possible ways to describe the 'ecclesial location' of Methodism.[2] Each has had its proponents at one time or another, but not all remain valid options today.

First of all, it is an historical fact that Methodism began as a network or connexion of religious societies within the Church of England. Therefore an obvious way to describe the ecclesial location of Methodism would be as a continuing network of religious societies within the Anglican Church, assuming that the historic breech could be repaired. This option has long held an appeal for some British Methodists, who would point out that the separation was an unfortunate accident of history which did not involve a formal schism. Neither the urging of a number of his preachers nor the hostile reaction from some of the bishops could persuade Wesley to separate from the Church of England, though he conceded that a certain 'unstitching' had already begun.[3] Nevertheless, after the Plan of Pacification (1795) had provided a comprehensive settlement for the Methodist societies, the re-absorption of Methodism into the Church of England was always a remote possibility. By the middle of the nineteenth century, Methodism had become so unstitched from the Church of England that the separation was irreversible, except in the mind of a few romanticists. Moreover, as Methodists grew increasingly confident of their own ecclesial identity, they sensed to their consternation that the Church of England was steadily moving in the direction of Rome. The history of Methodism in the nineteenth century can be described as the transition of a connexion of religious societies into a fully-fledged denomination with an established place in British society. In the United States the situation was even more clear-cut: after 1784, Methodism swiftly became the indigenous American church, its transatlantic roots in the Church of England having little relevance in the New World. For American Methodists, it makes little sense to describe the ecclesial location of Methodism by making any kind of reference to the Church of England.

Ironically, the recent Anglican–Methodist Covenant in Britain more or less closes this option. For the Covenant includes a series of mutual affirmations and commitments, the first of which indicates that Anglicans no longer regard Methodism as simply a network of religious societies: 'We affirm one another's churches as true churches belonging to the One, Holy, Catholic and Apostolic Church of Jesus Christ and as truly participating in the apostolic mission of the whole people of God.'[4] This affirmation of Methodism as a 'true church', though at first sight welcome to Methodists, poses a problem so far as ecclesiology and ecumenical method are concerned. In particular, it would seem that the criteria used to identify a 'true church' in the Anglican–Methodist Covenant are somewhat different to those generally employed in dialogue between Anglicans and Roman Catholics. This inconsistency is bound to complicate future ecumenical dialogue for all the parties concerned. In his address to the Methodist Conference in 1998, Cardinal Cassidy warned of the need for consistency across bilateral dialogues, if there is to be real progress towards unity.[5]

The second option for describing the ecclesial location of Methodism is a variation on the first. If it is no longer appropriate to describe Methodism in terms of a connexion of religious societies, is it possible instead to regard Methodism as a hitherto unrecognised province of the Anglican Communion? At the time of the abortive Anglican–Methodist unity scheme in the early 1970s, C. J. Bertrand, an historian of Methodism, described how the early Methodist movement exhibited the same family characteristics later evident in the various Anglican provinces that developed outside England.[6] These traits comprise a common doctrinal kernel within Anglican comprehensiveness, an independent liturgy with roots in the Book of Common Prayer, a spirituality and ministry adapted to the needs of the people, autonomous administration, and an undefined 'Englishness'.

This option also presents its problems, however. While Bertrand correctly identified the affinity between the Methodist movement and the spread of Anglicanism, there is one significant difference between Methodism and autonomous Anglican provinces which casts doubt on the value of his hypothesis. Ever since the Oxford Movement in the nineteenth century, Anglicans have tended to interpret the historic succession in terms of the *juridical* continuity of bishops under English canon law. The fact remains that the various Anglican provinces were all duly established by canon law, whereas Methodism was a canonically irregular movement. Therefore it would be inconsistent for Anglicans to sit lightly to the juridical status of Methodism, while defending their own historic succession by appealing to canon law. Even if British Methodism should at some time in the future adopt an episcopate acceptable to Anglicans, this would not remove the anomaly caused by the rupture in orderly succession. Whether the affirmations contained in the Anglican–Methodist Covenant alter the position is possible, though it seems doubtful.

A third way to describe the ecclesial location of Methodism would be to regard it as a church within the Holy Catholic Church, a 'sister' to the Roman Catholic Church and other churches, including the Anglican Communion. If autonomous Methodist conferences could be persuaded to fuse their authority into a strengthened World Methodist Council for the sake of greater unity, then the comparison with the Roman Catholic Church would be even more appropriate. Interestingly, the Anglican Communion is currently exploring whether the Archbishop of Canterbury might exercise a more authoritative ministry of primacy for its member churches. However, the basic problem with this option is that the New Testament refers only to the universal Church and local churches. Wainwright puts it bluntly: 'The existence of *denominations* – which so far in history always implies *divisions* – calls into question the reality of *the Church*.'[7] Furthermore, the power of the Gospel to reconcile human beings to God is seriously compromised by structural disunity among Christians. The idea of Methodism as a separate church within the Holy Catholic Church fails to take account of the Gospel imperative for Christian unity. If Methodists take seriously Christ's call for unity in the Church, then they should be reluctant to describe Methodism as a church. From a Roman Catholic perspective, the ecclesiology of the Second Vatican Council, reinforced by *Dominus Iesus*, rules out this third option as a serious alternative for discussion.

The fourth, and in some respects the most promising, way to describe the ecclesial location of Methodism is by analogy with the various religious orders found in the Roman Catholic Church. The Nairobi report noted certain similarities between John Wesley and both Benedict of Norcia and Francis of Assisi, but did not go into any detail.[8] Pressing the comparison, Wainwright observed an affinity between the Wesleyan and Benedictine approaches to prayer and work.[9]

Admittedly, Wainwright's comparison of Methodism with the Franciscan and Benedictine orders seems remote from the experience of most Methodists. However, these are just two historical examples of a phenomenon that occurs in every age of the Church. Recent years have witnessed a burgeoning of ecclesial movements within the Roman Catholic Church, stemming from what Pope John Paul II described as 'the Holy Spirit's response to the dramatic challenges of the close of this millennium'. A quick glance at one of these movements suggests that the rise of Methodism in the eighteenth century was part of a recurring pattern within the Holy Catholic Church.

The Focolare movement (the name comes from an Italian word for 'hearth') arose from the work of Chiara Lubich in Italy during the Second World War. In 1943, during the German Occupation, Lubich rediscovered the Gospel ideals of unity and community, and with her companions she developed a peaceable way of life in the midst of hatred and violence. Her pioneering work eventually gave birth to an international movement with its own distinctive ethos of social commitment and domestic piety. The Holy See approved the Focolare movement in 1962, and today it has branches in eighteen countries.

From this thumbnail sketch certain similarities emerge with the rise of Methodism in the eighteenth century though it would be unwise to press the comparison too far. Wesley and Lubich were highly motivated leaders, who responded to what they perceived to be an urgent need within the Church of their day. They each gathered a group of followers around a particular Gospel emphasis and built up a lay movement. While neither movement is particularly original in its purpose or theology, each has extended the Church's mission to a section of the population which might otherwise not have been reached. Both movements have a distinctive ethos and a specific mission. Of course, unlike Methodism, the Focolare movement has remained within the structures of its parent church.

On the whole, the Roman Catholic Church has proved itself much more skilful than Protestant churches at harnessing the powerful forces at work in ecclesial movements. In Protestantism, revival and renewal have often led to separation. The most obvious example in Methodism concerns the evangelical ministry of William Booth, a minister in the Methodist New Connexion, whose unconventional methods proved troublesome. Finding the Methodist New Connexion inhibitive, Booth left to pursue an independent ministry, later becoming the founder of the Salvation Army. Had Booth been a Roman Catholic, the outcome might have been different. A surprising degree of flexibility in Roman Catholic structures enables religious orders and ecclesial movements to enjoy a high degree of autonomy. They are usually governed by a Convocation at which members gather to confer and make decisions affecting their common future. The territorial jurisdiction of the local Roman Catholic bishop does not usually extend to the internal affairs of recognised groups, as long as they maintain the faith of the Church and respect its overall life and structures.

Altogether, there is sufficient phenomenological evidence to warrant a theological study of Methodism in relation to the various religious orders and ecclesial movements within the Roman Catholic Church as a possible basis for describing the ecclesial location of Methodism. Furthermore, if Methodists are to retain their characteristic features within some future united Church, this may be the most realistic option to pursue. Methodists, fearful of being swallowed up by a larger entity, usually look with consternation at the monolithic structure of the Roman Catholic Church. But, this is because they fail to observe the immense diversity within Roman Catholicism, which enables people to belong to a wide variety of religious orders and ecclesial movements. Moreover, belonging to such a group is often an integral part of the ecclesial identity of Roman Catholics. One practical difficulty, of course, would be to maintain the necessary discipline in a movement of over 70 million people: in comparison with world Methodism, religious orders in the Roman Catholic Church are tiny. Theologically, however, there is nothing that would automatically prevent further study of the analogy between Methodism and the various religious orders within the Roman Catholic Church as a possible model for describing the ecclesial location of Methodism in the Holy Catholic Church.

Dialogue between Methodists and Roman Catholics does not take place in an ecumenical vacuum. Given the number of other possibilities on the ecumenical agenda, it is fair to ask whether the dialogue justifies the commitment of time and energy on both sides. While the present study assumes that dialogue between Methodists and Roman Catholics is an intrinsically worthwhile activity, it is important briefly to consider the alternatives. For instance, some would abandon bilateral dialogues altogether, in favour of the kind of multilateral conversations pioneered by the WCC Faith and Order Commission which led to the famous Lima text in 1982, *Baptism, Eucharist, Ministry*. What they often fail to realise, however, is that the negotiations to produce *BEM* took place over a period of more than thirty years, and the process of reception could take just as long – hardly a rapid rate of progress. In a paper presented to the English Methodist–Roman Catholic Committee in 1979, Rupert Davies argued that bilateral dialogues offer the most realistic chance of advancing the cause of Christian unity, since representatives of two churches are more likely to be able to establish and build on common ground.[10]

Still, even if bilateral conversations are the best way forward, is Methodist–Roman Catholic dialogue a sensible option for both parties? In Eastern and Central Europe, many Roman Catholics would naturally regard dialogue with the Orthodox churches as potentially the most productive possibility. However, formal conversations between Roman Catholics and Orthodox ground to a halt some years ago and have not been resumed because of tensions in Eastern Europe following the collapse of the Soviet Union. For Roman Catholics in Western Europe, where Methodism is a relatively small community, dialogue with Lutherans and Reformed is more immediately relevant. What is more, the recent Joint Declaration on the Doctrine of Justification (see below) is a promising omen for future dialogue between Roman Catholics and Lutherans. In the diverse ecumenical scene in North America, Roman Catholic dialogue with Methodists makes sense to both parties because of their shared interests in education and health care provision.

In Britain, Roman Catholics tend to regard Anglicans as their most suitable dialogue partner, for obvious historical reasons. Here great hopes have been pinned on the Anglican–Roman Catholic International Commission. However, in some ways ARCIC has failed to live up to early expectations, which were probably unrealistic given the severity of the obstacles to be overcome. At the same time, the reports produced by ARCIC have been overly optimistic in their assessment of the level of agreement that currently exists between Anglicans and Roman Catholics. For instance, in February 2004 the General Synod of the Church of England noted that the most recent ARCIC report, *The Gift of Authority*, made no reference to the contested claim of universal, ordinary and immediate jurisdiction for the Bishop of Rome. Observing that the statement's treatment of teaching authority was 'not sufficiently clear', the General Synod requested 'that ARCIC clarify in what sense this is "a gift to be received by all the churches" '.[11] For Roman Catholics, the strains and ruptures within the Anglican Communion following the ordination of a practising homosexual, Gene Robinson, as a bishop in the United States in November 2003 threatens to scupper the work of ARCIC.

For British Methodists, the Church of England is the most obvious choice of dialogue partner. At the present time, ecumenical hopes and fears among Methodists in Britain are firmly fixed on the Anglican–Methodist Covenant with its joint commitment 'as a priority, to work to overcome the remaining obstacles to the organic unity of our two Churches'.[12] For this reason, many Methodists would be inclined to regard dialogue with Roman Catholics as of considerably less importance for the foreseeable future. Some Methodists (and Anglicans) would see the Church of England as a bridge between Methodism and the Roman Catholic Church. In some respects this may be true. Yet, as I hope has become clear in the course of the present study, Methodists

257

and Roman Catholics have a great deal more in common than is some-times supposed, not least in their understanding of holiness and grace. Furthermore, as a movement that is both Catholic and Reformed, Methodism is in some respects a bridge between Roman Catholicism and other Protestant churches.

Admittedly, there are sound strategic reasons for Anglicans and Methodists in England to devote time and energy to developing closer bilateral relations. The history of the Church in England suggests that repairing the breech between Anglicans and Methodists is the most realistic of all the possible options for establishing greater unity. All the same, the continuing conversations between Anglicans and Methodists need not be at the expense of other ecumenical opportunities, since insights from one bilateral dialogue can inform and stimulate another. Those Methodists who would prefer to concentrate on dialogue with the Church of England must remember that Anglicans are also in dialogue with Roman Catholics. For Methodists fully to appreciate what Anglicans and Roman Catholics are saying to each other, it is important for Methodism to remain in bilateral dialogue with both churches. Of course, consistency between these various dialogues is essential, if there is to be genuine progress towards full visible unity.

From the perspective of the Vatican, the dialogue with the World Methodist Council is just one among a number of bilateral conversa-tions that were established in the aftermath of the Second Vatican Council. This particular dialogue can be justified for a number of reasons. First, Methodism is a significant world communion, approxi-mately equal in size to the Anglican Communion. What is more, the doctrinal differences separating Roman Catholics and Methodists are no more serious than those between Roman Catholics and Anglicans. During the past forty years, Methodist–Roman Catholic dialogue has exceeded all expectations. Today, the Joint Commission enjoys the respect of serious ecumenists and the Pontifical Council for Promoting Christian Unity, because of its maturity and the realism with which it approaches its task. While it would be exaggerating to claim that the dia-logue with the World Methodist Council was any more significant for the Vatican than its other bilateral conversations, nevertheless it is fair to say that the talks with Methodists have at least as much potential as any of these others.

From the perspective of the World Methodist Council, the dialogue with the Vatican makes sense for much the same reasons. As the largest body of Christians in the world, the Roman Catholic Church is the obvious choice of dialogue partner. Also, Methodists and Roman Catholics share an undivided history of fifteen centuries, even if the traditions subsequently diverged following the Reformation. Furthermore, since the deepest division in the Western Church is that between Roman Catholic and Protestant, the dialogue with Roman Catholicism is far and away the most challenging, yet potentially the most rewarding, of all Methodism's ecumenical conversations. In some respects, Methodism remains an ecclesial renewal movement in search of a church. In other respects it is a *de facto* church that has yet to come to terms fully with the ecclesiological implications of its status. Either way, theological dialogue with Roman Catholics will enable Methodists to continue to explore in greater depth what it means for Methodism to claim and cherish its place in the Holy Catholic Church.

We have charted the course of controversy and dialogue between Methodists and Roman Catholics from John Wesley's letter 'To a Roman Catholic Priest' (1735) to the British Methodist Conference's 2003 response to the international dialogue. Along the way we have observed how two centuries of controversy finally gave way to a constructive theological dialogue following the Second Vatican Council. As a result of the Council and its stimulus to ecumenical dialogue, relations between Methodists and Roman Catholics are better now than they have ever been before, though there are still tensions in some countries due to local circumstances. The rapid thaw in relations between Methodists and Roman Catholics in the relatively short period of time since Vatican II is a cause for joy and confidence that future years will see even greater co-operation, though the remaining obstacles to unity are not insignificant.

Since its inaugural meeting in 1967, the international dialogue, ably supported by the national conversations, has made considerable progress in identifying areas of doctrinal agreement and disagreement, convergence and divergence. A feature of the Joint Commission is its painstaking methodology and cautious assessment of what has been achieved and what remains to be done. Over the years, the Joint Commission has consistently avoided presenting its sponsoring churches with rashly optimistic reports.

In the course of conversations between Methodists and Roman Catholics, certain aspects of doctrine emerge time and again as requiring further investigation, notably ordination, authority in the Church, and the universal primacy of the Bishop of Rome. Future conversations will have to overcome substantial disagreements in these areas before there can be significant progress towards full communion in faith, mission and sacramental life. The Joint Commission sensibly takes the view that to tackle these contentious issues head-on would lead to stalemate. The task of the Joint Commission therefore is to develop an appropriate theological framework in which the remaining areas of doctrinal disagreement between Methodists and Roman Catholics can be reduced and eventually resolved.

If full communion between Methodists and Roman Catholics lies some considerable distance ahead, what practical steps could be taken in the mean time to assist the dialogue? A recent development in the bilateral conversations between the Roman Catholic Church and the Lutheran World Federation offers an intriguing possibility for Methodist–Roman Catholic dialogue. The 'Joint Declaration on the Doctrine of Justification between the Roman Catholic Church and the Lutheran World Federation' was signed in Augsburg, Germany, on 31 October 1999. This agreement is a significant ecumenical landmark which has resolved certain historic differences between Roman Catholics and Lutherans concerning justification by faith.[13] Since Methodism was not a party to the sixteenth-century disputes between Roman Catholics and Lutherans, the agreement is not directly relevant to the World Methodist Council. However, for Methodism to find some form of association with the Joint Declaration on the Doctrine of Justification would deepen the communion in faith between Methodists, Lutherans and Roman Catholics in what historically has been a divisive matter. Needless to say, any form of association with the Joint Declaration on Justification would be an ambitious project, involving the World Methodist Council in delicate tripartite conversations, though the English Methodist–Roman Catholic convergence statement on justification might provide a useful starting-point. From his initial survey of the topic, Geoffrey Wainwright concludes that the Joint Declaration is a concise summary of the Wesleyan doctrine of salvation.[14]

The dialogue between Methodists and Roman Catholics in Britain would be enhanced by one small but significant gesture of goodwill on the part of the British Methodist Conference. The Deed of Union defines the Methodist doctrinal standards in terms of the historic creeds and the fundamental principles of the Protestant Reformation in conjunction with Wesley's Sermons and his Notes on the New Testament. Nowhere, however, is there an authoritative statement of how these elements are to be interpreted. To complicate matters, the doctrinal standards are not intended to impose any particular system of thought, but instead set up standards for Methodist belief and practice. Still, there is no escaping the fact that the Methodist doctrinal standards include Wesley's anti-Catholic statements, even if few Methodists would consider these to be entirely applicable today. Following the example of the United Methodist Church, the Methodist Church of Great Britain could usefully make its own Declaration of Intent concerning the appropriate interpretation of the anti-Catholic content of Wesley's Sermons and his Notes on the New Testament. Such a gesture would demonstrate beyond all doubt that British Methodism has distanced itself from its founder's hostile attitude towards the Roman Catholic Church.

For their part, Roman Catholics might also seek a fresh perspective on past controversies with Methodists. Cardinal Walter Kasper, President of the Pontifical Council for Promoting Christian Unity, graciously acknowledged the task facing Roman Catholics in his sermon to celebrate the tercentenary of the birth of John Wesley. 'A Catholic reflection on John Wesley needs to grapple with his ambivalent understanding of the Catholic Church, but cannot stop there; we must also seek a wider view, to see what dynamized Wesley's ministry, to see the evangelical passion which gave direction to his life and the movement he started. Furthermore, we do so today in a new context, engaging in a reassessment of John Wesley's life and ministry from a very different starting point.'[15] A commitment to renewed engagement with John Wesley would be a fitting way for Roman Catholics to mark this special anniversary for world Methodism.

John Wesley's mixed legacy to theological dialogue between Methodists and Roman Catholics has been referred to more than once in the course of this study. At its best however Wesley's vision of the Church was truly catholic, embracing all Christians within the communion of saints. Although sadly not typical of his writings on Roman Catholicism, the letter 'To a Roman Catholic' transcends the limitations imposed by the eighteenth century to provide an inspiring appeal for Methodists and Roman Catholics to 'reason together'. Undoubtedly, Wesley's enduring gift to ecumenism is his sermon on the catholic spirit, which called for catholic love and forbearance among Christians. The history of dialogue between Methodists and Roman Catholics reveals two communities each in their individual way in search of this catholic spirit.

We conclude with Charles Wesley's poem on 'Catholic Love', which John Wesley appended to the earliest published versions of his sermon on the 'Catholic Spirit'.[16] Superficially, the words might sound mawkish. At a deeper level, they bear eloquent testimony to the catholic spirit at work in John Wesley and his professed 'unbounded love' for the members of the Holy Catholic Church.

> WEARY of all this wordy strife,
> These notions, forms, and modes, and names,
> To Thee, the Way, the Truth, the Life,
> Whose love my simple heart inflames,
> Divinely taught, at last I fly,
> With Thee, and Thine to live, and die.
>
> Forth from the midst of *Babel* brought,
> Parties and sects I cast behind;
> Enlarged my heart, and free my thought,
> Where'er the latent truth I find,
> The latent truth with joy to own,
> And bow to Jesu's name alone.
>
> Redeem'd by Thine almighty grace,
> I taste my glorious liberty,
> With open arms the world embrace,
> But *cleave* to those who cleave to Thee;
> But only in Thy saints delight,
> Who walk with God in purest white.
>
> One with the little flock I rest,
> The members sound who hold the Head;
> The chosen few, with pardon blest,
> And by the anointing Spirit led

Into the mind that was in Thee,
Into the depths of Deity.

My brethren, friends, and kinsmen these,
Who do my heavenly Father's will;
Who *aim* at perfect holiness,
And all Thy counsels to fulfil,
Athirst to be whate'er Thou art,
And love their God with all their heart.

For these, howe'er in flesh disjoin'd,
Where'er dispersed o'er earth abroad,
Unfeign'd unbounded love I find,
And constant as the life of God;
Fountain of life, from thence it sprung,
As pure, as even, and as strong.

Join'd to the hidden church unknown
In this sure bond of perfectness,
Obscurely safe, I dwell alone,
And glory in the uniting grace,
To me, to each believer given,
To all thy saints in earth and heaven.

Postscript
A Parable

The original monastery at Buckfast in Devon was founded by Benedictine monks during the reign of King Cnut in 1018.[1] The Domesday Book of 1086 records its endowments at the time of the Norman Conquest. In comparison with the fifty or so other abbeys in England in the eleventh century, Buckfast was small and relatively poor. The rule of life followed by the monks was the *Regularis Concordia*, drawn up in Winchester in about 970 for the English Benedictine monasteries. Apart from a few fragments of stone, which may have been part of the Saxon church, no other evidence of the original monastery has so far been found.

At the beginning of the twelfth century, a series of reforms was initiated at the abbey of Cîteaux in France. These led to the creation of a new 'Cistercian' Order, which was intended to be a return to the Rule of St Benedict in its original and more austere form. All luxuries were prohibited, the rule of silence was reinstated, and a vegetarian diet enforced. Worship occupied the monks for six hours a day, the elaborate Gregorian chant being replaced with a simpler form of prayer. Buckfast became a Cistercian abbey in 1147, whereupon it was immediately rebuilt in stone, following the Cistercian pattern. The arch of the north gate and part of the undercroft by the west cloister are the only buildings to survive from the Cistercian abbey, though excavations have uncovered almost all of the original foundations from this period.

The peak period in the history of Buckfast Abbey occurred during the thirteenth century. At one time there may have been as many as sixty choir monks and possibly twice as many lay brothers. Through their skills and enterprise, the abbey thrived as a farming community and wool producer, exporting quantities of wool to Italy. By the fifteenth century, Buckfast had become a wealthy landowner and centre for a substantial business, maintaining parishes, manors, almshouses and a school.

For reasons that are not entirely clear, by the beginning of the sixteenth century the monasteries in England were generally in a state of decline, though they possessed considerable wealth in the form of land and treasures. Attracted by the vast prize on offer, Henry VIII appointed Thomas Cromwell as Vicar General in 1535 with instructions to visit and reform the monastic houses. The king's commissioners travelled the length and breadth of the country, closing monasteries and confiscating their lands and resources for the Crown. Buckfast was dissolved on 25 February 1539 and its treasures transferred to the Tower of London.

The abbey church and buildings at Buckfast were stripped and left to decay for more than two centuries, though some were converted for other uses. Eventually, in 1800 the Crown sold the ruined site of the abbey church, and the new owner cleared away the rubble to build a mansion. After changing ownership four times in the course of the next eighty years, in 1882 the property once again came into the ownership of the Benedictines, who immediately set about restoring it to its former use. After a gap of 343 years, Buckfast Abbey resumed its monastic way of life.

In 1907 the foundation stone of a new abbey church was laid, and a small group of monks began the huge task of constructing the sanctuary in twelfth-century Cistercian style. Finally, on 25 August 1932 the abbey church was consecrated in the presence of a large congregation with thousands more listening outside via loudspeakers. The service was also broadcast live on BBC radio. These days the abbey church is at the centre of a flourishing religious community. During the summer months, nearly half a million visitors flock to the tranquil surroundings of the abbey.

Unusually, the history of Buckfast Abbey includes Methodism. In 1881, just twelve months before the monks unexpectedly returned, the Wesleyans built a small chapel on part of the site of the ruined monastery. At that time, no one could have imagined that one day a new abbey would rise from the ruins of the old. If the Methodists gave any thought to the ruined abbey, it was probably to reflect on the English Reformation and the triumph of Protestant truth. Fittingly, the Methodist chapel, a symbol of Protestant ascendancy, stood foursquare near the site of the former abbey church. Had they but known it, these Devon Methodists were building on a Catholic foundation in more ways than one. What these Methodists thought as they watched the rebuilding of the abbey church is not recorded, though most likely there was great consternation at the prospect of a Roman Catholic revival in Devon. It would be understandable if the monks felt a surge of pride as the new abbey church, an icon of resurgent Roman Catholicism in England, gradually came to tower over the tiny Methodist chapel.

Today, Buckfast Methodist Church still stands resolutely on its small freehold site within the abbey grounds directly opposite the magnificent abbey church, presenting the bemused visitor with an architectural and theological contrast. What message the two buildings convey will depend to a large extent on the preferences of the visitor. Aesthetically, the austere beauty of the abbey church is more pleasing to the eye than the Methodist chapel. However, a theology of sacred space is not simply a theology of aesthetics. The Methodist chapel, as much as the abbey church, constitutes sacred space, which has been hallowed by the prayers of the faithful down the years. Interestingly, the visitors' book in the Methodist chapel records the appreciative comments of some of its many visitors, a surprising number of whom mention the prayerful atmosphere. A service of the word is held in the chapel on Sunday afternoons throughout the year for a small number of worshippers, though the Buckfast Abbey guidebook makes no mention of this unusual feature of the landscape.

To some extent, the respective histories of Buckfast Abbey and Buckfast Methodist Church mirror the fluctuating fortunes of Roman Catholicism and Protestantism in England. Sacred to their respective communities, these two liturgical spaces represent antithetical approaches to Christian worship and spirituality. Thus, at first sight, they have very little in common. Could it be however that the abbey church and the Methodist chapel, together with their respective communities and distinctive forms of worship and spirituality, complement each other? Might not each need the contribution of the other to enhance its own catholicity? Hopefully, in a future century in the long history of Buckfast Abbey, the two local Christian communities represented by the abbey church and the Methodist chapel will exist in full communion in faith, mission and sacramental life within the Holy Catholic Church in England.

Notes

Introduction

1 The only other entries in the 'Top One Hundred Great Britons' noted for their contribution to religion in Britain were the Bible translator William Tyndale (26) and the founder of the Salvation Army, William Booth (71).

2 Roy Hattersley, *A Brand from the Burning: The Life of John Wesley* (London: Little, Brown, 2002), p. 411.

3 For example, Kenneth J. Collins, *John Wesley: A Theological Journey* (Nashville: Abingdon, 2003); Richard P. Heitzenrater, *The Elusive Mr Wesley*, 2nd edn (Nashville: Abingdon, 2003); Stephen Tomkins, *John Wesley: A Biography* (Oxford: Lion, 2003); Ralph Waller, *John Wesley: A Personal Portrait* (London: SPCK, 2003); John Kent, *Wesley and the Wesleyans* (Cambridge: Cambridge University Press, 2002); John Munsey Turner, *John Wesley: The Evangelical Revival and the Rise of Methodism in England* (Peterborough: Epworth, 2002); Ronald H. Stone, *John Wesley's Life and Ethics* (Nashville: Abingdon, 2001). See also Richard P. Heitzenrater, *Wesley and the People Called Methodists* (Nashville: Abingdon, 1995); and Henry Rack, *Reasonable Enthusiast: John Wesley and the Rise of Methodism* (London: Epworth, 1989).

4 For the text of the Covenant see *An Anglican–Methodist Covenant: Common Statement of the Formal Conversations between the Methodist Church of Great Britain and the Church of England* (Peterborough: Methodist Publishing/ London: Church House Publishing, 2001).

5 Notable exceptions are John M. Todd, *John Wesley and the Catholic Church* (London: Hodder & Stoughton, 1958), and David Butler, *Methodist and Papists: John Wesley and the Catholic Church in the Eighteenth Century* (London: Darton, Longman & Todd, 1995). However, both studies deal exclusively with the eighteenth century.

6 For a useful introduction see David Hempton, *Methodism and Politics in British Society 1750–1850* (London: Hutchinson, 1984).

7 Sermon 39, *WJW* 2, pp. 79–99.

1 John Wesley and Roman Catholicism

1 'Homily of Cardinal Walter Kasper, Ponte Sant'Angelo Methodist Church, Rome, June 22nd 2003', *Pontifical Council for Promoting Christian Unity Information Service* 114 (2003/IV), pp. 183–6 (p. 183).

2 *Journal*, 24 May 1738. Several editions of the *Journal* have been published. For ease of reference, quotations from the *Journal* cite the date.

3 'Farther Thoughts on Separation from the Church', 11 December 1789. Printed in the *Arminian Magazine*, April 1790.

4 Letter, 8 April 1788, *LJW* 8, p. 52.

5 Letter, 29 April 1788, *LJW* 8, p. 57.

6 'Thoughts on the consecration of churches and burial grounds' (14 May 1788), *Works* 10, pp. 509–11 (p. 511).

7 'Thoughts on the consecration of churches and burial grounds', p. 511.

8 'A Word to a Protestant', *Works* 11, pp. 187–95 (pp. 192, 195).

9 R. A. Knox, *Enthusiasm: A Chapter in the History of Religion* (Oxford: Clarendon, 1950), p. 435.

10 Eamon Duffy, 'Wesley and the Counter-Reformation', in Jane Garnett and Colin Matthew (eds), *Revival and Religion since 1700: Essays for John Walsh* (London: Hambledon, 1993), pp. 1–19 (p. 1).

11 John Todd, *John Wesley and the Catholic Church* (London: Hodder & Stoughton, 1958), p. 29.

12 Augustin Cardinal Bea in the Introduction to Michael Hurley (ed.), *Wesley's Letter to a Roman Catholic* (London: Geoffrey Chapman, 1968).

13 David Butler, *Methodists and Papists: John Wesley and the Catholic Church in the Eighteenth Century* (London: Darton, Longman & Todd, 1995), p. 202.

14 'A Disavowal of Persecuting Papists', *Works* 10, pp. 173–5 (p. 174).

15 Henry Rack, *Reasonable Enthusiast: John Wesley and the Rise of Methodism* (London: Epworth, 1989), p. 309.

16 John Munsey Turner, *John Wesley: The Evangelical Revival and the Rise of Methodism in England* (Peterborough: Epworth, 2002), p. 113.

17 For an account of this process in an English parish see Eamon Duffy, *Voices of Morebath: Reformation and Rebellion in an English village* (London: Yale University Press, 2002).

18 Cf. William P. Haugaard, 'From the Reformation to the Eighteenth Century', in Stephen Sykes and John Booty (eds), *The Study of Anglicanism* (London: SPCK, 1988), pp. 3–28.

19 For a general introduction see H. Kamen, *The Rise of Toleration* (London: Weidenfeld & Nicolson, 1967).

20 Butler, *Methodists and Papists*, p. 10.

21 Butler, *Methodists and Papists*, pp. 47ff.; cf. *The Works of John Locke* (London, 1801), vol. 6.

22 'A Disavowal of Persecuting Papists', p. 174.

23 'A Disavowal of Persecuting Papists', p. 173.

24 'A Disavowal of Persecuting Papists', p. 174.

25 'A Letter to the Printer of the Public Advertiser', *Works* 10, pp. 159–61 (p. 160).

26 This was the substance of a correspondence between Wesley and a Roman Catholic priest by the name of Joseph Berington. Cf. W. L. Doughty, 'John Wesley's Letters to Mr Berington, 1780', *PWHS* 26 (1947), pp. 38–45, 68.

27 Doughty, 'John Wesley's Letters to Mr Berington, 1780'.

28 Letter to the Editor of the *Freeman's Journal*, Dublin, 23 March 1780, *Works* 10, pp. 162–6 (p. 166).

29 Arthur O'Leary, 'Remarks on Rev. John Wesley's Letters on the Civil Principles of Roman Catholics and his Defence of the Protestant Association', in *Miscellaneous Tracts* (London, 1781). Wesley's reply to the *Freeman's Journal* is printed in *LJW* 7, pp. 3–8.

30 Butler, *Methodists and Papists*, p. 123.

31 'A Short History of the People called Methodists' (1781), *WJW* 9, pp. 424–503 (p. 449).

32 *Journal*, 15 August 1747.

33 'A Short Method of Converting all the Roman Catholics in the Kingdom of Ireland', *Works* 10, pp. 129–33.

34 *Journal*, 3 April 1748.

35 *Journal*, 1 April 1748.

36 *Journal*, 3 June 1758

37 *Journal*, 26 April 1778.

38 *Journal*, 17 May 1762.

39 *Journal*, 19 July 1756. Cited in David Hempton, *Methodism and Politics in British Society 1750–1850* (London: Hutchinson, 1984), p. 37.

40 *Journal*, 1 May 1789.

41 Rack, *Reasonable Enthusiast*, pp. 97f.

42 For a more 'Lutheran' interpretation of Wesley see Franz Hildenbrandt, *From Luther to Wesley* (London: Lutterworth, 1951); for a more 'Calvinist' interpretation of Wesley see G. Croft Cell, *The Rediscovery of John Wesley* (New York: H. Holt & Company, 1935).

43 For a more thorough treatment see Geoffrey Wainwright, *Methodists in Dialogue* (Nashville: Abingdon, 1995), pp. 143–58.

44 Sermon 4, 'Scriptural Christianity', *WJW* 1, pp. 159–80 (p. 161).

45 'Advantage of the Church of England over the Church of Rome', *Works* 10, p. 139.

46 Sermon 61, 'The Mystery of Iniquity' (1783), *WJW* 2, pp. 451–70 (p. 463). In sermon 68, 'The Wisdom of God's Counsels', the Church was already corrupted in the first century when the love of money made 'the first breach in

the community of goods'. *WJW* 2, p. 555.

47 Sermon 22, 'Sermon on the Mount II' (1748), *WJW* 1, pp. 488–509 (p. 508).

48 'The Character of a Methodist' (1742), *WJW* 9, pp. 31–46 (p. 34).

49 Sermon 16, 'The Means of Grace', *WJW* 1, pp. 376–97 (p. 383).

50 Sermon 1, 'Salvation by Faith' (1738), *WJW* 1, pp. 117–30 (p. 118).

51 Sermon 91, 'On Charity', *WJW* 3 pp. 290–307 (p. 299).

52 Sermon 1, 'Salvation by Faith' (1738), *WJW* 1, pp. 117–30 (pp. 128ff.).

53 'A Letter to a Gentleman at Bristol', 6 January 1758, *LJW* 3, pp. 244ff.

54 *Journal*, 4 April 1739.

55 Sermon 85, 'On working out our own salvation', *WJW* 3, pp. 199–209.

56 Sermon 85, p. 202.

57 Sermon 85, p. 205.

58 Sermon 85, p. 208.

59 Sermon 85, p. 204. Cf. Ezekiel 11.19; Ephesians 2.8; Matthew 13.31–2; Ephesians 4.15; 4.13.

60 *A Plain Account of Christian Perfection*, *Works* 11, pp. 366–446 (pp. 441f.).

61 *A Plain Account of Christian Perfection*, p. 444.

62 Printed in the *Journal*, 14 May 1765. Cf. *LJW* 4, pp. 296–300. Jeremy Taylor, *The Rule and Exercises of Holy Living* (London, 1650), and *The Rule and Exercises of Holy Dying* (London, 1651).

63 Letter to John Newton, 9 April 1765. *LJW* 4, pp. 292–3 (p. 293).

64 Letter to John Newton, 14 May 1765. *LJW* 4, p. 298.

65 Letter to John Newton, 14 May 1765. *LJW* 4, p. 298.

66 'Serious Thoughts upon the Perseverance of the Saints', *Works* 10, pp. 284–98 (p. 285).

67 Croft Cell, *The Rediscovery of John Wesley*, p. 361.

68 Sermon 101 (1732), *WJW* 3, pp. 427–39.

69 *WJW* 25, pp. 428–30. Printed in the *Journal* entry for 27 August 1739. First published in 1742.

70 *WJW* 25, p. 429.

71 Cf. Sermon 78, 'Spiritual Idolatry', *WJW* 3, pp. 103–14. As examples of idolatrous worship in the Roman Catholic Church, Wesley cites angels; souls of the departed; and images of gold, silver, wood or stone.

72 'A Farther Appeal to Men of Reason and Religion, Part III', *WJW* 11, pp. 272–325 (p. 290). Wesley was responding to the papal Bull *Super forma juramenti professionis fidei* which was appended to the *Canones et Decreta*. All holders of ecclesiastical office were obliged to subscribe to it.

73 *Works* 10, pp. 133–9.

74 The same point is made at greater length in Wesley's *Explanatory Notes upon the New Testament* (1754).

75 *Works* 10, pp. 86–128.

76 *Works* 10, pp. 140–58.

77 'Popery Calmly Considered', *Works* 10, p. 152.

78 'Popery Calmly Considered', pp. 153f.

79 Sermon 74, *WJW* 3, pp. 45–57.

80 Sermon 74, *WJW* 3, p. 50.

81 Sermon 74, *WJW* 3, p. 51. Article XIX was taken from the Augsburg Confession (1530).

82 Sermon 74, *WJW* 3, p. 52.

83 Sermon 74, *WJW* 3, p. 56.

84 Sermon 39, 'Catholic Spirit', *WJW* 2, pp. 79–95 (p. 82).

85 *Journal*, 25 March 1743.

86 *Works* 10, p. 142.

87 Sermon 22, 'Upon our Lord's Sermon on the Mount', *WJW* 2, pp. 488–509 (p. 508).

88 Sermon 4, 'Scriptural Christianity', *WJW* 1, pp. 159–80 (p. 175).

89 'The Character of a Methodist' (1742), *WJW* 9, pp. 31–46 (p. 34).

90 Sermon 55, 'On the Trinity', *WJW* 2, pp. 373–86 (p. 374).

91 Sermon 55, p. 376.

92 Sermon 20, 'The Lord our Righteousness', *WJW* 1, pp. 449–65 (p. 454).

93 Sermon 38, *WJW* 2, pp. 61–78 (p. 71). The commandment supposedly dropped by Roman Catholics was the second. *The Catechism of the Council of Trent for Parish Priests* (1566) took the whole of Exodus 20.2–6 as the first commandment and made Exodus 20.17 into two commandments. Protestants claimed the second commandment had been dropped.

94 *Works* 10, pp. 80–6.

95 Cf. Albert Outler, *John Wesley* (New York: Oxford University Press, 1964), p. 492.

96 Sermon 39, *WJW* 2, pp. 79–95.

97 Sermon 39, p. 90.

98 Sermon 39, p. 86.

99 Sermon 39, p. 94.

100 See below, p. 262.

101 See Chapter 6.

102 Frank Baker, *John Wesley and the Church of England* (Nashville: Abingdon, 1970), p. 86.

103 'To Dr Lavington, Bishop of Exeter', *LJW* 3, pp. 295–331 (p. 326).

104 For example, *The Jesuit detected; or, The Church of Rome discover'd in the guise of a Protestant under the guise of an answer to all that is material in the Rev. Mr Hervey's eleven letters to the Rev. Mr John Wesley* (London, 1768); and *Methodism and popery dissected and compared, and the doctrines of both proved to be derived from a pagan origin, including an impartial and candid enquiry into the writings of St Paul with general remarks on the nature of and affinity between*

enthusiasm and superstition (London, 1779).

105 For a complete bibliography of anti-Methodist publications in the eighteenth century see Clive Field, 'Anti-Methodist publications of the eighteenth century: a revised bibliography', *Bulletin of the John Rylands University Library of Manchester* 73 (1991), pp. 159–280.

106 Cf. A. M. Lyles, *Methodism Mocked: The Satiric Reaction to Methodism in the Eighteenth Century* (London: Epworth, 1960).

107 For a vivid account of an anti-Methodist riot in Wednesbury, see Wesley's *Journal* entry for 20 October 1743.

108 For a full account of the controversy between Wesley and Challoner see Butler, *Methodists and Papists*, chs 7 and 8.

109 Butler, *Methodists and Papists*, pp. 81f.

110 Reproduced in the *Journal* entry for that day. See *WJW* 21, pp. 303–8.

111 *WJW* 21, pp. 304f. (emphasis in original).

112 *WJW* 21, p. 305.

113 *WJW* 21, p. 305. 'Look at the Romanists in London or Dublin. Are these the "Holy", the only "Holy" Church? Just such holiness is in the bottomless pit.'

114 *WJW* 21, p. 305.

115 *WJW* 21, p. 306.

116 Pierre François le Courayer, *Dissertation on the Validity of English Ordinations and of the Succession of Bishops in the Church of England*, trans. Daniel Williams (London, 1725). Le Courayer was a French Augustinian canon who escaped from France after his works were condemned and lived in England until his death in 1776. *WJW* 21, p. 307, note 70.

117 *WJW* 21, p. 307.

118 Cf. *Catechism of the Catholic Church* (London: Geoffrey Chapman, 1994), para. 1256.

119 *WJW* 21, p. 307.

120 *WJW* 21, pp. 307f.

121 Joint Commission for Dialogue between the World Methodist Council and the Roman Catholic Church, *Growth in Understanding* (Dublin, 1976), p. 29, note 6.

122 Joint Commission for Dialogue between the World Methodist Council and the Roman Catholic Church, *Towards an Agreed Statement on the Holy Spirit* (Honolulu, 1981), para. 24.

123 Sermon 106, 'On Faith', *WJW* 3, pp. 491–501 (p. 500). The archbishop in question was François de Salignac de la Mothe-Fénelon.

124 'A Disavowal of Persecuting Papists', *Works* 10, p. 174.

125 'Letter to the Editor of the London Chronicle', reproduced in the *Journal*, 19 February 1761.

126 Cf. *Journal*, 13 May 1762.

127 Rack, *Reasonable Enthusiast*, p. 400.

128 Outler, *John Wesley*, p. viii.

129 Outler, *John Wesley*, p. viii.

2 From the Death of Wesley to 1900

1 *Minutes* (1791). Extract reprinted in Rupert Davies, A. Raymond George and Gordon Rupp (eds), *A History of The Methodist Church in Great Britain*, vol. 4 (London: Epworth, 1988), p. 245.

2 *Minutes* (1795). The Plan of Pacification is reprinted in Davies *et al.*, *A History of The Methodist Church in Great Britain*, vol. 4, pp. 264–7.

3 *Minutes* (1807). Extract reprinted in Davies *et al.*, *A History of The Methodist Church in Great Britain*, vol. 4, p. 320.

4 David Hempton, *Methodism and Politics in British Society 1750–1850* (London: Hutchinson, 1984), pp. 42f.

5 Hempton, *Methodism and Politics*, p. 117.

6 Untitled article in *The Methodist Magazine* (1810), pp. 118–20. The extract from the oath is reprinted from the *Christian Guardian* (1809).

7 *The Methodist Magazine* (1810), p. 119.

8 *The Methodist Magazine* (1810), p. 120.

9 'The Truth of God Defended: Review of the Catholic Magazine', *The Methodist Magazine* (1812), pp. 493–504. There have been several periodicals entitled *The Catholic Magazine*. Unfortunately, I have not been able to locate the periodical featured in *The Methodist Magazine*. The Methodist reviewer quotes the editor as declaring its 'sole aim is to remove, or at least diminish, those numberless false fabricated notions and prejudices forged against Catholics, so deeply rooted in the minds of many Protestants, and as infused, drop by drop, from early infancy, by lists of popish abominations, fees, pecuniary absolutions, indulgences, Fox's romancing Martyrology, and the whole train of controvertible artillery, all pointed at the Catholic faith.' *The Catholic Magazine* (1811?), p. 51.

10 *The Methodist Magazine* (1812), p. 493. Cf. *The Catholic Magazine* (1811?), p. 3.

11 *The Methodist Magazine* (1812), p. 496.

12 *The Methodist Magazine* (1812), p. 496.

13 *The Methodist Magazine* (1812), p. 501; Cf. *The Catholic Magazine* (1811?), p. 16.

14 *The Methodist Magazine* (1812), p. 501; Cf. John Tillotson, *Works* (London, 1728), pp. 252f.

15 *The Methodist Magazine* (1812), p. 499. Cf. *The Catholic Magazine* (1811?), p. 62. Milner was Vicar Apostolic of the Midlands District between 1803 and 1826, and the author of *The Divine Right of Episcopacy addressed to the Catholic laity of England, in answer to the Layman's* [i.e. Sir John Throck-

273

morton's] *second letter to the Catholic clergy of England; with remarks on the Oaths of Supremacy and Allegiance* (London, 1791).

16   *The Methodist Magazine* (1812), p. 499.

17   'The Scarcity of the Bible in Rome', *The Primitive Methodist Magazine* (1851), p. 479; 'The Romish Persecution in France', *The Methodist Magazine* (1812), pp. 301f.

18   *The Methodist Magazine* (1820), p. 509.

19   'Popery Illustrated: The Santiago Conflagration', *The United Methodist Free Churches' Magazine* (1864), pp. 137–45 (p. 142).

20   *The United Methodist Free Churches' Magazine* (1863), p. 670.

21   J. P. Gledstone, 'A Romish Seminary in England', *Methodist Monthly* (July 1895), pp. 207–9.

22   Gledstone, 'A Romish Seminary in England', p. 208.

23   D. G. Paz, *Popular Anti-Catholicism in Mid-Victorian England* (Stanford: Stanford University Press, 1992), p. 161.

24   e.g. *The substance of a letter to the Rev. Mr Fitzsimmons, Roman Catholic Priest of Ballymena, in Ireland, on some chief pillars or prime articles of his faith, especially transubstantiation, propitiatory sacrifice of the mass, and divine worship of the host etc. These are proved beyond a possibility of contradiction never to have been taught by Christ or his apostles, and to be necessarily subversive of Christianity* (Dublin, 1816); *Letters to Dr Doyle on the Doctrines of his Church with an easy and effectual plan to obtain Immediate Emancipation* (Dublin, 1824); *Error Unmasked* (Dublin, 1828).

25   David Hempton, *The Religion of the People: Methodism and Popular Religion c. 1750–1900* (London: Routledge, 1996), p. 136.

26   Hempton, *Methodism and Politics*, p. 136.

27   Cited in David Carter, *Love Bade be Welcome: A British Methodist Perspective on the Church* (Peterborough: Epworth, 2002), p. 51.

28   The titles of many of these tracts admirably sum up their content. For example, *A speech delivered in the Town Hall, Sheffield on Wednesday, February 18, 1829 at a Public Meeting convened to Petition the Legislature against the admission of Roman Catholics to Legislative and Political Power by Rev. George Cubitt, a Wesleyan minister.*

29   Hempton, *Methodism and Politics*, p. 138.

30   Hempton, *Methodism and Politics*, p. 140.

31   Reprinted in Davies *et al.*, *A History of the Methodist Church in Great Britain*, vol. 4, pp. 434–6 (p. 436).

32   *The Watchman*, 20 February 1839, p. 61. Cited in John T. Smith, *Methodism and Education 1849–1902* (Oxford: Clarendon, 1989), p. 7. *The Watchman* was the first Methodist newspaper. A semi-official organ, it was launched to defend the Wesleyan leadership from its critics and appeared weekly from 1835 to 1884. *DMBI*, p. 372.

33 For Example, George Osborne, *No popery in schools supported by the state: an address at the Wesleyan Chapel, Horseferry Road, Westminster on Tuesday May 28th 1839 with reference to the proposed Government scheme of Public Education.*

34 *The Watchman*, 12 June 1839, p. 202. Cited in Smith, *Methodism and Education 1849–1902*, p. 7.

35 *Minutes of the Wesleyan Conference 1839.* Extract reprinted in Davies *et al.*, *A History of the Methodist Church in Great Britain*, vol. 4, pp. 437f.

36 Smith, *Methodism and Education 1849–1902*, p. 12.

37 T. J. Graham, *To the Ministers, Leaders and Members of the Wesleyan Methodist Connexion* (1849). Cited in Smith, *Methodism and Education 1849–1902*, p. 14.

38 J. H. Rigg, 'Denominational and National Education', report from the *London Quarterly Review* (January 1870), pp. 26, 30. Cited in Smith, *Methodism and Education 1849–1902*, p. 54.

39 *School Board Chronicle*, 11 March 1871, p. 107. Cited in Smith, *Methodism and Education 1849–1902*, p. 80.

40 J. H. Rigg, *Oxford High Anglicanism and its Chief Leaders* (London, 1894), p. 125.

41 J. H. Rigg, *A Comparative View of Church Organisations, Primitive and Protestant* (London, 1878), p. 171.

42 Rigg, *A Comparative View of Church Organisations*, p. 223.

43 Rigg, *A Comparative View of Church Organisations*, p. 223.

44 Cited in David L. Edwards, *Christian England*, vol. 3 (London: Collins, 1984), p. 280.

45 'The Papal Aggression, and the Duties of Protestants at this crisis', *The Methodist New Connexion Magazine and Evangelical Expository* (1850), pp. 566–76. The name of the author is not given.

46 'The Papal Aggression', p. 566.

47 'The Papal Aggression', p. 566.

48 'The Papal Aggression', p. 567.

49 'The Papal Aggression', p. 567.

50 'The Papal Aggression', p. 569.

51 'The Papal Aggression', p. 574.

52 'The Papal Aggression', p. 573.

53 'The Papal Aggression', p. 568.

54 'The Papal Aggression', p. 574.

55 'The Papal Aggression', p. 576.

56 Paz, *Popular Anti-Catholicism*, p. 169.

57 *The Wesleyan Times*, 25 November 1850. Cited in Paz, *Popular Anti-Catholicism*, p. 169.

58 Paz, *Popular Anti-Catholicism*, p. 169.

59 Paz, *Popular Anti-Catholicism*, p. 174.

60 Henry Rack, *Reasonable Enthusiast: John Wesley and the Rise of Methodism* (London: Epworth, 1989), p. 516.

61 Articles XIV, XIX, XXI, XXII, XXIV, XXV, XXVIII, XXX, XXXI, XXXIV.

62 Emory Stevens Buckle (ed.), *The History of American Methodism*, vol. 2 (New York: Abingdon, 1964), pp. 332f.

63 Buckle, *American Methodism*, vol. 2, p. 333.

64 J. A. Phillips, 'The Holy Catholic Church', *Methodist Review* [published by the Methodist Episcopal Church, South] April 1922, pp. 217–19. Cited in Karen B. Westerfield Tucker, *American Methodist Worship* (New York: Oxford University Press, 2001), p. 40.

65 G. Bromley Oxenham opposed electing a Roman Catholic as President of the United States, fearing that a Catholic president would be in constant touch with the pope. See Robert Dallek, *John F. Kennedy: An Unfinished Life 1917–1963* (London: Allen Lane, 2003), p. 231.

66 Charles Elliott, *The Delineation of Roman Catholicism*, 4th edn (London, 1877), preface.

67 Elliott, *Roman Catholicism*, preface.

68 Elliott, *Roman Catholicism*, pp. 285, 501.

69 Elliott, *Roman Catholicism*, pp. 442–7.

70 Elliott, *Roman Catholicism*, p. 450.

71 Elliott, *Roman Catholicism*, p. 451.

72 Elliott, *Roman Catholicism*, p. 453.

73 Elliott, *Roman Catholicism*, p. 492.

74 Elliott, *Roman Catholicism*, p. 495.

75 Elliott, *Roman Catholicism*, p. 500.

76 Hempton, *Methodism and Politics*, p. 118.

77 Dr Thomas Coke in a report to the Wesleyan Missionary Society in 1806. Cited in Hempton, *Methodism and Politics*, p. 121.

78 W. Crook, *Ireland and the Centenary of American Methodism* (London, 1866), p. 31; cited in Norman W. Taggart, *The Irish in World Methodism 1760–1900* (London: Epworth, 1986), p. 43.

79 C. H. Crookshank, *History of Methodism in Ireland* (London, 1886), vol. 2, p. 167. Cited in Taggart, *The Irish in World Methodism 1760–1900*, p. 143.

80 A. Stevens, *History of the Methodist Episcopal Church* (New York, 1865), vol. 1, p. 48. Cited in Taggart, *The Irish in World Methodism 1760–1900*, p. 6.

81 'Methodist Foreign Missionary Enterprise', in W. J. Townsend, H. B. Workman and George Eayrs (eds), *A New History of Methodism* (London: Hodder & Stoughton, 1909), vol. 2, pp. 283–416.

82 'Methodist Foreign Missionary Enterprise', pp. 400f.

83 Taggart, *The Irish in World Methodism 1760–1900*, p. 142.

84 Taggart, *The Irish in World Methodism 1760–1900*, p. 142.

85 Taggart, *The Irish in World Methodism 1760–1900*, pp. 168–80.

86 W. C. Barclay, *History of Methodist Missions* (New York, 1950), vol. 3, p. 834. Cited in Taggart, *The Irish in World Methodism 1760–1900*, p. 179.

87 'From 1868 to 1892 he was connexional editor and played a leading part in the 1882 revision of the "Book of Offices", being keen to eliminate anything "unscriptural" or "sacerdotalist" from the services derived from the Book of Common Prayer.' Article on Gregory in *DMBI*, p. 141.

88 Benjamin Gregory, *The Holy Catholic Church: The Communion of Saints* (London, 1873), p. 7.

89 Gregory, *The Holy Catholic Church*, p. 31.

90 Gregory, *The Holy Catholic Church*, p. 32.

91 Gregory, *The Holy Catholic Church*, p. 10.

92 Gregory, *The Holy Catholic Church*, p. 173.

93 Gregory, *The Holy Catholic Church*, p. 177.

94 Gregory, *The Holy Catholic Church*, p. 143.

95 Gregory, *The Holy Catholic Church*, p. 95. Cf. *Evidences of Christianity*, pt. I, ch. 1.

96 Gregory, *The Holy Catholic Church*, p. 93.

97 Gregory, *The Holy Catholic Church*, p. 101.

98 Gregory, *The Holy Catholic Church*, p. 59.

99 Gregory, *The Holy Catholic Church*, p. 209.

100 Gregory, *The Holy Catholic Church*, p. 228.

101 Gregory, *The Holy Catholic Church*, pp. 231f.

102 Gregory, *The Holy Catholic Church*, p. 166.

103 Gregory, *The Holy Catholic Church*, p. 205.

104 Gregory, *The Holy Catholic Church*, pp. 208f.

105 Carter, *Love Bade me Welcome*, p. 82.

106 D. Hughes, *The Life of Hugh Price Hughes* (London: Hodder & Stoughton, 1904), p. 222.

107 Hughes, *The Life of Hugh Price Hughes*, p. 635.

108 Hughes, *The Life of Hugh Price Hughes*, p. 424.

109 Hughes, *The Life of Hugh Price Hughes*, p. 629.

110 Hughes, *The Life of Hugh Price Hughes*, pp. 394–5.

111 Carter, *Love Bade me Welcome*, p. 85.

112 Francis Martyn, *Lecture I (–VIII) being . . . a series of lectures delivered in the Catholic Chapel, St Mary's Mount, Walsall on the infallibility of the Church, and other important points of Controversy* (Walsall, 1830?); cf. William Dalton, *The Doctrine of the Cross compared with the Sacrifice of the Mass . . . in reply to Rev. F. Martyn*, 4th edn (London, 1830).

113 Francis Martyn, *A sermon preached at the funeral obsequies of the Right Reverend John Milner: Bishop of Castabala, and Vicar Apostolic of the Midland District, on the 27th day of April, 1826, at the Catholic Chapel, Wolverhampton*

(London, 1826).

114 Cf. J. A. Mason, *The Perpetuity of Revealed Religion, and uniformity of her spirit and worship; a sermon* (London, 1839).

115 e.g. *A touchstone for Methodism; or, A dialogue on the forgiveness of sins, between farmer Lovegood, a Catholic, and William Pearcival and Timothy Scattergood, of the Methodist persuasion* (London, 1835)

116 John Chettle, *Protestant Objections, against the Romish Doctrine of Transubstantiaion; addressed to the Rev. F. Martyn, and to the inhabitants of Walsall and Bloxwich*, 2nd edn (Walsall, 1827).

117 J. A. Mason, *A shaver for John Chettle, Methodist preacher; or, a vindication of the doctrine of the real presence of Jesus Christ in the holy eucharist, as taught by the Catholic Church* (London, 1827).

118 J. A. Mason, *The Conversion of Edward Corser, Esq. of Stourbridge, in the County of Worcester, to the Catholic faith: with remarks thereon, as connected with the mission of that place by J. A. Mason . . .; also the address delivered to Mr Corser on the morning of his communion by Rev. Francis Martyn* (London, 1838). Cf. *Wonderful discoveries and portentous disclosures elicited from a ghost by . . . J. A. Mason's pamphlet on Mr Corser's conversion to catholicity, together with a review of the said pamphlet, and of certain letters to the author* (London, 1839).

119 J. A. Mason, *Strictures on the First part of Wesley's Roman catechism* (London, 1828); *Strictures on the Second part of Wesley's Roman catechism* (London, 1830); *Strictures on the third and fourth parts of Wesley's Roman catechism* (London, 1830).

120 *Dialogues on the spirit of the Methodist preachers towards the catholic religion and clergy* (Tract 35); *Dialogues of the spirit of the new birth exemplified in Methodist preachers towards the Catholic religion and clergy* (Tract 37).

121 Advertisement to vol. 1 of the *Tracts for the Times* (London, 1834).

122 'Selina, Countess of Huntingdon', in J. H. Newman, *Essays Critical and Historical*, vol. 1 (London, 1871), pp. 387–425 (pp. 387f).

123 Newman, *Essays Critical and Historical*, p. 388. 'May my soul be with Wesley [rather] than with Luther or with Calvin, and with many others whom it would be tedious to list now.'

124 Newman, *Essays Critical and Historical*, pp. 404f.

125 Newman, *Essays Critical and Historical*, p. 424.

126 Newman, *The Present Position of Catholics in England* (London, 1851, reprinted 1899), p. 364.

127 English translation, *Symbolism* (New York: Crossroad, 1997). I am indebted to Revd Professor George H. Tavard for permission to use material relating to the continental perception of Methodism from his as yet unpublished paper 'How Catholics have seen Methodists', written for the international Methodist–Roman Catholic dialogue (2002).

128 *Symbolism*, p. 436. Cited in Tavard, 'How Catholics have seen

Methodists'.

129 *Symbolism*, p. 437. Cited in Tavard, 'How Catholics have seen Methodists'.

130 *Symbolism*, p. 439. Cited in Tavard, 'How Catholics have seen Methodists'.

131 *Symbolism*, p. 444. Cited in Tavard, 'How Catholics have seen Methodists'.

132 J.-P. Migne, *Encyclopédie Théologique*, vol. 11 (1847), col. 1004. Cited in Tavard, 'How Catholics have seen Methodists'. Author's translation.

133 René Rohrbacher, *Histoire universelle de l'Eglise catholique*, vol. 13, p. 767. Cited in Tavard, 'How Catholics have seen Methodists'.

134 Rohrbacher, *Histoire universelle de l'Eglise catholique*, vol. 13, p. 766. Cited in Tavard, 'How Catholics have seen Methodists'.

135 Rohrbacher, *Histoire universelle de l'Eglise catholique*, vol. 13, p. 768. Cited in Tavard, 'How Catholics have seen Methodists'.

136 Rohrbacher, *Histoire universelle de l'Eglise catholique*, vol. 13, p. 778. Cited in Tavard, 'How Catholics have seen Methodists'.

3 The Twentieth Century to the Second Vatican Council

1 Gordon Wakefield, 'Roman Catholicism', in *DMBI*, p. 300.

2 Henry Bett, *The Spirit of Methodism* (London: Epworth, 1937), p. 144.

3 Bett, *The Spirit of Methodism*, p. 145.

4 Bett, *The Spirit of Methodism*, pp. 64–70, 71, 85.

5 David Carter, *Love Bade me Welcome: A British Methodist Perspective on the Church* (Peterborough: Epworth, 2002), p. 85.

6 J. Agar Beet, *The Church, the Churches and the Sacraments* (London: Hodder & Stoughton, 1907), p. 106.

7 Beet, *The Church, the Churches and the Sacraments*, pp. 68ff.

8 Beet, *The Church, the Churches and the Sacraments*, p. 99.

9 Beet, *The Church, the Churches and the Sacraments*, pp. 80f.

10 W. J. Townsend, H. B. Workman and George Eayrs, *A New History of Methodism* (London: Hodder & Stoughton, 1909), Preface.

11 H. B. Workman, 'The Place of Methodism in the Life and Thought of the Christian Church', in Townsend *et al.*, *A New History of Methodism*, pp. 39f.

12 Workman, 'The Place of Methodism in the Life and Thought of the Christian Church', p. 40.

13 Workman, 'The Place of Methodism in the Life and Thought of the Christian Church', p. 43.

14 Workman, 'The Place of Methodism in the Life and Thought of the Christian Church', p. 44.

15 For a biography see Alan Turberfield, *John Scott Lidgett: Archbishop of*

British Methodism? (Peterborough: Epworth, 2003).

16 John Scott Lidgett, *God, Christ and the Church* (London: Hodder & Stoughton, 1927), p. 230.

17 Lidgett, *God, Christ and the Church*, p. 231.

18 Lidgett, *God, Christ and the Church*, p. 266.

19 Lidgett, *God, Christ and the Church*, pp. 272f.

20 Lidgett, *God, Christ and the Church*, p. 312.

21 Lidgett, *God, Christ and the Church*, p. 320.

22 Clause 4 of the Deed of Union.

23 R. Newton Flew, 'Methodism and the Catholic Tradition', in N. P. Williams and Charles Harris (eds), *Northern Catholicism* (London: SPCK, 1933), pp. 515–30.

24 'One of the sublimest passages in Newman's writings is that wherein he takes his stand on holiness as the single mark of the true Church.' Flew, 'Methodism and the Catholic Tradition', p. 515.

25 Flew, 'Methodism and the Catholic Tradition', p. 530.

26 *Conference Agenda* (1937), pp. 365–402; reprinted in *Statements of the Methodist Church on Faith and Order 1933–1983* (London: Methodist Conference, 1984), pp. 5–42.

27 *The Nature of the Christian Church*, section II, paragraph 1.

28 *The Nature of the Christian Church*, Section II, paragraph 3.

29 Revd A. W. Harrison, *PWHS* 16 (1927), p. 1.

30 Maximin Piette, *John Wesley in the Evolution of Protestantism* (London: Sheed and Ward, 1937), p. 473.

31 Piette, *John Wesley in the Evolution of Protestantism*, p. 476.

32 Piette, *John Wesley in the Evolution of Protestantism*, p. 478.

33 Piette, *John Wesley in the Evolution of Protestantism*, p. 475.

34 Piette, *John Wesley in the Evolution of Protestantism*, p. 476.

35 R. A. Knox, *Enthusiasm: A Chapter in the History of Religion, with special reference to the XVII and XVIII centuries* (Oxford: Clarendon, 1950).

36 Knox, *Enthusiasm*, p. 450.

37 Knox, *Enthusiasm*, p. 581.

38 Knox, *Enthusiasm*, p. 589.

39 *Journal*, 26 April 1739. Cf. Knox, *Enthusiasm*, p. 521.

40 *Journal*, 15 June 1739.

41 Knox, *Enthusiasm*, pp. 451f.

42 *Journal*, 8 September 1784; 5 February 1786. Cf. Knox, *Enthusiasm*, p. 531.

43 Knox, *Enthusiasm*, p. 535.

44 Knox, *Enthusiasm*, p. 589.

45 Knox, *Enthusiasm*, p. 547.

46 Knox, *Enthusiasm*, p. 423.

47 Knox, *Enthusiasm*, p. 454.

48 Knox, *Enthusiasm*, p. 589.

49 Knox, *Enthusiasm*, p. 590.

50 Knox, *Enthusiasm*, p. 590.

51 Knox, *Enthusiasm*, p. 435.

52 Henry Rack, *Reasonable Enthusiast: John Wesley and the Rise of Methodism* (London: Epworth, 1989), p. 276.

53 Rack, *Reasonable Enthusiast*, pp. 552f.

54 Louis Bouyer, *Du Protestantisme à l'Église* (Paris, 1954). Trans. A. V. Littledale, *The Spirit and Forms of Protestantism* (London: Harvill, 1956).

55 Bouyer, *The Spirit and Forms of Protestantism*, p. 30.

56 Bouyer, *The Spirit and Forms of Protestantism*, p. 30.

57 Bouyer, *The Spirit and Forms of Protestantism*, p. 183.

58 *Hymns and Psalms: A Methodist and Ecumenical Hymnbook* (London: Methodist Conference, 1983), No. 528.

59 Bouyer, *The Spirit and Forms of Protestantism*, p. 32.

60 Bouyer, *The Spirit and Forms of Protestantism*, p. 184.

61 Bouyer, *The Spirit and Forms of Protestantism*, p. 184.

62 Bouyer, *The Spirit and Forms of Protestantism*, p. 182.

63 John Todd, *John Wesley and the Catholic Church* (London: Hodder & Stoughton, 1958), p. 11.

64 Todd, *John Wesley and the Catholic Church*, p. 15.

65 Todd, *John Wesley and the Catholic Church*, p. 12.

66 Todd, *John Wesley and the Catholic Church*, p. 12.

67 Todd, *John Wesley and the Catholic Church*, p. 19.

68 Todd, *John Wesley and the Catholic Church*, p. 23.

69 Todd, *John Wesley and the Catholic Church*, pp. 13–15.

70 Todd, *John Wesley and the Catholic Church*, p. 22.

71 Todd, *John Wesley and the Catholic Church*, p. 122.

72 *Journal*, 22 June 1739. Cf. Todd, *John Wesley and the Catholic Church*, p. 125.

73 *Journal*, 6 September 1742.

74 Todd, *John Wesley and the Catholic Church*, pp. 125f.

75 Todd, *John Wesley and the Catholic Church*, p. 119.

76 Knox, *Enthusiasm*, pp. 538f.

77 Todd, *John Wesley and the Catholic Church*, p. 130.

78 e.g. 'A Roman Catechism', in *Works* 10, pp. 86–128, Question 24.

79 Todd, *John Wesley and the Catholic Church*, p. 29.

80 Todd, *John Wesley and the Catholic Church*, p. 32.

81 Todd, *John Wesley and the Catholic Church*, p. 11.

82 Todd, *John Wesley and the Catholic Church*, p. 11.

83 Todd, *John Wesley and the Catholic Church*, p. 100.

84 Todd, *John Wesley and the Catholic Church*, p. 101.

85 Todd, *John Wesley and the Catholic Church*, pp. 102–20. Cf. Ole E. Borgen, *John Wesley on the Sacraments* (Zurich: United Methodist Publishing House, 1972). Borgen concludes that, although there is an affinity between Wesley and the continental Reformers, Wesley's understanding of the sacraments was wholly derived from the English Reformation.

86 Todd, *John Wesley and the Catholic Church*, p. 192.

87 Cf. 'A Roman Catechism', in *Works* 10, pp. 86–128, Question 19.

88 Todd, *John Wesley and the Catholic Church*, p. 16.

89 Cf. Edward C. Butler, *The Vatican Council 1869–70*, ed. Christopher Butler (London: Collins Harvill, 1962).

90 Yves Congar, *Chrétiens désunis* (Paris, 1937); ET *Divided Christendom* (London: Geoffrey Bles, 1939), pp. 191, 253–4, 271–2.

91 *The Tablet*, 26 October 2002, p. 11.

92 The Council did not actually define the meaning of *aggiornamento*, but it involved a return to the sources of the Christian life and an adjustment to changed circumstances. Cf. Christopher Butler, *The Theology of Vatican II* (London: Darton, Longman & Todd, 1967; revised edn 1981), p. 18.

93 Peter Hebblethwaite, *John XXIII: Shepherd of the Modern World* (London: Geoffrey Chapman, 1984), p. 196.

94 *The Tablet*, 26 October 2002, p. 11.

95 See J. R. H. Moorman, 'Observers and Guests of the Council', in Alberic Stacpoole (ed.), *Vatican II by Those Who Were There* (London: Geoffrey Chapman, 1986), pp. 155–69.

96 Cf. Albert Outler, ' "Strangers within the Gates": An Observer's Memories', in Stacpoole, *Vatican II by Those Who Were There*, pp. 170–83; and Albert Outler, *Methodist Observer at Vatican II* (Westminster, Md.: Newman Press, 1967). The following Methodists were authorised substitutes for the three delegated observers: José Miguez-Bonino (Argentina), Emerito Nacpil (Philippines), Alan Keithley (Great Britain), Gordon Rupp (Great Britain), William Cannon (United States), Robert Cushman (United States), Max Woodward (British Secretary of the World Methodist Council).

97 *Lumen Gentium*, para. 8. Emphasis added. All quotations from the conciliar texts are taken from the English translation by Walter M. Abbott, *The Documents of Vatican II* (London: Geoffrey Chapman, 1967).

98 For a helpful discussion see Francis A. Sullivan, 'Subsistit in', *One in Christ* 22 (1986), pp. 115–23.

99 Cited in Paul McPartlan, *Sacrament of Salvation: An Introduction to Eucharistic Ecclesiology* (Edinburgh: T & T Clark, 1995). The reference is elusive. Dr McPartlan suggests that the remark was adapted from a comment by the distinguished Orthodox theologian Paul Evdokimov in his book *L'Orthodoxie* (Neuchatel: Delachaux et Niestlé, 1959), p. 343: 'We know where the Church is;

it is not for us to say and judge where the Church is not.' Curiously, in *The Theology of Vatican II*, Butler records Endokimov's comment on p. 119, but does not repeat the famous statement that has been widely attributed to himself.

100 *Lumen Gentium*, 14.

101 *Lumen Gentium*, 15.

102 *Unitatis Redintegratio*, 1.

103 *Unitatis Redintegratio*, 3.

104 *Unitatis Redintegratio*, 8.

105 *Unitatis Redintegratio*, 9.

106 *Unitatis Redintegratio*, 4.

107 *Unitatis Redintegratio*, 3.

108 *Unitatis Redintegratio*, 4.

109 *Unitatis Redintegratio*, 15.

110 Herbert Vorgrimler (ed.), *Commentary on the Documents of Vatican II* (London: Burns & Oates, 1968), vol. 2, pp. 77–8.

111 *Unitatis Redintegratio*, 19.

112 'A response' to *Lumen Gentium*, in Abbott, *The Documents of Vatican II*, pp. 102–06.

113 For an assessment of the Council's achievement 25 years afterwards see the collection of essays, Adrian Hastings (ed.), *Modern Catholicism: Vatican II and After* (London: SPCK, 1991).

4 International Methodist–Roman Catholic Dialogue

1 Since 1967 the Methodist co-chairs have been: Bishop William R. Cannon (1967–86) and Professor Geoffrey Wainwright (1986–). The Roman Catholic co-chairs have been: Rt Revd J. Murphy (1967–71), Rt Revd Michael Bowen (1971–6), Rt Revd Francis Stafford (1976–86), Rt Revd James W. Malone (1986–96) and Rt Revd Michael Putney (1996–).

2 Richard Stewart, 'Dialogue with Methodism', *One in Christ* 18 (1982), pp. 223–36.

3 Stewart, 'Dialogue with Methodism', p. 225.

4 Geoffrey Wainwright, *Methodists in Dialogue* (Nashville: Abingdon, 1995), p. 39.

5 Tom Stransky, 'Ecumenism (*Unitatis Redintegratio*)', in Adrian Hastings (ed.), *Modern Catholicism: Vatican II and After* (London: SPCK, 1991), pp. 113–17 (p. 116). Stransky is a former member of the Vatican Secretariat for Promoting Christian Unity.

6 Paragraph 15 cites the Rio report (1996) and the Nairobi report (1986); paragraph 44 cites the Singapore report (1991); paragraph 53 cites the Dublin report (1976).

7 For a retrospective of the Joint Commission's work up to 1991 see Wain-

wright, *Methodists in Dialogue*, especially ch. 1, 'Roman Catholic–Methodist Dialogue: A Silver Jubilee' pp. 37–56. For a commentary on the reports since 1986 see Geoffrey Wainwright, ' "Can two walk together except they be agreed?" Progress between Methodists and Catholics on the Way of Unity', in Peter Walter, Klaus Krimer and George Augustine (eds), *Kirche in ökumenischer Perspektive: Kardinal Walter Kasper zum 70. Geburtstag* (Freiburg: Herder, 2003), pp. 275–89. Also, David Carter, 'The Roman Catholic–Methodist Dialogue', *Exchange: Journal of Missiological and Ecumenical Research* 28 (1999), pp. 363–80.

8 The published title was simply 'Denver Report'. Retrospectively, it was referred to as *Growth in Agreement*. This later title is used in the present volume as an aide-memoire to the content of the report.

9 'A Methodist Statement on Euthanasia' adopted by the Methodist Conference of 1974, in *Declarations and Statements* (London: Methodist Conference, 1981), pp. 19–24.

10 Cf. *Lumen Gentium*, 10.

11 'Towards an Agreed Statement on the Holy Spirit', *One in Christ* 15 (1979), pp. 274–81; 'The Holy Spirit, Christian Experience and Authority', *One in Christ* 16 (1980), pp. 225–33.

12 Cf. Max Thurian, 'Baptism, Eucharist and Ministry ("The Lima Text")', in Nicholas Lossky, José Miguez Bonino, John S. Pobee *et al.* (eds), *A Dictionary of the Ecumenical Movement* (Geneva: WCC, 1991), pp. 80–3.

13 Cf. Honolulu report, 57.

14 *BEM*, 37.

15 The Munich Report (1982) of the Catholic–Orthodox dialogue was also a landmark in introducing the concept of *koinonia* into bilateral dialogues.

16 Geoffrey Wainwright (ed.), *A. Raymond George: Memoirs Methodist and Ecumenical* (Buxton: Church in the Market Place Publications, 2003), p. 193.

17 *United Methodist Book of Discipline* (2000), paras 503 and 504.

18 See 'Episcopacy (1998)', in *Statements and Reports of the Methodist Church on Faith and Order*, vol. 2: *1984–2000* (Peterborough: Methodist Conference, 2000), pp. 370–82 (p. 382).

19 J. M. R. Tillard, 'Commentary on "Towards a Statement on the Church" ', *One in Christ* 22 (1986), pp. 259–66.

20 Tillard, 'Commentary on "Towards a Statement on the Church" ', p. 260.

21 Tillard, 'Commentary on "Towards a Statement on the Church" ', p. 265.

22 Tillard, 'Commentary on "Towards a Statement on the Church" ', p. 261.

23 Tillard, 'Commentary on "Towards a Statement on the Church" ', p. 265.

24 Tillard, 'Commentary on "Towards a Statement on the Church" ', p. 265.

25 Raymond George, 'The Apostolic Tradition', *One in Christ* 28 (1992), pp. 82–6 (p. 85).

26 George, 'The Apostolic Tradition', p. 86.

27 Jared Wicks, 'Commentary and Assessment of the Apostolic Tradition', *One in Christ* 28 (1992), pp. 74–81.

28 Wicks, 'Commentary and Assessment of the Apostolic Tradition', p. 79.

29 Wicks, 'Commentary and Assessment of the Apostolic Tradition', p. 80.

30 *Towards a Statement on the Church*, 9.

31 *The Apostolic Tradition*, 89.

32 William Henn, 'Reflections on the *Word of Life*', *One in Christ* 32 (1996), pp. 363–77 (p. 365).

33 Cf. T. F. Best and G. Gassmann, *On the Way to Fuller Koinonia: Report of the Fifth World Conference on Faith and Order* (Geneva: WCC, 1994), pp. 228–62.

34 Henn, 'Reflections on the *Word of Life*', p. 368.

35 ARCIC, *The Gift of Authority* (London: CTS/Church House Publishing, 1999), para. 28.

36 *Dei Verbum*, 10.

37 Ralph Del Colle, 'Commentary and Reflections on *Speaking the Truth in Love: Teaching Authority among Catholics and Methodists* Report of the Joint Commission between the Roman Catholic Church and the World Methodist Council 1997–2001 Seventh Series', *Pontifical Council for Promoting Christian Unity Information Service* 107 (2001/II–III), pp. 118–26.

38 *The Word of Life*, 131–2.

39 *Growth in Agreement*, 5.

40 Geoffrey Wainwright, ' "Can two walk together except they be agreed?" Progress between Methodists and Catholics on the Way of Unity', in Walter *et al.*, *Kirche in ökumenischer Perspektive*, p. 286.

41 Report on the 'Meeting of the International Methodist–Roman Catholic Dialogue, October 24–31, [2003] York, England', *Pontifical Council for Promoting Christian Unity Information Service* 114 (2003/IV), p. 196.

42 'Message from Cardinal Walter Kasper on the occasion of the 225th anniversary of Wesley's Chapel and the ongoing celebration of the 300th anniversary of John Wesley's birth', *Pontifical Council for Promoting Christian Unity Information Service* 114 (2003/IV), p. 185.

5 National Methodist–Roman Catholic Dialogues

1 The first co-chairs were Revd Dr Harold Roberts (Methodist) and Bishop Mervyn Alexander (Roman Catholic). The present co-chairs are Revd Dr Richard G. Jones (Methodist) and Bishop Ambrose Griffiths (Roman Catholic). David Butler was the Methodist co-secretary between 1984 and 2000. His reminiscences of the committee during this period are recorded with humour in his article 'The British Roman Catholic–Methodist Dialogue 1984–2000', *Epworth Review* 29/3 (2002), pp. 9–15.

2 The final versions of both statements were also published separately in Britain, along with an English Methodist–Roman Catholic statement on authority in *Eucharist, Ministry, Authority: Statements Agreed by Roman Catholics and Methodists* (Catholic Information Service, 1978)

3 Cf. Richard Stewart, *Catholics and Methodists: An Introduction to the Work of the Joint Commission Between the World Methodist Council and the Roman Catholic Church* (London: CTS, 1974); David Butler and Michael Jackson, *Catholics and Methodists: The Work of the International Commission* (London: CTS/Methodist Publishing House, 1986).

4 e.g. David Carter, 'Catholics, Methodists and Reception', *One in Christ* 28 (1992), pp. 232–47; John Newton, 'Spirituality and Sanctification', *One in Christ* 24 (1988), pp. 218–22; Marion Morgan, 'The Sacred Heart of Jesus in Catholic Devotion', *One in Christ* 24 (1988), pp. 223–36; Cf. John Newton and Marion Morgan, *Will you Walk a Little Faster: Letters between a Methodist and a Roman Catholic* (London: Epworth, 1984); Emmanuel Sullivan and Gordon Wakefield, 'Towards a Spirituality for Today', *Epworth Review* 4 (1977), pp. 61–7.

5 Conference Agenda, 1978; reprinted as 'Conversations between Methodists and Roman Catholics in England 1967–78', *One in Christ* 15 (1979), pp. 348–53. Cf. D. Alan Keighley, 'Pursuing the Roman Catholic–Methodist Dialogue', *Epworth Review* 4 (1977), pp. 33–41.

6 Conference Agenda (1975).

7 The text can be found in *Eucharist, Ministry, Authority: Statements Agreed by Roman Catholics and Methodists* (Catholic Information Service, 1978), pp. 16–26.

8 'English Roman Catholic–Methodist Committee: Justification – A Consensus Statement', *One in Christ* 24 (1988), pp. 270–3.

9 'English Roman Catholic–Methodist Committee: Justification – A Consensus Statement', *One in Christ* 28 (1992), pp. 87–91.

10 'Justification – A Consensus Statement' (1992), p. 89.

11 'Justification – A Consensus Statement' (1992), p. 88.

12 e.g. Proverbs 19.17; Deuteronomy 5.28–33; Exodus 23.20–2; Matthew 5.3–12, 46; 6.1, 18; 7.21; 11.29; 25.34; Luke 12.8; John 4.36; Romans 2.2, 6; 1 Corinthians 3.8; 2 Timothy 4.8; Revelation 2.10; 14.3.

13 'Justification – A Consensus Statement' (1992), p. 89. Cf. Augustine, *On Grace and Free Will* (VI, 15).

14 For a fuller treatment of this subject from a Methodist perspective see David M. Chapman, 'Rest and Light Perpetual: Prayer for the Departed in the Communion of Saints', *One in Christ* 34 (1998), pp. 39–49.

15 Owen Chadwick, *The Reformation* (London: Penguin, 1972), p. 42.

16 'Justification – A Consensus Statement' (1992), p. 90.

17 'Justification – A Consensus Statement' (1992), p. 90.

18 'Justification – A Consensus Statement' (1992), p. 90. Cf. Geoffrey Wainwright (ed.), *A. Raymond George: Memoirs Methodist and Ecumenical* (Buxton: Church in the Market Place Publications, 2003), p. 200.

19 Conference Agenda (1992), pp. 202–6. Reprinted, *One in Christ* 29 (1993), pp. 165–9. David Butler was the principal author.

20 Conference Agenda (1996), pp. 260–1.

21 Conference Agenda (1996), p. 261.

22 Pius IX, *Ineffabilis Deus*, 8 December 1854.

23 There is a wealth of published material on the Marian doctrines. For a general overview of the subject see Michael Schmaus, 'Mariology', in Karl Rahner (ed.), *Encyclopedia of Theology: A Concise Sacramentum Mundi* (London: Burns & Oates, 1975), pp. 893–901. Also, Alberic Stacpoole (ed.), *Mary and the Churches* (Blackrock, Co. Dublin: Columba, 1987).

24 Gordon Wakefield, 'The Virgin Mary in Methodism', *One in Christ* 4 (1968), pp. 156–64 (p. 161).

25 John Wesley, 'A Word to a Protestant', *Works* 11, pp. 187–95 (pp. 188f.).

26 John Wesley, 'A Word to a Protestant', p. 190.

27 John Wesley, 'Letter to a Roman Catholic', *Works* 10, pp. 80–6 (p. 81).

28 Neville Ward, *Five for Sorrow, Ten for Joy* (London: Epworth, 1971), p. ix.

29 Ward, *Five for Sorrow, Ten for Joy*, p. ix.

30 Geoffrey Wainwright, 'Mary in Relation to Methodism', *One in Christ* 11 (1975), pp. 121–44.

31 Wainwright, 'Mary in Relation to Methodism', p. 123.

32 Wainwright, 'Mary in Relation to Methodism', p. 123.

33 The principal author was Revd Michael Evans (Roman Catholic). Discussion began with two background papers from committee members: Eamon Duffy, 'The Place of the Blessed Virgin Mary in Roman Catholicism', *Epworth Review* 16 (1989), pp. 51–68; and Roger Stubbings, 'The Blessed Virgin Mary: A Methodist Contribution', unpublished paper for the English Methodist–Roman Catholic Committee, May 1988. Cf. Pauline Warner, 'Mary, a Two-Edged Sword to Pierce our Hearts?' *Epworth Review* 18 (1991), pp. 67–79.

34 *Matrimonia Mixta*. Cited in *Mixed Marriages: The Revised Directory promulgated by the Bishops' Conference of England and Wales 30th April 1990.*

35 Wainwright (ed.), *A. Raymond George: Memoirs Methodist and Ecumenical*, p. 197.

36 *Marriages with Roman Catholics* is available from the Methodist Publishing House, Peterborough.

37 The 'open table policy' of Methodism has been much debated in recent years. In theory, there has been some tightening of rules. For instance, baptism is supposed to be the essential prerequisite for receiving Holy Communion. See 'Children and Holy Communion (2000)', in *Statements and Reports of the*

Methodist Church on Faith and Order, vol. 2: *1984–2000* (Peterborough: Methodist Conference, 2000), pp. 176–88.

38 From the preamble to the *Resolution of Intent*, printed in Albert C. Outler, 'Discovery: An Olive Branch to the Romans, 1970's-style: United Methodist Initiative, Roman Catholic Response', *Methodist History* 13 (1975), pp. 52–6 (p. 53).

39 'Disavowing the traditional polemical understanding of those among its "articles of religion" which were part of an anti-Catholic inheritance from a less happy age, the resolution gives courageous practical and public expression of that "change of heart" which the Second Vatican Council saw as the soul of the ecumenical movement, and a solemn responsibility in every Church.' Denver report (1971), 130.

40 For a useful summary see *Methodist–Catholic Dialogues: Thirty Years of Mission and Witness* (The General Commission on Christian Unity and Inter-religious Concerns of the United Methodist Church and the United States Catholic Bishops' Conference, 2001).

41 *Methodist–Catholic Dialogues*, p. 17.

42 The text can be found in Joseph A. Burgess and Jeffrey Gros, *Building Unity: Ecumenical Dialogues with Roman Catholic Participation in the United States* (New York: Paulist Press, 1989), pp. 295–6.

43 Reprinted in Burgess and Gros, *Building Unity*, pp. 297–306.

44 Burgess and Gros, *Building Unity*, pp. 304f.

45 Burgess and Gros, *Building Unity*, p. 305.

46 Reprinted in Burgess and Gros, *Building Unity*, pp. 307–22.

47 Burgess and Gros, *Building Unity*, p. 315.

48 Joseph Dalaney and Benjamin Oliphant (eds), *Holy Living, Holy Dying* (Cincinnati: General Board of Global Ministries, 1988), reprinted in Joseph A. Burgess and Jeffrey Gros, *Growing Consensus: Church Dialogues in the United States 1962–1991* (New York: Paulist Press, 1995), pp. 529–42.

49 Methodist General Conference Minutes (1973).

50 Methodist General Conference Minutes (1973).

51 *Proceedings of the Second Assembly of the Uniting Church in Australia* (1979), pp. 41–2.

52 *Interchurch Marriages: Their Ecumenical Challenge and Significance for our Churches, Report of the National Dialogue between the Roman Catholic Church and the Uniting Church in Australia* (1999), p. 29.

53 *Interchurch Marriages*, p. 27.

54 *Interchurch Marriages*, p. 90.

55 *Report on the Methodist–Roman Catholic Dialogue 1995–1999 to the Conference of the Methodist Church of New Zealand Te Haa, hi Weteriana o Aotearoa and the Bishops' Conference of the Roman Catholic Church 1999*, p. 3.

56 *Report on the Methodist–Roman Catholic Dialogue 1995–1999*, p. 4.

57 Terry Wall, 'Speaking the Truth in Love, Teaching Authority Among Catholics and Methodists (November 2000) A New Zealand Response (April 2002)'. Unpublished paper from the Methodist–Roman Catholic dialogue in New Zealand.

58 *Report on the Methodist–Roman Catholic Dialogue 1995–1999*, p. 12.

59 *Report on the Methodist–Roman Catholic Dialogue 1995–1999*, p. 12.

60 *Report on the Methodist–Roman Catholic Dialogue 1995–1999*, p. 13.

61 *Report on the Methodist–Roman Catholic Dialogue 1995–1999*, p. 13.

62 *Report on the Methodist–Roman Catholic Dialogue 1995–1999*, p. 14.

6 Towards Catholicity

1 Cardinal Edward Cassidy, 'Reflections on the Ecumenical Movement and Catholic–Methodist Relations', *Epworth Review* 25 (1998), pp. 13–22.

2 Cassidy, 'Reflections on the Ecumenical Movement and Catholic–Methodist Relations', p. 15.

3 'There is an urgent need for us, my dear brothers and sisters, to move away from the shore, to move out into the deep, to have the courage to question our status quo and to give the quest for unity a much higher place in our priorities.' Cardinal Edward Idris Cassidy, 'Ecumenical Message' to the World Methodist Conference, Brighton, 2001, in *Proceedings of the 18th World Methodist Conference, Brighton 2001* (Lake Junaluska: World Methodist Council, 2001), pp. 59–62 (p. 60).

4 Sermon 39, 'Catholic Spirit', *WJW* 2, pp. 79–95 (p. 94).

5 Geoffrey Wainwright, ' "The Gift Which He on One Bestows, We All Delight to Prove" A Possible Methodist Approach to a Ministry of Primacy in the Circulation of Love and Truth', in James F. Puglisi (ed.), *Petrine Ministry and the Unity of the Church* (Collegeville,: Liturgical, 1999), pp. 59–82.

6 Geoffrey Wainwright, ' "The Gift Which He on One Bestows, We All Delight to Prove" ', p. 62; cf. *Ut Unum Sint*, 97.

7 Response to *Ut Unum Sint* (1997). *Statements and Reports of the Methodist Church on Faith and Order*, vol. 2: *1984–2000* (Peterborough: Methodist Conference, 2000), pp. 430f.

8 (Further) Response to *Ut Unum Sint* (1998), *Statements and Reports of the Methodist Church on Faith and Order*, vol. 2: *1984–2000*, pp. 432–4.

9 Cf. *Note on the Expression Sister Churches* issued by the CDF on 30 June 2000. 'One cannot properly say that the Catholic Church is the sister of a particular Church or group of Churches' (note 11). 'In the proper sense, sister churches are exclusively particular Churches or groupings of particular Churches' (note 10).

10 'A Statement in Response to the Vatican's *Dominus Iesus* From the Methodist Members of the Joint Commission for Dialogue Between the World

Methodist Council and the Roman Catholic Church, 7 September 2000'. Cf. Geoffrey Wainwright, '*Dominus Iesus,* A Methodist Response', *Pro Ecclesia* 10 (2001), pp. 11–13.

11 'A Statement in Response to the Vatican's *Dominus Iesus*'.

12 'A Statement in Response to the Vatican's *Dominus Iesus*'.

13 The concept of 'sufficient authority' is taken from R. E. Davies, *Religious Authority in an Age of Doubt* (London: Epworth, 1968), pp. 212ff. Roman Catholics will want to ask Methodists just what this 'sufficient authority' guarantees to the Church (if anything) and how it is exercised. *Called to Love and Praise* interprets the Roman Catholic concept of infallibility in maximalist terms (i.e. as 'absolute'). In fact, infallibility should be interpreted in minimalist terms as being just enough to enable the Church to continue in its providential way. Whether it is possible to find a convergence between the concepts of sufficient authority and infallibility would be worth studying further.

14 Cf. *Towards Koinonia in Faith, Life and Witness: A Discussion Paper, April 1993* (Geneva: WCC, 1993), pp. 8–9.

15 Cf. *Towards a Statement on the Church,* Nairobi report (1986), para. 23.

16 For a critique of *Called to Love and Praise* from a Methodist perspective, see David Carter, *Love Bade Me Welcome: A British Methodist Perspective on the Church* (Peterborough: Epworth, 2002), ch. 4.

17 Conference Agenda (2003), pp. 161–80.

18 This was one of the concerns expressed by Methodists in response to *BEM.*

19 Conference Agenda (2003), pp. 175–80.

20 Conference Agenda (2003), p. 178.

21 Conference Agenda (2003), p. 178.

22 For a useful introduction and bibliography see H. Ellsworth Chandlee, 'The Liturgical Movement', in J. G. Davies (ed.), *A New Dictionary of Liturgy and Worship* (London: SCM Press, 1986), pp. 307–14.

23 Chandlee, 'The Liturgical Movement', pp. 310f.

24 For a short commentary see Aidan Kavanagh, 'Liturgy (*Sacrosanctum Concilium*)', in Adrian Hastings (ed.), *Modern Catholicism: Vatican II and After* (London: SPCK, 1991), pp. 68–73; ch. 8, 'Liturgy; Church and World; Reflections', in Christopher Butler, *The Theology of Vatican II* (London: Darton, Longman & Todd, 1967; revised edn, 1981), pp. 170–202.

25 Ernest Rattenbury, *Wesley's Legacy to the World* (London, 1938), p. 198. Cited in Geoffrey Wainwright, *The Ecumenical Moment: Crisis and Opportunity for the Church* (Grand Rapids: Eerdmans, 1983), p. 196.

26 For useful background see Geoffrey Wainwright, 'The Ecumenical Scope of Methodist Liturgical Revision', in the *Centro Pro Unione Bulletin* (Fall 2002), pp. 16–26. For a study of the Eucharist in Methodism see John C. Bowmer, *The Sacrament of the Lord's Supper in Early Methodism* (London: Epworth, 1951),

and the sequel, *The Lord's Supper in Methodism 1791–1960* (London: Epworth, 1960).

27 Sermon 101, *WJW* 3, pp. 427–39.

28 Wesleyan Methodists sometimes made use of 'The Order for Morning Prayer', in *The Book of Offices* (London: Methodist Conference, 1936) for their main Sunday morning service. In a few Methodist churches, the Order for Morning Prayer remained in use until the 1980s.

29 'The worship of the Church is the offering of praise and prayer in which God's Word is read and preached, and in its fullness it includes the Lord's Supper, or Holy Communion.' *The Methodist Service Book* (London: Methodist Conference, 1975), p. B1. The service book also included an order for 'The Sunday Service without the Lord's Supper'. In practice, this was used less frequently since many ministers and congregations did not feel the need to use a printed liturgy for a preaching service.

30 *BEM*, Section II, para. 28.

31 *BEM*, Section II, para. 31.

32 The text can be found in Max Thurian (ed.), *Churches Respond to BEM* (Geneva: WCC, 1986–8), vol. 2, pp. 210–29 (p. 215).

33 Thurian, *Churches Respond to BEM*, p. 222.

34 Thurian, *Churches Respond to BEM*, p. 223.

35 Thurian, *Churches Respond to BEM*, p. 224.

36 Thurian, *Churches Respond to BEM*, p. 223.

37 For a useful introduction to *The Methodist Worship Book* in relation to previous Methodist service books see Neil Dixon, *Wonder, Love and Praise: A Companion to the Methodist Worship Book* (Peterborough: Epworth, 2003).

38 *The Book of Offices*, p. 51.

39 There were two possible forms: (1) 'Lord, confirm your servant N. by your Holy Spirit that *he* may continue to be yours for ever' (2) 'Lord, confirm *these* your servants by your Holy Spirit that *they* may continue to be yours for ever.' Only the first form was accompanied by the laying on of hands. *The Methodist Service Book*, pp. A23, A24. The rubrics make it clear that 'confirmation' refers to the Holy Spirit who confirms the gifts he has given (p. A15).

40 *The Methodist Worship Book* (Peterborough: Methodist Conference, 1999), p. 61; cf. *The Methodist Service Book*, p. B2.

41 Cf. Wainwright, 'The Ecumenical Scope of Methodist Liturgical Revision', p. 18.

42 *His Presence Makes the Feast: Holy Communion in the Methodist Church* (Peterborough: Methodist Conference, 2003).

43 *His Presence Makes the Feast*, paras 24–62.

44 *His Presence Makes the Feast*, para. 61.

45 *His Presence Makes the Feast*, para. 11.

46 Cf. *His Presence Makes the Feast*, para. 205.

47 For a history of Methodist worship in North America see K. Westerfield Tucker, *American Methodist Worship* (New York: Oxford University Press, 2001).

48 For instance, Wesley removed most of the holy days; he altered 'priest' to 'presbyter'; the pronouns in the prayer of absolution were changed from 'you' to 'us'; the Nicene Creed, exhortations and second post-communion prayer were dropped. Tucker, *American Methodist Worship*, pp. 5f.

49 Tucker, *American Methodist Worship*, p. 12.

50 Four years later, in 1880, the recommendation to use unfermented wine became a requirement 'wherever possible'. This loophole was finally closed in 1916. See Susan J. White, *Christian Worship and Technological Change* (Nashville: Abingdon, 1994) p. 85.

51 Paul Bradshaw has challenged the view that Christian liturgy has evolved from a single primitive form. Instead he argues that ancient Christian worship took various forms. The implications for the Liturgical Movement lie outside the scope of the present study. See Paul F. Bradshaw, *The Search for the Origins of Christian Worship: Sources and Methods for the Study of early Liturgy* (London: SPCK, 1992).

52 *The United Methodist Book of Worship* (Nashville: United Methodist Publishing House, 1992), p. 14.

53 To 'Our Brethren in America', *LJW* 7, pp. 238–9 (p. 239). Cited in Tucker, *American Methodist Worship*, p. 23.

54 The text can be found in Max Thurian, *Churches Respond to BEM*, vol. 2, pp. 177–99 (p. 188).

55 Thurian, *Churches Respond to BEM*, vol. 2, p. 189.

56 Thurian, *Churches Respond to BEM*, vol. 2, p. 189.

57 I am indebted to Revd John Bradley, Field Officer (South) for Churches Together in England, for providing me with a complete list of Local Ecumenical Partnerships involving both Roman Catholics and Methodists.

58 Taken from a submission to the British Methodist–Roman Catholic Committee.

Conclusion

1 *WJW* 21, p. 305.

2 Geoffrey Wainwright, 'Ecclesial Location and Ecumenical Vocation', in *The Ecumenical Moment: Crisis and Opportunity for the Church* (Grand Rapids: Eerdmans, 1983), pp. 189–221.

3 Frank Baker, *John Wesley and the Church of England* (Nashville: Abingdon, 1970), p. 311. 'Dr Coke puts me in mind of a German proverb, which I may apply to himself and to myself. "He skips like a flea; I creep like a louse." He would tear all from top to bottom. I will not tear, but unstitch.' Cited in

Wainwright, 'Ecclesial Location and Ecumenical Vocation', p. 193, note 10.

4 'An Anglican–Methodist Covenant: Common Statement of the Formal Conversations between the Methodist Church of Great Britain and the Church of England' (London: Methodist Publishing/Church House Publishing, 2001), para. 194.

5 Cardinal Edward Cassidy, 'Reflections on the Ecumenical Movement and Catholic–Methodist Relations', *Epworth Review* 25 (1998), pp. 13–22 (pp. 20f.).

6 C. J. Bertrand, 'Le méthodisme, "province" méconnue de la communion anglicane?', in *Aspects de l'Anglicanisme: Colloque de Strasbourg 14–16 Juin 1972* (1974), pp. 103–22. Cited in Wainwright, 'Ecclesial Location and Ecumenical Vocation', pp. 193–4.

7 Wainwright, 'Ecclesial Location and Ecumenical Vocation', p. 195.

8 See above, ch. 5. More recently, Francis Frost, a Roman Catholic writer, has suggested that Methodism owes its spirit to John Wesley in the same way that a religious order within the Roman Catholic Church owes its spirit to its founder. Francis Frost, 'Méthodisme', in G. Jacquement *et al.* (eds), *Catholicisme, hier, aujourd'hui et demain*, vol. 9 (Paris: Cerf, 1982), pp. 48–71.

9 Geoffrey Wainwright, '*Ora et labora*: Benedictines and Wesleyans at Prayer and at Work', in *Methodists in Dialogue* (Nashville: Abingdon, 1995), pp. 89–106.

10 Rupert Davies, 'Multilateral and Bilateral Conversations', *One in Christ* 15 (1979), pp. 334–5.

11 '*The Gift of Authority*: Report of the Council for Christian Unity', General Synod, 13 February 2004.

12 *An Anglican–Methodist Covenant*, para. 194.

13 The text can be found in *Origins* 28/8 (16 July 1998), pp. 120–7.

14 Geoffrey Wainwright, 'The Lutheran–Roman Catholic Agreement on Justification: Its Ecumenical Significance and Scope from a Methodist Point of View', *One in Christ* 37 (2003), pp. 3–31 (p. 8).

15 'Homily of Cardinal Walter Kasper, Ponte Sant' Angelo Methodist Church, Rome June 22nd 2003', *Pontifical Council for Promoting Christian Unity Information Service* 114 (2003/IV), pp. 183–5 (p. 183).

16 G. Osborn (ed.), *The Poetical Works of John and Charles Wesley*, vol. 6 (London, 1870), pp. 71f.

Postscript

1 See Robin Clutterbuck, 'Buckfast Abbey: A History' (Buckfast: Buckfast Abbey, 1994).

Select Bibliography

Primary Sources

(a) General Church Reports and Statements

Abbott, Walter M. *The Documents of Vatican II* (London: Geoffrey Chapman, 1967)

An Anglican–Methodist Covenant: Common Statement of the Formal Conversations between the Methodist Church of Great Britain and the Church of England (Peterborough: Methodist Publishing/London: Church House Publishing, 2001)

ARCIC I, *The Final Report* (1981)

ARCIC, *The Gift of Authority* (London: CTS/Church House Publishing, 1999)

Baptism, Eucharist and Ministry (Geneva: WCC, 1982)

Best, T. F. and G. Gassmann (eds), *On the Way to Fuller Koinonia: Report of the Fifth World Conference on Faith and Order* (Geneva: WCC, 1994)

Called to Love and Praise (British Methodist Conference, 1999)

Declaration 'Dominus Iesus': On the Unicity and Salvific Universality of Jesus Christ and the Church (CDF, 2000)

Declarations and Statements (Methodist Conference, 1981)

His Presence Makes the Feast: Holy Communion in the Methodist Church (Peterborough: Methodist Conference, 2003)

'International Roman Catholic/Methodist Conversations 1967–2001' (Faith and Order Report to the British Methodist Conference 2003), in *Conference Agenda* (2003), pp. 161–80

'Mixed Marriages: The Revised Directory promulgated by the Bishops' Conference of England and Wales 30th April 1990'

Note on the Expression Sister Churches (CDF, 30 June 2000)

Statements of the Methodist Church on Faith and Order, vol. 1: *1933–1983* (London, 1984)

Statements and Reports of the Methodist Church on Faith and Order, vol. 2: *1984–2000* (Peterborough: Methodist Conference, 2000)

Ut Unum Sint, Encyclical Letter of The Holy Father John Paul II on Commitment to Ecumenism (1995)

294

(b) **Reports of the Joint Commission for Dialogue between the World Methodist Council and the Roman Catholic Church (in chronological order):**

Growth in Agreement (Denver, 1971)
Growth in Understanding (Dublin, 1976)
Towards an Agreed Statement on the Holy Spirit (Honolulu, 1981)
Towards a Statement on the Church (Nairobi, 1986)
The Apostolic Tradition (Singapore, 1991)
The Word of Life: A Statement on Revelation and Faith (Rio de Janeiro, 1996)
Speaking the Truth in Love: Teaching Authority among Catholics and Methodists (Brighton, 2001)

(c) **Reports from National Methodist–Roman Catholic Dialogues (in chronological order)**

In Great Britain

Christian Belief: A Catholic/Methodist Statement (1970)
Eucharist, Ministry, Authority: Statements agreed by Roman Catholics and Methodists (Catholic Information Service, 1978)
'English Methodist–Roman Catholic Committee: Conversations between Methodists and Roman Catholics in England 1967–78', *One in Christ* 15 (1979), pp. 348–53
Marriages of Methodists with Roman Catholics (1980)
'English Roman Catholic–Methodist Committee: Justification – A Consensus Statement', *One in Christ* 24 (1988), pp. 270–3
Marriages with Roman Catholics (1990)
'English Roman Catholic–Methodist Committee: Justification – A Consensus Statement', *One in Christ* 28 (1992), pp. 87–91
'Can the Roman Catholic and Methodist Churches be Reconciled?' *Methodist Conference Agenda* (1992), pp. 202–06
Mary, Sign of Grace, Faith and Holiness: Towards a Shared Understanding (1995)

In the United States:

Shared Convictions about Education (1970)
Holiness and Spirituality of the Ordained Ministry (1976)
Eucharistic Celebration: Converging Theology – Divergent Practice (1981)
(The text of the above reports can be found in Joseph A. Burgess and Jeffrey Gros, *Building Unity: Ecumenical Dialogues with Roman Catholic Participation in the United States* (New York: Paulist Press, 1989), pp. 295–6.)
Holy Living, Holy Dying (1988); reprinted in Joseph A. Burgess and Geoffrey

Gros, *Growing Consensus: Church Dialogues in the United States, 1962–1991* (New York: Paulist Press, 1995), pp. 529–42

Yearning to be One: Spiritual Dialogue between Catholics and United Methodists (United Methodist/Catholic Bishops' Conference, 2000)

Methodist–Catholic Dialogues: Thirty Years of Mission and Witness (The General Commission on Christian Unity and Inter-religious Concerns of the United Methodist Church and the United States Catholic Bishops' Conference, 2001)

In Australia:

Joint Statement on Baptism (1973)

Christian Marriage: Its Meaning and Pastoral Implications (1973)

An Agreed Statement on Baptism (1979)

Make Straight his Way: Stages on the Road to Unity (c.1981)

Towards Agreement on Marriage (1989)

Interchurch Marriages: Their Ecumenical Challenge and Significance for our Churches (1999)

In New Zealand:

Report on the Methodist–Roman Catholic Dialogue 1995–1999 to the Conference of the Methodist Church of New Zealand Te Haa, hi Weteriana o Aotearoa and the Bishops' Conference of the Roman Catholic Church

(d) Denominational Magazines

Methodist Magazine
Methodist Monthly
Methodist New Connexion Magazine
Primitive Methodist Magazine
United Methodist Free Churches Magazine

(e) Other Primary Sources

Beet, J. Agar *The Church, the Churches and the Sacraments* (London: Hodder & Stoughton, 1907)

Bergier, Nicholas *Dictionnaire de théologie* (Paris, 1788)

Bett, Henry *The Spirit of Methodism* (London: Epworth, 1937)

Bouyer, Louis *Du Protestantism à l'église* (Paris, 1954). English Translation, *The Spirit and Forms of Protestantism* (London: Harvill, 1956)

Cassidy, Cardinal Edward 'Reflections on the Ecumenical Movement and Catholic–Methodist Relations', *Epworth Review* 25 (1998), pp. 13–22

Chettle, John *Protestant Objections, against the Romish Doctrine of Transubstantiation; addressed to the Rev. F. Martyn, and to the inhabitants of Walsall and Bloxwich*, 2nd edn (Walsall, 1827)

Cubitt, George 'A speech delivered in the Town Hall, Sheffield on Wednesday, February 18, 1829 at a Public Meeting convened to Petition the Legislature against the admission of Roman Catholics to Legislative and Political Power by Rev. George Cubitt, a Wesleyan minister'

Declaration of the Catholic bishops, the vicars apostolic and their coadjutors in Great Britain (1829)

Dutton, Anne *A Letter to the Rev. Mr J. Wesley. In vindication of the Doctrines of Absolute Election, Particular Redemption, Special Vocation, and Final Perseverance. Occasioned chiefly by some things in his Dialogue between a Predestinarian and his friend; and in his Hymns on God's Everlasting Love* (1742)

Flew, R. Newton 'Methodism and the Catholic Tradition', in N. P. Williams and Charles Harris (eds), *Northern Catholicism* (London: SPCK, 1933), pp. 515–30

Gregory, Benjamin *The Holy Catholic Church: The Communion of Saints* (London, 1873)

Holroyd, J. B. *Remarks and Illustrations on a Letter from the Rev. J. L., Roman Catholic Priest, at Scarborough to a member of the Methodist Society, in that town* (1827)

—*A Reply to Methodism Unmasked by the Rev. J. L. Roman Catholic priest at Scarborough, in which the abominations of the Church of Rome are further exposed by J. B. Holroyd Wesleyan Methodist minister* (1828)

Hughes, D. *The Life of Hugh Price Hughes* (London: Hodder & Stoughton, 1904)

J. L., Revd, *A Refutation of Remarks and Illustrations by J. B. Holroyd (Wesleyan Methodist Minister) on a Letter to A Member of the Methodist Society in which his Glaring Blunders, and Total Ignorance of Canons, Councils, Bulls etc. are exposed* (1827)

—*Methodism Unmasked* (1828)

Knox, R. A. *Enthusiasm: A Chapter in the History of Religion* (Oxford: Clarendon, 1950)

Lidgett, John Scott *God, Christ and the Church* (London: Hodder & Stoughton, 1927)

Martyn, Francis 'A sermon preached at the funeral obsequies of the Right Reverend John Milner: Bishop of Castabala, and Vicar Apostolic of the Midland District, on the 27th day of April, 1826, at the Catholic Chapel, Wolverhampton' (London, 1826)

—'Lecture I (–VIII) being . . . a series of lectures delivered in the Catholic Chapel, St Mary's Mount, Walsall on the infallibility of the Church, and other important points of Controversy' (1830?)

297

J. A. Mason, *An Earnest Appeal to the People called Methodists and to the nation at large by the Rev. J. A. Mason formerly a Methodist preacher* (1827)

—*The Triumph of Truth in the Conversion of the Rev. J. A. Mason from the Errors of Methodism to the Catholic Faith* (1827)

—*Strictures on the First part of Wesley's Roman Catechism* (London, 1828)

—*Strictures on the Second part of Wesley's Roman Catechism* (London, 1830)

—*Strictures on the Third and Fourth Parts of Wesley's Roman Catechism* (London, 1830)

—*The Conversion of Edward Corser, Esq. of Stourbridge, in the County of Worcester, to the Catholic faith: with remarks thereon, as connected with the mission of that place by J. A. Mason . . . ; also the address delivered to Mr Corser on the morning of his communion by Rev. Francis Martyn* (London, 1838)

—*Wonderful discoveries and portentous disclosures elicited from a ghost by . . . J. A. Mason's pamphlet on Mr Corser's conversion to catholicity, together with a review of the said pamphlet, and of certain letters to the author* (London, 1839)

—*The Perpetuity of Revealed Religion, and uniformity of her spirit and worship; a sermon* (London, 1839)

—*Dialogues on the spirit of the Methodist preachers towards the catholic religion and clergy* (n.d.)

—*Dialogues of the spirit of the new birth exemplified in Methodist preachers towards the Catholic religion and clergy* (n.d.)

Migne, J.-P. *Encyclopédie théologique* (Paris, 1847)

Möhler, Johann *Symbolik* (1838); ET *Symbolism* (New York: Crossroad, 1997)

Newman, J. H. *Essays Critical and Historical* (London, 1871)

—*The Present Position of Catholics in England* (London, 1851; reprinted 1899)

O'Leary, Arthur 'Remarks on Rev. John Wesley's Letters on the Civil Principles of Roman Catholics and his Defence of the Protestant Association', in *Miscellaneous Tracts* (London, 1781)

Ouseley, Gideon *The substance of a letter to the Rev. Mr Fitzsimmons, Roman Catholic Priest of Ballymena, in Ireland, on some chief pillars or prime articles of his faith, especially transubstantiation, propitiatory sacrifice of the mass, and divine worship of the host etc These are proved beyond a possibility of contradiction never to have been taught by Christ or his apostles, and to be necessarily subversive of Christianity* (1816)

Piette, Maximin *John Wesley in the Evolution of Protestantism* (London: Sheed & Ward, 1937)

Rigg, J. H. *A Comparative View of Church Organisations, Primitive and Protestant* (London, 1878)

Rohrbacher, René *Histoire universelle de l'Eglise catholique* (Paris, 1849)

Tavard, George H. 'How Catholics have seen Methodism' (Joint Commission for Dialogue between the World Methodist Council and the Roman Catholic Church, 2002)

Thurian, Max (ed.) *Churches Respond to BEM* (Geneva: WCC, 1986–8), 6 vols

Todd, John *John Wesley and the Catholic Church* (London: Hodder & Stoughton, 1958)

Townsend, W. J., H. B. Workman and George Eayrs (eds) *A New History of Methodism* (London: Hodder & Stoughton, 1909)

Vickers, John (ed.) *A Dictionary of Methodism in Britain and Ireland* (Peterborough: Epworth, 2000)

Wainwright, Geoffrey 'A Statement in Response to the Vatican's *Dominus Iesus* From the Methodist Members of the Joint Commission for Dialogue Between the World Methodist Council and the Roman Catholic Church, 7 September 2000'

Wesley, John *The Journal of the Rev. John Wesley A. M.*, ed. Nehemiah Curnock (London: Epworth, 1938), 8 vols

—*Letters of John Wesley*, ed. John Telford (London: Epworth, 1931)

—*Works of John Wesley*, various editors (Nashville: Abingdon, 1984–2003)

—*The Works of Rev. John Wesley A. M.*, ed. Thomas Jackson (London, 1872), vols. 1–13

—*Explanatory Notes upon the New Testament* (1754, reprinted 1976)

Workman, Herbert *The Place of Methodism in the Catholic Church* (London: Epworth, 1921)

Secondary Sources

Baker, Frank *John Wesley and the Church of England* (Nashville: Abingdon, 1970)

Borgen, Ole E. *John Wesley on the Sacraments* (Zurich: United Methodist Publishing House, 1972)

Bowmer, John C. *The Sacrament of the Lord's Supper in Early Methodism* (London: Epworth, 1951)

—*The Lord's Supper in Methodism 1791–1960* (London: Epworth, 1960)

Buckle, Emory Stevens (ed.), *The History of American Methodism*, (New York: Abingdon, 1964)

Butler, Christopher *The Theology of Vatican II* (London: Darton, Longman & Todd, 1967; revised edition 1981)

Butler, David *Methodists and Papists: John Wesley and the Catholic Church in the Eighteenth Century* (London: Darton, Longman & Todd, 1995)

—'The British Roman Catholic–Methodist Dialogue 1984–2000', *Epworth Review* 29/3 (2002), pp. 9–15

Butler, David and Michael Jackson *Catholics and Methodists: the Work of the International Commission* (CTS and Methodist Publishing House, 1986)

Butler, Edward C. *The Vatican Council 1869–70*, ed. Christopher Butler (London: Collins Harvill, 1962)

Carter, David *Love Bade me Welcome: A British Methodist Perspective on the Church* (Peterborough: Epworth, 2002)

—'Catholics, Methodists and Reception', *One in Christ* 28 (1992), pp. 232–47

—'The Roman Catholic–Methodist Dialogue', *Exchange: Journal of Missiological and Ecumenical Research* 28 (1999), pp. 363–80

Cell, G. Croft *The Rediscovery of John Wesley* (New York: H. Holt & Company, 1935)

Chadwick, Owen *The Reformation* (London: Penguin, 1972)

Chapman, David M. 'Mary, Icon of the Covenant', *One in Christ* 33 (1997) pp. 55–66

Congar, Yves *Divided Christendom* (London: Geoffrey Bles, 1939)

Davies, Rupert 'Multilateral and Bilateral Conversations', *One in Christ* 15 (1979), pp. 334–5

Davies, Rupert, A. Raymond George and Gordon Rupp (eds), *A History of the Methodist Church in Great Britain*, vol. 4 (London: Epworth, 1988)

Del Colle, Ralph 'Commentary and Reflections on *Speaking the Truth in Love: Teaching Authority among Catholics and Methodists* Report of the Joint Commission between the Roman Catholic Church and the World Methodist Council 1997–2001 Seventh Series', *Information Service – Pontifical Council for Promoting Christian Unity* 107 (2001/II–III), pp. 118–26

Doughty, W. L. 'John Wesley's Letters to Mr Berington 1780', *PWHS* 26 (1947), pp. 38–45, 68

Duffy, Eamon 'The Place of the Blessed Virgin Mary in Roman Catholicism', *Epworth Review* 16 (1989), pp. 51–68

—'Wesley and the Counter-Reformation', in Jane Garnett and Colin Matthew (eds), *Revival and Religion since 1700: Essays for John Walsh* (London: Hambledon, 1993), pp. 1–19

Edwards, David L. *Christian England*, vol. 3 (London: Collins, 1984)

Field, Clive 'Anti-Methodist publications of the eighteenth century: a revised bibliography', *Bulletin of the John Rylands University Library of Manchester* 73 (1991), pp. 159–280

Frost, Francis 'Méthodisme', in G. Jacquement *et al.* (eds), *Catholicisme, hier, aujourd'hui et demain*, vol. 9 (Paris: Cerf, 1982), pp. 48–71

George, Raymond 'The Apostolic Tradition', *One in Christ* 28 (1992), pp. 82–6

Hastings, Adrian (ed.), *Modern Catholicism: Vatican II and After* (London: SPCK, 1991)

Hattersley, Roy *A Brand from the Burning: The Life of John Wesley* (London: Little, Brown, 2002)

Haugaard, William P. 'From the Reformation to the Eighteenth Century', in Stephen Sykes and John Booty (eds), *The Study of Anglicanism* (London: SPCK, 1988), pp. 3–28

Hebblethwaite, Peter *John XXIII: Shepherd of the Modern World* (London:

Geoffrey Chapman, 1984)

Heitzenrater, Richard P. *Wesley and the People Called Methodists* (Nashville: Abingdon, 1995)

Hempton, David *Methodism and Politics in British Society 1750–1850* (London: Hutchinson, 1984)

—*The Religion of the People: Methodism and Popular Religion c. 1750–1900* (London: Routledge, 1996)

Henn, William 'Reflections on the *Word of Life*', *One in Christ* 32 (1996), pp. 363–77

Hildebrandt, F. *From Luther to Wesley* (London: Lutterworth, 1951)

Kamen, H. *The Rise of Toleration* (London: Weidenfeld & Nicolson, 1967)

Keighley, D. Alan 'Pursuing the Roman Catholic–Methodist Dialogue', *Epworth Review* 4 (1977), pp. 33–41

Lyles, A. M. *Methodism Mocked: The Satiric Reaction to Methodism in the Eighteenth Century* (London: Epworth, 1960)

Moorman, J. R. H. 'Observers and Guests of the Council', in Alberic Stacpoole (ed.), *Vatican II by Those Who Were There* (London: Geoffrey Chapman, 1986), pp. 155–69

Morgan, Marion 'The Sacred Heart of Jesus in Catholic Devotion, *One in Christ* 24 (1988), pp. 223–36

Nelson, J. R. 'Methodism and the Papacy', in P. J. McCord (ed.), *A Pope for all Christians? An Enquiry into the Role of Peter in the Modern Church* (London: SPCK, 1977), pp. 148–75

Newton, John 'Spirituality and Sanctification', *One in Christ* 24 (1988), pp. 218–22

Newton, John and Marion Morgan, *Will you Walk a Little Faster: Letters between a Methodist and a Roman Catholic* (London: Epworth, 1984)

Outler, Albert *John Wesley* (New York: Oxford University Press, 1964)

—'Discovery: An Olive Branch to the Romans, 1970's-style: United Methodist Initiative, Roman Catholic Response', *Methodist History* 13 (1975), pp. 52–6 (p. 53)

Paz, D. G. *Popular Anti-Catholicism in Mid-Victorian England* (Stanford: Stanford University Press, 1992)

Rack, Henry *Reasonable Enthusiast: John Wesley and the Rise of Methodism* (London: Epworth, 1989)

Smith, John T. *Methodism and Education 1849–1902: J. H. Rigg, Romanism and Wesleyan Schools* (Oxford: Clarendon, 1998)

Stewart, Richard *Catholics and Methodists: An Introduction to the Work of the Joint Commission Between the World Methodist Council and the Roman Catholic Church* (London: CTS, 1974)

—'Dialogue with Methodism', *One in Christ* 18 (1982), pp. 223–36

Stransky, Tom 'Ecumenism (*Unitatis Redintegratio*)', in Adrian Hastings (ed.),

Modern Catholicism: Vatican II and After (London: SPCK, 1991), pp. 113–17

Stubbings, Roger 'The Blessed Virgin Mary: A Methodist Contribution', (English Methodist–Roman Catholic Committee, May 1988)

Sullivan, Emmanuel and Gordon Wakefield, 'Towards a Spirituality for Today', *Epworth Review* 4 (1977), pp. 61–7

Sullivan, Francis A. 'Subsistit in', *One in Christ* 22 (1986), pp. 115–23

Taggart, Norman W. *The Irish in World Methodism 1760–1900* (London: Epworth, 1986)

Thurian, Max 'Baptism, Eucharist and Ministry ("The Lima Text")', in *A Dictionary of the Ecumenical Movement*, ed. Nicholas Lossky *et al.* (Geneva: WCC, 1991), pp. 80–3

Tillard, J. M. R. 'Commentary on "Towards a Statement on the Church"', *One in Christ* 22 (1986), pp. 259–66

Tucker, K. Westerfield *American Methodist Worship* (New York: Oxford University Press, 2001)

Turberfield, Alan *John Scott Lidgett: Archbishop of British Methodism?* (Peterborough: Epworth, 2003)

Turner, John Munsey *John Wesley: The Evangelical Revival and the Rise of Methodism in England* (Peterborough: Epworth, 2002)

Vorgrimler, Herbert (ed.), *Commentary on the Documents of Vatican II*, vol. 2 (London: Burns & Oates, 1968)

Wainwright, Geoffrey *The Ecumenical Moment: Crisis and Opportunity for the Church* (Grand Rapids: Eerdmans, 1983)

—*Methodists in Dialog* (Nashville: Abingdon, 1995)

—'"The Gift Which He on One Bestows, We All Delight to Prove": A Possible Methodist Approach to a Ministry of Primacy in the Circulation of Love and Truth', in James F. Puglisi (ed.), *Petrine Ministry and the Unity of the Church* (Collegeville: Liturgical Press, 1999), pp. 59–82

—'The Ecumenical Scope of Methodist Liturgical Revision', *Bulletin of the Centro Pro Unione* (Fall 2002), pp. 16–26

—(ed.), *A. Raymond George: Memoirs Methodist and Ecumenical* (Buxton: Church in the Market Place Publications, 2003)

—'"Can two walk together except they be agreed?" Progress between Methodists and Catholics on the Way of Unity', in Peter Walter, Klaus Krimer and George Augustine (eds), *Kirche in ökumenischer Perspektive: Kardinal Walter Kasper zum 70. Geburtstag* (Freiburg: Herder, 2003)

—'The Lutheran–Roman Catholic Agreement on Justification: its ecumenical significance and scope from a Methodist point of view', *One in Christ* 37/2 (2003), pp. 3–31

Wakefield, Gordon 'The Virgin Mary in Methodism', *One in Christ* 4 (1968), pp. 156–64

Wall, Terry, 'Speaking the Truth in Love, Teaching Authority Among Catholics and Methodists'(November 2000); 'A New Zealand Response' (April 2002) (Methodist–Roman Catholic dialogue in New Zealand)

Ward, Neville *Five for Sorrow, Ten for Joy* (London: Epworth, 1971)

Warner, Pauline 'Mary, a two-edged sword to pierce our hearts?' *Epworth Review* 18 (1991), pp. 67–79

White, Susan J. *Christian Worship and Technological Change* (Nashville: Abingdon, 1994)

Wicks, Jared 'Commentary and Assessment of the Apostolic Tradition', *One in Christ* 28 (1992), pp. 74–81

Index of Names and Subjects